Cultural Property Law and Restitution

IHC SERIES IN HERITAGE MANAGEMENT

Series Editor: Evangelos Kyriakidis

Cultural Property Law and Restitution
A Commentary to International Conventions and European Union Law
Irini A. Stamatoudi

Cultural Property Law and Restitution

A Commentary to International Conventions and European Union Law

Irini A. Stamatoudi

LL.M, Ph.D

IHC SERIES IN HERITAGE MANAGEMENT

Edward Elgar

Cheltenham, UK • Northampton, MA, USA

Published by
Edward Elgar Publishing Limited
The Lypiatts
15 Lansdown Road
Cheltenham
Glos GL50 2JA
UK

Edward Elgar Publishing, Inc.
William Pratt House
9 Dewey Court
Northampton
Massachusetts 01060
USA

A catalogue record for this book
is available from the British Library

Library of Congress Control Number: 2010934018

MIX
Paper from
responsible sources
FSC® C018575
FSC
www.fsc.org

ISBN 978 1 84844 661 8

Typeset by Servis Filmsetting Ltd, Stockport, Cheshire
Printed and bound by MPG Books Group, UK

To my little beloved Anastassis, born together with this book.

Contents

Preface

Dealing with issues of cultural property law is not an easy task. This area of law combines aspects from many separate areas of law, which only recently took on a more rigid form under the label of cultural property law. On top of this, the interests at stake as well as the stakeholders (states, museums, galleries, collectors, art dealers and so on) are numerous. On the one hand, some of the issues raised are, strictly speaking, legal; on the other hand, this area of law depends heavily on ethics, morality and personal convictions, which, by definition, do not involve pure objectivity, unaffected by emotion.

My involvement with cultural property law, from different perspectives and on different occasions, has allowed me to develop a considerable degree of understanding of the different views and approaches. I studied this area of law in England, with an emphasis on the common law liberal approach and practised it in Greece, with an emphasis on the protective approach. I have participated in negotiations on the Parthenon Marbles issue; acted as a legal advisor for the return of artefacts to Greece from abroad including returns from the J.P. Getty Museum in Los Angeles and the Leon Levy and Shelby White collection in New York; negotiated bilateral agreements on the protection of cultural treasures between Greece and other states; represented Greece in UNESCO; and participated in the drafting Committee of the most recent Act on Measures for the Protection of Cultural Goods and Other Provisions enacted in Greece (Law 3658/2008).

This book was written while I was pregnant with my son Anastassis: in many ways, its writing may be compared to a pregnancy. For this book to be published, many people have played their part. The first ones to thank are the Initiative for Heritage Conservancy (IHC), Lloyd Cotsen, Evangelos Kyriakides and Edward Elgar Publishing for making the publication of this book possible. I also wish to thank Wendy Addison for editing the manuscript, Maria Tzima for editing other smaller parts and the bibliography of this book and Polyxeni Veleni (Director of the Archaeological Museum of Thessaloniki, Greece) for providing the photo which became the cover of this book. Many thanks also to my two other children, Fotini and Manthos: though they did not always manage to keep quiet and behave themselves during its writing, they did, however, try hard to do so. Last but not least, I am especially grateful to my husband, Angelos, for his unfailing patience and support during the writing of this book.

Introduction

Cultural property law is a rather recent and fast evolving area of law. Its origins date back to the mid nineteenth century when the first legal instruments were drafted.[1] It has essentially developed around two main areas of interest: the protection of cultural treasures both in times of war and in times of peace. In the latter case, emphasis was placed on incidents of theft, illegal excavation and export of cultural treasures from their countries of origin. Cultural property law, however, encompasses other interests in culture, such as the protection and preservation of cultural goods in general. Although cultural property has developed as a niche area in international law, it involves national and regional laws too. It is a hybrid area of law, in the sense that it involves principles from various hard core

[1] See some examples during this period: The Lieber Code (Francis Lieber, Instructions for the Government of Armies of the United States in the Field,1863); International Convention with Respect to the Law and Customs of War by Land (Hague II), 29 July 1899; Convention Respecting the Laws and Customs of War on Land (Hague IV), 18 October 1907; Article 238 of the Treaty of Peace between the Allied & Associated Powers and Germany, Versailles, 28 June 1919 and Protocols; Inter-Allied Declaration Against Acts of Dispossession Committed in Territories under Enemy Occupation or Control, London, 5 January 1943; Judgment of the International Military Tribunal, 30 September 1946; Convention for the Protection of Cultural Property in the Event of Armed Conflict (1954 Hague Convention on Cultural Property), 14 May 1954; Statutes of the International Centre for the Study of the Preservation and Restoration of Cultural Property, 5 December 1956 (as revised, 24 April 1963, and 14–17 April 1969); Convention on the Means of Prohibiting and Preventing the Illicit Import, Export and Transfer of Ownership of Cultural Property, 14 November 1970; Convention Concerning the Protection of the World Cultural and Natural Heritage, 23 November 1972; Recommendation Concerning the International Exchange of Cultural Property, adopted by the General Conference at its Nineteenth Session, Paris, 30 November 1976; Recommendation for the Protection of Movable Cultural Property, adopted by the General Conference at its Twentieth Session, Paris, 28 November 1978; European Cultural Convention, 19 July 1954; European Convention on Offences Relating to Cultural Property, 23 June 1985; Convention for the Protection of the Architectural Heritage of Europe, 3 October 1985; European Convention on the Protection of the Archaeological Heritage (Revised), 16 January 1992; Resolution 1205, Looted Cultural Property, Parliamentary Assembly of the Council of Europe, 4 November 1999.

areas of law, such as public international law, private law, private international law and so on.

This book does not intend to cover all issues pertaining to cultural property law; that would be an extremely optimistic exercise. It will limit itself to issues of restitution and return of cultural treasures, alienated from their countries of origin in times of peace. It sets out the basics, that is the notions of 'cultural property', 'return' and 'restitution'. The two theories in the area, namely that of cultural nationalism and that of cultural internationalism, are also explored (Chapter 1).

Chapter 2 of the book deals with the most important international legal instruments in this field,[2] that is the 1970 UNESCO Convention on the Means of Prohibiting and Preventing the Illicit Import, Export and Transfer of Ownership of Cultural Property and the 1995 Unidroit Convention on Stolen or Illegally Exported Cultural Objects.[3] Primary and secondary European Union legislation is examined. This comprises the relevant provisions in the Treaty on the Functioning of the European Union (TFEU) and Regulations 116/09 on the Export of Cultural Goods and 752/93 laying down provisions for the implementation of Council Regulation 3911/92 on the Export of Cultural Goods, as well as Directive 7/93 on the Return of Cultural Objects Unlawfully Removed from the Territory of a Member State (Chapter 3).

---

[2] For example, the 1985 European Convention on Offences Relating to Cultural Property (Delphi, 23 July 1985) is not discussed since it never entered into force.

[3] The 2001 UNESCO Convention on the Protection of Underwater Cultural Heritage is not discussed because it does not fall squarely within this particular field. For the 2001 UNESCO Convention on the Protection of Underwater Cultural Heritage see Camarda, G. & T. Scovazzi (eds) (2002), *The Protection of the Underwater Cultural Heritage – Legal Aspects*, Milan; O'Keefe, P. (2002), *Shipwrecked Heritage: A Commentary on the UNESCO Convention on Underwater Cultural Heritage*, Leicester; Carducci, G. (2002) 'New Developments in the Law of the Sea: The UNESCO Convention on the Protection of the Underwater Cultural Heritage, *American Journal of International Law* 419; Garabello, R. & T. Scovazzi (eds) (2003), *The Protection of the Underwater Cultural Heritage – Before and After the 2001 UNESCO Convention*, Leiden; Dromgoole, S. (ed.) (2006), *The Protection of the Underwater Cultural Heritage – National Perspectives in Light of the UNESCO Convention 2001*, Leiden. See also the Italian cases on the Melquart of Sciacca (9 January, 1963, Tribunal of Sciacca) and the victorious Athlete (two cases 12 June, 2009 and 10 February, 2010, Tribunal of Pesaro) as discussed in Scovazzi, T. (2010) 'A Second Italian Case on Cultural Properties Enmeshed in Fishing Nets' http://www.mepielan-ebulletin.gr/default.aspx?pid=18&CategoryId=4&ArticleId=17&Article=A-Second-Italian-Case-on-Cultural-Properties-Enmeshed-in-Fishing-Nets.

Cultural property law is, to a large extent, affected and shaped by soft law, since it is often expressed as a compromise between the various interests involved, and many acts take place on an ethical and voluntary basis. This is especially so because cultural property law touches on state sovereignty, meaning that, on most occasions, particularly on those falling outside the scope of international conventions and those concerning states with differing national legislation or attitudes, claims involving two or more states are processed on the basis of ethics, mutual agreement and co-operation. To this end, the most important codes of ethics are examined on a par with the role of international organisations, such as UNESCO, ICOM, ICCROM and so on. Reference is also made to registers of stolen and illegally exported cultural objects, which play an increasingly significant role in the tracking down of those objects (Chapter 4).

Dispute resolution in cultural property claims is another significant area which is developed at length. More than in any other field of law, disputes in this field do not necessarily find their way to courts but, because of the particularities and sensitivities they engender, are solved through alternative dispute resolution, such as arbitration, mediation and especially through negotiations. Cultural diplomacy and its role are also examined (Chapter 5).

Chapter 6 of this book explores the basic principles and trends in cultural property law and draws some conclusions as to where we stand today and where we are heading. This is done on the basis of discussions in preceding chapters of the book, but takes a step back from the bulk of law and ethics, in an attempt to assess them as a whole. At the end of the book conclusions are drawn. An Appendix enables the reader to refer to particular provisions of instruments discussed.

1. Cultural property and restitution: the theories of cultural nationalism and cultural internationalism

1.1 THE NOTION OF CULTURAL PROPERTY

There is no internationally accepted definition of cultural property. Cultural property is a notion which differs according to the point of view taken, to the legal instrument applied and to the intended result. It is also a notion which is subject to evolution,[1] whilst in bilateral or multilateral relations it forms the subject of mutual agreement or compromise respectively. Therefore the definition of a state's cultural property varies according to whether it is the state itself which defines that property, or whether it is defined by another state involved in a claim for return or restitution. Does that mean that 'cultural property' is a term which is vague and flexible and cannot be subject to an objective definition?[2] Not entirely. Although cultural property is a general notion familiar to the layperson,

[1] Especially after the growth of interest in anthropology and ethnography. Askerud P. & E. Clément (1997), *Preventing the Illicit traffic in Cultural Property. A Resource Handbook for the implementation of the 1970 UNESCO Convention*, Paris: UNESCO, 5. Indicative also is the fact that cultural objects are no longer approached on the basis of their aesthetic value but as evidence of particular cultures and times in history. This is also the reason why their preservation in their context carries so much weight. Preserving cultural objects in context allows one to use them as testimonies of particular habits of their time in order to advance research and contribute to the knowledge of our history. See also Francioni, Fr., 'A Dynamic evolution of concept and scope: from cultural property to cultural heritage', in Yusuf, A. (ed.), *Standard-setting in UNESCO, volume I: normative action in education, science and culture, essays in commemoration of the Sixtieth Anniversary of UNESCO*, Paris, p.221.

[2] Some countries chose a general definition (especially countries in continental Europe) whilst some others (especially common law countries) an enumerative one according to their legal tradition and the items they want to cover. See Lalive, P. (1993), 'Le projet de Convention de l'Unidroit sur les biens culturels volés ou illicitement exportés', in M. Briat and J. Freedberg (eds), *Legal Aspects of International Art Trade*, The Hague: Kluwer Law International, 26–27.

it can still be specified by means of the standpoint taken, the aims pursued and the politics followed.[3] Cultural property is occasionally classified into categories according to time spans (cut-off dates in history), monetary values, types of use, types of material and so on. These categories have much to do with cultural conceptions as to what is worth protecting and what is not, depending primarily on each state's interests and culture. That means that a cultural object may be considered in one state as *res extra commercium*, as non-exportable in another and of no significance to a third. In general, however, one could define cultural property as anything which bears witness to the artistry, history and identity of a particular culture.[4] That includes objects that are considered cultural by nature (for

---

3 As Scovazzi points out, 'cultural heritage is too important to be understood only in the light of legal technicalities'. He also refers to article 4, paragraphs 1 and 2 of the Statutes of the Intergovernmental Committee for Promoting the Return of Cultural Property to its Countries of Origin or Its Restitution in Case of Illicit Appropriation where it is indicated that the Committee seeks 'ways and means of facilitating bilateral negotiations for the restitution or return of cultural property to its countries of origin' and promotes 'multilateral and bilateral cooperation with a view to the restitution and return of cultural property to its countries of origin'. In fact he wants to indicate that this Committee takes into consideration not solely the law but ethical and moral issues, too. See Scovazzi, T. (2009), 'Diviser c'est détruire: ethical principles and legal rules in the field of return of cultural properties', Paper presented in the 16th Session of the Intergovernmental Committee for Promoting the Return of Cultural Property to Its Countries of Origin or Its Restitution in Case of Illicit Appropriation (21–23.9.2010), Paris: UNESCO, at 2.

4 Specialised categories such as archaeology, prehistory, history, religion, literature, science, anthropology and ethnology are included in the aforementioned general categories. Also included is anything which qualifies as intellectual property according to national and European Union laws and international conventions. Interesting in this respect is also the definition of 'movable cultural property' according to the 1978 Recommendation for the Protection of Movable Cultural Property.

> I.1.For the purposes of this Recommendation: (a) 'movable cultural property' shall be taken to mean all movable objects which are the expression and testimony of human creation or of the evolution of nature and which are of archaeological, historical, artistic, scientific or technical value and interest, including items in the following categories: (i) products of archaeological exploration and excavations conducted on land and under water; (ii) antiquities such as tools, pottery, inscriptions, coins, seals, jewellery, weapons and funerary remains, including mummies; (iii) items resulting from the dismemberment of historical monuments; (iv) material of anthropological and ethnological interest; (v) items relating to history, including the history of science and technology and military and social history, to the life of peoples and national leaders, thinkers, scientists and artists and to events of national importance; (vi) items of artistic interest, such as: paintings and drawings, produced entirely by hand on any support and

example a painting) as well as objects, which by reason of time and evolution of beliefs have been rendered cultural (such as, for example, utensils).[5]

'Cultural property' is not a term identical to 'cultural heritage'. In practice though, these two terms are used interchangeably. Cultural property is a western concept with commercial connotations and direct reference to property law and thus ownership.

> The fundamental policy behind property law has been seen as the protection of the rights of the possessor. If this policy is carried to its logical conclusion then the owner can be buried with a painting that he purchased for millions of dollars but which represents a peak achievement of human culture. The fundamental policy behind cultural heritage law is protection of the heritage for the enjoyment of present and later generations.[6]

---

in any material (excluding industrial designs and manufactured articles decorated by hand); original prints, and posters and photographs, as the media for original creativity; original artistic assemblages and montages in any material; works of statuary art and sculpture in any material; works of applied art in such materials as glass, ceramics, metal, wood, etc.; (vii) manuscripts and incunabula, codices, books, documents or publications of special interest; (viii) items of numismatic (medals and coins) and philatelic interest; (ix) archives, including textual records, maps and other cartographic materials, photographs, cinematographic films, sound recordings and machine-readable records; (x) items of furniture, tapestries, carpets, dress and musical instruments; (xi) zoological, botanical and geological specimens; (b) 'protection' shall be taken to mean the prevention and coverage of risks as defined below: (i) 'prevention of risks' means all the measures required, within a comprehensive protection system, to safeguard movable cultural property from every risk to which such property may be exposed, including those resulting from armed conflict, riots or other public disorders; (ii) 'risk coverage' means the guarantee of indemnification in the case of damage to, deterioration, alteration or loss of movable cultural property resulting from any risk whatsoever, including risks incurred as a result of armed conflict, riots or other public disorders whether such coverage is effected through a system of governmental guarantees and indemnities, through the partial assumption of the risks by the State under a deductible or excess loss arrangement, through commercial or national insurance or through mutual insurance arrangements. 2. Each Member State should adopt whatever criteria it deems most suitable for defining the items of movable cultural property within its territory which should be given the protection envisaged in this Recommendation by reason of their archaeological, historical, artistic, scientific or technical value.

[5] Derout, A. (1993), *La protection des biens culturels en droit communautaire*, Rennes: Editions Apogée.

[6] Prott, L.V. and P.J. O'Keefe (1992), '"Cultural Heritage" or "Cultural Property"?', *International Journal of Cultural Property* 1, 307. The authors refer to two characteristic cases: *Milirrpum v. Nabalco Pty. Ltd* (1971) 17 F.L.R. 141 and *Mullick v. Mullick* (1925) LR LII Indian Appeals 245. In the first case it was noted

Cultural property law, if seen restrictively, can be put alongside real property,[7] personal property[8] and intellectual property.[9] [10] However, cultural property law only contains parts of these fields of law (for example only parts of 'real property law' are relevant to cultural property law since not all cultural property is immovable property) and at the same time presents particularities that cannot be accommodated by these fields of law (for example certain aspects of intangible cultural property, which are not protected by intellectual property, i.e. ideas, languages and so on).

Cultural property law has seen an evolution towards cultural heritage law.[11] The term 'cultural property', though known in civil law tradition,[12] was used for the first time in English in a legal context in the 1954 Hague Convention for the Protection of Cultural Property in the Event of Armed Conflict. After that it was again used in the 1970 UNESCO Convention on the Means of Prohibiting and Preventing the Illicit Import, Export and Transfer of Ownership of Cultural Property. The term 'cultural heritage' is found in the 1969 European Convention on the Protection of the Archaeological Heritage (revised in 1992), the 1972 UNESCO Convention concerning the Protection of the World Cultural and Natural Heritage and the 1985 Convention for the Protection of the Architectural Heritage of Europe, as well as in many regional and national legal instruments. The

---

that the Australian aboriginals, rather than believing that the land belonged to them, believed that they belonged to the land. In the second case the Privy Council held that a Hindu family idol was not a mere chattel which was owned and could be dealt with by its owner as he pleased, but a legal entity in its own right to which duties were owed and which was entitled to have its own interests represented in court.

7 Which stands for interests in land.

8 Which stands for everything else but interests in land.

9 Which stands for interests in the fruits of the intellect.

10 Crewdson, R. (1984), 'Cultural Property – a Fourth Estate?', *Law Society Gazette*, 126.

11 Prott, L.V. and P. O'Keefe, n. 6 above. See also Frigo, M. (2004), 'Cultural property v. cultural heritage: a "battle of concepts" in international law?' *International Review of the Red Cross*, 86 (854), 367; Przyborowska-Klimczak, A. (1989–1990), 'Les notions de "biens culturels" et de "patrimoine culturel mondial" dans le droit international', *Polish Yearbook of International Law*, XVIII, 51; Blake, J. (2000), 'On defining the cultural heritage', *International & Comparative Law Quarterly* 61; O'Keefe, R. (1999), 'The meaning of "cultural property" under the 1954 Hague Convention', *Netherlands International Law Review*, 26.

12 E.g. 'biens culturels' in French, 'beni culturali' in Italian and 'politistika agatha' in Greek. The Greek term is a term which though translated in English as 'cultural goods', is however wider than that, since it refers to goods in the wider sense of the word and not as mere commodities. Yet, all these terms cannot incorporate the full notion of cultural heritage.

1995 Unidroit Convention on Stolen or Illegally Exported Cultural Objects also uses primarily the term 'cultural heritage'. In the secondary European Union legislation the terms 'goods' and 'objects' are used, which come closer to the 'property' term. The reason for that is that a) in practice the two terms ('property' and 'heritage') are used interchangeably[13] (this is also the reason why some states, parties to the aforementioned Conventions, have incorporated them into their national laws by using the term 'cultural heritage' (e.g. Australia and Greece));[14] b) the term 'property' is a term with particular connotations in law and therefore seems to prevail in strictly legal instruments; and c) the international instruments concerning the illegal trade in cultural goods refer to the tangible, rather than to the intangible, part of cultural heritage. In any case, however, the term 'cultural heritage' is a wider term,[15] which moves away from the strictly legal notion of ownership and property[16] towards a broader scope, encompassing a duty to safeguard[17] this inheritance and hand it down to future generations.

Cultural property can be divided into tangible (for example monuments and movable goods, such as antiquities, paintings, statues and so on) and intangible property (intellectual property law subject matter as well as folklore, traditional knowledge and so on).[18] Yet, cultural property law at national and international level focuses primarily on the protection of tangible cultural goods. There is also a distinction between movable

---

[13] See in this respect article 1 paragraph 1 of an earlier draft of the 2001 UNESCO Convention on the Protection of the Underwater Cultural Heritage, which refers to both terms interchangeably: 'For the purposes of the Convention all remains and objects and any other traces of human existence [. . .] shall be considered as being part of the underwater cultural heritage, and are hereinafter referred to as "underwater cultural property"'. The final text of article 1 is changed and has solely kept the notion of 'cultural heritage'.

[14] See the (Australian) Movable Cultural Heritage Act 1986 and the Greek law 3028/2002 on the protection of antiquities and cultural heritage in general.

[15] Prott, L. and P. O'Keefe (n. 6 above) define 'cultural heritage' in the following manner: 'The cultural heritage consists of manifestations of human life which represent a particular view of life and witness the history and validity of that view. The expression of culture or evidence of a way of life may be embodied in material things such as monuments or sites.'

[16] Property law traditionally gives priority to the rights of the possessor: one can do what one wishes with one's own property (including one's right to destroy it) excluding all others. Cultural heritage law avoids the strict commoditisation of cultural objects and also takes other values and interests apart from the commercial value into account, such as the interests of society, community and those of mankind in general.

[17] i.e. protect and preserve.

[18] See in this respect the 2003 UNESCO Convention for the Safeguarding of Intangible Cultural Heritage and its definitions: Article 2:

and immovable property. However, this distinction is not always easy to make. It is not, for example, easy to tell whether a part of a sculpture detached from a permanent building is considered movable property after its detachment or whether it continues to qualify as immovable property. In English law there is the concept of 'fixtures' (objects which are attached in a permanent way to the building and cannot be separated from the immovable and therefore are susceptible to any rules relating to it). Two English cases that had to deal with cultural property of this kind held that a door and a door frame that had been designed by the famous architect Adam and that had been detached from the house, should be returned and re-installed as they constituted an integral part of it and continued to

---

> For the purposes of this Convention, 1. 'intangible cultural heritage' means the practices, representations, expressions, knowledge, skills – as well as the instruments, objects, artefacts and cultural spaces associated therewith – that communities, groups and, in some cases, individuals recognize as part of their cultural heritage. This intangible cultural heritage, transmitted from generation to generation, is constantly recreated by communities and groups in response to their environment, their interaction with nature and their history, and provides them with a sense of identity and continuity, thus promoting respect for cultural diversity and human creativity. For the purposes of this Convention, consideration will be given solely to such intangible cultural heritage as is compatible with existing international human rights instruments, as well as with the requirements of mutual respect among communities, groups and individuals, and of sustainable development. 2. 'intangible cultural heritage', as defined in paragraph 1 above, is manifested inter alia in the following domains: (a) oral traditions and expressions, including language as a vehicle of the intangible cultural heritage; (b) performing arts; (c) social practices, rituals and festive events; (d) knowledge and practices concerning nature and the universe; (e) traditional craftsmanship. [. . .].

See also the 1989 UNESCO Recommendation for the Safeguarding of Traditional Culture and Folklore and the 2006 Council of Europe Recommendation on the Protection of Old and Traditional Crafts (Doc. 11072/2006). The latter makes reference to the European Cultural Convention (signed in Paris on 19 December 1954), Recommendation No. R (81) 13 of the Committee of Ministers to Member States on action in aid of certain declining craft trades in the contexts of craft activity (adopted on 1 July 1981), the Parliamentary Assembly Resolution 782 (1982), on craftsmanship (adopted on 30 September 1982), the Parliamentary Assembly Resolution 798 (1983) on 1983 'European Year of the small and medium-sized enterprises and craft trades' (adopted on 29 April 1983) and Council of Europe Framework Convention on the Value of Cultural Heritage for Society (signed in Faro on 27 October 2005). See also the 2001 Council of Europe European Convention for the Protection of Audiovisual Heritage (Strasbourg 8 November 2001). See also Article 4 of the 2005 UNESCO Convention on the Protection and Promotion of the Diversity of Cultural Expressions (Paris, 20 October 2005).

do so after their unauthorised removal (*Phillips v Lamdin*).[19] In *Norton v Dashwood*,[20] tapestries, that had been affixed to the walls of a house for more than one hundred years were also considered an integral part of it and therefore could not be separated without causing damage to their context. The most interesting case though, albeit a French one, is *Ville de Genève et Fondation Abegg v Consorts Margail.*[21] In this case the French court held that the frescoes detached from a building and sold outside the country remained immovables even after their detachment and therefore were subject to the rules relating to immovables. This case and its outcome bear strong similarities to the English *Phillips v Lamdin* case.[22]

Another distinction is between land and underwater cultural heritage. The notion of underwater cultural heritage has been defined in article 1(1)(a) of the 2001 UNESCO Convention on the Protection of Underwater Cultural Heritage (Paris, 2 November 2001): 1. (a) 'Underwater cultural heritage' means all traces of human existence having a cultural, historical or archaeological character which have been partially or totally under water, periodically or continuously, for at least 100 years such as: (i) sites, structures, buildings, artefacts and human remains, together with their archaeological and natural context; (ii) vessels, aircraft, other vehicles or any part thereof, their cargo or other contents, together with their archaeological and natural context; and (iii) objects of prehistoric character. (b) Pipelines and cables placed on the seabed shall not be considered as underwater cultural heritage. (c) Installations other than pipelines and cables, placed on the seabed and still in use, shall not be considered as underwater cultural heritage.[23]

A further theoretical distinction is made between cultural and natural

---

19 [1949] 2 KB 33.

20 [1896] 2 Ch 497.

21 D 1985.208.

22 See Stamatoudi, I. (2002), 'Legal Grounds for the Return of the Parthenon Marbles', *Revue Hellénique de Droit International*, 2, 513, at 519–520.

23 See also the Council of Europe Recommendation 848 (1978) on underwater cultural heritage. A draft Convention on underwater heritage was drafted in 1985 by the Council of Europe but could not be opened for signature. Also article 1 of the Valetta Convention, in the definition of archaeological heritage, makes reference to heritage situated on land or under water in the area under the jurisdiction of the parties to the Convention. The 'area' includes the territorial sea, the contiguous zone and the continental shelf. See also the 1982 United Nations Convention on the Law of the Sea, the ICOMOS Charter on Underwater Cultural Heritage (1996), the 1989 International Salvage Convention, the Council of Europe Recommendation 1486 (2000) on Maritime and Fluvial Cultural Heritage. See Pickard, R. (2003), *European Cultural Heritage: A review of Policies and Practice*, Strasbourg: Council of Europe Publishing, vol. II, 53.

heritage, as in the 1972 UNESCO Convention Concerning the Protection of the World Cultural and Natural Heritage (Paris, 16 November 1972). However, in practice this distinction is not always followed given the fact that many items coming within the concept of natural heritage are considered to be cultural objects according to the 1970 UNESCO Convention and the 1995 Unidroit Convention.[24] Also, the European Convention on the Protection of the Archaeological Heritage (Council of Europe, London, 6 May 1969 as revised in Valetta, 16 January 1992) refers to the protection and enhancement of the archaeological heritage in the context of town and country planning operations (Preamble).

The notion of 'cultural property' has been defined in various national, regional (including European Union) or international legal instruments, for the purposes of these instruments. With regard to international conventions, I shall only refer to those concerned with the illegal trade in art in times of peace, which forms the subject of this book. Article 1 of the 1970 UNESCO Convention, dealing with the prevention of the illicit export, import and transfer of ownership of cultural property, defines 'cultural property' as property which, on religious or secular grounds, is specifically designated by each state as being of importance for archaeology, prehistory, history, literature, art or science and belongs to a number of categories that are specifically set out in the same article.[25] In other words, according to this Convention states parties to the Convention are free to

---

[24] See e.g. article 1(a) of the 1970 UNESCO Convention and Annex (a) in the 1995 Unidroit Convention: 'Rare collections and specimens of fauna, flora, minerals and anatomy, and objects of palaeontological interest'.

[25] (a) Rare collections and specimens of fauna, flora, minerals and anatomy, and objects of palaeontological interest; (b) property relating to history, including the history of science and technology and military and social history, to the life of national leaders, thinkers, scientists and artists and to events of national importance; (c) products of archaeological excavations (including regular and clandestine) or of archaeological discoveries; (d) elements of artistic or historical monuments or archaeological sites which have been dismembered; (e) antiquities more than one hundred years old, such as inscriptions, coins and engraved seals; (f) objects of ethnological interest; (g) property of artistic interest, such as: (i) pictures, paintings and drawings produced entirely by hand on any support and in any material (excluding industrial designs and manufactured articles decorated by hand); (ii) original works of statuary art and sculpture in any material; (iii) original engravings, prints and lithographs; (iv) original artistic assemblages and montages in any material; (h) rare manuscripts and incunabula, old books, documents and publications of special interest (historical, artistic, scientific, literary, etc.) singly or in collections; (i) postage, revenue and similar stamps, singly or in collections; (j) archives, including sound, photographic and cinematographic archives; (k) articles of furniture more than one hundred years old and old musical instruments.

define their own cultural property as long as this definition comes within the specifically designated categories of article 1.[26] Almost the same list of objects is also found in the 1995 Unidroit Convention on Stolen or Illegally Exported Cultural Objects without, however, any reference made this time to the contracting states' competence to define their cultural treasures.[27] This can be considered as retrogression compared to the 1970 UNESCO Convention.[28] These definitions constitute the compromise reached between two views: on the one hand, the most 'protective' view of culture, which favours a broad definition of cultural objects held by states that regard themselves as victims of plunder and spoliation and want to protect their treasures as effectively as possible, and on the other hand, the view of the so-called 'art market' states, which favour a narrow definition, including only a limited number of cultural objects and therefore not jeopardising the free trade in art and their extensive museum and privately owned collections containing items with a foreign provenance.[29]

---

[26] For an extensive analysis see 2.1.3. below

[27] Article 2: 'For the purposes of this Convention, cultural objects are those which, on religious or secular grounds, are of importance for archaeology, prehistory, history, literature, art or science and belong to one of the categories listed in the Annex to this Convention.'

[28] For an extensive analysis see section 2.2.3 below.

[29] See also Article 1 of the 1954 Hague Convention:

> For the purposes of the present Convention, the term 'cultural property' shall cover, irrespective of origin or ownership: (a) movable or immovable property of great importance to the cultural heritage of every people, such as monuments of architecture, art or history, whether religious or secular; archaeological sites; groups of buildings which, as a whole, are of historical or artistic interest; works of art; manuscripts, books and other objects of artistic, historical or archaeological interest; as well as scientific collections and important collections of books or archives or of reproductions of the property defined above; (b) buil dings whose main and effective purpose is to preserve or exhibit the movable cultural property defined in subparagraph (a) such as museums, large libraries and depositories of archives, and refuges intended to shelter, in the event of armed conflict, the movable cultural property defined in subparagraph (a); (c) centres containing a large amount of cultural property as defined in subparagraphs (a) and (b), to be known as 'centres containing monuments';

Article 1 of the1972 UNESCO Convention Concerning the Protection of the World Cultural and Natural Heritage:

> For the purpose of this Convention, the following shall be considered as 'cultural heritage': monuments: architectural works, works of monumental sculpture and painting, elements or structures of an archaeological nature, inscriptions, cave dwellings and combinations of features, which are of outstanding universal

The aforementioned states are also known as 'export' states and 'import' states respectively.

Regulation 116/09 and Directive 7/93 refer to 'cultural goods' and 'cultural objects' respectively. Both are considered to have defined 'national treasures' (as these are provided for in article 36 TFEU)[30] which, by derogation from the rules on the free movement of goods, are subject to their 'protective regime'. According to the Regulation 'cultural goods' are considered those items listed in the Regulation's Annex.[31] The Directive provides for two conditions: the object has to be (a) included in the list in the Annex (which is the same as the Regulation's list) or in that of article 1 (that is it must form an integral part of a public collection, or of inventories of ecclesiastical institutions) and (b) classified among the 'national treasures' under national legislation or administrative procedures within the meaning of article 36 TFEU.[32] Both legal instruments refer to the

---

> value from the point of view of history, art or science; groups of buildings: groups of separate or connected buildings which, because of their architecture, their homogeneity or their place in the landscape, are of outstanding universal value from the point of view of history, art or science; sites: works of man or the combined works of nature and man, and areas including archaeological sites which are of outstanding universal value from the historical, aesthetic, ethnological or anthropological point of view.

The definitions found in regional Conventions are also relevant. See e.g. article 5 of the 1954 European Cultural Convention, article 1 of the 1969 European Convention on the Protection of the Archaeological Heritage as revised in Valetta, 16 January 1992, article 1 of the 1985 Convention for the Protection of the Architectural Heritage of Europe, article 2 and the Annex to the 1985 European Convention on Offences Relating to Cultural Property (which has never entered into force) and article 2 of the 1976 Convention on the Protection of the Archeological, Historical, and Artistic Heritage of the American Nations (Convention of San Salvador) signed in Washington, D.C., on 16 June 1976.

30 See section 3.1.2 below.

31 Regulation 116/09: Article 1: 'Without prejudice to Member States' powers under Article 30 of the Treaty, the term "cultural goods" shall refer, for the purposes of this Regulation, to the items listed in Annex I'. See section 3.2.2 below.

32 Directive 93/7/EEC: Article 1

> For the purposes of this Directive: 1. 'Cultural object' shall mean an object which:—is classified, before or after its unlawful removal from the territory of a member state, among the 'national treasures possessing artistic, historic or archaeological value' under national legislation or administrative procedures within the meaning of Article 36 of the Treaty, and—belongs to one of the categories listed in the Annex or does not belong to one of these categories but forms an integral part of:—public collections listed in the inventories of museums, archives or libraries' conservation collections. For the purposes of

Member States' competence in the area, albeit to different degrees. In the case of the Regulation the Member States' competence is mentioned as a reminder that Member States can designate a higher or lower number of goods as cultural, although these will not be subject to the Regulation's regime if they do not come within the Annex. In the case of the Directive, the competence of the Member States has a decisive role to play. It forms one of the conditions in order for an object to be protected under the Directive. Only when both conditions are met (an object is both defined by the Member State as a national treasure and included in the list of the Directive) can the object be the subject of restitution.

It can be derived from the above that a) variations in terms are not as important as variations in definitions, and b) the significant limiting factor in relation to a definition is not so much whether it is set out as a list of objects or categories (an enumerative definition) or as a general definition or a combination of the two, but whether a state's competence in defining its own cultural treasures is taken into account. In the aforementioned definitions the competence of the state varies. That means in practice that there will be cases where there will be no agreement as to whether an object falls within the ambit of a legal instrument or not, if the parties come from different traditions or do not share the same values, mentalities or interests (i.e. divergent views between source states and import states). Such instances may slow down or otherwise affect the application of the legal instruments in the field.

1.2 RETURN AND RESTITUTION

Cultural property law uses a variety of terms to indicate claims of relocation of cultural property at the request of a prior possessor, be it the state of origin or other entity or person. The terms used are 'return', 'recovery', 'retrieval', 'recuperation', 'restitution' and 'repatriation'. Although in practice all these terms are used interchangeably, there were originally

---

this Directive, 'public collections' shall mean collections which are the property of a member state, local or regional authorities within a member state or an institution situated in the territory of a member state and defined as public in accordance with the legislation of that member state, such institution being the property of, or significantly financed by, that member state or a local or regional authority;—the inventories of ecclesiastical institutions.

The Annex to the Directive is the same as the one found in Regulation 116/09. See section 3.3.2 below.

differences in substance, since some of these terms have particular legal connotations.

'Restitution' or '*restitutio in integrum*' are terms with origins in Roman law, which are nowadays often found in both civil and common law legal systems. The main meaning behind these terms is the complete (or almost complete, where complete is not possible in the circumstances) restoration of the previous state of affairs (*status quo ante*) and reparation for an injury. That means that the term 'restitution' presupposes that an unlawful act has taken place, which has created an injury that needs to be restored.[33] If this is transposed to cultural objects, alienated from their countries of origin (especially during periods of colonisation or under dubious legal circumstances), restitution should mean that the object should either be returned to the dispossessed owner or (where this is not possible) an object identical or equivalent should be given back. According to W. Kowalski, the term 'restitution', as a term usually used for the return of property looted in times of war, should be distinguished from the term 'reparations'. The latter is only used to compensate for the loss in an approximate manner and it is usually accomplished by handing over money or goods of equivalent value.[34]

The term 'restitution' evolved in the nineteenth century, when claims

---

[33] According to Barkan, E. ('The Guilt of Nations: Restitution and Negotiating Historical Injustices', in L.V. Prott (ed.), (2009) *Witnesses to History*, Paris: UNESCO, at 78) restitution

> include[s] the entire spectrum of attempts to rectify historical injustices, including not only the return of the specific belongings that were confiscated, seized, or stolen, such as land, art, ancestral remains, and so on, but also 'reparations' (some form of material recompense for that which cannot be returned, such as human life, a flourishing culture and economy, and identity), and 'apology' (an admission of wrongdoing, a recognition of its effects, and, in some cases, an acceptance of responsibility for those effects and an obligation to its victims). For him the concept means something more like 'making amends' and as the result of guilt. He sees restitution not just as a legal but also as a cultural concept.

Prott, L.V. (2009), 'Note on Terminology', *ibid*, xxii.

[34] Kowalski, W. (2009), '"Restitution": Art Treasures and War' (extract from (2002), *Restitution of Works of Art pursuant to Private and Public International Law, Recueil des Cours 80–90*,The Hague: Martinus Nijhoff), in L.V. Prott (ed.), *Witnesses to History*, n. 33 above, 163. See also Barkan, E. (2009), 'The Guilt of Nations', n. 33 above, 80, where he mentions that 'Restitution strictly refers to the return of the specific actual belongings that were confiscated, seized, or stolen, such as land, art, ancestral remains, and the like. Reparations refers to some form of material recompense for that which cannot be returned, such as human life, a flourishing culture and economy, and identity.'

for the repatriation of cultural objects augmented. It was based on the principle of identification, which provided for the return of the cultural object that had been removed and the principle of territoriality, according to which an item is returned to the place from which it was taken. This latter principle was also connected with the protection of the integrity of national cultural heritage, and has increasingly influenced both bilateral and multilateral international agreements.[35] Apart from the peace treaties signed after the First World War, it is also found in the 1970 UNESCO Convention with regard to cultural objects which are illicitly imported, exported and have their ownership transferred.[36] It is also found in the 1995 Unidroit Convention but only with regard to cultural objects that are stolen.[37] In both the 1970 UNESCO Convention and the 1995 Unidroit Convention, however, the notion of restitution allows for the return of the removed cultural object, irrespective of the particular requirements applying in each case.

Despite the fact that in many national systems the term 'restitution' is closely linked to ownership, it is argued that in modern cultural property law it should not be seen 'as one of ownership but as one of justice; not as a matter of legality, but as one of legitimacy'.[38] That means that 'restitution' is gradually being taken out of its narrow legal context, whilst ethical values and principles (as well as cultural arguments)[39] are being attached to it. Yet, reservations about the unbridled use of this term seem to survive even today, as for example in the title of the Intergovernmental Committee for Promoting the Return of Cultural Property to its Countries of Origin

---

[35] 'As early as the nineteenth century, [the obligation of the restitution of looted art] was based on the principle of identification, which provided for the return of exactly the same and only the same objects which had been removed, as well as on the principle of territoriality, according to which an item is returned to the place from which it was taken. In many cases, when claims were examined, the period of time that had passed since the loss of the object was not taken into account. From the beginning of the nineteenth century, claims relating to cultural heritage emerged, indicating the development of the principle of the special territorial bonds attaching to works of art, which had previously applied only to archives. This principle is connected with the protection of the integrity of national cultural heritage, and has increasingly influenced both bilateral and multilateral international agreements.' *Ibid.*, 164.

[36] See e.g. articles 13(b) and 15.

[37] See e.g. the Preamble to the Convention and articles 1(a), 3(3),(4),(5),(8), 4(1), 8(3), 9(1), 10(3), 16(1),(2), and 19(3).

[38] See Prott, L.V. (2009), 'Note on Terminology', n. 33 above, xxi.

[39] L. Prott mentions that 'restitution' is not a question of reparation of injury but rather one of ensuring adequate national collections of local cultures. *Ibid.*

or its Restitution in Case of Illicit Appropriation.[40] Indicative in this respect is also the distinction followed in the 1995 Unidroit Convention (discussed below[41]) with regard to stolen and illegally exported cultural objects.

'Recovery', 'retrieval', 'recuperation' and 'repatriation' are more neutral terms, which incorporate 'pre-return' efforts, such as identification, location and request of the cultural object through particular processes.[42] The term 'repatriation' in particular is firmly based on the principles of cultural integrity and territoriality, which dictate the return of the cultural object to its place of origin. In that sense it puts forward the territory instead of the dispossessed owner and in these instances claims by countries of origin are based on this particular principle, that is the return of the object to its place of origin, and not on 'ownership'. Repatriation is not a concept relating solely to inter-state relocation of cultural objects but to intra-state relocation too. An example of such is the Stone of Scone, used for centuries in the coronation of monarchs of Scotland and returned from England to Scotland in November 1996. Another example is the return of manuscripts from the canton of Zurich to the canton of Saint Gall in 2006 from which they were taken during the Toggenburg War of 1712 when the Prince-Abbot of St. Gall was defeated by the forces of Zurich and Bern. The manuscripts were returned to St. Gall on long-term loan and on the condition that it would digitize them and make them available on the Internet by the end of 2007. In that sense the concept of 'repatriation' carries with it cultural values and principles. There exists a potential problem with this terminology. This lies in the fact that it does not cover cases of return which relate to people and their connection to history, religion and identity as is the case with indigenous communities and human remains. However, there is nothing to preclude the term 'territory' from being conceived broadly so as to include people, their contribution to their identities and their role in time and history.

'Return' is the most neutral term of all and, to a certain extent, incorporates the interests of both the requesting and the requested party in the sense that it takes account of both of them (on the one hand, the need for

---

40 The phrase 'in case of illicit appropriation' was put there as a compromise between the joint French and German suggestion to delete the word 'restitution' and the view of those who wanted it to remain in the title of the Committee. For more historical details as to this controversy see Prott, L.V., *ibdi*, xxi–xxii.

41 See section 2.2 below

42 There is also the view that they relate to major losses of cultural goods and specific programmes set up for their retrieval. Prott, L.V. (2009), 'Note on Terminology', n. 33 above, xxiii.

repatriation of the object and on the other hand, the acknowledgment of the ethical, moral, archaeological, ethnographical or other values in order for such repatriation to take place). The term 'return' is widely used in requests for relocation and specifically in the area of illegal trade in cultural property (as is the case, for example, with the 1970 UNESCO Convention, the 1995 Unidroit Convention and Council Directive 93/7/EEC on the return of cultural objects unlawfully removed from the territory of a Member State). In these cases return is justified on the basis of an illegal act having preceded the request. However, this term is not generally associated with the rectification of a 'wrong' or the amendment of an 'injury'. Rather, it unequivocally signifies an obligation for the physical return of the displaced object with the ultimate aim of achieving the integrity of the site or that of the cultural context from which the object has been removed. Self-evidently such an outcome cannot be achieved if the displaced cultural object no longer survives. It is not, therefore, the unlawful act as such that dictates return (which can be considered as a form of restitution) but the ethical and moral principles attached to it. These principles are particular to cultural property law, because they have been directly or indirectly recognised in international conventions. They are discussed in detail in chapter 6.[43] Therefore 'return' is subject to a 'cultural philosophy', which puts forward the protection of national cultural heritage as a vehicle for the protection of the world's heritage, in the sense that countries of origin are the best placed trustees for such property (irrespective of issues of ownership) particularly by reason of the fact that cultural objects are best conceived in their cultural context and they should not operate merely on the basis of their aesthetic values. Cultural objects also serve as information for archaeological, historical, ethnographic or other finds. On top of that, unequivocal and unreserved return of cultural objects, which have been illegally displaced, works as a means of discouraging the illegal trade in art.

The neutrality of the term 'return' is also indicated by the fact that this term is used in cases of relocation of cultural objects, irrespective of time limitations or other legal constraints, where the objects have been displaced under unethical circumstances. These circumstances include cases where the object's removal may not have been illegal at the time of its removal, but was nonetheless unethical (for example removals during periods of war, belligerent occupation, colonisation or when a nation had no control

---

[43] See O'Keefe, P.J. and L.V. Prott (1989), *Law and the Cultural Heritage: Volume I: Discovery and Excavation* and *Volume III: Movement*, London: Butterworths, 830.

over its cultural treasures).[44] These cases cover art looted during the Nazi period and human remains of indigenous people. They also include several other cases such as the Parthenon Marbles case. The Utimut project was one such, involving the repatriation of a large number of artefacts from Denmark to Greenland that were displaced during the Danish colonial reign in Greenland (1721–1953)[45] irrespective of the legal case for such a return (permanent loans, reservation of propriety, shared ownership and so on).

1.3 THE THEORIES OF CULTURAL NATIONALISM AND CULTURAL INTERNATIONALISM

Two important theories underline the area of cultural property law: cultural nationalism and cultural internationalism. These theories were initially developed alongside the emergence of the international legal instruments in the area (such as the Convention for the Protection of Cultural Property in the Event of Armed Conflict, known as the 1954 Hague Convention)[46] in the mid nineteenth century. They were developed further later on with the drafting of the 1970 UNESCO Convention on the Means of Prohibiting and Preventing the Illicit Import, Export and Transfer of Ownership of Cultural Property and the 1995 Unidroit Convention on Stolen or Illegally Exported Cultural Objects, and were called upon/relied upon to a large extent to work as justifying bases for two different approaches to the trade in art.

International instruments in the area of protection of cultural property,

---

[44] J. H. Merryman refers to return of works of art and antiquity that were taken from their sites during the Age of Imperialism which extends (according to him) from the Roman sack of Veii in 396 B.C., through Napoleon's Northern, Italian and Egyptian campaigns and the US suppression of American Indian cultures, to the fall of the Third Reich at the end of the Second World War. He also argues that some of the forms art imperialism has taken are aggression, opportunism, partage (according to which objects found during excavations conducted by a foreign archaeological team were divided equally between this team and the source nation) and accretion (for example the suppression of American Indian nations by the colonists since 1533). Merryman, J.H. (ed.) (2006), *Imperialism, Art and Restitution*, Cambridge University Press, 1 and 3 *et seq*.

[45] See Thorleifsen, D. (2009), 'The Repatriation of Greenland's Cultural Heritage', *Museum International*, 61 (1–2), 25; and, Mille G. (2009), 'The Return of Cultural Heritage from Denmark to Greenland', *ibid*, 30.

[46] The 1954 Hague Convention also indicated the developments concerning the protection of cultural property in the international law of war.

as well as the international interest, were initiated when certain countries became victims of spoliation and removals of their cultural property, either by reason of war, belligerent occupation, colonisation, turbulent political or other circumstances or by reason of their actual incapacity to protect their treasures from vandalism or organised crime. These countries (at the beginning of the nineteenth century), after having emerged from these circumstances or after having gained their independence, started claiming back their lost treasures in an effort to reconstruct their national identity. This new state of affairs contrasted with what had been going on for several years, and was to a certain degree feeding the former situation: the high demand in Europe and other developed countries for antiquities and artefacts in general by private collectors and museums. Private collectors and museums acted as potential buyers in a flourishing market largely operating illegally or semi-legally. A number of traders, such as antiquarians, gallery owners, dealers and auction houses survived by means of these activities. The absence of any national binding legal rules to this end let things develop in their own way.

These two realities (that of retention of cultural objects within the territory of their nation of origin and that of their retention within the territory of the acquiring nation by private collectors or museums and/or the free trading in these cultural objects) contradicted each other. The interests involved were mostly financial since the art market constituted one of the most lucrative markets comparable with those in drugs and weapons. At the same time collectors and museums needed desperately to find a basis to justify their collections, which were 'collected' under dubious circumstances and contained objects which were unprovenanced. 'Internationalism' or 'Cosmopolitanism' could serve both as an ideal basis and an answer to those claiming the return of these objects.

The role of museums cannot be disregarded. These entities had brought together significant works of art, which otherwise may have been lost or destroyed. They preserved and cared for them, researched them, educated and sensitised their visitors and provided access to them in an era when travelling was not easy. This argument also applies to collectors who provided public access to their collections.

Thus, on the one side there were wealthy states (also known as 'import' or 'market' states), wealthy museums and wealthy collectors. The interests of these states were the undisturbed import of and trade in antiquities.[47] On the other side there were essentially poor, developing states or states particularly rich in cultural property which could not always effectively

---

[47] UK, France, Switzerland, Thailand, Hong Kong, Singapore, Japan and so on.

control their cultural heritage (also known as 'export' or 'source' states),[48] most of them just emerging from turbulent situations. Their interests were the return and restitution of their missing cultural property. This latter group occasionally included developed 'import' states, too, such as France, Canada and Australia.

Two theories have emerged in cultural property law, known by different terms or labels, depending on whether or not reference to them is made by their detractors or not. On the one hand, there is the theory of cultural nationalism, with direct references to retentionism, protectionism, particularism and so on. On the other hand, there is the theory of national internationalism or cosmopolitanism,[49] with direct references to imperialism and to a form of 'de-contextualisation'.

These theories are not cast in stone. It can be argued that each one of them has a core that is shared by all those who adhere to it but there are also variations between the various writers or commentators as well as variations dictated by actual practice and reality. The core of these theories can be described as follows:

According to cultural internationalism (the international expression of which, according to one view, is found in the 1954 Hague Convention), cultural property is not linked to a state or nation nor to a particular territory. It forms part of the cultural heritage of the world and as such belongs to all mankind. Therefore claims for restitution and return are not justified unless the objects at issue have been acquired as a result of theft. There have occasionally been some reservations about this theory, even by its supporters. Some of them argue that it should not apply to archaeological objects, which come from an unauthorized, clandestine excavation and an undocumented removal. J. H. Merryman provides the following example:

---

48 Such as Greece, Italy, Cambodia, Peru, Mali, Turkey, Mexico, Afghanistan, China, Bolivia, Colombia and so on.

49 Other terms are 'supranationalism' and 'meta-nationalism', which again try to reflect the idea that humanity, independently of nations, is the party in inte rest. See Merryman, J. H. (1986), 'Two ways of thinking about cultural property', *American Journal of International Law*, 80 (4) 831, at 842, n. 37. See also Nafziger, J.A.R., 'Cultural Heritage Law: The International Regime', in Nafziger & T. Scovazzi (eds) (2008), *Le patrimoine culturel de l'humanité – Cultural Heritage of Mankind*, Leiden, p.147, at 203 where he refers to the fact that 'The term 'cultural internationalism', then, cleverly pirates a commonly understood and venerated term – internationalism – to justify practices that actually defy the fundamental requirements of co-operation and collaboration underlying internationalism in the normal sense of the term.'

> A Mayan stele torn from an undeveloped, undocumented site in the jungle of Belize and smuggled to Switzerland to be sold becomes anonymous. Both, it and the site, have been deprived of valuable archaeological and ethnological information that would have been preserved had the removal been properly supervised and documented or had the stele remained in place.[50]

This, however, relates to a small proportion of cultural objects, and there is no reason to prevent the rest from being traded or exported.

According to cultural internationalism the activities of *huaqueros* (in Mexico and Central America) and *tombaroli* (in Italy) should be legalised and supervised by professionals in order for the damage to cultural objects found or excavated in this manner to be prevented. That, of course, relies on these activities being sponsored by collectors or museums that will be prepared to buy the aforementioned objects. In other words, the state will first, be able to minimise illegal excavations by legalising and supervising them, and second, by trading in its cultural objects it will be able to better preserve antiquities already in its collections, as well as newly found ones (since the state will not trade in all of them but only in those existing in surplus).

According to this theory cultural property should be traded freely. The countries of origin should not be the ones to decide whether a cultural object has left their territory illegally or not. In that sense national export laws as well as national laws providing for state ownership in cultural treasures should not be enforced by third countries. The supporters of this theory do not feel comfortable with the 1970 UNESCO Convention. If, however, their countries (usually 'import' states) have ratified it, they attempt interpretations reflecting the aforementioned spirit. The same applies to the 1995 Unidroit Convention. Yet in this case the situation is somewhat different in the sense that only very few states have ratified it. Both Conventions provide expressly for return of cultural objects to their countries of origin and mutual co-operation in the area of illicit export, import and trade of cultural objects.[51]

---

50 *Ibid*, at 843. Merryman also provides for other examples such as the Native American Graves Protection and Repatriation Act (NAGPRA) and the Afo-A-Kom case without, however, offering guidelines as to why he distinguishes these particular cases. Merryman, J.H. (2006), 'Whither the Elgin Marbles?', in J.H. Merryman (ed), *Imperialism, Art and Restitution*, Cambridge University Press, 98, at 112. For the Afo-A-Kom case see J.H. Merryman (2002), 'Who Owns the Past?' in J.H. Merryman and A.E. Elsen (eds.), *Law, Ethics and the Visual Arts*, 4th edition, the Netherlands: Kluwer Law International, 161, at 267.

51 There is very little merit in the attitude of those who, in the name of an alleged principle of "cultural internationalism", plead for an uncontrolled movement of cultural properties. It is not by chance that such a movement goes always

Lastly, this theory bears considerable resemblance to the theory of 'universal' museums. According to that, cultural objects originating from other countries and acquired in earlier times, after they have been displaced from their original source, have become part of the museums that have cared for them and by extension part of the heritage of the nations that house them. Retention of those objects by museums, irrespective of the way in which they have been acquired, is important for the interests of all people.[52] Universal museums have also been referred to

---

in the same direction, following the rules of the market, to the benefit of those who can invest huge amounts of money in purchasing foreign cultural properties and to the detriment of the countries of origin. If cultural internationalists start from the objective of preventing "retention" by the countries of origin and reach the result of blessing "retention" by the States of import, in particular the States where those people and institutions are located that are prepared to pay the most and do their best to protect their investments, there is a dubious exercise of logic, to say the least. [. . .] In the field of cultural heritage, the word "internationalism", which instinctively implies a positive meaning, should be understood not in the sense of unbridled international trade, but in the sense of international cooperation with countries of origin to prevent and sanction illegal trade, as well as in the sense of international financial and technical assistance to developing countries of origin to allow them to protect their cultural heritage in the place where it has been created. After all, nothing prevents those who are interested in cultural internationalism to move, to cross a boundary and to admire the cultural heritage in its most appropriate context.

Scovazzi, T. (2009), 'Diviser c'est détruire: ethical principles and legal rules in the field of return of cultural properties', paper presented in the 16th Session of the Intergovernmental Committee for Promoting the Return of Cultural Property to Its Countries of Origin or Its Restitution in Case of Illicit Appropriation (21–23.9.2010), Paris: UNESCO, at 40–41.

52 See the Declaration on the Importance and Value of Universal Museums, 10 December 2002. Eighteen major museums have signed it: The Art Institute of Chicago; Bavarian State Museum, Munich (Alte Pinakothek, Neue Pinakothek); State Museums, Berlin; Cleveland Museum of Art; J. Paul Getty Museum, Los Angeles; Solomon R. Guggenheim Museum, New York; Los Angeles County Museum of Art; Louvre Museum, Paris; The Metropolitan Museum of Art, New York; The Museum of Fine Arts, Boston; The Museum of Modern Art, New York; Opificio delle Pietre Dure, Florence; Philadelphia Museum of Art; Prado Museum, Madrid; Rijksmuseum, Amsterdam; State Hermitage Museum, St. Petersburg; Thyssen-Bornemisza Museum, Madrid; Whitney Museum of American Art, New York.

> The international museum community shares the conviction that illegal traffic in archaeological, artistic, and ethnic objects must be firmly discouraged. We should, however, recognize that objects acquired in earlier times must be viewed in the light of different sensitivities and values, reflective of that earlier era. The

as 'encyclopedic' museums in the sense that they try to exhibit examples from as many cultures as possible in order for the visitor to be able to see, understand and compare the various cultures. From the above it may be deduced that not all museums can qualify as 'universal' museums since they do not all exhibit examples of different cultures.

The 2002 Declaration (setting up the notion of the 'universal museum') is quite confusing. It seems to adhere to the notion of 'national heritage' meaning the heritage of the country on whose territory the museum is ('part of the heritage of the nations which house them'), whilst at the same time it refers to the cultural heritage of all mankind ('museums serve not just the citizens of one nation but the people of every nation'). Given also the fact that they unequivocally state that the 'illegal traffic in archaeological, artistic, and ethnic objects must be firmly discouraged', one could easily reach the conclusion that this declaration was drafted by museums which possess the largest collection of cultural objects of an ambiguous provenance.[53] These museums want to find a legitimising basis in order to

---

> objects and monumental works that were installed decades and even centuries ago in museums throughout Europe and America were acquired under conditions that are not comparable to those of today.
>
> Over time, objects so acquired, whether by purchase, gift, or partage, have become part of the museums that have cared for them, and by extension part of the heritage of the nations which house them. Today we are especially sensitive to the subject of a work's original context, but we should not lose sight of the fact that museums too provide a valid and valuable context for objects that were long ago displaced from their original source. The universal admiration for ancient civilisations would not be so deeply established today were it not for the influence exercised by the artefacts of these cultures, widely available to an international public in major museums. [. . .] Calls to repatriate objects that have belonged to museum collections for many years have become an important issue for museums. Although each case has to be judged individually, we should acknowledge that museums serve not just the citizens of one nation but the people of every nation. Museums are agents in the development of culture, whose mission is to foster knowledge by a continuous process of reinterpretation. Each object contributes to that process. To narrow the focus of museums whose collections are diverse and multifaceted would therefore be a disservice to all visitors

(Extracts from the 2002 Declaration).

[53] According to statistics released by the Chinese Society of Cultural Relics, China's cultural relics have been lost in amazing figures calculated by the million pieces, including hundreds of thousands of works of superb quality, scattered in forty-seven countries, some of them being taken away in wartime. In terms of Chinese paintings alone, the Metropolitan Museum of Art in New York claims the biggest number, while the British Museum boasts the best quality paintings. As for porcelain, le Musée Guimet of France is famed for its best collection of Asian

rebut criticism and requests emerging during the last decades, for repatriation of treasures in their collections originating from other countries and acquired under dubious circumstances and traumatic events, such as conquest or colonialism. In this climate, museums have tried to disassociate their collections from imperialism (the circumstances under which most of the exhibited artefacts have been acquired)[54] and articulate a new role for themselves as places that preserve diversity and foster mutual respect among civilisations and people. [55]

The concept of universal museums, which only emerged very recently and corresponds to those museums that could be made only at a particular juncture in history when there was a convergence of wealth, power, physical

---

art works. In America, over a thousand large bronze wares of ancient China can be found, including at least one thousand extraordinary pieces. Among European countries, Britain has the richest collection of Chinese cultural objects, next comes France. In its Guimet museum over half of the works collected are of Chinese origin, more than 30,000 pieces in number.

See L.V. Prott (ed.), *Witnesses to History*, n. 33 above, 119. See also Abungu, G. (1994), 'The Declaration: A Contested Issue', ICOM News as referred to in L.V. Prott (ed.), *ibid*, 121.

[54] See the comment by W. St Clair (2006) in relation to the Parthenon Marbles exhibited in the British Museum where he mentions that the British Museum celebrates 'British national and imperial success', 'Imperial Appropriations of the Parthenon', in J.H. Merryman (ed), *Imperialism, Art and Restitution*, n. 44 above, 82. He later on (at 94–95) offers more arguments against the notion of 'universal museum'. He first refers to the fact that the ideal of the universal museum was part of the aspiration of the European Enlightenment with the aim that the general public should have access to artistic achievements of the present and the past by plaster casts or copies. The signatories to the Declaration are only interested in exhibiting originals (it could perhaps be added to that that today no problems of accession to artistic achievements are encountered as was the case during the European Enlightenment). Second, he finds it absurd that a museum in a northern country is the best place in which to appreciate an ancient monument, especially if this is to be compared to its original cultural context, just because it presents examples from other cultures (in this sense one could argue, let's destroy to compare). Third, not all cultures bear resemblances and are comparable to each other. On the contrary, a visitor seeing artefacts decontextualised, can only compare their aesthetics and no other values. (The comments in brackets are the author's and not W. St Clair's.)

[55] Singh, K. 'Universal Museums: The View From Below', Speech given at the Salzburg Global Seminar 'Achieving the Freer Circulation of Cultural Artefacts'. A condensed version entitled 'National patrimony in a global environment' was published in *The Art Newspaper*, No. 192, June 2008, as published in L.V. Prott (ed.), n. 33 above 123 *et seq*., at 126. See also Boyd, W. (2006), 'Museums as Centers of Cultural Understanding', in J.H. Merryman (ed), *Imperialism, Art and Restitution*, n. 44 above, 56 *et seq*.

contact with far-off lands, and an intellectual interest in encyclopaedism,[56] does not seem to find/attract any support in international law[57] or ethics as they have been formed and transformed so far. First, it seems to create two classes of museums: museums with universal value for humanity and others. However, most museums offer something special, which may be of universal value. Therefore this distinction does not seem justified, whilst the criteria used for this classification are unknown.[58] Second, exhibiting other people's cultures separated from their traditions, religions, language and so on can only be done in a sterile way. It is half of the information, if not the wrong information, which is conveyed to the visitor. It is a de-contextualised aesthetic picture, which misses the values and the messages incorporated in the object.[59] This, of course, does not mean that there do not exist objects that can be exhibited as such, if these objects do not function in a whole or constitute parts of it and if they are well

---

56 *Ibid.*

57 'In 1954 the United Nations Educational, Scientific and Cultural Organization (UNESCO) adopted the Convention on Stolen and Illegally Exported Cultural Objects, stipulating that any cultural object looted or lost due to reasons of war should be returned without any limitation of time span. Apparently the Declaration by 18 museums runs counter to the spirit of the international convention.' See Prott, L.V. n. 33 above, 119–120.

58 See Abungu, G. (1994) who brings up in this respect the example of the National Museums of Kenya, 'The Declaration: A Contested Issue' ICOM News as referred to in L.V. Prott (ed.), n. 33 at 121.

59 Great and important indigenous collections were gathered for the Melbourne Museum and they are still held by the Museum today although it is in a dramatic new site. Although the collections were made with a dutiful, high-minded idea of the universalist museum, when presented in the way they were in 1929, they show only the memory patterns of one culture at work – the collecting culture – and demonstrate the loss and erasure of the memory structures of the cultures collected. Therefore, for me, Philippe de Montebello's metaphor of the universalist museum as the cultural family tree where all people can find their roots cannot possibly express what is happening in this situation. All of these spears and shields and other things that were shown in this exhibition have come from different peoples of different kinship, different traditions, different languages, and the original producers would have been horrified to find their cultural items mixed up with foreign items in this way, destroying all meanings that are important to the producing cultures, or what is here being called the 'source cultures'. The producing cultures – many of them continuing and flourishing today – give meaning to any particular item only through the total ensemble of living relationships and practices that emanate from one particular people, language and tradition.

Bernice Murphy in Museums, Memory and Universality, UNESCO Forum on Memory and Universality, UNESCO Headquarters, Paris, 5 February 2007, in L.V. Prott (ed.), n. 33 above, 45, at 57.

documented. Third, this declaration seems to imply that the best place to preserve cultural treasures is the 'Universal Museum'. However, this absolute way of approaching all treasures, irrespective of their particularities, seems to promote one single way of approaching cultural property. And that is through its function as art. In other words the theory of 'universal museum' privileges the physical object ('the primacy of the object') over its original functions (for example religious sentiment) that may correspond to human rights expressions. Such an approach, however, neglects other, at least equal, approaches to cultural property, such as, for example, its ethnographic, anthropocentric or religious connotations or functions or its contribution to a nation's identity. It may be hard for some to see exhibited in a museum window, as common works of art, utensils for religious ceremonies or objects buried with their ancestors. Acknowledging other approaches to cultural property denotes respect for people from which this property originates. And it is highly significant that museums are as respectful to people as they are to their artistic masterpieces. As K. Singh puts it:

> It's not just the universal museum that is being challenged here – your right to represent my ancestors – but it is the museum mode. And it is the museum mode whether this lives in the British Museum, or in the Bangladesh National Museum, or in a tiny site museum in the wilderness of Central India. And by the museum mode I mean the lifting out of the object from its particular context of use – domestic use, ritual use, courtly use, which made the object accessible and useful to a small group – and the transformation of the object into 'art' – desacralized, secularized, rationalized; turned into heritage; fitted into an intellectual structure in which it can become meaningful or interesting to a larger group; to the public.[60]

In this light '[t]he museum's 'universalism' is an ideological position that has its own history and its own politics, and the universal museum is fighting to protect its own heritage, not the world's'.[61]

On the other side of the spectrum stands the theory of cultural nationalism. According to this theory, states aim to retain their cultural treasures within their territory as part of their national cultural heritage. They also pursue the return of cultural objects that have left their territory either

---

60 Singh, K. 'Universal Museums', n. 33 above, at 128.

61 *Ibid.*, at 126. See also Lewis, G. (2006), 'The "Universal Museum": a case of special pleading?' in B. T. Hoffman (ed), *Art and Cultural Heritage. Law, Policy and Practice*, Cambridge University Press, 379 where he mentions that 'the real purpose of this declaration is to establish for "universal museums" a higher degree of immunity from claims of repatriation from their collections'.

illegally (according to their national laws) or unethically (in periods where such laws did not exist or could not have been enforced by reason of special circumstances).[62] These are usually the states that are rich in cultural treasures but that do not always possess the financial means or simply it is not always possible to protect these treasures from being stolen, illegally excavated or illegally exported. These states are usually victims of spoliation and plunder. Spoliation is the result of the international demand for cultural objects. The opponents of this theory argue that these states ('source' or 'export' states) are 'maximalist' in their requests (and 'particularist' in their attitudes) in the sense that they, on the one hand, request back all treasures originating from them (that is, the treasures found in their soil) and on the other hand, they provide for an extensive regime of protection for a wide range of cultural treasures, impeding the market in art unnecessarily. This policy has also been accused of forming one of the reasons that gives rise to the illegal trade in art.[63] The more severe the laws are, the more people use illegal methods to acquire what they desire. The theory of cultural nationalism does not always favour state ownership of cultural treasures. It may also favour private ownership by owners that are based in the state of origin on condition that they keep these treasures within the country.

There are variations with regard to these two theories, mainly due to state policies or commentators' views. That means that these views can be taken to the extreme but they can also exist in moderate forms. There are cases where cultural property issues are not approached according to objective theories or precast beliefs, but rather on the basis of their own facts and circumstances,[64] in other words from the problem-solver's subjective theory of justice or point of view.[65] In any case, of course, international Conventions work as the minimum acceptable standard for

---

[62] Egypt, for example, requests the return of six significant cultural treasures irrespective of the manner in which they left the country. These treasures are the Rosetta Stone in the British Museum in England, the statue of Hemiun in Roemer- and Pelizaeusmuseum in Hildesheim, Germany, the Nefertiti bust in the Berlin Museum in Germany, the Denderra Zodiac in the Louvre Museum in Paris, the Anchaf bust in the Museum of Fine Arts, Boston in the US and the Ramsay II statue in the Egizio Museum in Turin, Italy.

[63] Illicit trafficking in cultural property is the second most lucrative underground market after illegal drug trafficking. Charter of Courmayeur, 25–27, June 1992 <http://www.icomos.org/unesco/cormayeur.html>.

[64] Such as the circumstances of the object's removal, its importance for the requesting state (on historic, humanitarian, religious or other grounds) and so on.

[65] See Koskenniemi, M. (1989), *From Apology to Utopia: The Structure of International Legal Argument*, Cambridge University Press, 456–7.

the return of an object to its country of origin. Also, retention of a cultural object may be justified under both theories: both from a *nationalist* perspective which appreciates it as part of a wider cultural context and from an *internationalist* perspective which seeks to preserve the information, which would otherwise be lost if a significant cultural object is at issue and runs the risk of being displaced by means of illegal excavation (see the Merryman statement above). The same applies in relation to the movement of cultural objects. Their movement could be justified both on the basis of the distribution of the world's cultural heritage (internationalist approach) as well as on the basis of 'missionary art' (nationalist approach).[66]

The same applies with regard to the various arguments which may be used to support both theories depending on the point of view taken. For example, *preservation* is used to indicate the protection of cultural objects from destruction and damage. On this basis a cultural object may be alienated from its site in order to be protected. These cases, however, can only be very specific and relate to actual situations of danger (for example war). In any other case a cultural object, whose cultural context survives, can be returned in order to be intergrated into that context again. Therefore preservation should be regarded in a wider sense: not only the preservation of the object itself, but also the preservation of its surviving context. *Truth* and *access* form other important arguments. Truth has been referred to as meaning the information and insight that can be derived from the study of objects[67] and contexts, whilst accessibility is linked to the needs of scholars and the public for study and enjoyment.[68] Although these arguments are meant to be object-oriented, they very much refer to the preservation of cultural contexts in the sense that truth can be appreciated only if an object is found in its original site and a scholar or the public can best appreciate it in this particular original cultural context. This context necessarily represents the object's place of origin, whilst the object serves a wider aim by representing a brick in a wider construction. And it is this construction as a whole that one should appreciate and study if one is to derive conclusions about the original functions and aesthetics of the object.

Overall, however, and especially after the enactment of the 1970

---

[66] Barker, L. (2000–2003), 'Indeterminacy in International Legal Discourse', *Auckland University Law Review*, 9, 334, at 369.

[67] It is a fact that most museums are trying to recreate the original circumstances in exhibiting their objects and/or offer as much information as possible to the visitor concerning these circumstances. In that sense, by exhibiting the object in its original cultural context, the principle of truth can only be better served.

[68] J.H. Merryman n. 44 above, at 12 and n. 31.

UNESCO Convention and the 1995 Unidroit Convention, cultural nationalism has gained ground over cultural internationalism. In fact, it has been widely recognised that countries have legitimate interests in their cultural heritage and are the best-placed custodians to preserve it for the sake of humanity. It is in this context that cultural property is linked to certain territories and people and not seen in isolation from the soil or context in which it is found. In this way information is preserved, integrity, continuity and truth are served, whilst humanitarian principles are given priority.[69]

---

[69] See Brodie, N. (2006), 'An Archaeologist's View of the Trade in Unprovenanced Antiquities', in B.T. Hoffman (ed.), *Art and Cultural Heritage. Law, Policy and Practice*, Cambridge University Press, 52; Brodie, N. (2004), 'Export Deregulation and the Illicit Trade in Archaeological Material', in J.R. Richman and M.P. Forsyth (eds.), *Legal Perspectives on Cultural Resources*, Walnut Creek: AltaMira; Elia, R. (2001), 'Analysis of Looting, Selling and Collecting of Apulian Red-Figure Vases: A Quantitative Approach', in N. Brodie, J. Doole & C. Renfrew (eds.), *Trade in Illicit Antiquities: The Destruction of the World's Archaeological Heritage*, Cambridge: McDonald Institute for Arcaheological Research; Chippindale C. & D.W. Gill, (2000), 'Material consequences of Contemporary Classical Collecting', *American Journal of Archaeology*, 104; Renfrew, C. (2000), *Loot, Legitimacy and Ownership*, London: Duckworth; Wyliw, A. (1995), 'Archaeology and the Antiquities Market: The Use of 'Looted' Data', in M.J. Lynott and A. Wylie (eds.), *Ethics in American Archaeology: Challenges for the 1990s*, Washington D.C.: Society for American Archaeology.

2. International Conventions

2.1 THE 1970 UNESCO CONVENTION

2.1.1 General Remarks

The 1970 UNESCO Convention was the result of a long process of forming mentalities towards the protection of cultural property, which had taken place both in the League of Nations (predecessor of the United Nations) and in UNESCO itself.[1] It was also the outcome of an era during which illegal trade in art was flourishing and claims for the return and restitution of cultural objects were augmenting. The late 1960s in particular was a time when many objects, removed during the colonial period, were being claimed back. Many states, such as Greece (1834), Italy (1872) and France (1887), had already enacted laws in the late nineteenth and early twentieth centuries, with the aim of protecting their cultural property.[2] The first discussions in the League of Nations were initiated after the First World War with the co-ordination of the Office International des Musées (OIM) and gave rise to two draft conventions which, however, never became proper conventions because of the reluctance of the Netherlands, the United Kingdom, Sweden and the United States. The Second World War put an end to those negotiations.[3]

The two most important and influential instruments in this respect were two Recommendations. The 1956 Recommendation on International Principles Applicable to Archaeological Excavations aimed at encouraging

---

[1] UNESCO was founded in 1945.

[2] O'Keefe, P.J. (2000), *Commentary on the UNESCO 1970 Convention on Illicit Traffic*, Leicester: Institute of Art and Law, 3.

[3] The first draft convention was entitled 'Convention on the Repatriation of Objects of Artistic, Historical or Scientific Interest, which have been Lost, Stolen or Unlawfully Alienated or Exported'. It was submitted to the League of Nations in 1933 but it was not adopted because the Netherlands, the UK and the US opposed it. A second draft entitled 'Convention for the Protection of National, Historic and Artistic Treasures' was submitted to the League of Nations in 1936. Negotiations started on this draft, but the Second World War put an end to the process.

states to adopt measures against clandestine excavation, damage to monuments and export of material so obtained. It also urged museums, when they are offered archaeological objects, to ascertain that these objects have not been procured by clandestine excavation, theft or by any other method regarded as illicit by the country of origin.[4] The second Recommendation (the 1964 Recommendation on the 'Means of Prohibiting and Preventing the Illicit Export, Import and Transfer of Ownership of Cultural Property') aimed at encouraging states to adopt, within the limits of their national competence, measures to prevent illicit dealings in cultural property and pave the way towards the adoption of an international convention.

From that point onwards the preparation of the Convention was initiated by means of a series of processes and acts. It was not an easy progression since it was difficult to reconcile the views of the 'import' states with those of the 'export' states. At that stage, any state obligation towards the protection of cultural property appeared to be huge and constitute an insurmountable obstacle against the free market. However, after all those years and after a series of concessions, a 'Convention on the Means of Prohibiting and Preventing the Illicit Import, Export and Transfer of Ownership of Cultural Property' was adopted at the 16th General Conference of UNESCO in November 1970 by a majority of the states that were present.[5] The Convention entered into force on 24 April 1972.

Due to the lengthy negotiations, the divergence of views and mentalities, and the conflict of the various interests on the one hand, and the need to attain a final draft, which would be acceptable to both 'import' and 'export' states on the other, the content of the Convention is at times confusing and the obligations set out are very general and somewhat vague. This, of course, does not mean that these obligations do not exist for States Parties. On the contrary, according to article 31(1) of the 1969 Vienna Convention on the Law of Treaties 'a Treaty shall be interpreted in good faith in accordance with the ordinary meaning to be given to the terms of the Treaty in their context and in the light of its object and purpose'. In *Commonwealth of Australia v. State of Tasmania*,[6] a case which did not involve the 1970 UNESCO Convention, though of a similar nature, Judge Mason noted that 'however loosely such obligations may be defined, it is apparent that [a state], by depositing its instrument of ratification, bound itself to observe the terms of the Convention and assumed

---

4 See in particular articles 29, 30 and 31 of the Recommendation.

5 Seventy seven states voted in favour of its adoption, one against and eight states abstained. There is, however, no record of which states these were, because the vote was carried out by a show of hands.

6 46 A.L.R. 625.

real and substantive obligations under them'. It is, however, still difficult to define the scope of the obligations enshrined in the 1970 UNESCO Convention and ascertain how much these obligations can be manipulated by the interests and mentalities of the various states. This is especially so because there is no indicative case law relating to the UNESCO Convention. Some conclusions could possibly be drawn by examining the legislation implemented by States Parties. Yet this task is difficult, if such legislation has not been enacted solely for the purpose of implementing the 1970 UNESCO Convention, but reflects a State's intention to protect its cultural property.

2.1.2 Aims and Scope of the Convention (Preamble, Articles 2, 3, 11 and 12)

The 1970 UNESCO Convention aims to attain a minimum level of uniform protection against the illicit trafficking of cultural objects and a certain degree of international co-operation and solidarity in this respect. States Parties can provide for more protection if they wish. This Convention is not a self-executing legal instrument. It is a public law instrument which deals with relations between States Parties and requires action between national administrations or governments. Private parties do not derive rights directly from it and cannot sue another state's citizens or the state itself on the basis of this Convention.

Some legal instruments complement the Convention by providing for the protection of cultural property in particular circumstances. Examples include the 1954 Hague Convention for the Protection of Cultural Property in the Event of Armed Conflict and its two Protocols and the 2001 UNESCO Convention on the Protection of the Underwater Cultural Heritage. The 1970 UNESCO Convention is, however, independent from these legal instruments. The Convention that is most closely linked to the 1970 UNESCO Convention is the 1995 Unidroit Convention and this is discussed in section 2.2 below. These two Conventions are complementary to each other in the sense that they serve a common purpose albeit by different means. The 1995 Unidroit Convention, based on article 7(b)(ii) of the 1970 UNESCO Convention, regulates matters of private law regarding the *bona fide* possessor, his right to compensation, time limitations and so on. The 1995 Unidroit Convention is relevant to both private parties and states.

The 1970 UNESCO Convention refers to cultural property as this is defined in article 1 (and analysed in the next section). Articles 2, 3, 11 and 12 specify the particular aims and purpose of the Convention. According to this Convention States Parties *recognise* a) that the illicit import, export and transfer of ownership of cultural property is one of the main causes of the impoverishment of the cultural heritage of countries of origin of such property and b) that international co-operation constitutes one of the most efficient means of protecting each country's cultural property against all the dangers resulting from the illicit trafficking.[7] To this end, the states parties undertake to *oppose* such practices with the means at their disposal, in particular by removing their causes, putting a stop to current practices, and by helping to make the necessary reparations.[8]

Articles 3 and 11 provide clarification of which kind of import, export and transfer of ownership of cultural property is considered to be illicit. Anything which is effected contrary to the provisions of the Convention,[9] including the export and transfer of ownership of cultural property under compulsion arising directly or indirectly from the occupation of a country by a foreign power[10] is deemed to be illicit.

Article 3 should be read in conjunction with articles 6, 7, 9 and 13 regarding illicit exports and imports. However, it seems that its scope is wider compared to these articles, in the sense that it creates obligations in its own right. According to O'Keefe[11] it requires states, in their national laws, to regard as illicit transactions that breach the national law of another state party, whose law is in accordance with the Convention. This view is contested in the literature. Three alternative views have been put forward, one of which constitutes a variation of O'Keefe's view.

According to the first view (the variation on O'Keefe), article 3 requires states who are party to the Convention to hold void any contract between a party in the country of origin and a party in another state, where the object is still within the country of origin and completion of the contract would involve the breach of export regulations.[12] However, the distinction between the situation where a cultural object has already been exported at the time of the conclusion of a contract and the situation where such export has not yet taken place, is not apparent. In both circumstances, whether the object is outside its country of origin or is due to leave its country of origin, an illicit export will either have taken place or will be

---

7 Article 2(1).
8 Article 2(2).
9 Article 3.
10 Article 11.
11 O'Keefe, P.J., n. 2 above, 41–44 as he refers to other views, too.
12 Sandrock, O. (1988), 'Foreign Laws Regulating the Export of Cultural Property: The Respect Due to them by the Judge of the Lex Fori', in P. Lalive (ed.), *International Sales of Works of Art*, Paris: Institute of International Business Law & Practice and Geneva: Faculté de Droit de Genève, 457, at 460, 464 and 478.

about to take place. The underlying reasons for considering such an act as illicit are in both cases the same.

Of the other two views, the first alleges that this provision does not mean anything at all.[13] The other view ties the illicit character of the import to the particular provisions of the Convention and specifically to articles 6(b) (export without an export certificate), 7(b)(i) (import of property stolen from a museum or other institution) and 13(a) (transfers of ownership likely to promote illicit import and export). According to this view, these acts become unlawful acts in international law and should be treated as illicit transactions by other States Parties to the Convention.[14] However, if one considers that according to article 1 it is the export state that designates the cultural property that is of importance to it and requires (according to article 6) a certificate for its export, it will be difficult for the import state (which is party to the Convention) to argue that an export, which is considered illicit according to the export state's regulations is licit according to the import State's regulations, without infringing the substantive provisions of the Convention and without impinging on the Convention's spirit. If the same export of a cultural object is considered illegal in the country of origin and legal in the country of import, no international co-operation is achieved. The designation by a state of its cultural property is not respected, whilst information regarding an object's origin, history and traditional setting is lost (Preamble). This also seems to be the view followed by Canada, Greece and Australia in their national laws.[15]

Article 12 provides that States Parties shall respect the cultural heritage of the territories for which they are responsible for international relations, and shall take all appropriate measures to prohibit and prevent the illicit

---

[13] Bator, P.M. (1982), 'An Essay on the International Trade in Art', *Stanford Law Review*, 275, at 377.

[14] Fraoua, R. (1986), *Convention concernant les mesures à prendre pour interdire et empêcher l'importation, l'exportation et le transfert de propriété illicites de biens culturels (Paris, 1970) – Commentaire et aperçu de quelques mesures nationales d'exécution*, Paris: UNESCO Doc. CC – 86/WS/40, at 57.

[15] See section 31 of the Canadian Cultural Property Export and Import Act 1975; sections 3 and 14 of the Australian Protection of Movable Cultural Heritage Act 1986 and Greek Ministerial Decisions YA ΥΠΠΟ/ΔΟΕΠΥ/ΤΟΠΥΝΣ/17764 and 17759/5.3.2004. In other countries the situation seems to be unclear. There are, however, bilateral agreements between various states, which set out detailed rules and lists of cultural objects, whose import is restricted to the territory of the contracting states. Such agreements have been concluded between the US and a number of countries (Bolivia, Cambodia, Canada, China, Colombia, Cyprus, El Salvador, Guatemala, Honduras, Iraq, Italy, Mali, Nicaragua and Peru) <http://exchanges.state.gov/heritage/culprop.html>, between Greece and Switzerland, and between Italy and Switzerland.

import, export and transfer of ownership of cultural property in such territories. In conclusion one could argue that all these provisions come down to one main commitment: States Parties should try by any means possible to oppose practices involving the illicit import, export and transfer of ownership of cultural property taking place contrary to this Convention.

2.1.3 The Notion of 'Cultural Property' (Articles 1, 4 and 13(d))

The definition of cultural property is vital because it predefines the scope of the Convention. Significantly it was one of the most contested points in the Convention. Article 1 contains a general definition and an enumerative one, both of which complement each other. According to this article, '"cultural property" means property which, on religious or secular grounds, is specifically designated by each State as being of importance for archaeology, prehistory, history, literature, art or science and which belongs to the following categories . . .'. Then a number of categories follow.[16] States are free to define the scope and content of their own

---

16

(a) Rare collections and specimens of fauna, flora, minerals and anatomy, and objects of paleontological interest;
(b) property relating to history, including the history of science and technology and military and social history, to the life of national leaders, thinkers, scientists and artists and to events of national importance;
(c) products of archaeological excavations (including regular and clandestine) or of archaeological discoveries;
(d) elements of artistic or historical monuments or archaeological sites which have been dismembered;
(e) antiquities more than one hundred years old, such as inscriptions, coins and engraved seals;
(f) objects of ethnological interest;
(g) property of artistic interest, such as:
    (i) pictures, paintings and drawings produced entirely by hand on any support and in any material (excluding industrial designs and manufactured articles decorated by hand);
    (ii) original works of statuary art and sculpture in any material;
    (iii) original engravings, prints and lithographs;
    (iv) original artistic assemblages and montages in any material;
(h) rare manuscripts and incunabula, old books, documents and publications of special interest (historical, artistic, scientific, literary, etc.) singly or in collections;
(i) postage, revenue and similar stamps, singly or in collections;
(j) archives, including sound, photographic and cinematographic archives;
(k) articles of furniture more than one hundred years old and old musical instruments.

cultural property subject to two reservations. First, it has to be of importance for archaeology, prehistory, history, literature, art and science, and second, it has to belong in one of the categories of cultural objects enumerated in article 1.

One could argue that two more reservations are possible: a) the designation of cultural objects by the States Party should be a 'specific' designation and b) it should take place on religious or secular grounds. On this last point one could argue that there is, in practice, not much interest in it. It has perhaps been put there to exclude objects which cannot be considered cultural in the common sense of the word. However, the term 'specifically designated' has given rise to some literature in the area. The views are divided between those who argue that in order for an object to be protected under the scope of this Convention, it has to be particularly and specifically designated by the State and not just be part of a general category of objects or contained in a regime of classification of cultural objects. Yet, this view did not gain ground. States have chosen different ways to designate their cultural property, some of them being the ones just mentioned. From this point of view both these reservations do not seem to carry any special weight.[17]

According to the general definition found in article 1, in order for a cultural object to come under the scope of the Convention, it has to fall under both the general definition and the enumerative one. The reason for this is that some states were wary that a general definition would be too wide, whilst others that an enumerative one would be too restrictive. Of course, if an object has to fall under both a wide and a restrictive definition, the

---

[17] According to Askerud, P. and E. Clément (1997), *Preventing the Illicit Traffic in Cultural Property: A Resource Handbook for the Implementation of the 1970 UNESCO Convention*, Paris: UNESCO, 6 *et seq.*,

> A definition of cultural property like the one given above [article 1] is, however, so wide and normative that it is only useful if national Governments specifies what national cultural property should be protected by their legislation by designating the items which are to be considered so. It is therefore a requirement of each State party to the 1970 UNESCO Convention, that they establish and update a list of protected property whose export would constitute an appreciable impoverishment of the national cultural heritage. Not all objects can be mentioned in such a list (e.g. archaeological objects which have been plundered from illegal excavations and are therefore not registered) and objects can belong to more than one national heritage. To deal with objects which for one reason or another are not mentioned in the list, the 1970 UNESCO Convention stipulates that a State, in addition to the objects mentioned in Article 1, is entitled to consider an object as part of its cultural heritage if it falls in the categories provided by the Convention's Article 4.

restrictive one prevails. This seems to be the case here. In other words, even if an object comes within the general definition, it also needs to be included in the enumerative one and *vice versa*. So if an object comes within the enumerative definition, as being of importance for archaeology, prehistory, history, literature, art or science, it will not be covered by the Convention unless it has been designated as such by the State.

Apart from the definition enshrined in article 1, there are also articles 4 and 13(d) which provide for the notion of cultural property. These two provisions complement the original one in the sense that they clarify certain points, which otherwise may have been disputed. In particular article 4 sets out certain categories of cultural objects which form part of a State's cultural heritage.

First, included within the notion of cultural property is property created by nationals of the state as well as non-nationals, where this is of importance to the State concerned. The precondition that a cultural object has to be of importance to the State concerned refers only to property created by non-nationals and probably implies that a special link is required between that property and the State concerned.[18] Therefore it is not between the non-national and the State that this special link should be established but between the property and the State concerned.[19]

---

[18] There is also an argument that in order for cultural property created by non-nationals to be 'important' and therefore protectable, there needs to be a close relationship between the State concerned and the non-national. In this light it is argued that someone who lives only briefly in a particular country does not possess the required link. Fraoua, R. (n. 14 above), at 60. However, there is no justifying reason for such an approach given the fact that there are cultural objects which have been created by non-nationals who were only briefly resident in a country (e.g. English travellers who had visited Greece during Ottoman occupation and designed landscapes). No particular interpretation can be inferred from the use of the term 'importance'.

[19] See also Article 1(1)(b) of the Resolution of the Institut de Droit International (Session of Basel – 1991) 'The International Sale of Works of Art from the Angle of the Protection of the Cultural Heritage' according to which 'country of origin' of a work of art means the country with which the property concerned is most closely linked from the cultural point of view. http://www.idi-iil.org/idiE/resolutionsE/1991_bal_04_en.PDF

Cornu, M. & M.-A. Renold (2010) attempt some examples ('New Developments in the Restitution of Cultural Property: Alternative Means of Dispute Resolution', *International Journal of Cultural Property*, **17**(1), 16–17). They refer to archives or manuscripts, which can be considered to be closely linked to the history of a state or community and should naturally be held in that state or community. They also refer to objects of sacred or symbolic value including human remains, objects found in archaeological excavations, which are essential not only to an understanding of states and their history but also to their construction and founda-

For example, cultural objects created by immigrants or colonialists may be important to the history of the colony, which has in the meantime turned into an independent State. That is the case for many States in Africa as well as States in Latin America.

Second, cultural property found within the national territory of a State is also included in that State's cultural heritage. This class of property essentially refers to objects which are the result of an archaeological or other excavation, are found in the waters of a State or form part of archaeological remains. In other words they form an integral part of the state's 'soil'. Objects which are found in this way are thought to belong to the cultural heritage of the State in which they were found even if their initial origin is linked to another State or community which no longer exists or has moved territories. For example, Greek Attic amphorae excavated from the soil of Northern Italy or the coasts of Asia Minor belong to Italy's and Turkey's cultural heritage irrespective of their Greek origin and irrespective of the fact that these countries in their present form did not exist at the time.[20]

Third, cultural property acquired by archaeological, ethnological or natural science missions, with the consent of the competent authorities of the country of origin of such property is also considered part of that country's cultural heritage. This provision is also reflected in many national laws dealing with archaeological excavations conducted by foreign schools or archaeologists who are foreigners and conduct the excavation under a foreign programme.[21]

Fourth, cultural property which has been the subject of a freely agreed exchange is also included. This provision does not specify whether this exchange should be one between states or individuals or a mix of the two. There is of course nothing in this provision to exclude individuals. If, however, the cultural object at issue is state property, it cannot be the subject of a freely agreed exchange between individuals.

Fifth, cultural property received as a gift or purchased legally with the

---

tions, and lastly to elements removed from monuments where the link of origin is clearly strengthened by the natural attachment of the detached part to its original support.

[20] This is also the reason why newly independent states have brought claims against their former colonial states or states which occupied them or formed part of them but no longer do for the return of cultural properties which are today found in the territories of these latter states and outside the territories that have created them.

[21] See also article 23 of the 1956 Recommendation on International Principles Applicable to Archaeological Excavations.

consent of the competent authorities of the country of origin of such property is covered too.[22]

Article 4 does not provide for any time limits. Time limits in this respect may impinge on the effective application of the article in the sense that many countries' recent history may be as important as other countries' ancient history. In this sense O'Keefe alleges that US implementing legislation concerning the 1970 UNESCO Convention, which provides that protection extends only to archaeological objects which are more than 250 years old, does not conform to the State's obligations under article 4.[23]

Article 13(d) refers to a special category of cultural objects, which a state may declare as inalienable. This cultural property cannot be exported, and if exported, States Parties to the Convention need to facilitate its recovery.[24] Many States consider that that part of their cultural property is so important that they have an imprescriptible and inalienable right over it. This means that the State cannot be alienated from its rights whilst third parties cannot gain ownership of it by way of short- or long-term possession, irrespective of whether they are in good faith or not, or by any other way. These cultural objects cannot be transferred. This notion, subject to concessions, is also found in the 1995 Unidroit Convention in relation to certain categories of cultural objects which are particularly mentioned,[25] such as cultural objects forming an integral part of an identified monument or archaeological site, or belonging to a public collection. However,

---

22 Article 4: 'The States Parties to this Convention recognize that for the purpose of the Convention property which belongs to the following categories forms part of the cultural heritage of each State: (a) Cultural property created by the individual or collective genius of nationals of the State concerned, and cultural property of importance to the State concerned created within the territory of that State by foreign nationals or stateless persons resident within such territory; (b) cultural property found within the national territory; (c) cultural property acquired by archaeological, ethnological or natural science missions, with the consent of the competent authorities of the country of origin of such property; (d) cultural property which has been the subject of a freely agreed exchange; (e) cultural property received as a gift or purchased legally with the consent of the competent authorities of the country of origin of such property'.

23 O'Keefe, P.J., n. 2 above, 47.

24 Article 13: 'The States Parties to this Convention also undertake, consistent with the laws of each State: . . . (d) to recognize the indefeasible right of each State Party to this Convention to classify and declare certain cultural property as inalienable which should therefore ipso facto not be exported, and to facilitate recovery of such property by the State concerned in cases where it has been exported'.

25 Article 3 of the 1995 Unidroit Convention.

since consensus could not be achieved in this respect, the imprescriptibility of those objects was reduced to a time limit of 75 years from the time of their theft for putting forward a claim.

The definition of cultural property that is enshrined in the Convention is exhaustive compared to the ones found in the 1954 Hague Convention for the Protection of Cultural Property in the Event of Armed Conflict and the UNESCO Recommendations. The reason for that is that the former is the result of a compromise between importing and exporting States whilst the latter were linked to aims for which there was a general consensus from the participating States.

2.1.4 States Parties' Obligations

2.1.4.1 Establishment of national services (articles 5 and 14)

Amongst States Parties' obligations is also the establishment within their territories of national services, with the aim of protecting their cultural heritage (i.e. against the illicit import, export and transfer of ownership). These services (one or more) should be adequately staffed in order to meet their aims. Their functions are set out specifically in articles 5 and 14 of the Convention. Before we explore their functions, we need to mention that these services are to be set up 'as appropriate for each country'. This phrase works perhaps as a reservation for those countries that do not have the financial means to support such services. However, they are under a clear obligation to direct their best efforts towards such an aim. The same phrase could also be held to mean that according to each country's administration system, such national services may differ. This is of course no problem as long as the substantive aim of this provision is served. In many instances such services may already be there and there may be no need to set them up, apart from reviewing and updating them for their proper and efficient function.

Such services should be there (a) to contribute to the drafting of laws and regulations serving the aims of the Convention (i.e. the protection of cultural property) and (b) to establish and keep up to date a national inventory of protected property (a list of important public and private cultural property) whose export would constitute an appreciable impoverishment of the national cultural heritage. This obligation should not be narrowly construed because such a construction would jeopardise rather than protect a state's cultural property. Such an inventory does not necessarily mean that it only includes particular, isolated, specifically designated items. It may also include categories of items, newly excavated or newly created objects and/or whole collections, as well as the exhibits of various museums or other institutions and so on. This is a list that is not only inventoried for customs use but also for scientific purposes. It aims to encourage the study and classification of the various items that make up a country's cultural heritage and determine those objects, which should be preserved and become subject to export prohibition as well as those for which the legal transfer from the country can be authorized.[26] In any case, such an inventory helps the restitution and return of cultural objects which have left the country under suspicious circumstances. These national services should also (c) promote the development or the establishment of scientific and technical institutions, such as museums, libraries, archives, laboratories, workshops and so on with a view to ensuring the preservation and presentation of cultural property; and (d) organise the supervision of archaeological excavations and ensure the preservation *in situ* of certain cultural property as well as protecting certain areas reserved for future archaeological research. These functions relating to archaeological excavations and *in situ* preservation of cultural objects reflect principles found in international legal and soft law instruments pertaining to archaeological excavations and are directed towards the prevention of clandestine excavation.[27] (e) These national services should also establish rules reflecting the ethical principles set out in this Convention (and ensure the observance of those rules) for the benefit of those involved in the art trade such as curators, collectors, antique dealers and so on. This function/obligation presents an interesting point. It makes reference to ethical principles enshrined in the Convention and links them to rules. However, it is not only ethical principles that are provided for. There are also hard core obligations, which bind States Parties (though not private parties). Therefore it is the States that need to force the Convention's principles onto of the agents of the art trade by the establishment of rules. Given, however, the fact that laws are not ethical principles but legally enforceable rules, it seems that the Convention does not necessarily provide for the establishment of laws but rather for soft laws, such as codes of ethics, best practices, guidelines, and so on. These rules are also necessary in order to create a uniform environment of practice, which will not favour certain agents at the expense of others. In other words we should not be able to envisage instances where the museums will have to conform to certain rules and practices, whilst private collectors do not. If museums are not allowed to acquire cultural objects that are not fully documented as regards their provenance, then collectors will have a greater choice at the expense of museums and other institutions because

---

26 Views of the Secretariat. UNESCO Doc. SHC/MD/5 Annex II at p.5.

27 E.g. 1956 UNESCO Recommendation on International Principles Applicable to Archaeological Excavations, article 4 of the European Convention on the Protection of the Archaeological Heritage, revised in 1992 and article 2(5) of the 2001 Convention on the Protection of the Underwater Cultural Heritage.

cultural objects which have left a country illicitly will still find their way into the market. (f) Also included amongst the functions is the taking of educational measures. This notion is rather a vague one. However, the aim of this provision is to stimulate and develop respect for the cultural heritage of all States and communicate knowledge of the Convention's principles. (g) Lastly, it is provided that publicity should be given to the disappearance of cultural property. This last provision is particularly important in the sense that publicising such disappearances may deter potential 'clients' from acquiring objects, fearing that they may have to return them to their countries of origin. This provision has a triple aim. First, it diminishes the clientele for those objects; second, it allows experts as well as non-experts to inform the interested state if such an object is located; and third, publication equals knowledge in many instances. That means that if the disappearance of an object is widely publicised, it will be difficult for a purchaser to invoke his or her good faith in acquiring it. Thus, it will be more likely for the dispossessed State to take it back without paying any compensation to the possessor of the object. To that end it is vital that effective and wide publication takes place through mass communication media and the internet, perhaps as part of an international campaign. Special services exist to bring this about. There are, for example, national databases (which one can consult by sending a request to the state of origin of the object), the Art Loss Register, the INTERPOL database, the ICOM database and information made available by UNESCO. (h) A last function, which is enshrined in article 14, is the provision of an adequate budget and/or a fund to those services to enable them to serve the purposes of the Convention. Although this provision makes direct reference to the prevention of illicit export, it could be held to include all the obligations under the Convention due to the fact that this is mentioned later on in the provision.[28] It would indeed be difficult for one to imagine that any national services would be capable of delivering their tasks without appropriate financial support. It has also been argued that such a fund could be used by the State in order to buy back (or help a museum or other institution accessible to the public to acquire) cultural objects that are of significant importance to it and whose export cannot be prevented by other means. This is especially true for States Parties to the Convention such as the

---

[28] Article 14: 'In order to prevent illicit export *and to meet the obligations arising from the implementation of this Convention*, each State Party to the Convention should, as far as it is able, provide the national services responsible for the protection of its cultural heritage with an adequate budget and, if necessary, should set up a fund for this purpose' (emphasis added).

UK,[29] which have a cultural property export system under which they can prevent the export of a significant cultural object for a particular period of time. If during this period no buyer within the country is found, then the object is freed for export. This would not be the case for countries such as Greece and Italy, which prevent the export of particular objects by law, whether these objects are in private collections or owned by public bodies.[30]

There are two essential points that one needs to clarify. First, the national services referred to in these articles (5 and 14) concern the protection of cultural property in general and not only in relation to the import, export and transfer of ownership of cultural objects. These aims cannot be attained in isolation without a general plan of protection of a state's cultural property, which will be supported by national services set up in proportion to a state's capacity. It would be absurd to argue that only a part of cultural property should be protected while, at the same time, that protection may be flawed in relation to other parts, especially where any acts in this respect are closely linked.[31] The second point requiring clarification is that a State's responsibility for the protection of its cultural property is not, strictly speaking, a responsibility linked to its own interests. It is a responsibility towards the protection of cultural heritage for the interests of humanity. It is each State's cultural heritage which makes a contribution to the world's cultural heritage and impoverishment of a State's heritage necessarily also constitutes an impoverishment of the world's heritage.[32]

2.1.4.2 Export certificate (articles 6 and 7(b)(i), 3)

Amongst States Parties' obligations are a) the introduction of an export certificate for cultural property, [33] b) the prohibition of export of cultural

---

[29] See the Waverley criteria <www.culture.gov.uk/images/publications/waverley_ criteria.pdf>.

[30] These cases do not include the issuance of temporary permits for export in order, for example, for the cultural objects to be exhibited in other museums.

[31] O'Keefe, P.J., n. 2 above, 53.

[32] See in this respect, the 1954 Hague Convention (para 2 of the Preamble), the 1972 UNESCO Convention on the Protection of the World Cultural and National Heritage (para 2 of the Preamble) and the 2001 Universal Declaration on Cultural Diversity (article 1). See also Article 167 (ex 151) para 1 TFEU: 'The Community shall contribute to the flowering of the cultures of the Member States, while respecting their national and regional diversity and at the same time bringing the common cultural heritage to the fore.' 29.12.2006 EN Official Journal of the European Union C 321 E/113.

[33] For the situation in various countries see the International Law Association Draft Report on National Controls over the Export of Cultural Material, The Hague, 2010, http://www.ila-hq.org/en/committees/index.cfm/cid/13.

property without this export certificate, and c) the publication of this prohibition by appropriate means (article 6).[34] Although this seems to be a clear-cut obligation, its inclusion in the Convention when coupled with article 7(b)(i) is somehow problematic. Article 7(b)(i) provides that States Parties are not under an obligation to prohibit any import designated by other states as an illegal export according to their laws but only imports relating to cultural property stolen from a museum or a religious or secular public monument or similar institution in another State Party, provided that such property is inventoried by that institution. Therefore private property, even if it is considered important, is not covered. This leaves one wondering what the reason would be for introducing an export certificate and a prohibition of export, if such a prohibition is not equally accompanied by a prohibition of import on the same grounds. Article 6 would indeed form a meaningless provision if seen in this light. However, according to many commentators,[35] it should not be seen in conjunction with article 7(b)(i) but in conjunction with article 3 of the Convention. According to article 3,[36] as was explained above,[37] and according to a preferable interpretation of the reasons discussed in the relevant section, there is also an obligation for States Parties to regulate their exports in order to protect cultural property which has been designated by them as protectable or which has been listed as requiring an export certificate, according to the system followed by each State. [38] Given also the fact that article 6

---

34 Article 6: 'The States Parties to this Convention undertake: (a) to introduce an appropriate certificate in which the exporting State would specify that the export of the cultural property in question is authorized. The certificate should accompany all items of cultural property exported in accordance with the regulations; (b) to prohibit the exportation of cultural property from their territory unless accompanied by the above-mentioned export certificate; (c) to publicize this prohibition by appropriate means, particularly among persons likely to export or import cultural property.'

35 O'Keefe, P.J., n. 2 above, 54 as he refers to Raschèr, Andrea F.G., Marc Bauen, Yves Fischer and Marie-Noëlle Zen-Ruffinen (2005), *Cultural Property Transfer*, Zürich: Schulthess, at 20.

36 Article 3: 'The import, export or transfer of ownership of cultural property effected contrary to the provisions adopted under this Convention by the States Parties thereto, shall be illicit.'

37 Under section 2.

38 Several national systems, encouraged by the 1970 UNESCO Convention, have established procedures and facilities for registering significant objects or national treasures, such as Brazil's *tombamento* and Germany's comprehensive list of nationally important cultural objects and archives that is prepared by the Länder (constituent states). South Africa's broad inventory of the 'national estate' takes the form of a data base of information that purports to identify all heritage

does not restrict the issuing of export certificates (and consequently the prohibition of export) to certain cases only, combined with the fact that we cannot have a provision in the Convention which contradicts other provisions in the same Convention (according to article 31 of the 1969 Vienna Convention on the Law of Treaties an interpretation which makes sense is preferred over a meaningless one), one can draw the conclusion that States Parties' obligations in this respect should not be minimised and that States Parties to the Convention should respect other States Parties' export regulations by introducing an equivalent prohibition of import in their own laws.

Export certificates form a practice nowadays, which is widely accepted both at international[39] and at European Union level.[40]

---

resources worthy of consideration. Such registration provides a reliable basis for determining the exportability of material. Mexico's system of Registers, beginning under 1972 law, offers a tool to reconcile private ownership with national sovereignty over immovable monuments.

As an example of one registration process, the recent law governing the Swiss inventory of cultural objects stipulates the following effects: listed objects cannot be acquired by a third party, even if the purchaser is in good faith; claims for the restitution or return of looted objects are not subject to a time limitation; listed objects cannot be exported from Switzerland, except for very specific reasons and on a temporary basis; if a listed object is illicitly exported, the Swiss government can claim its return from another state party to the 1970 UNESCO Convention; temporary export of listed objects is possible; and the illegal export of listed material is a criminal offense.

The International Law Association Draft Report on National Controls over the Export of Cultural Material, The Hague, 2010, http://www.ila-hq.org/en/committees/index.cfm/cid/13.

[39] In 2005 UNESCO and the World Customs Organization have introduced such certificates. CLT-2005/WS/5. See also the 'Object ID' initiated in 1993 by the Getty Information Institute and endorsed by UNESCO in its 30th General Conference in 1999.

[40] See Regulation 116/2009 on the export of cultural goods of 18 December 2008 (Council Regulation 3911/92 of 9 December 1992 on the export of cultural goods, OJ L 395/1 (Corrigendum OJ L267/30, 19/10/1996), as amended by Council Regulation 2469/96 of 16 December 1996 OJ L 335/9, Council Regulation 974/2001 of 14 May 2001 OJ L 137/10 and Council Regulation 806/2003 of 14 April 2003 OJ L 122/1. Council Regulation (EC) No 116/2009 of 18 December 2008 on the export of cultural goods (codified version)). See also Commission Regulation 752/93 of 30 March 1993 laying down provisions for the implementation of Council Regulation 3911/92 on the export of cultural goods, as amended by Commission Regulation (EC) 1526/98 of 16 July 1998, OJ L 201/47 and Commission Regulation (EC) 656/2004 of 7 April, 2004, OJ L104/50 (Corrigendum, OJ L 203, 8.6.2004, p.14 (656/2004)).

2.1.4.3 Measures against stolen and illegally exported cultural objects (articles 7 and 13)

Articles 7 and 13 provide for measures against stolen and illegally exported cultural objects. According to article 7, States Parties undertake to *take the necessary measures*, consistent with national legislation, to prevent museums and similar institutions within their territories from acquiring cultural property originating in another State Party, which has been illegally exported from it after the Convention entered into force. They are also under an obligation, whenever possible, to *inform a State of origin of an offer of such cultural property illegally removed from that State*.

It is clear from the above that in order for the aforementioned obligations to apply, the States involved have to be Parties to the Convention. Other States, non-Parties to the Convention, may choose to submit to these obligations, but this is a matter entirely left to their discretion. Being a Party to the Convention, however, is not the only requirement. The Convention should also have entered into force for States Parties. In other words, in order for a State Party to be under an obligation to inform the State of origin that a cultural object has been offered for sale to one of its museums, the cultural property at issue needs to have been exported from the State of origin after the Convention entered into force for that State. It goes without saying that the Convention should also have entered into force for the State informer.

These obligations are also subject to various interpretations by reason of their phrasing. In particular, in relation to the first obligation it is not clear whether all museums and similar institutions within the territory of the State Party are included or whether it is only public museums and institutions that are included. If it is only public museums that are included, then the notion of 'public' is not a clear one.[41] Also the phrasing 'consistent with national legislation' is thought to somehow weaken the ultimate result of the provision. P. Bator justifies the presence of this phrase as limiting the obligations at issue, only to the extent that such obligations are recognised by the country's national law and do not run contrary to it. In other words, according to his view, this provision does not oblige States Parties to introduce into their national laws, further obligations beyond those existing already.[42] It is argued here that this view does not, however,

---

[41] See the also the relevant section on the 1995 Unidroit Convention (2.2 below).

[42] Bator, P.M. (1982), 'An Essay on the International Trade in Art', *Stanford Law Review*, 275, at 380. See also Abramson, Ronald D. and Stephen B. Huttler (1973), 'The Legal Response to the Illicit Movement of Cultural Property', *Law and Policy in International Business*, 5, 932, at 951, as they are referred to in

correspond to the provision's spirit. When a State agrees to become a party to the Convention, it is in full knowledge and conscience of the obligations it undertakes. Therefore it is expected that it will fulfil these obligations to the maximum so far as this is consistent with its national laws. In other words a particular method of fulfilment is not required. What is required is an effective result.[43]

States Parties are also obliged to prohibit the import of stolen cultural property. However, this prohibition should not be interpreted as general in nature. It only covers cultural objects stolen from a museum or a religious or secular public monument or similar institution[44] in a State Party which are inventoried by that institution.[45] Cultural objects which are clandestinely excavated and illegally exported are not covered since they

---

O'Keefe, P.J. (2007), *Commentary on the UNESCO 1970 Convention on Illicit Traffic*, 2nd edition, Crickadarn: Institute of Art and Law, 56–7. Specifically O'Keefe mentions that the phrase 'consistent with national legislation' was inserted at the request of the US delegation and it was stated that 'the section would be interpreted so as to confine the effect of this measure to museums whose acquisition policies are controlled by the State. Such museums in the US are only two, i.e. the Library of Congress and the National Archives, since the status of the Smithsonian Institution and the National Gallery in Washington is not clear. However, Nafziger, J.A.R. (1975), 'Article 7(a) of the UNESCO Convention', in L.D. DuBoff, *Art Law: Domestic and International*, South Hackensack: Fred B. Rothman & Co., 387, at 388–9, argues that even the museums that are not considered public can be tied to analogous obligations as a prerequisite to receiving public funding. This is also the case in the UK where adherence to codes of ethics (International Council of Museums and Museums Association) forms a precondition for receiving funding. O'Keefe, P.J. (2007), *op.cit*, 57.

43 Article 7(a): 'The States Parties to this Convention undertake: (a) To take the necessary measures, consistent with national legislation, to prevent museums and similar institutions within their territories from acquiring cultural property originating in another State Party which has been illegally exported after entry into force of this Convention, in the States concerned. Whenever possible, to inform a State of origin Party to this Convention of an offer of such cultural property illegally removed from that State after the entry into force of this Convention in both States.'

44 The notions of 'religious or secular public monument or similar institutions' are not entirely clear as to their meaning. Are village churches administered by local communities included or not?

45 Article 7(b)(i): 'The States Parties to this Convention undertake: (b) (i) to prohibit the import of cultural property stolen from a museum or a religious or secular public monument or similar institution in another State Party to this Convention after the entry into force of this Convention for the States concerned, provided that such property is documented as appertaining to the inventory of that institution.'

could not have been inventoried.[46] This limitation to a particular category of stolen objects is a rather unfortunate one since it restricts effective protection of cultural property and also runs contrary to a widely accepted notion that stolen objects should be returned to their countries of origin. This notion, however, is reflected in the 1995 Unidroit Convention.[47] An argument which can be put forward is that the issue here is not about return, but rather about regulating import. And the regulation of imports is not an easy task. Yet, prohibiting imports equates with return. In any case it will be hard to imagine a situation where a country would police all imports of cultural objects coming from other States. It will only be imports of objects which are found as a result of a random check or about which there is prior information before or upon their entry into the country.[48] If these objects clear customs then the State of origin can only claim them back by using the regular route and applying the country's laws for stolen objects, which in most cases will be more protective (even extending to include more objects than the ones provided for in this article of the Convention) compared with an application for return on the basis of an illegal import; unless of course the claims for return of a stolen object have been statute barred whilst the claims based on illegal import have not.

According to the same provision (article 7(b)(ii))[49] a State Party should

---

[46] See, however, article 3(2) of the Unidroit Convention according to which 'a cultural object which has been unlawfully excavated or lawfully excavated but unlawfully retained shall be considered stolen, when consistent with the law of the State where the excavation took place'.

[47] Article 3(1) of the Unidroit Convention 1995: 'The possessor of a cultural object which has been stolen shall return it'.

[48] According to Canadian (Cultural Property Export and Import Act 1975, section 31(3)) and Australian (Protection of Movable Cultural Heritage Act 1986, section 41(1)) law, countries can only act on a formal request by another country. The same applies for the US which considers this provision as creating a juridical basis for later actions to recover cultural property (US Report of the United States Delegation to the Special Committee of Governmental Exports to Examine the Draft Convention on the Means of Prohibiting the Illicit Import, Export and Transfer of Ownership of Cultural Property, UNESCO House, 13–14 April 1970, Paris, at 14).

[49] Article 7(b)(ii): 'The States Parties to this Convention undertake: (b) (ii) at the request of the State Party of origin, to take appropriate steps to recover and return any such cultural property imported after the entry into force of this Convention in both States concerned, provided, however, that the requesting State shall pay just compensation to an innocent purchaser or to a person who has valid title to that property. Requests for recovery and return shall be made through diplomatic offices. The requesting Party shall furnish, at its expense, the documentation and other evidence necessary to establish its claim for recovery and

take appropriate steps to recover and return stolen cultural property (within the meaning of the previous paragraph) that has been imported illegally into that State.[50] However, a request of the State Party of origin is presupposed. The 'taking of appropriate steps' by the State from which the cultural object is requested, forms rather a vague obligation. Would it suffice for it to advise the State of origin to take legal action? This course of action would, of course, not need an express provision in the Convention since everyone knows that s/he has a right to pursue litigation. Therefore the drafters of the Convention must have had something more effective in mind in the sense that it would either facilitate the return of the cultural object to its country of origin, or at least secure its presence in a particular jurisdiction until a court decision is delivered. A seizure or confiscation of the artefact, either on the grounds of existing laws or as laws implementing the Convention, or a facilitation of the process of turning to national courts would come closer to the spirit of the Convention and would fulfil, to a greater or lesser extent, the State's obligation to act (take appropriate steps) in such a situation. In any case it seems to be clear that such measures should not replace existing measures of recovery but rather should supplement them either by introducing new, more effective ones[51] or by rendering current procedures more effective.

The requesting State should also pay just compensation to an innocent purchaser or to a person who has valid title to that property. The precise meaning of this compensation is not set out. Would such compensation involve the purchase price, the market price, expenses for the conservation or for insuring the cultural object and so on? This article has formed the basis for the drafting of the 1995 Unidroit Convention, which refers in its article 4 to 'fair and reasonable compensation'. The same should apply with regard to the interpretation of an 'innocent purchaser'. There is a view that an 'innocent purchaser' is someone who has acquired the object without knowing that this acquisition was contrary to law, whilst a 'person who has valid title' means a person who has acquired a valid title to the property at issue by reason of time limitations or lapse of time.[52] In

---

return. The Parties shall impose no customs duties or other charges upon cultural property returned pursuant to this Article. All expenses incident to the return and delivery of the cultural property shall be borne by the requesting Party'.

[50] Cultural property should be imported after the entry into force of this Convention in both States concerned.

[51] An example of such is considered to be the Commonwealth Scheme. For details see O'Keefe, P.J. (1995), 'Protection of the Material Cultural Heritage: The Commonwealth Scheme', *International and Comparative Law Quarterly*, 147.

[52] Fraoua, R. (1986), n. 14 above, 75.

any event, the payment of just compensation should be a matter of 'good faith' acquisition. 'Good faith' is a legal concept which varies between the different legal systems. To a certain extent in this respect the 1995 Unidroit Convention in article 4(4) seems to conflate the different traditions by providing for particular requirements and also by reversing the burden of proof, if the purchaser has to prove the existence of all these circumstances.[53]

Although a small number of the States that have ratified the 1970 UNESCO Convention have also ratified the 1995 Unidroit Convention, the latter should form a basis for the interpretation of the notions which appear in the UNESCO Convention. The Unidroit Convention, where these notions are further elaborated, is the outcome of meticulous study and consideration and is the more specialized international legal instrument in the area. Any requests for compensation have to be made through diplomatic offices. The requesting Party should also furnish, at its own expense, the documentation and other evidence necessary to establish its claim for recovery and return. The cultural objects will be recovered/returned without the payment of any customs duties or other charges. However, all expenses incidental to the return and delivery of the cultural property are to be borne by the requesting Party.

Another article which provides explicitly for measures against stolen and illegally exported cultural objects is article 13 of the Convention. According to this article States Parties undertake a number of obligations, which should be consistent with the laws of those States. This requirement was also considered earlier in the same section to be interpreted in a sense that diminishes States' obligations since these obligations are subject to their existing laws. According to this interpretation put forward by Bator,[54] States Parties do not have to undertake any further action beyond what is already provided for in their laws. However, such an interpretation would significantly impinge on the regular way in which we understand the adoption of an international Convention, whereby States should make their best efforts to conform to these obligations, even if

---

53 Article 4(4): 'In determining whether the possessor exercised due diligence, regard shall be had to all the circumstances of the acquisition, including the character of the parties, the price paid, whether the possessor consulted any reasonably accessible register of stolen cultural objects, and any other relevant information and documentation which it could reasonably have obtained, and whether the possessor consulted accessible agencies or took any other step that a reasonable person would have taken in the circumstances.' See the discussion in the relevant section in the chapter on the 1995 Unidroit Convention.

54 Bator, P.M. (1982), n. 13 above, at 378.

conformity impels them to supplement, update or otherwise make their existing laws more effective.

In the first place States Parties should, by all appropriate means, prevent transfers of ownership of cultural property that are likely to promote the illicit import or export of such property. It is not very clear in this obligation what these measures are and how they can work against illicit import and export of cultural property. Because of this, some States have chosen to ban exports of cultural property in general,[55] prohibit all trade in antiquities,[56] regulate the transfer and collection of certain classes of cultural goods[57] or goods above a certain value and so on. States Parties have done this because they had to comply with their own or another system in terms of transfers, exports and imports of cultural property (article 13(a)).

Secondly, States Parties need to ensure that their competent services co-operate in facilitating the earliest possible restitution of illicitly exported cultural property to its rightful owner (article 13(b)). This article is, to a certain extent, incomprehensible because it does not add anything to what already applies in all States. If something is considered as illicitly exported then it shall be restored according to the laws of this State. If, however, such a procedure has not been legislated for, States Parties are obliged to introduce one. What creates further difficulties in the understanding of this provision is the notion of 'rightful owner'. It is not easy to assess who the rightful owner of a cultural object is. Which law would one apply to define the rightful owner and what if the rightful owner himself or herself has illicitly exported the object at issue? Should the cultural object be returned to him/her? The cases that will be uncontested in this area are those cases where a cultural object belongs to the requesting State and should not have left this State without an authorisation or an export permit.[58] In such a case the object should be returned as early as possible and the competent authorities of the two States should co-operate to this end.

Thirdly, States Parties should admit actions for recovery of lost or stolen items of cultural property brought by or on behalf of the rightful owners (article 13(c)). This is also an obligation which is either provided for or implied by the laws of most States anyway, and there was no need for a further particular reference. As analysed earlier, the notion of 'stolen' is not defined in the Convention. It will therefore be subject to the appli-

---

[55] i.e. China.

[56] E.g. Egypt and Jordan.

[57] E.g. Greece, Italy and Cyprus.

[58] It means perhaps, in particular, cultural objects that are 'inalienable' according to article 13(d).

cable law.[59] However, there have been cases where it has been recognised (both in the US and in the UK) that objects which were considered to be State property (including cultural objects found in the soil of a State before they were excavated) and have been removed without this State's authorisation, are considered to be stolen.[60]

Fourthly, States Parties are obliged to recognise the indefeasible right of each State Party to classify and declare certain cultural property as inalienable. That means that this cultural property should not be exported. In addition they have to facilitate recovery of such property by the State concerned, in cases where it has been exported (article 13(d)).[61]

This provision is rather complicated; it lacks clarity and precision and the obligations on States Parties look vague. However, this should not deprive states of the ability to enforce these obligations, as they were explained above. This provision should also be considered in conjunction with other provisions in the Convention which seek the same end, such as articles 3 and 6, explained above.

2.1.4.4 Imposition of sanctions (article 8)

Article 8 of the Convention[62] is the only provision which makes reference to penalties and administrative sanctions. These sanctions are provided in relation to the prohibition of particular acts, i.e. the acts provided in articles 6(b)[63] and 7(b)[64] in relation to the export of cultural property from

---

59 See for example, *Winkworth v. Christie Manson and Woods Ltd*, (Ch D) 5 November 1979, [1980] Ch. 496, [1980] 2 W.L.R 937, [1980] 1 All E.R. 1121 where Japanese cultural objects were stolen in England, sold to a *bona fide* purchaser in Italy and sent back to London for auction. The case was brought before an English Court which, however, applied Italian law, which was the *lex rei sitae*.

60 *United States v. Schultz* 178 F.Supp.2d 45 (2002); 333 F.3d 393 (2003). See also K. Chamberlain, 'UK accession to the 1970 UNESCO Convention' (2002) *Art, Antiquity and Law* 231, at 251–2.

61 See section 2.2.3 below.

62 Article 8: 'The States Parties to this Convention undertake to impose penalties or administrative sanctions on any person responsible for infringing the prohibitions referred to under Articles 6(b) and 7(b) above'.

63 Article 6(b): 'The States Parties to this Convention undertake: (b) to prohibit the exportation of cultural property from their territory unless accompanied by the above-mentioned export certificate.'

64 It probably refers to article 7(b)(i): 'The States Parties to this Convention undertake: (b)(i) to prohibit the import of cultural property stolen from a museum or a religious or secular public monument or similar institution in another State Party to this Convention after the entry into force of this Convention for the States concerned, provided that such property is documented as appertaining to the inventory of that institution'.

their territory without an export certificate and the import of cultural property stolen from a museum, a religious or secular public monument or similar institution.

The nature of those penalties/sanctions is not set out. That means that States Parties are free to adopt the measures they wish as long as these measures are thought to serve effectively the aims provided for. States Parties have adopted different systems so far. They have regulated exports either in relation to certain objects or classes of objects designated by the States Parties as being of importance to their cultural heritage[65] or in relation to categories of objects (which are also defined chronologically) for which export is prohibited unless a permit is obtained.[66]

2.1.4.5 International co-operation (articles 9, 15 and 17)

International co-operation constitutes one of the principal foundations of the Convention. In fact, it runs through the whole Convention (by reason of its very nature as an international legal instrument) as well as through the basic purpose for its adoption. Nevertheless, articles 9 and 15 provide for more specific obligations in this respect, whilst article 17 sets out the role of UNESCO.

According to article 9, States Parties whose cultural patrimony is in jeopardy from pillage of archaeological or ethnological materials may call upon other States Parties who are affected. In fact they undertake to participate in a concerted international effort to determine and then to institute the necessary concrete measures, including the control of exports and imports and international commerce in those materials and put in place provisional measures to prevent irremediable injury to the cultural heritage of the requesting State.[67]

Although the word 'cultural patrimony' is used for the first time in this

---

[65] E.g. Canada, according to the law of which specified classes of objects included in the Control List cannot be exported unless a permit is obtained in accordance with its Act.

[66] E.g. Australia, Greece and Italy. These countries provide for total prohibition of certain objects whilst for some others a permit may be obtained.

[67] Article 9: 'Any State Party to this Convention whose cultural patrimony is in jeopardy from pillage of archaeological or ethnological materials may call upon other States Parties who are affected. The States Parties to this Convention undertake, in these circumstances, to participate in a concerted international effort to determine and to carry out the necessary concrete measures, including the control of exports and imports and international commerce in the specific materials concerned. Pending agreement each State concerned shall take provisional measures to the extent feasible to prevent irremediable injury to the cultural heritage of the requesting State'.

Convention, it does not seem to imply something different from 'cultural heritage' (the wording used later in the same article) or 'cultural property', used repeatedly within the Convention. However, in order for this article to apply, a State's cultural patrimony has to be in jeopardy. Since the term 'jeopardy' is not a term of art or a legal notion, it should be accorded its common meaning. In other words, it should mean 'danger'. When combined with the prerequisite of pillage, this situation should be considered to occur at least a) when the remains of a particular civilisation are threatened with destruction or shrinkage of vital information by reason of an extensive movement abroad, or b) when the demand for certain archaeological or ethnological objects on the international market renders clandestine excavations a prime aim and when these clandestine excavations, if successful, would lead to the destruction of important archaeological sites.[68] As is clear from its text, the scope of this article does not seek international co-operation over all cultural objects designated by States Parties, but only over archaeological and ethnological material.[69]

The aim of this article is to make market States enter into bilateral agreements and co-operate in general with States Parties facing problems with the protection of their cultural property (i.e. export States) in order to determine (set out in detail) concrete measures which would put a stop to this pillage or would limit it considerably. These market States will likely be the States that market cultural material from the States that request such co-operation. Article 9 refers to the nature of such measures without limiting its scope only to those. It refers to control of exports and imports and international commerce in those materials and the provision of provisional measures. These latter measures are provided to the extent feasible to prevent irremediable injury to the cultural heritage of the requesting State.

There is a view that such measures should form the object of a bilateral agreement between the States involved, so that particular objects or classes of objects for which special import, export or other measures are required,

---

[68] See also in this respect Fraoua, R. n. 14 above, at 80. See also the (US) Senate Committee on Foreign Relations, Convention on Ownership of Cultural Property S. Exec. Rep. No. 29, 92nd Congress, 2nd session (1972), at 5, where almost the same approach is followed in relation to the last part of article 9, though referring to 'provisional measures *to the extent feasible* to prevent *irremediable injury* to the cultural heritage of the requesting State'. According to O'Keefe, P.J. (2007), at 72, 'a general trade in unprovenanced objects from various sites in a country or countries of the same region may destroy any national efforts to properly survey, date and verify the development of national culture'.

[69] The US has restricted these categories even further by its implementing legislation. O'Keefe, P.J. *ibid*, 69.

are identified.[70] However, the conclusion of an agreement as a prerequisite for the activation of the clause is not expressly required. In addition, if a State has a total import or export ban on cultural objects that have been illegally exported from another State Party or any State,[71] it does not have to enact further legislation in this respect. However, it cannot maintain that this legislation suffices in relation to the rest of the obligations provided under the Convention. These obligations might also consist of acts such as public campaigns or other informative actions in relation to risks linked to the acquisition of unprovenanced cultural objects from a particular part of the world. Therefore article 3 may or may not be capable of covering the scope of article 9. Greece, in this respect, has concluded one agreement with Switzerland (15 May 2007) and one Memorandum of Understanding (MoU) (not strictly speaking within the ambit of article 9 of the 1970 UNESCO Convention) with China (26 February 2008), whilst agreements are underway between Greece and the US and Greece and Italy. Italy has also concluded agreements with the US (19 January, 2001), Switzerland (20 October, 2006) and China (20 January, 2006).

Apart from article 9, some States Parties, especially those which request the conclusion of an agreement for offering the full protection provided for under article 9, also use article 15[72] as a basis for the conclusion of bilateral agreements. However, this article has been included in the Convention in order to clarify that States Parties a) are free to conclude other special agreements among themselves, and b) that they are free to continue implementing agreements (regarding the restitution of cultural property) to which they were Parties upon the coming into force of the 1970 UNESCO Convention. It is clear from the Convention that the discretion for States Parties to conclude bilateral agreements in no way affects the implementation of the Convention and the obligations deriving from it, making these agreements a point of activation for such obligations. Agreements (in the narrow sense of the word, or MOUs) should supplement the Convention and not replace or substitute it.

Article 17 also falls within the ambit of international co-operation, but from the angle of co-operation with the United Nations Educational,

---

70 See, for example, the US, the Swiss and the German legislation in this respect.

71 See, for example, Canada (Cultural Property Export and Import Act 1975, s. 31) and Australia (Protection of Movable Cultural Heritage Act 1986, s. 14).

72 Article 15: 'Nothing in this Convention shall prevent States Parties thereto from concluding special agreements among themselves or from continuing to implement agreements already concluded regarding the restitution of cultural property removed, whatever the reason, from its territory of origin, before the entry into force of this Convention for the States concerned'.

Scientific and Cultural Organization. In fact this article provides for the technical assistance that could be offered by UNESCO to States Parties either on its own initiative or when it is called on. Technical assistance, which is offered when States Parties call for it, covers the following fields: (a) information and education, (b) consultation and expert advice, and (c) co-ordination and good offices, while UNESCO may, on its own initiative, conduct research and publish studies on matters relevant to the illicit movement of cultural property, call on the co-operation of any competent non-governmental organisation (such as ICOM and ICOMOS with whom it has an existing co-operation), and make proposals to States Parties concerning the implementation of the Convention.[73]

In this way UNESCO has been active and has undertaken particular action in the field of protection of cultural property. P. O'Keefe, who has been involved in many UNESCO projects, paints a good picture of these activities.[74] UNESCO has published national laws on cultural heritage[75] and has also created the Cultural Heritage Laws Database.[76] It has published a study on national controls,[77] a handbook on national regulations concerning the export of cultural property,[78] a commentary of the 1970 Convention,[79] a resource handbook for the implementation of the 1970 Convention,[80] a study of the trade in antiquities (1997), educational material,[81] and has conducted a number of regional workshops with the co-operation of INTERPOL and ICOM.

UNESCO's most important arm in the area of return and restitution of cultural property to its country of origin is the Intergovernmental Committee for Promoting the Return of Cultural Property to its

[73] So far nothing has been done in this field apart from the adoption of the Recommendation of the Committee of Experts in 1983.

[74] O'Keefe, P.J. (2007), n. 42 above, 92.

[75] UNESCO Docs. CLT-85/WS (the 'red leaflet' series).

[76] Cultural Heritage Laws Database at: http://www.UNESCO.org/culture/natlaws.

[77] Prott, L.V. and P.J. O'Keefe (1983), *Implementation of the 1970 Convention on the Means of Prohibiting and Preventing the Illicit Import, Export and Transfer of Ownership of Cultural Property*, UNESCO doc. CLT-83/WS/16, Paris: UNESCO.

[78] Prott, L.V. and P.J. O'Keefe (1988), *Handbook of National Regulations Concerning the Export of Cultural Property*, UNESCO doc. CC.88/WS/27, Paris: UNESCO.

[79] Fraoua, R. (1986), n. 14 above.

[80] Askerud, P. and E. Clément (1997), *Preventing the Illicit Traffic in Cultural Property: A Resource Handbook for the Implementation of the 1970 UNESCO Convention*, Paris: UNESCO.

[81] Posters and leaflets on the illicit traffic of cultural property as well as manuals for national workshops in this field. They are all available on its website.

Countries of Origin or its Restitution in Case of Illicit Appropriation. This Committee deals also with cases outside the ambit of the 1970 UNESCO Convention where property has been alienated from its country of origin under suspicious circumstances.[82] This Committee has been particularly active in offering technical assistance. It has endorsed an international code of ethics for dealers, the 'Object ID' identification system, to help trace missing objects. This was developed at the Getty Museum initiative and, on the recommendation of the General Conference of UNESCO, the initiative has established a fund to assist poor countries to recover their cultural treasures.[83] The first and only country up to now to contribute to this fund is Greece. The money has been used by UNESCO to co-organise, with the Hellenic Ministry of Culture, an International Conference on the Return of Cultural Objects to their Countries of Origin in Athens (Greece) on 17 and 18 March 2008 in the New Acropolis Museum. The conclusions of this Conference were very interesting in the sense that they placed cultural property in context and indicated how the Committee's role would develop.[84] These conclusions were more or less

---

82 In fact it was originally set up to deal with cases of restitution arising from colonial occupation. During recent years it has also dealt with cases of illicit traffic.

83 O'Keefe, P.J. (2007), n. 42 above, 93.

84 The Conclusions from this Conference are the following:

Experts on the issue of the return of cultural objects to their countries of origin, who participated in the first International Conference held in Athens, on 17th and 18th March 2008, within the framework of the meeting co-organized by the Intergovernmental Committee of UNESCO for Promoting the Return of Cultural Property to its Countries of Origin or its Restitution in case of Illicit Appropriation, and the Hellenic Ministry of Culture, in the presence of the Member-States of the Committee have reached the following conclusions:

It is important that UNESCO organise international conferences, so that experts intensify their study of the issue of the return of cultural property to its country of origin, in order to produce viable and realistic solutions.

Cultural heritage constitutes an inalienable part of a people's sense of self and of community, functioning as a link between the past, the present and the future.

It is essential to inform and sensitise the public, especially the younger generation, about this issue. An information campaign may prove very effective toward that end.

Certain categories of cultural property are irrevocably identified by reference to the cultural context in which they were created (unique and exceptional artworks and monuments, ritual objects, national symbols, ancestral remains,

repeated and confirmed at the Extraordinary Session of the Committee in Seoul in November 2008 commemorating its 30th anniversary.[85]

---

dismembered pieces of outstanding works of art). It is their original context that gives them their authenticity and unique value.

The role of the Intergovernmental Committee for Promoting the Return of Cultural Property to its Countries of Origin or its Restitution in Case of Illicit Appropriation must be strengthened through the necessary means, resources and infrastructure. Effort should be made to encourage mediation either through the Committee or by other means of alternative dispute resolution.

Requests and negotiations for the return of cultural goods can work as a vehicle for cooperation, collaboration, sharing, joint research and economic promotion.

In recent years a clear tendency towards the return of cultural objects to their countries of origin has been developed on legal, social and ethical grounds. The return of cultural objects is directly linked to the rights of humanity (preservation of cultural identity and preservation of world heritage).

Museums should abide by codes of ethics. On this basis, museums should be prepared to initiate dialogues for the return of important cultural property to its country or community of origin. This should be undertaken on ethical, scientific, and humanitarian principles. The cooperation, partnership, goodwill and mutual appreciation between the parties concerned could lead to joint research programs and exchange of technical expertise.

[85] Recommendation adopted at the Extraordinary Session of the Committee in Seoul in November 2008:

The ICPRCP ('the Committee'),
Expressing its appreciation to the Korean authorities for organizing this Extraordinary Session of the Committee commemorating its 30th anniversary;
Welcoming a recent increase in the number of returns of cultural property to its countries of origin, and *acknowledging* a rise in awareness of the general public, researchers and institutions, in the return of cultural property to its countries of origin or its restitution in case of illicit appropriation as well as the fight against illicit traffic;
Recognizing that in its 30 years of existence, the Committee has made substantial achievements in the raising of awareness concerning the return of cultural property to its countries of origin or its restitution in case of illicit appropriation and concerning the fight against illicit traffic;
Mindful of the need to further strengthen the role of the Committee as a facilitator for the return of cultural property to its countries of origin or its restitution in case of illicit appropriation, including through bilateral negotiations;
Taking note of the discussions and the Conclusions of the Athens International Conference on the Return of Cultural Objects to their Countries of Origin (March 2008) and of the meeting of the non-governmental experts held in Seoul in November 2008 (reservations by Japan);

The Committee has also recently adopted Rules of procedure for mediation and conciliation.[86]

Lastly, at the request of at least two States Parties, which are engaged in a dispute over its implementation, UNESCO may extend its good offices to reach a settlement between them. This is the only mechanism found in the Convention for the resolution of disputes and from the way it is set out (as the fifth paragraph of an article on technical assistance) it seems as if it is of secondary importance, especially when compared to the resolution of disputes usually found in other Conventions. UNESCO is the most appropriate forum for the resolution of disputes because of its expertise in the field but in no case does it form a court.

Reaffirms that certain categories of cultural property fully reveal their authenticity and unique value only in the cultural context in which they were created,
Encourages the States concerned to continue and intensify their efforts with a view to resolving disputes on the return of cultural property or restitution in case of illicit appropriation, by amicable means through bilateral negotiations complemented by other means, such as mediation and conciliation, bearing in mind that in many cases this may involve non-state actors;
Encourages international cooperation with a view to assisting developing countries in building their capacity to facilitate restitution of their cultural property;
Encourages States through international cooperation to develop inventories of their cultural property wherever located and to make better use of existing databases of stolen works of art;
Suggests collecting information on successful restitutions and setting up a database thereon;
Invites States to consider becoming [become] parties to the international instruments relating to the return of cultural property to its countries of origin or return in case of illicit appropriation and the fight against illicit traffic;
Invites States to consider a more active use of the Committee;
Considers that adoption of rules of procedure on mediation and conciliation will be a significant step to strengthen the role of the Committee;
Urges the development of innovative ways to raise awareness for the return of cultural property to its countries of origin or restitution in case of illicit appropriation, and the fight against illicit trafficking;
Suggests that the International Code of Ethics for Dealers in Cultural Property be amended and *considers* that further efforts should be made to encourage the art market to respect it;
Encourages contributions to the International Fund for the Return of Cultural Property to its Countries of Origin or its Restitution in Case of Illicit Appropriation;
Invites the Director-General to include an item in the agenda of the Committee's 15th Ordinary Session concerning a strategy for the future work of the Committee, within the framework of its mandate, and to prepare a document to that end'.

86 See section 5.2.2 below.

It is instead a political organisation which tries to maintain balance at all times. A better forum could perhaps be the International Court of Justice in the Hague. This provision in the Convention does not preclude its jurisdiction. If both (or more) States involved in the dispute submit to it (or are subject to the compulsory jurisdiction of the Court), then the Court can deliver a judgment. Also UNESCO (as a United Nations Specialized Agency), according to its Statutes, can turn to it for advisory opinions.[87]

2.1.4.6 Education and public sensitisation (article 10)

It has been understood by the drafters of the Convention that narrow legal obligations do not suffice when trying to convince the players in the illicit trade in art and the public that the trade in unprovenanced antiquities is capable of impoverishing and destroying civilisations, of limiting the sources of history and the references to national identity as well as the richness of the world's culture. It is because of this that States Parties undertake three main obligations. First, they undertake to restrict the illicit trade in art (referred to as movement of cultural property illegally removed from any State Party to this Convention) by education, information and vigilance.[88] Second, 'as appropriate for each country', they oblige antique dealers, subject to penal or administrative sanctions, to maintain a register recording the origin of each item of cultural property, names and addresses of the supplier, description and price of each item sold and to inform the purchaser of the cultural property of the export prohibition to which such property may be subject. Third, States Parties undertake to provide for general educational measures in order to create and develop in the public mind a realisation a) of the value of cultural property and b) of the threat to the cultural heritage created by theft, clandestine excavations and illicit exports.

All these obligations leave considerable discretion to States Parties as to their implementation. However, this does not detract in any respect from the fact that the States Parties are obliged to conform. In relation to the second obligation concerning antique dealers, however, there are a couple

---

[87] Constitution of UNESCO, article V and Charter of the United Nations, article 96. The International Court of Justice has delivered one judgment in the area of cultural property, Temple of Preah Vihear, Merits, Judgment (*Cambodia v. Thailand*) I.C.J. Reports 1962.

[88] This may include educational seminars, workshops, competitions, films, visits to archaeological sites, publications, exhibitions, national campaigns and so on. The same applies for the obligation concerning general educational measures and the sensitisation of the public.

of issues which merit clarification. First, the meaning of the phrase 'as appropriate for each country' is not very clear. It would not be logical to allege that there may be situations where such an obligation is not appropriate because that would invalidate the existence of the obligation itself. It should rather be interpreted in such a way as to mean that it is up to States Parties to choose the way, method or procedure by which to implement this provision.[89]

It is also difficult to understand why this obligation refers only to antique dealers (which in my opinion should be read as 'dealers in antiquities'[90] otherwise it seems to refer to dealers in only recent works of art, which would make no sense in relation to the purpose of the Convention) and not to dealers in cultural property in general.

The obligation on dealers in antiquities is rather an interesting one since it makes direct reference to penal and administrative sanctions and it is rather detailed in the way it is described. In fact it breaks new ground in the sense that up to this point, and even until today, many dealers avoid keeping any records (or better, avoid admitting keeping any records) on the basis of confidentiality, data protection, security from thefts, tax reasons and even to aid clients who buy objects in order to launder their money. Yet, none of these reasons should be held to be unjustifiable in relation to the promotion of unprovenanced and undocumented cultural objects. The reason for that of course is that cultural objects are not 'any' objects. They bring with them values (over and above the aesthetic ones) which are closely linked to the public interest. It also goes without saying that the registration of those objects facilitates their tracing and restitution and throws light onto a grey area of trade.

Dealers who have not complied with this obligation cannot invoke their good faith in relation to the acquisition of a cultural object against a requesting State. This, of course, cannot be derived directly from the Convention since this Convention binds States Parties and not individuals. However, it should carry weight in private transactions since this provision is enshrined in a widely accepted Convention which forms one of the basic (if not the basic) Conventions in the area.[91]

---

[89] According to Bator, P.M. (1982), n. 13 above, 275, and Abramson, Ronald D. and Stephen B. Huttler (1973), n. 42 above, at 963, this obligation is severely restricted by the aforementioned phrase. However, Fraoua, R. (1986), n. 14 above, at 84 and O'Keefe, P.J. (2007), n. 41 above, 75 take the opposite view.

[90] Fraoua, R. (1986), n. 14 above, at 83, according to which this article covers all dealers in cultural goods.

[91] It could be seen in conjunction with the relevant provisions of the 1995 Unidroit Convention.

2.1.5 Retroactivity and Time Limitations

The 1970 UNESCO Convention contains no provisions on retroactivity or time limitations, which means that in relation to retroactivity the 1969 Vienna Convention on the Law of Treaties[92] applies. The Vienna Convention stipulates that a Convention applies from the moment it enters into force for the State which either accedes to it or ratifies it. Therefore the Convention has no retroactive effects and States Parties cannot claim cultural objects which have been stolen, imported or exported before the Convention entered into force. This of course does not mean that these objects have been lost. It means that they can only be requested under the existing laws of the States and not under the special provisions of the Convention.

The Convention does not refer to time limitations either. This again means that States Parties can apply their own time limitations, without the need to make a reservation or declaration in this respect.[93] The issue of time limitations was dealt with in detail during the drafting of the 1995 Unidroit Convention and evoked a lot of controversy. It is discussed in section 2.2.

2.1.6 Final Remarks

By today's standards, the 1970 UNESCO Convention is not a legal instrument containing radical measures for the protection of cultural property.[94] Its provisions constitute the basic provisions necessary for the least possible protection of cultural objects. Yet at the time, when there was no common agreement or even awareness that the illicit trafficking in art was harming national cultural property and by extension the world's cultural heritage (for which the protection of national heritage is the mechanism and vehicle for its safeguarding and promotion), it was a decisive step in this direction. The significance of the 1970 UNESCO Convention essentially lies in the bridging of the very different views in this field. It promoted the encouragement of co-operation between States with a common

---

92 Vienna Convention on the Law of Treaties, 23 May 1969, 1155 U.N.T.S. 331, articles 28 and 100.

93 When the UK ratified the Convention, it declared that it would interpret article 7(b)(ii) to the effect that it may continue to apply its existing rules on limitation to claims made under the article for the recovery and return of cultural objects.

94 For the monitoring of the Convention and relevant Resolutions see http://portal.unesco.org/en/ev.php-URL_ID=13039&URL_DO=DO_TOPIC&URL_SECTION=201.html.

aim and understanding, the enactment of codes of ethics, the establishment of agreed ethics and customs, the softening of attitudes, the end of the 'blessing' of bad and immoral acquisition policies by museums and collectors and the reconciliation between the principles of archaeology and history and those of the art trade and collection. For the first time it was shown that these two worlds were not that far apart and they could co-exist on the premise that there would be common moral and legal grounds which would be internationally respected.[95]

It is significant that, at its outset, no one believed that this Convention would be successful. Initially only a small number of States ratified or acceded to it. Today the States Parties to the Convention number 120. Among these States are major market States such as the United States, the United Kingdom, Switzerland, Japan and so on. From the European Union alone, 21 out of 27 States have ratified it.[96]

However, today, almost 40 years after its adoption, the 1970 UNESCO Convention seems outdated. Morals and attitudes have developed since then, whilst many national laws have incorporated provisions which go a lot further than the ones enshrined in the Convention. During the first years of the Convention, the discussion of cultural property protection was rather vague, limiting itself to general theoretical principles. In recent years the discussion has become more specific with reference to particular obligations and duties, as well as measures and methods that have been tested over time and can help to combat the illicit trade in art effectively. Technologies have also developed in terms of real time exchange of information, as well as international and regional mechanisms of co-operation. By today's standards the 1970 UNESCO Convention looks vague, weak and rather complex.[97] Its complexity is essentially due to the fact that, at the stage of its drafting, mentalities and attitudes were not as mature as they are now. Its wording was the outcome of the concessions that had to

---

95 It can even be considered to reflect international public policy. See in this respect, O'Keefe, P.J. (2007), n. 42, 163 *et* seq referring to *Allgemeine Versicherungsgesellschaft v. E.K.* BGHZ 59, at 83 (Germany); *L. v. Chambre d'accusation du canton de Genève* BGE 123 II 134 (Switzerland), and *Autocephalous Greek-Orthodox Church of Cyprus v. Goldberg and Feldman Fine Arts* 917 F.2d 278 (1990) at p.296 (US).

96 Greece, Italy, Cyprus, Spain, Portugal, Slovakia, Slovenia, France, Finland, UK, Sweden, Denmark, Germany, Poland, Romania, Bulgaria, Estonia, Hungary, the Netherlands, Belgium and Lithuania have ratified the 1970 UNESCO Convention.

97 Gordon, J.B. (1971), 'The UNESCO Convention on the Illicit Movement of Art Treasures', *Harvard International Law Journal*, 12, 537, at 554.

be made. Since then the landscape has changed considerably and a lot of expertise has been gained from its implementation.[98]

According to article 25, this Convention may be revised. Any such revision, however, would only bind the States which become Parties to it and not the States Parties to the 1970 UNESCO Convention.[99] There was an initial very premature attempt[100] at revision in 1983 but it was still early days for the Convention. Today even market States have become well disposed to the idea of protecting other States' cultural property and have enacted laws to this end. Cultural diplomacy, bilateral agreements within the ambit of the 1970 Convention, publications, a series of return and restitution cases, the adoption of codes of ethics, best practices by museums and dealers as well as the offices and activities of UNESCO and its Intergovernmental Committee for Promoting the Return of Cultural Property to its Countries of Origin or its Restitution in Case of Illicit Appropriation, have shaped a new landscape. It is in this new landscape that the 1995 Unidroit Convention was concluded, even though the number of States ratifying it comes nowhere near that which ratified the 1970 UNESCO Convention. Perhaps the time is ripe for the convergence of the two Conventions into one international legal instrument, which will rub out inconsistencies, contradictions and complexities running contrary to the aims served by these instruments. The experience gathered over time can be incorporated into this instrument and certain issues can be taken further with less prejudice and fear, whilst others can become more concrete in order to avoid large differences and variations in national implementation laws.[101] Most countries have some cultural property to

---

[98] See in particular article 16, which provides that 'The States Parties to this Convention shall in their periodic reports submitted to the General Conference of the United Nations Educational, Scientific and Cultural Organization on dates and in a manner to be determined by it, give information on the legislative and administrative provisions which they have adopted and other action which they have taken for the application of this Convention, together with details of the experience acquired in this field.' On the basis of this article collections of national reports were published in 1987 (UNESCO Doc. 24 C/24), 1995 (UNESCO Doc. 28 C/35) and 2003 (UNESCO Doc. 32 C/24).

[99] According to article 25 paragraph 2 '[i]f the General Conference should adopt a new convention revising this Convention in whole or in part, then, unless the new convention otherwise provides, this Convention shall cease to be open to ratification, acceptance or accession, as from the date on which the new revising convention enters into force'.

[100] There were only suggestions for revision. At that time the States Parties to the Convention were only 50 while many more ratifications were expected.

[101] E.g. Japan and Sweden take the minimalist approach as regards the prohibition of imports of objects illegally exported from other States Parties. That

protect that is linked to their tradition, history, identity and culture. And the way to protect it in a globalised environment is necessarily through international co-operation and respect of their laws by other States.

2.2 THE 1995 UNIDROIT CONVENTION

2.2.1 General Remarks[102]

The Unidroit Convention was signed in Rome on 24 June 1995. Its origins are found in the 1970 UNESCO Convention on the Means of Prohibiting

---

means that on many occasions objects smuggled out of a State Party can be legally imported into Japan or Sweden. Such provisions probably infringe the principle of reciprocity applying between States Parties to an international convention.

[102] See, Bator, P.M. (1996), *The International Trade in Art*, 2nd ed., Chicago, London: University of Chicago Press, 107; Bibas, St. (1996), 'The Case against Statutes of Limitations for Stolen Art', *International Journal of Cultural Property*, 5, 73; Byrne-Sutton, Q. (1992), 'The Goldberg Case: A Confirmation of the Difficulty in Acquiring Good Title to Valuable Stolen Cultural Objects', *International Journal of Cultural Property*, 1; Coggins, C. (1995), 'A Licit International Traffic in Ancient Art: Let There Be Light!', *International Journal of Cultural Property*, 4; Crewdson, R. (1996), 'On the Making of Conventions', *International Legal Practitioner*, 21; Droz, G. (1997), 'Convention d'UNIDROIT sur les biens volés ou illicitement exportés', *Revue Critique de Droit International Privé*, 1; Fraoua, R. (1995), 'Le projet de convention de l'UNIDROIT sur le retour international des biens culturels volés ou illicitement exportés', *Aktuelle Juristische Praxis*, 317; Greenfield, J. (2007), *The Return of Cultural Treasures*, 3rd revised edition, Cambridge University Press; Jenkins, P. (1996), 'The UNIDROIT Convention on Stolen and Illegally Exported Cultural Objects', *Art Antiquity and Law*, 1; Hawkins, Ashton (1995), 'A Tale of Two Innocents: Creating an Equitable Balance between the Rights of Former Owners and Good Faith Purchasers of Stolen Art', *Fordham Law Review*, 64; Hughes, V. (1994), 'International Efforts to Secure the Return of Stolen or Illegally Exported Cultural Objects: Has Unidroit Found a Global Solution?' *The Canadian Yearbook of Int'l Law* 219; Lalive, P. (1996), 'Une avancée du droit international: la convention de Rome d'UNIDROIT sur les biens culturels volés ou illicitement exportés', *Uniform Law Review*, 1; Lalive, P. (1997), 'La convention d'UNIDROIT sur les biens culturels volés ou illicitement exportés (du 24 juin 1995)', *Revue Suisse de Droit International et de Droit Européen*, Geneva, (1), 13; Lenzner, N. (1994), 'The Illicit International Trade in Cultural Property: Does the UNIDROIT Convention Provide an Effective Remedy for the Shortcomings of the UNESCO Convention?', *University of Pennsylvania Journal of International Business Law*, 15, 469; Marks, P. (1998), 'The Ethics of Art Dealing', *International Journal of Cultural Property*, 7, 116; Merryman, J.H. (1996), 'The UNIDROIT Convention: Three Significant Departures from the Urtext', *International Journal of Cultural Property*, 5, 1–18; Montagu, A. (1993–1994), 'Recent Cases on the Recovery of Stolen Art – The Tug

and Preventing the Illicit Import, Export and Transfer of Ownership of Cultural Property.[103] In other words it can be called a follow-up to, or a Convention complementing, the 1970 UNESCO Convention.[104] From a

---

of War between Owners and Good Faith Purchasers', *Columbia VLA (Volunteer Lawyers for the Arts) Journal of Law and the Arts*, 18; Nafziger, J.A.R. (1987), 'Repose Legislation: A Threat to the Protection of the World's Cultural Heritage', *California Western International Law Journal* 250; Nott, S. (1984), 'Title to Illegally Exported Items of Historic or Artistic Worth', *International Comparative Law Quarterly*, 206; O'Keefe, P.J. and L.V. Prott (1989), *Law and the Cultural Heritage: Volume I: Discovery and Excavation* and *Volume III: Movement*, London: Butterworths; Palmer, N. (ed.) (1998), *The Recovery of Stolen Art: A Collection of Essays*, London: Kluwer Law International; Prott, L.V. (1992), 'The Preliminary Draft UNIDROIT Convention on Stolen or Illegally Exported Cultural Objects', *International and Comparative Law Quarterly*, 41, 160; Prott, L.V (1996), 'UNESCO and UNIDROIT: A Partnership against Illicit Trafficking', *Uniform Law Review*, 59; Prott, L.V. (1989), 'Problems of Private International Law for the Protection of Cultural Heritage', *Recueil des Cours*, 215; Prott, L.V. (1997), *Commentary on the UNIDROIT Convention on Stolen and Illegally Exported Cultural Objects 1995*, Leicester: Institute of Art and Law; *Report of the UK Department of National Heritage on the 1970 UNESCO Convention concerning the Illicit Import, Export and Transfer of Cultural Property*, 21 March 1996; Schneider, M. (1997), 'The UNIDROIT Convention on Cultural Property: State of Play and Prospects for the Future', *UNIDROIT Research Officer*, 494; Sidorsky, E. (1996), 'The 1995 UNIDROIT Convention on Stolen or Illegally Exported Cultural Objects: The Role of International Arbitration', *International Journal of Cultural Property*, 5, 19; Siehr, K. (1992), 'The UNIDROIT Draft Convention on the International Protection of Cultural Property', *International Journal of Cultural Property*,1(2) 321; Siehr, K. (1997), 'The Protection of Cultural Heritage and International Commerce', *International Journal of Cultural Property*, 304; Stamatoudi, I. (1997), 'The Law and the Ethics Deriving from the Parthenon Marbles Case', *Web Journal of Current Legal Issues*, (www.ncl.ac.uk/~nlawwww/) and (1998) *Yearbook of Current Legal Issues*, Blackstone Press; Stamatoudi, I. (1998), 'The National Treasures Exception in Article 36 EC: How Many of them Fit the Bill?', *Art, Antiquity and Law*, 39; Stamatoudi, I. (2000), 'Restitution of Stolen and Illegally Exported Cultural Objects', in P. Torremans (ed.), *Legal Convergence in the Enlarged Europe of the New Millennium,* The Netherlands: Kluwer Law International, 109; The Law Reform Commission Report on the Unidroit Convention on Stollen or Illegally Exported Cultural Objects, Ireland, 1997; von Plehwe, T. (1995), 'European Union and the Free Movement of Cultural Goods', *European Law Review*, 431; Wyss, M. (1992), 'The Protection of the Cultural Heritage and its Legal Dimensions: The Heidelberg Symposium 22–23 June 1990', *International Journal of Cultural Property*, 232.

[103] Precisely in article 7(b)(ii) of the 1970 UNESCO Convention, which raises a number of important issues of private law. The Unidroit Convention has undertaken to make the obligations of the parties clearer and effective.

[104] A report to UNESCO on national legal control of illicit traffic in cultural property in 1982 recommended that UNESCO take up this issue with an

comparative point of view, the purpose of these two legal instruments is not identical, since Unidroit's purpose is not only '*to contribute effectively to the fight against illicit trade in cultural objects*', but also to '*establish common, minimal legal rules for the restitution and return of cultural objects between Contracting Parties*'.[105] Essentially it seeks to harmonise the various national rules on the issue of good faith acquisition. It was clear that the short time limitations in many countries[106] in favour of a good faith purchaser (such as 3 years after the purchase of an object by a buyer unaware that it had been stolen), which applied for chattels in general, only favoured the illegal trade in art. The protection of cultural property demanded more extensive time limitations and a tailor-made legal treatment.

The UNESCO Convention, in order to combat the illicit traffic in art, provides for State action through administrative procedures. The Unidroit Convention provides for direct access to the courts of one state by the owner of a stolen cultural object or by a state from which the cultural object has been illegally exported[107].[108]

The final text of the Unidroit Convention was the outcome of a confrontation between two extreme views: on the one hand the view of the 'importing' States,[109] which possess a strong art market and therefore favour the protection of the *bona fide* possessor, and on the other hand the 'exporting' or 'source' States,[110] which are usually victims of spoliation, and have a more protective attitude towards the dispossessed owner of the cultural object. From the very beginning of this initiative, it was obvious that the drafters of this Convention would have to make compromises in

---

international body specialised in private law. Prott, L.V. and P.J. O'Keefe (1983), *National Legal Control of Illicit Traffic in Cultural Property* UNESCO doc. CLT/83/WS/16, Paris: UNESCO.

105 The Preamble to the 1995 Unidroit Convention.

106 E.g. Poland.

107 Prott, L.V. (1997), *Commentary on the Unidroit Convention,* n. 99 above, 15.

108 The dramatic increase in art theft and illegal export in the 1980s all over the world contributed significantly to the idea of drafting a legal instrument which would put an end to this situation. See Report on the situation of cultural heritage in central and eastern Europe, Council of Europe, Parliamentary Assembly, Doc. 6538, Strasbourg, 1991, Recommendation 1172 (1992) on the situation of cultural heritage in central and eastern Europe.

109 For the purpose of this chapter I we will include in this category the States which throughout the drafting of the Convention favoured a restricted protection of cultural property. i.e. Germany, Austria, Belgium, Denmark, Finland, Ireland, Holland, Poland, United Kingdom, Sweden and Switzerland.

110 The States with a more protective attitude towards cultural property, i.e. Greece, Iran, Mexico, Nepal, Turkey and Canada.

order to achieve consensus and ratification by as many States as possible. To this end, the study group charged with this task had to face not only the difficulty of harmonising the various legal systems on good faith acquisition, but it also had to reconcile the political rhetoric and the conflicting interests of delegations. The fact that the 1970 UNESCO Convention had been in existence for almost 25 years made things easier in this regard, since it had formed mentalities and made many states better disposed towards the idea of protecting other states' cultural property.

2.2.2 Claims of an 'International' Character

The Unidroit Convention does not apply to all thefts of cultural objects. Domestic thefts, which lead to a claim that lacks an international character, are not covered.[111] However, it applies to all illegal exports of cultural goods. Article 1 of the Convention provides that it only applies to claims of an international character. Although this prerequisite refers to both stolen and illegally exported cultural goods, it seems to have been added rather superfluously in relation to the latter category, since the exportation of an object necessarily leads to an international claim.

Yet it is not very clear from the Convention how far the notion of a claim of an 'international character' is meant to go. If article 1 of the Convention is read in conjunction with article 10,[112] the following conclusion can be drawn. In the case of stolen cultural treasures, what is decisive for the application of this Convention is the State where the good is located. This State has to be a contracting party to the Convention, otherwise the requesting State has no right to invoke the application of the Convention. The requesting State is under no obligation in these circumstances to be a contracting party to the Convention. In other words, the place from which the cultural object is stolen is of no relevance in the application of the Convention. Although this State might not be a contracting party to the Convention it can still bring its suit before the courts of the State

---

[111] However, domestic claims will also be affected indirectly in those States where the legal situation applying is less favourable compared to that of the Convention. What usually happens is that States find it almost impossible to afford a protection which is more favourable to other countries than it is to their own citizens.

[112] Article 10 provides that: '(1) The provisions of chapter II shall apply only in respect of a cultural object that is stolen after this Convention enters into force in respect of the State where the claim is brought, provided that: (a) the object was stolen from the territory of a Contracting State after the entry into force of this Convention for that State; or (b) the object is located in a Contracting State after the entry into force of the Convention for that State . . .'

where the good is located,[113] if the latter has ratified the Convention or has acceded to it. This conclusion is also strengthened by the fact that the drafters of the final text of Unidroit chose to omit from the earlier draft of the Convention the requirement that the stolen cultural object had to be removed from the territory of a Contracting State.[114]

The case is different with regard to illegally exported cultural goods. Both States that are involved, the source State and the State where the object is found, have to be contracting parties to the Convention (article 1(b)). As long as a cultural object has been stolen from one State and has been (illegally) exported to another the situation is always clear. Problems arise, however, in cases where the cultural object at issue returns to the State from which it has been stolen or never manages to leave the State in which it was stolen in the first place. Let us assume, for example, that an American steals a Picasso in France, exports it to the US and the purchaser of the Picasso reimports it to France. Consider also an alternative scenario in which the American, though he steals the Picasso in France, locks it in a bank vault in France until he finds a buyer for it abroad. The question is whether the claims arising from these situations are held to be claims having an 'international character'.

The answer to this question, which in the final resort will have to be given by the national courts before which the case will be brought, depends on whether the claim having an international character is, in substance, the same as a claim which involves an international aspect. In the cases at issue we have two States involved, France and the US. It is very likely that the person suing (the State will not be the one suing in this instance) will choose to sue in the country where the object is located.[115] From a

---

113 Article 18(1).

114 Third session of the Unidroit Study Group on 26 January 1990. The 1990 preliminary draft of the Unidroit Convention provided in its first article that the Convention applies 'to claims for the restitution of stolen cultural objects *removed from the territory of a Contracting State* contrary to its export legislation'. According to this wording, an international transaction had to take place in cases regarding illegally exported objects. However, the rules regarding stolen cultural objects were applicable in both international and domestic transactions and this was not seen as fully desirable by all the national delegations. The effect of the rules of the Convention on domestic transactions was a very delicate issue, which touched on private law matters, and demanded amendments in the national laws, which the States were not willing to adopt.

115 Article 8 of the Convention provides that 'a claim . . . may be brought before courts or other competent authorities of the Contracting State where the cultural object is located, additionally to the courts or other competent authorities otherwise having jurisdiction under the rules in force in Contracting States'.

private international law point of view, any claim which involves nationals of two different States is always an international claim. Yet many would argue that such a claim should not be covered by the Convention, or that the Convention at least does not fulfil its main objective in such a case. That main objective was the return or restitution of stolen cultural objects between States. The scope of the Convention was widened in order to allow private parties as well as the States to make the claim for such a return. Nevertheless it was always the intention that the cultural good was found in the territory of one State and should be returned to the territory of the other State from which it was stolen.

Both in the case where the foreign thief never removes the stolen cultural good from the territory of the State from which it was stolen and in the case where, irrespective of the nationality, domicile or residence of the thief, the stolen cultural object has been returned to the territory of the State where it was stolen before the claim is brought, that intended international aspect is absent. One could nevertheless argue that these cases still involve an international claim. In the second case such an argument may seem rather plausible, since at one stage the cultural object did cross borders and it could be said that the return of the cultural object to the territory of the State where the theft took place simply facilitates things by removing one factual hurdle.[116]

The first case is slightly more problematic. The international character of the claim cannot be derived from the wording of the Convention in this case. One has to rely on general principles of private international law and argue that that international nature can be derived from the fact that a foreign defendant is involved, just as that fact would bring a case within the scope of private international law. It is not clear, however, that the Convention ought to be applied in such a situation and that this was the concept of an international claim that the drafters of the Convention had in mind.

That means that the State where the cultural object is located is not the only forum available under the Convention.

[116] Similar to this case was the *Winkworth v Christie Manson and Woods Ltd* case [1980] 1 Ch. 496 [England], where the cultural objects of an English collector, two years after the theft had taken place, offered them for sale at Christie's in London. Although there were reservations by some governmental experts during the working sessions of the drafting of the Unidroit Convention, L. Prott alleges that the Convention should apply, even if the litigation takes place in the first jurisdiction, since an international transaction has taken place. 'If it does not, there will be an incentive for dishonest dealers to "launder" goods through any convenient foreign jurisdiction and return the goods with impunity to the jurisdiction where the original owner was deprived of them.' Prott, L.V. (1997), *Commentary on the Unidroit Convention*, n. 102 above, 22.

If one accepts that the crucial point in time, when the assessment as to the applicability of the Convention is made, is the moment at which the claim is brought, one could just as easily argue that the first and the second scenarios really amount to the same thing. The cultural object no longer has to be returned to the territory of the State in which it was stolen. In other words it no longer has a foreign situs, and the claim merely amounts to a prosecution for theft of a national or foreign defendant. Both cases could be seen as domestic cases and lacking the international element which the Convention requires in order to qualify as an international claim. As such both would necessarily fall outside the scope of the Convention. This conclusion would fit in with the objectives of the Convention, but one could equally arrive at the conclusion that, in the absence of a special definition in the Convention, the word 'international' should be given its normal meaning. That would mean that the excluded category of domestic claims should be restricted to a theft in the forum, by a local thief, all in circumstances where the stolen cultural object never leaves the territory of the forum State.[117]

2.2.3 The Notion of 'Cultural Objects'

The definition of cultural objects which come within the ambit of protection of the Convention is an issue which has been most controversial in the drafting of the Unidroit Convention. Basically the decision had to be made between two solutions: a general definition of cultural objects, which would, it was feared, be too wide,[118] or an enumerative indication of cultural objects, which ran the risk of being too restricted. The solution that was finally adopted was a combination of the two. A general definition was inserted in article 2 of the main body of the Convention and an enumerative[119] one was annexed to it in a separate text at the end of the Convention. The adoption of this combined definition was thought to be

---

[117] See also Kowalski, W.W. (2002), *Restitution of Works of Art Pursuant to Private and Public International Law in Hague Academy of International Law – Recueil de cours 2002*, The Hague: Martinus Nijhoff, 147.

[118] A general list of cultural objects, instead of an enumerative one, would be a simpler solution and would also favour States such as the US and the UK, which in view of the enumerative list, will find many of their cultural objects unprotected, since they do not have the system of classification of movables that is used in many civil law systems, such as the French one. In the end, the fear of such a solution, favouring essentially the States that designate large amounts of cultural property, prevailed. See Prott, L.V. (1997), *Commentary on the Unidroit Convention*, n. 102 above, 26.

[119] Which is, also, an exhaustive list of cultural objects.

capable of avoiding the disadvantages that the separate implementation of each of the definitions would bring. On top of that, the adoption of a list of cultural objects as an Annex to the Convention also served the purpose of linking the 1995 Unidroit Convention to the 1970 UNESCO Convention. Although this was not done expressly[120] by coordinating their definitions, the two instruments could be made to work together.[121]

Article 2 of the Unidroit Convention reads as follows: 'cultural objects are those which, on religious or secular grounds, are of importance for archaeology, prehistory, history, literature, art or science *and* belong to one of the categories listed in the Annex to this Convention'. The wording of article 2 leads us to think that, in order for a cultural object to qualify as such under the Convention, it has to meet two tests. First, it has to come within the general definition enshrined in article 2 of the Convention *and* it also has to be included in the list of cultural objects which is annexed to the Convention. One out of the two does not suffice. Thus, no questions should arise regarding which of the two definitions should prevail in case of conflict. The reason for the inclusion of the general definition in the Convention is, in this context, rather ambiguous. What happens in reality is that article 2 works primarily as a signpost to the list of cultural objects found in the Annex, since these objects have in advance been found to be of importance for archaeology, prehistory, history, literature, art or science on religious or secular grounds. The general definition enshrined in article 2 of the Convention has probably been put there in order to convince those States that had a strong preference for it to agree with this part of the Convention. In practice it is only the enumerative definition of cultural objects that is of importance.

The enumerative list of cultural objects found in the Unidroit Convention coincides to a large extent with that of the UNESCO Convention. Although the cultural objects enshrined in the Unidroit and UNESCO Conventions are the same, the UNESCO definition demands an additional element. Each state is required to designate which cultural objects are of importance to its archaeology, literature, art, etc and they have to be included in the above list.[122]

---

120 There is only a reference to the 1970 UNESCO Convention in the Preamble of the 1995 Unidroit Convention.

121 See also article 13 of the Unidroit Convention, which reads '[t]his Convention does not affect any international instrument by which any Contracting State is legally bound and which contains provisions on matters governed by this Convention . . .'.

122 One of the arguments was that the Unidroit Convention operates on the basis of private law and not on a State-to-State level. Therefore the Unidroit

Although most International[123] and European Union[124] legal instruments in this area provide for States Parties' competence to define their cultural treasures, the Unidroit Convention does not allow for such a competence. This seems to be a serious retrogression with regard to the protection of cultural heritage.[125] And this is not only so by reason of the

---

Convention should be able to cover all cultural objects and not just the designated ones. Prott, L.V. (1997), *Commentary on the Unidroit Convention*, n. 102 above, 26.

[123] i.e. article 1 of the UNESCO Convention, 'the term "cultural property" means property which, on religious or secular grounds, is specifically designated by each State as being of importance to archaeology, prehistory, history, literature, art or science . . .'; see also, paragraph 2c of the UNESCO Recommendation (9th session, N. Delhi, 5.12.1956): 'the provisions of the present Recommendation apply to any remains whose preservation is in the public interest from the point of view of history or art and architecture, each Member State being free to adopt the most appropriate criterion for assessing the public interest of objects found in its territory'; and paragraph 2 of the UNESCO Recommendation (13th session, Paris, 19.2.1978): 'each Member State should adopt whatever criteria it deems most suitable for defining the items of movable cultural property within its territory which should be given the protection envisaged in the Recommendation, by reason of their archaeological, historical, artistic, scientific or technical value'; also, article 2(3) of the European Convention of Delphi of 23.6.1985 on offences relating to cultural property, according to which a State may declare at any time that it also considers as cultural property, besides the (vast) categories of objects mentioned in Appendix II of the Convention, any other category of movable or immovable property, presenting artistic, historical, archaeological, scientific or other cultural interest. This provision is also interesting from the point of view that it recognises, by its flexible definition of cultural property, the evolutionary character culture may have throughout the years.

[124] Directive 93/7/EEC of 15 March, 1993 on the return of cultural objects unlawfully removed from the territory of a Member State (OJ L 74/74, 27.3.1993), amended by Directive 96/100/EC of 17 February, 1997 (L 60/59, 1.3.1997) and Directive 2001/38/EC of 5 June, 2001 (L 187/43, 10.7.2001). Specifically it provides that 'Member States will retain the right to define their national treasures'. See also Council Regulation 3911/92 of 9 December, 1992 on the export of cultural goods, OJ L 395/1 (Corrigendum OJ L267/30, 19/10/1996), as amended by Council Regulation 2469/96 of 16 December, 1996 OJ L 335/9, Council Regulation 974/2001 of 14 May, 2001 OJ L 137/10 and Council Regulation 806/2003 of 14 April, 2003 OJ L 122/1. Council Regulation (EC) No 116/2009 of 18 December, 2008 on the export of cultural goods (codified version) where it is provided in article 1 that 'Without prejudice to Member States' powers under Article [36] of the Treaty, the term 'cultural goods' shall refer, for the purposes of this Regulation, to the items listed in Annex I'.

[125] As Professor Dolzer mentioned in his speech at the Heidelberg Symposium in June 1990 on the protection of cultural heritage and its legal dimensions, 'cultural property can be important in connection with national rights of self-determination and identification', in Wyss's summary of the Symposium, Wyss, M. (1992), 'The Protection of the Cultural Heritage and its Legal Dimensions:

fact that it is rather inconsistent to draft a Convention whose scope of application differs compared to pre-existing legal instruments in the area, but also because by 'protection of cultural property' we mainly assume the recognition of, and support for, the interest of the State of origin to retain and conserve its cultural objects within its territory, preventing their illicit removal. This goal is difficult to attain if a State's role in defining its own cultural heritage is not recognised.[126] It is very likely that the different historical, cultural and religious backgrounds of the States will prompt different judgments as to whether something is of minor or major importance to someone else.[127] So far it is obvious that the only competent authority, and the one that is best equipped to define its important cultural property, is the State of origin itself. Thus, recommendations favouring a common definition of cultural property for reasons of uniformity lack the power to persuade, since uniformity is both impossible and undesirable in the area of culture.[128] The Convention leaves it to the courts of the country of the *lex situs* to operate their own definition under the rules of the Annex and assumes that a uniform approach will necessarily emerge. It might have been a better idea to refer to the law of the country from which the object was taken (within the guidelines set out in the Annex) in relation to this preliminary point.

There is also the view, however, that since no designation is required, this definition is wider compared to the one found in the 1970 UNESCO Convention. In addition the Unidroit Convention applies to all stolen cultural objects whilst the 1970 UNESCO Convention (according to article

---

The Heidelberg Symposium 22–23 June 1990', *International Journal of Cultural Property*, 232. In other words, the State's competence to define its own cultural property involves also dimensions inextricably linked with national identification and sovereignty.

126 A cultural object can more effectively be protected by the State of its origin. Common and international obligations sometimes turn out to be vague and inoperative. An example of this is the 1954 Hague Convention on the protection of cultural property in the event of armed conflict. Wyss, M. *ibid*, observes, 'it is unlikely that the notion of "common heritage of the mankind" will have any normative or descriptive content beyond its declaratory effect in specific treaties'.

127 An international judiciary, dealing with international claims regarding cultural property, could be a solution at this point.

128 See also article 167 TFEU paragraph 5: 'In order to contribute to the achievement of the objectives referred to in this Article: the European Parliament and the Council acting in accordance with the ordinary legislative procedure and after consulting the Committee of the Regions, shall adopt incentive measures, excluding any harmonisation of the laws and regulations of the Member States [. . .]'.

7(b)(i))[129] applies only to objects stolen from museums, religious, secular or other similar institutions that have been inventoried in these institutions. The Unidroit Convention therefore encompasses a wider scope of stolen artefacts that can be recovered. The reason for this is that Unidroit aims to cover any artefact, including univentoried items, which could be stolen from private parties (in these cases inventories make no sense), whilst the UNESCO Convention is a Convention which only applies between States. For illegally exported cultural objects it is the requesting state (and no private parties) which need to establish that the removal of the object from its territory significantly impairs one or more of the designated in Article 5 interests.[130],[131]

For the purposes of the Unidroit Convention 'stolen' is also considered to mean the cultural objects which have been unlawfully excavated or lawfully excavated but unlawfully retained when this is consistent with the law of the State where the excavation took place.[132]

2.2.4 Restitution of Stolen Cultural Objects

2.2.4.1 Restitution

According to article 3(1) of the Unidroit Convention 'the possessor of a cultural object which has been stolen shall return it'. This is a very important provision since it provides for an unequivocal obligation on the possessor who holds an artefact that is stolen to return it. This provision presents a departure from those legal systems (essentially civil law systems)[133] which favour the good faith purchaser against the dispossessed

---

129 Article 7(b)(i): 'The States Paries to this Convention undertake . . . to prohibit the import of cultural property stolen from a museum or a religious or secular public monument or similar institution in another State Party to this Convention after the entry into force of this Convention for the States concerned, provided that such property is documented as appertaining to the inventory of that institution.'

130 See articles 5 and 7.

131 'In effect, all States were in agreement on the need to co-operate with a view to penalising theft committed abroad as theft was universally considered to be a criminal act, whereas only a few States would, in the state of the law, be prepared to undertake an obligation to sanction customs offences committed abroad.' Doc. 48 §§ 52, 100–102, 105–108.

132 Article 3(2).

133 For example in an Italian case [Tribunale di Roma of 27 June 1987 *(Stato francese c. Ministero per I beni culturali e ambientali e De Contessini)*, (1988) 71 *Rivista di Diritto Internazionale* 920, confirmed by Corte di Cassazione of 24 November 1995, n. 12166, (1997) 33 *Rivista di Diritto Internazionale Privato e Processuale* 427] where tapestries were stolen in France and bought by a *bona fide* purchaser in Italy, the Italian Court found that according to Italian law the pur-

owner, by allowing him to keep the good he purchased after the lapse of a considerably short period of time (from 3 to 6 years) or, in certain instances, return it against compensation[134].[135] By contrast, in common law systems the *nemo dat quod non habet* rule prevailed according to which no one can pass a title he does not possess and therefore one cannot become the owner of an object he acquired from a thief[136].[137]

In the end the absolute duty of return was accepted due to a number

---

chaser could keep them. An English Court came to the same conclusion in a case concerning Japanese drawings (*Winkworth v. Christie, Manson & Woods Ltd* [1980] 1 All ER. 1121, [1980] 2 WLR. 937 (ChD)). The drawings were stolen in England and sold in Italy to a *bona fide* purchaser. They were then given to Christie's in London to be auctioned. The English Court applied Italian law to the case at issue. According to this law the *bona fide* purchaser had acquired title to the drawings. We should note here that according to private international law, suits concerning the return of an object are usually brought before the courts of the country where the object is situated, whilst the law applicable to *bona fide* purchases is usually the law of the country where the purchase took place.

134 According to the French civil code (arts 2279 and 2280) a good faith purchaser – if s/he has acquired the goods at auction or though a dealer – may have to return them to the dispossessed owner (if the latter acts quickly) against the payment of compensation. In Greek law the good faith purchaser may under certain circumstances (ordinary acquisition by possession – art. 1041 GCC) become the owner of them after three years. According to English law (Limitation Act 1980) the good faith purchaser becomes an owner after the lapse of six years. These provisions, however, do not apply in all cases to cultural property objects. For example in Greece, according to Law 3028 of 2002 'movable ancient monuments up to 1453 belong to the State in terms of ownership and possession, are imprescriptible and *extra commercium* according to article 966 of the Civil Code' (article 21).

135 In civil law traditions damages are the rule, whilst *in natura* compensation forms the exception. See in this respect Stamatoudi, I. (1997), 'Specific performance in non-contractual obligation. A comparative study in French and Greek law', *Nomiki Epitheorissi*, 50.

136 However, time limitations may apply to claims for the recovery of stolen objects. For example, in an American case (*DeWeerth v. Baldinger* 658 F. Supp. 688 (S.D.N.Y. 1987), 836 F.2d 103 (2d Cir. 1987), relief granted under Rule 60 F.R.C.P., 804 F. Supp. 539 (S.D.N.Y. 1992), rev'd, 38 F.3d 1266 (2d Cir. 1994)) concerning a Claude Monet painting that had been stolen in Germany in 1945, the Court found against the original owner because she did not bring her replevin suit in time as she was proven to be negligent in tracing her painting.

137 Other legal bases that can be brought forward against the recovery of stolen cultural objects are in civil law countries acquisitive prescription (usucapio) and statute limitations. In common law countries apart from time limitations, there is also estoppel, laches or prescription. See Siehr, K. (1997), 'The Protection of Cultural Heritage and International Commerce', *International Journal of Cultural Property*, 306.

of factors. Amongst those was the fact that it had become clear to most delegations that unless a duty of return was provided, the illicit trade in stolen artefacts would not be affected, particularly in relation to cultural objects of an outstanding aesthetic or other value. Even the provision of compensation instead of return would leave this kind of trade unaffected.[138] The solution put forward was a combination of the two, i.e. return and compensation. And that was so because it was difficult to combine two different legal traditions in any other way.

The word 'possessor' was preferred over any other word (acquirer or holder) since it was neutral enough to accommodate both legal systems; those which provide that the good faith purchaser of a stolen artefact becomes an owner and those which do not.

Though not mentioned, the return should be effected towards the dispossessed owner, that is the owner of the cultural object, the museum which has the cultural object on loan, the creditor with whom it was deposited and so on. In any case this shall be an issue for the national court to decide.[139]

2.2.4.2 'Stolen' cultural objects

As mentioned above[140] stolen cultural objects for which there is an obligation to return covers all cultural objects which have been stolen, regardless of whether they have been inventoried in an institution (as is the case with the 1970 UNESCO Convention) or been designated as cultural objects by the State in which the theft has taken place. Therefore all cultural objects are covered given that they first come within the definition of 'cultural objects' as this is provided in article 2 of the Unidroit Convention and explained above. Also included are objects which have been unlawfully excavated or lawfully excavated and unlawfully retained (article 3(2)). This provision (article 3(2)) reflected a view which had already been

---

138 Bibas, St. (1996), 'The Case against Statutes of Limitations for Stolen Art', *International Journal of Cultural Property*, at 76–77 and 81–91. Other factors which worked in favour of the adoption of these provisions were the Draft Uniform Law of the Acquisition in Good Faith of Corporeal Movables (LUAB), which was completed in 1974 and departed from the protection of the *bona fide* possessor towards a more balanced approach which would also take into account the interests of the disposessed owner. Civil law lawyers, experts in the field, also played their role, i.e. Chatelain, J., Rodotà, St. and J. Kohler (1904), 'Das Recht an Denkmälern und Alertumsfunden' *Deutsche Juristenzeitung*, 771, at 775.

139 Lalive, P. (1997), n. 102 above, at 33.

140 Section 2.2.3.

accepted by some courts in various countries[141] and underlined various national laws in the field. The latter either provided for State ownership of all subsoil archaeological resources[142] or vested ownership in the landowner.[143] Therefore their taking without authorisation is necessarily a wrongful taking which equals theft.

The notion of 'excavation' is understood, according to the 1956 UNESCO Recommendation on the International Principles Applicable to Archaeological Excavations, to also cover underwater sites.

One issue which is of interest, at this point, is whether the notion of theft includes kindred offences such as defalcation, conversion, fraud, intentional misappropriation of lost property and so on. The wording of 'unlawfully retained' in article 3(2) suggests that the interpretation of theft should include all these offences. This is also reinforced by the minutes of the Third Meeting of Governmental Experts where it was noted that 'the notion of theft, for the purpose of the Convention, was not the restrictive notion of certain national laws, but rather a broader, autonomous one which would of necessity encompass similar acts'.[144]

2.2.4.3 Time limitations

The issue of time limitations, which will rule out any claims of dispossessed owners with regard to their stolen cultural property, was basically a discussion between two extreme views: one favouring short time limits and one which was against any time limits at all. Short time limits were primarily favoured by 'importing' States and were based on the idea of maximum marketability, safety in transactions and stability in the presumptions which were publicly created, i.e. the one possessing the good is also the owner of the good. The view against any time limits was primarily based on morality, optimum marketability, justice and efficiency in transactions, as well as on the need to combat any recourse to illicit trade by legitimising stolen objects in the long term and sheltering superficial checks of titles.

The solution eventually adopted by the final provisions of the Unidroit Convention, is a revised version of the one in the preliminary Draft,[145] and provides for a period of three years from the time when the claimant knew

---

141 See a US case: *United States v. McClain* 545 F.2d 988 (1977); 551 F.2d 52 (1977); 593 F.2d 658 (1979).

142 Such as Greece and Italy

143 Such as the UK.

144 Doc. 39 § 60.

145 The Preliminary Draft of the Unidroit Convention provided for three years and thirty years respectively.

the location of the cultural object and the identity of the possessor,[146] and for an absolute period of fifty years from the time of theft.[147] This provision of time limitations does not follow any particular legal system. Rather it represents the average view of many existing legal systems, some of them more generous[148] towards the dispossessed owner and other less generous.[149]

The longer limitation periods were dictated by the need to combat the illicit trade in art effectively, since cultural objects are often the object of covert international transactions and the passage of time increases rather than decreases their value.[150] The provision that the dispossessed owner

---

146 G. Droz argued that in the event that the Convention required one only of the two prerequisites it presently requires for the time limitation to start running, we would end up with cases where the possessor of the cultural object, once alerted by a request for restitution, would transfer and place it in a bank vault in a non-Contracting State. Droz, G. (1997), 'Convention d'UNIDROIT sur les biens volés ou illicitement exportés', *Revue Critique de Droit International Privé*, §15, note 21. On top of that it would be rather absurd to expect someone to enter litigation before he or she has assembled all the information possible.

147 Article 3(3) of the Unidroit Convention.

148 In New York time limitations are calculated from the date of demand and refusal. There have also been cases where important cultural objects have been retrieved 21 and 36 years after the date of theft. See *Menzel v. List* 253 N.Y.S. 2d 43 Misc. 2d 300; 267 N.Y.S2d 804 aff'd 298 N.Y.S. 2d 979 (1969); *Kunstsammlung zu Weimar v. Elicofon* 536 F. Supp. 829 (1981) 678 F. 2d 1150 (1982); *Solomon R. Guggenheim Foundation v. Lubell* 567 N.Y.S. 2d 623 (1991) and *De Weerth v. Baldinger* 836 F. 2d 1150 (1987) respectively. See Prott, L.V. (1997), *Commentary on the Unidroit Convention*, n. 99 above, 35. See also the Commonwealth Scheme for the return of unlawfully exported cultural objects from one commonwealth country to another, which provides for a 5-year time limitation for making a claim calculated from the time the country of export had knowledge of the whereabouts of the item in the country of location. No maximum time limitations exist. According to O'Keefe, P.J. (1995), 'Protection of the Material Cultural Heritage: The Commonwealth Scheme', *International and Comparative Law Quarterly*, 147, at 158,

> The wording seems to suggest that subjective knowledge is necessary – that knowledge cannoy be imputed to the country concerned. It would thus be need to be proved in a substantive form such as overt action by the government or production documents indicating knowledge on the part of the appropriate authorities. The mere fact that, for example, the ambassador of the country of export saw the item in a collection in the country of location should not necessarily start the period running.

149 France takes as a starting point for the calculation of the time limitation the date of theft or loss (art. 22 79 FCC); England calculates it from the date the *bona fide* possessor acquired the object. There are diverging systems in the US. In New Jersey and California time limitations are calculated from the date of discovery of the object.

150 Although some States put forward the time limitation provided by the

needs to know both the identity of the possessor and the location of the cultural object for the time limitation to start running is a significant contribution against illicit art trade. If the identity of the possessor sufficed (as some States wanted it to), as soon as the possessor was notified of a request for the return of an object, he could easily be prompted to hide the object in a bank vault in a non-Contracting State.[151]

The issue of knowledge is one to be decided according to the law of the State which applies. In cases which have been decided so far, courts have been quite sensitive. The courts looked not only into whether information on the sale or auction of an object was available but also into whether this information was accessible to the claimant. In the same spirit, a bill which would have made it possible for a cultural object to be exhibited in a museum was not found to suffice in this respect.[152] Inclusion in a public collection, temporary exhibition or auction catalogue would not suffice either.[153] If, however, the purchaser tried to notify possible owners (including the dispossessed owner) or the State from whose territory the cultural object comes, he could then probably invoke the shorter limitation period.

Time limits are set out in the Convention in a very neutral and objective way without the provision of any exceptions with regard to force majeure or any other inability.[154] However, it is very likely that national courts will apply to claims concerning cultural objects the general (national) provisions applying to the interruption of the running of limitation periods as these provisions apply to any other claim. The fifty year period is subject to almost the same kind of limitations.[155] Yet here, the essential incapacity

---

European Directive EEC/93/7, which is no more than one year after the requesting Member State became aware of the location of the cultural object and of the identity of its possessor or holder, this was not accepted on the basis that the Unidroit Convention was a Convention of an international rather than regional character.

151 Droz, G. (1997), n. 102 above, at 22.

152 In relation to a New York case. Nafziger, J.A.R. (1987), 'Repose Legislation: A Threat to the Protection of the World's Cultural Heritage', *California Western International Law Journal* 250.

153 Prott, L.V. (1997), *Commentary on the Unidroit Convention*, n. 102 above, 38.

154 There are cases where a State on an individual, though they know where their stolen object is found, are not in a position to put a claim for its return forward. A State, either because it is at war, or because it has not been accepted as an independent State, might not have the right to recover its loss, whilst in the case of an individual the classic incapacities of infancy, insanity or imprisonment might prevent him or her from bringing a suit in support of a claim.

155 The UK has suggested an even shorter 'absolute' time limit than the one of thirty years provided in the Draft Convention. Specifically, it suggested six years from the time of theft or the illegal export of the cultural object.

or difficulty is the inability of an owner to trace his or her stolen cultural property. Even if an object is openly disposed of, it can well be the case that an owner cannot trace it, if this object is found at someone's house, private collection, or in the collection of a distant and unpopular museum somewhere in the world.[156] Apart from the difficulties one faces today, in tracing his property, by reason of the widespread international borderless trade in art and the covert nature of transactions, it is also well known how easy it is to hide an object in a museum's store or in a bank's vault, especially when this object is extremely valuable. If dealers and other persons engaged in such activities have to keep the object out of the market for some time or let it go 'underground',[157] they not only have nothing to lose, but in some cases they will even profit, since the passage of time may lead to an increase in the object's value. If the person who illegally acquired the object finally decides to sell it, a fifty-year period is not necessarily a deterrent for the purchaser. He or she may be willing to hide the object without exposing it publicly for the remainder of the fifty-year term if the purchase price is right. It may turn out to be a good and valuable long-term investment. This was proven to be the case with regard to artefacts stolen during or immediately after the Second World War, which have recently been discovered. As L. Prott, puts it 'long limitation periods have important reasons behind them, and it is noteworthy that neither the Declaration of London of 1943 concerning the restitution of cultural property taken under the Nazi occupation, nor the Protocol to the Convention on the Protection of Cultural Property in the Event of Armed Conflict 1954 (the "Hague Convention"), which concerns displaced cultural movables, has an expressed limitation period'.[158]

There is no doubt that long prescription of claims periods impede trade

---

[156] In the following cases American courts have held that cultural objects had been held openly by their possessors, even in cases where these objects were only held indoors. *Burroughs Adding Machine Co. v. Bivens-Corhn Co.* 119 P.2d 58, 59 (Okla. 1941); *Reynolds v. Bagwell*, 198 P.2d 215, 217 (Okla. 1948); cf. *United States v. One Stradivarius Kieserwetter Violin* 197 F. 157, 159 (2d Cir. 1912), about a violin held in the defendant's house; *Connor v. Hawkins* 9 S. W. 684, 685 (Tex. 1888), about a piano held in the defendant's house; *Joseph v. Lesnevich* 153 A.2d 349, 357 (N.J. Super. Ct. App. Div. 1959). As quoted in the article by Bibas, St. (1996), 'The Case against Statutes of Limitations for Stolen Art', *International Journal of Cultural Property*, 73, at 78.

[157] For an example of another type of mala fide activity see *Attorney General of New Zealand v. Ortiz* [1982] 2 WLR. 10; [1982] 3 WLR. 570; [1983] 2 WLR. 809; [1984] AC 1.

[158] Prott, L.V. (1997), *Commentary on the Unidroit Convention*, n. 102 above, 36. In any case cultural objects taken during conflict or occupation would fall within the ambit of the Hague Convention in any event. *Ibid.*

and create instability in law on certain occasions. Yet, in the area of culture there are other values to be found, the protection of which might eventually outweigh the facilitation of trade.[159] It has been observed that, 'the law's goal should not be to maximise marketability *per se*, but rather to achieve optimum marketability by inducing buyers to weigh the costs of investigation against its benefits. If art has a readily discernible, honourable provenance, there is no impediment to its sale. The cloud over an artwork's title arises when its provenance is unclear or questionable'.[160] Optimum marketability can only be achieved if the owner from whom the good is stolen is always given the opportunity to claim it back. Although this solution might be 'severe' on bona fide purchasers, it is the only way of making purchasers more diligent about the status of what they are buying.[161] If this policy is established, it is first the purchasers who will not be willing to take any risks and then the sellers who will have to engage themselves in legitimate activities only. Demand for stolen art in the black market will dry up[162].[163]

---

159 The recent discovery of large amounts of cultural property taken in the course of or in the immediate aftermath of World War II shows that long limitation periods have important reasons behind them, and it is noteworthy that neither the Declaration of London of 1943 concerning the restitution of cultural property taken under Nazi occupation nor the Protocol to the Convention on the protection of cultural property in the event of armed conflict 1954 (the 'Hague Convention'), which concerns displaced cultural movables, has an expressed limitation period.

Prott, L.V. (1997), *Commentary on the Unidroit Convention*, n. 102 above, 36.

160 Bibas, St. n. 153 above, 83.

161 Prott, L.V. (1989), 'Problems of Private International Law for the Protection of Cultural Heritage', *Recueil des Cours*, 215, at 275.

162 In any case, after a certain number of years the material evidence that is necessary to enable one to reclaim stolen artefacts will no longer be available in practice. Yet, it is inequitable to determine in advance in an arbitrary way that this period will be 50 years. It is interesting to note in this respect that the holocaust victims only now, almost 50 years after the end of the Second World War, have managed to trace some of their stolen paintings, and essentially only those in public museums or other places that are open to the public. Stolen artefacts in private collections are very difficult to trace. At a recent press conference they admitted that if the tracing of their stolen cultural objects does not take place soon, in a number of years there will be no survivors to claim them back.

163 It is interesting to note a recent decision of the High Court in London that dealt with time limitations and prescription periods in relation to the title of a painting which had been stolen almost 50 years ago (*City of Gotha v. Sotheby's and Cobert Finance SA*; *Federal Republic of Germany v. Sotheby's and Cobert Finance SA*. QBD (Moses J) 9/9/1998, nyr). Maybe somewhat surprisingly, Mr Justice Moses rules that he was not prepared to accept any absolute time limitations in relation to a stolen painting currently possessed by a purchaser in bad

We have to admit that apart from the general rules applying to most cultural objects, there is a special category of cultural objects, whose significance does not permit for any time limitations or the consideration of any market interests of the individuals concerned. Time cannot make up for the removal from their place of origin objects that are of extreme importance to a nation's history, culture and religion. Some national laws provide for the imprescriptibility of such objects.[164] Others categorise them as inalienable[165], as *res extra commercium,*[166] or *res sacrae*, the only legitimate possessor being the State, which preserves them for the common interest and benefit.

Article 3(4) of the Unidroit Convention comes close to such a regime, but not close enough. '[C]ultural object[s] forming an integral part of an identified monument or archaeological site, or belonging to a public collection, shall not be subject to time limitations other than a period of three years from the time when the claimant knew the location of the cultural object and the identity of the possessor'.[167] However, the lack of a general unreserved time limitation is not absolute. Paragraph (5) of the same article provides the opportunity to the Parties to unilaterally provide for a fixed time limitation of 75 years.[168] This term can be extended by the Parties, if they so wish.[169] In case they do, the principle of reciprocity applies as this is set out by article 3(5). 'A claim made in another Contracting State for

---

faith, because to accept such an outcome on the basis of the foreign applicable law would go against English public policy. On these grounds he refused to apply the 30-year German time limitation to stolen goods, because the rule in section 4 of the Limitation Act 1980 identified a public policy rule that in England time does not run in favour either of the thief or of any transferee who is not a purchaser in good faith. This conclusion is to be welcomed, but it comes as a surprise in a country where the government has consistently refused to accept instruments with more restrictive rules, such as the Unidroit Convention.

164 E.g. art.18 (1) of the French law for historical monuments of 1993: 'all the movable objects listed are imprescriptible'.

165 E.g. Mexico; Spain, in its Law on Historical Patrimony 1985 and the Law on National Patrimony 1982; Greece in its Law 3028 of 2002 and 3658/2008. See also, art. 28 of the relevant Portuguese law, which does not allow for any private ownership of works of art listed in a national registry.

166 This was also explained by Professor Mussgnug in the 1990 Heidelberg Symposium with reference to the German administrative law and to the broadly accepted concept of *res sacrae*.

167 This special category of objects undoubtedly leaves out many of the objects a State may consider as extremely important to its culture and therefore categorises as e.g. *res extra commercium.*

168 See also article 3(6).

169 Article 9(1).

restitution of a cultural object displaced from a monument, archaeological site or public collection in a Contracting State making such a declaration shall also be subject to that time limitation.'

This particular category of cultural objects, enshrined in article 3(4), which is subject to a special regime of time limitations, is not entirely clear. Paragraph (7) of the same article attempts a definition of 'public collection'. A 'public collection' consists of a group of inventoried or otherwise identified cultural objects owned by (a) a Contracting State, (b) a regional or local authority of a Contracting State, (c) a religious institution in a Contracting State or (d) an institution that is established for an essentially cultural, educational or scientific purpose in a Contracting State and is recognised in that State as serving the public interest[170].[171] It is not clear what is meant by 'cultural objects owned by a Contracting State' and whether authorities and institutions not totally owned but controlled by the State or institutions funded by the State are also included. This is essential in order to understand whether such cultural objects fall within the article 3(4) regime of protection or within the general regime subject to article 3(3). Especially with regard to article 3(7) (d) and the notion of 'public interest', Paul Jenkins[172] asks whether the UK would include under this article the National Trust or a charitable trust, say at Chatsworth, by according it charitable status.[173]

2.2.4.4 Compensation

As mentioned above, the possessor of a cultural object that has been stolen has to return it. However, upon the return of the artefact, the possessor who finds himself in good faith, shall be entitled to a 'fair and reasonable compensation' (article 4(1)).[174] A possessor is held to be in good faith if

---

[170] The latter paragraph was essentially inserted at the request of the US which feared that most of its museum collections, which are not state-owned, would fall outside the scope of 'public collections'. Doc. 48, §§ 63–8, 77–9.

[171] According to article 3(8), 'a claim for restitution of a sacred or communally important cultural object belonging to and used by a tribal or indigenous community in a Contracting State as part of that community's traditional or ritual use, shall be subject to the time limitation applicable to public collections'. For the notion of 'indigenous people' see United Nations Document E/CN.4/Sub.2/1994/2.

[172] Jenkins, P. (1995), *The UNIDROIT Convention on Stolen or Illegally Exported Cultural Objects*, London: UK Department of National Heritage.

[173] The same arguments also apply to the time limitations for the return of illegally exported cultural objects in article 5(5).

[174] It was argued by many national representatives during the drafting of the Convention that the only realistic and efficient way of combating illicit art trade would be an absolute provision for return of stolen artefacts, irrespective of the

he neither knew nor ought reasonably to have known that the object was stolen and can prove that he exercised due diligence when acquiring it.

Article 4,[175] which provides for the payment of compensation[176] to the *bona fide* purchaser, breaks new ground from two points of view.[177] First, it provides for compensation to the possessor in good faith, where most national laws do not; at least if the compensation is to be paid by the dispossessed owner. And secondly, it reverses the burden of proof, by requiring the possessor to prove that he did not know or could not have reasonably known that the object in his possession was stolen, and that he exercised due diligence when he acquired it.

In the final text of the Convention the term 'due diligence' was adopted, instead of the term 'good faith'. The latter would automatically refer one to the classical meaning afforded to it by civil law traditions and consequently to their existing domestic practice. The drafters of the Convention

---

good faith of the purchaser. That provision would become even more efficient, perhaps, if the requirement of compensation was absent, too. Prospective purchasers would refrain from buying artefacts without full documentation and they would question the statements of their sellers. Dealers and auction houses would have to be more diligent as to with what and whom they deal, and they would be more willing to disclose the names of their transferors and clients. In case something still goes wrong, the *bona fide* purchaser can always invoke his rights against the seller of the good. However the return of an artefact 'from a *bona fide* purchaser was already a very considerable change in a fundamental principle of law for a number of legal systems, and that to do so without compensation would be extremely difficult for political reasons'. Doc. 23 §§ 69–71, 73. Prott, L.V. (1997), *Commentary to the Unidroit Convention*, n. 102 above, 41.

175 Article 4 (1) reads: 'The possessor of a stolen cultural object required to return it shall be entitled, at the time of its restitution, to payment of a fair and reasonable compensation provided that the possessor neither knew not ought reasonably to have known that the object was stolen and can prove that he exercised due diligence when acquiring the object'.

176 Compensation should be paid at the time of an object's restitution (article 4(1)). However, the court may provide for some other payment arrangement. In any case the parties may negotiate other forms of compensation and come to a mutually acceptable solution such as the one reached in *Union of India v. The Norton Simon Foundation*, United District Court, Southern District of New York, 74 Cir. 5331; United States District Court, Central District of California, Case No. CV 74-3581-RJK, where a stolen Sina Nataraja from India was displayed by a US collector for ten years before it returned to India.

177 The innovation article 3(1) provides for, i.e. the return of a stolen object by the *bona fide* purchaser, breaks new ground, especially in relation to civil law systems. Civil law systems protect to varying degrees the *bona fide* purchaser of a stolen object, especially in situations where the object at issue has been purchased from a store or an auction. In most common law systems the *nemo dat quod non habet* rule applies, i.e. no one can transfer what he does not possess.

wanted to avoid that. They wanted to link this term to the needs and purpose of the Convention. However, the term 'due diligence' which was opted for is also a term of art in US law.

With regard to the first point, the drafters of the Convention clearly thought that it wouldn't be equitable simply to deprive someone of an asset that he had diligently acquired. On top of that, it would not be practical to depart considerably from the legal traditions of many States who favoured the good faith purchaser without providing some kind of compensation for him. According to Article 4(4) of the Convention, whether the possessor exercised due diligence[178] upon the acquisition of the object will be judged according to all the circumstances of the acquisition.[179] These include the character of the parties (reputed sellers, specialised dealers[180] and buyers who are connoisseurs should demonstrate a higher degree of diligence),[181] the price paid (which should not differ substantially from the normal market price for the artefact), whether the possessor consulted any reasonably accessible register of stolen cultural objects, and any other relevant

---

178 This provision incorporates the long-standing doctrine caveat emptor, according which it is always the purchaser who has the onus of investigating the title of the object he intends to buy.

179 According to Prott, L.V. (1997), *Commentary on the Unidroit Convention*, n. 99 above, 47–8, all the circumstances of the acquisition should be taken into account, such as an unusual place of transfer (e.g. the bond area of an airport (*Autocephalous Greek-Orthodox Church of Cyprus v. Goldberg & Feldman Fine Arts Inc.* 717 F.Supp 1374 (1989); 917 F.2d 278 (1990) (US)), or a trailer track in a loading dock (The Sevso treasure)) or time of day (*Reid v. Metropolis Police Comr.* [1973] 2 All ER 97 (UK). Undue haste to conclude the transfer would seem to indicate caution. Antiquities whose original container also revealed woodchips, soil and caterpillars (the Sevso treasure) or mud and straw (*United States v. McClain* 545 F.2d 988 (1977); 551 F.2d 52 (1977); 593 F.2d 658 (1979) (US)) must surely suggest the need for further inquiries, as would objects from some areas which have been heavily looted, such as Afghanistan or Iraq, and have been publicised as such. There are also certain classes of antiquities whose illicit origin should be presumed, e.g. Cycladic figures and Apulian vases. In any case antiquities are within this class of objects which require a special degree of care (*Versicherung X v. A.M.* (antique weapons case) BGE/ATF 122 III 1 (Federal Court Lausanne, 5 March 1996).

180 The fact that a dealer offers for sale an object which is undocumented or unprovenanced may come under the Sale of Goods Act 1979, according to which there is an implied warranty that the property was free from encumbrance, was of satisfactory quality and reasonably fit for its purpose.

181 Also the buyer who buys an artefact from a seller with whom he has never dealt before, who has no expertise in this kind of trade or who also trades in other objects, should make stringent inquiries into its provenance and legitimacy. If the object has been imported from another country he should also look for an export certificate.

information and documentation which he could reasonably have obtained, and whether the possessor consulted accessible agencies or took any other step that a reasonable person would have taken in the circumstances.[182] Although the list of conditions relating to the possessor's due diligence is quite lengthy, non-exhaustive and certainly non-cumulative in its application, the truth is that in reality hardly any search of title is undertaken and little attention is paid by the purchasers upon the purchase of an artefact.[183]

---

[182] Such information can either be, for example, a catalogue raisonné of an artist's work which is usually drafted by a prominent art expert listing every known artwork of a particular artist, and which can determine with a great degree of certainty the lineage and the most recent ownership of a work, or the international computerised database of stolen art, which is accessible to everyone subject to a fee from 1991.

[183] See Cuno, J. (2006), 'Beyond Bamiyan: Will the World be Ready Next Time?' in Hoffman, B.T. (ed), *Art and Cultural Heritage. Law, Policy and Practice*, Cambridge University Press, 41, at 45 where he claims that

> inherent in the concept of 'due diligence' is acceptance of the fact that at the time of acquisition all evidence may not be at hand regarding the legal standing of the work of art in question. A museum is free to make the acquisition without such evidence only after certain procedures have been followed. If, after making the acquisition, convincing evidence is brought forward to prove that the work of art was illegally exported from its country of origin, then one is obliged to return it to the proper authorities in that country. It may result in money spent inappropriately, but that is part of the cost of doing business as a museum.

See also DeAngelis, I.P. (2006), 'How Much Provenance is Enough? Post-schultz Guidelines for Art Museum Acquisition of Archaeological Materials and Ancient Art' in Hoffman, B.T. *ibid* at 398, where he discusses the due diligence tests that museums should undergo before they acquire objects. See the two decisions taken respectively on 12 June, 2009, as regards the question of jurisdiction, and on 10 February, 2010, as regards the merits by the Tribunal of Pesaro relating to the confiscation of a bronze statue of a victorious athlete, attributed to the Greek sculptor Lysippos which was found in August 1964 by the vessel *Ferruccio Ferri* flying the Italian flag and fishing in an area of high seas in the Adriatic Sea. It was introduced in Italy where it was kept for a certain time and then illegally exported to Munich, London and perhaps Brazil before it entered in 1977 the United States. It was finally bought by the J. Paul Getty Museum of Los Angeles. The Italian court found that 'the managers of the J. Paul Getty Museum had been at least grossly negligent in buying the statue, if they had not been fully aware of its illicit origin. They had acquired a work of inestimable value without making any serious control on the legality of its provenance and without having asked to check the title under which the seller had the possession of it. They had relied only on a legal advice given by the lawyers of the seller who had an evident interest in concluding the sale, without taking the care to ask the Italian authorities about the legality of the export of a work which had been the subject of a criminal proceeding before Italian

Nevertheless, these purchases qualify in some cases as purchases being made in good faith.[184]

If, of course, one buys a painting in suspicious circumstances from a person whose real profession is not an art dealer of any kind, at a price that one knows is not the right one for that kind of object, one is probably in trouble. But there are also circumstances where one buys a painting from a gallery which certifies that that painting is a perfectly legitimate painting, or one where the title has been checked, or one which has been bought directly from the artist or from a previous owner. In these cases the court is not bound to reach the conclusion that the buyer at issue was a bad faith buyer. Unfortunately, there have been cases in which even reputable auction houses have not been perfectly reliable.[185] As a commentator argues, 'the issue is not whether buyers *in fact* rely on merchants, but also whether we think that buyers *should* rely on merchants without seeing evidence of a title search'.[186]

The conclusion is that it is not unrealistic to argue that buyers who undertake just minimal investigation of title will stand a fair chance of being held to be *bona fide* purchasers, and will be entitled to the compensation provided for in the Unidroit Convention. However, the issue is how ethical, moral and just it is for this kind of purchaser to be entitled to

---

courts. The Tribunal adds that the museum in question is an institution particularly competent and qualified from which a higher degree of diligence has to be expected'. As discussed in Scovazzi, T. '*A Second Italian Case on Cultural Properties Enmeshed in Fishing Nets*', http://www.mepielan-ebulletin.gr/default.aspx?pid = 18&CategoryId = 4&ArticleId = 17&Article = A-Second-Italian-Case-on-Cultural-Properties-Enmeshed-in-Fishing-Nets

[184] See, for example, *O'Keefe v. Snyder* 416 A.2d 862, 872 (N.J. 1980); *Menzel v. List* 246 N. E.2d 742, 743 (N.Y. 1969).

[185] Sotheby's sold a cultural object which had not been checked for possible theft. G Glueck, 'Who owns stolen artifacts? College confronts a museum' N.Y. Times, 30 April 1991, at A1. The fact that purchasers tend to rely on the reputability of the gallery or the merchant where they buy their artefact from is shown in many cases. See, for example, *Menzel v. List* 246 N. E.2d 742, 743 (N. Y. 1969). See also what E des Portes, Secretary of ICOM, has pointed out in Le Monde, 14 January 1997, 'It is evident that one can no longer rely on the fame of certain salerooms or dealers for assurance of the provenance of objects. The very efficient French Office pour la repression de vol des oeuvres d'art, which makes seizures both at the Hotel Drouot as well as at the big names of the market place, is there to prove it'; and *Noce v. Libération* 15 September 1995, at 28, where it was published that Sotheby's Paris was offering for sale copies of books stolen during the 1970s from three French libraries, although inquiries could have established the dubious provenance of these books if one was a bit familiar with their history.

[186] Bibas St., n. 156 above, 84.

compensation that originates from the claimant,[187] if it is taken into account that he has in any case a full panoply of rights against the person who passed the object over to him. It is also easier for him, in comparison to any other party, to trace his merchants. If his merchants cannot be traced, that means he was not a sound person to deal with (which in fact is the fault of the possessor who chose to deal with him), or that the transaction took place under suspicious circumstances, where the purchaser could not have been in good faith and therefore should not be entitled to any compensation.[188]

Indeed, the issue here is not whether we punish the possessor of the stolen artefact or the dispossessed owner, but whether we are placing responsibility on the thief, the seller or any other intermediary merchant involved in the deceitful transaction. Sellers should logically be the ones to bear the responsibility because they are the ones that acquired the object either directly or indirectly from the thief in the first place. Furthermore, they are, from a commercial point of view, in a stronger position and they thus should be the ones to bear the risks of their commerce. In addition, they are the persons that are best equipped to do all the relevant checks of title or to undertake any other investigation in the area by reason of status and expertise. Art dealers are also usually covered by insurance with regard to the objects they trade in and their origins. On top of that, they would not be willing to risk trading in stolen or unverified artefacts, if they were responsible from a legal point of view and if that responsibility were to be reinforced by the provisions of the Convention.

Article 4(2) of the Convention tries to shift the problem wherever possible to the merchant involved in the transaction and away from the claimant. It provides that '[w]ithout prejudice to the right of the possessor to

---

[187] Although article 4(1) is not explicit as to who is obliged to pay the compensation to the possessor, paragraph (3) of the same article leads us to draw the conclusion that the claimant will be the one to pay. This becomes clearer if the provision is coupled with article 7(b)(ii) of the 1970 UNESCO Convention (which was also the starting point of the Unidroit Convention), which provides that 'the requesting State shall pay just compensation to an innocent purchaser or to a person who has valid title to that property'; and article 4(2) of the Resolution of the Institute of International Law of 3.9.1991, which provides that 'the country of origin should provide for equitable compensation to be effected to the holder who has proved in good faith'.

[188] See for example the *Goldberg* case, where the possessor met the purchaser for only a few minutes. This is an indication that the purchaser is not in good faith. For details regarding the *Goldberg* case, see Byrne-Sutton, Q. (1992), 'The Goldberg Case: A Confirmation of the Difficulty in Acquiring Good Title to Valuable Stolen Cultural Objects', *International Journal of Cultural Property*, 151.

compensation referred to in the preceding paragraph, reasonable efforts shall be made to have the person who transferred the cultural object to the possessor, or any prior transferor, pay the compensation where to do so would be consistent with the law of the State in which the claim is brought'. It seems that this provision does not solve the problem; it rather works as a panacea. Article 4(2) provides clearly that the efforts of tracing and making the merchant pay will be without prejudice to the right the possessor has to be compensated by the claimant. In other words, whether the claimant succeeds or does not succeed in tracing the intermediary person, concluding the transaction is basically a problem for the claimant himself. In either case, whether the merchant is found or not, the possessor will be paid. If the possessor has to engage himself in the tracing of the merchant, he might have to wait a lot longer in order to be compensated than if he seeks to be compensated by the claimant right away upon the return of the artefact. There is also no incentive for the possessor to help the claimant trace the merchant, since the claimant himself is the one who deprives the possessor of the artefact he acquired, and the latter will have to be compensated in any case if the cultural object is to be returned. Although the claimant has the right to recuperate the compensation he has paid to the possessor for taking back his stolen cultural object,[189] he will not find anybody sharing the same interest that is prepared to help him with his investigation. In addition, even if the merchant is traced, the owner may not be able to recuperate his costs, if the merchant is found to be in good faith. That means that an attempt should then be made to reconstruct a whole chain of transactions to find the original illicit transaction. This process might eventually lead to an unsuccessful result, either because the illicit transaction cannot be traced or because the original culprit is in no position to pay. It is highly unlikely in these circumstances that the claimant alone will be able to trace a person he has never dealt with, and who, according to his national law, will be the only person responsible for compensating his loss.[190,191]

---

[189] Article 4(3).

[190] Another possible model of compensation is perhaps the model where the seller will be the first responsible for compensating the purchaser. In case the seller can no longer be found, then the dispossessed owner should compensate the purchaser only if the latter fulfils a duty of information, i.e. hands over to the dispossessed owner all the necessary information and helps to trace the seller of the stolen artefact.

[191] The fact that, according to the Convention, the claimant is the first responsible for paying compensation to the *bona fide* possessor contradicts the principle of 'subsidiarity' as this is enshrined in the European Directive. '[T]he claimant would not necessarily be the person required to pay compensation to the *bona fide*

If the system of return of stolen cultural objects is left to operate in this way, purchasers will not have to undertake stringent investigations of titles because they know that they will either not be traced, or if they are traced they will be fairly and reasonably remunerated by one source or another, given they have made the basic typical checks in relation to the artefact they purchased.[192] It seems that the trade in stolen art in this case is anything but undermined since the parties involved do not run important risks that are capable of stopping them from trading in or buying objects of a dubious origin.[193]

Also the notion of 'fair and reasonable' compensation is vague. It is not defined in the Convention as the market price, the price the possessor paid to acquire the object, or the 'objective' value of the object as estimated by the national court. Several opinions and suggestions have been put forward during the drafting of the Convention. However, it was thought wiser to leave the whole issue to the national judge to decide by evaluating the circumstances of each case. Even so, no one has mentioned what the ceiling of such consideration should be, and whether in cases where this ceiling was held to be the price which the *bona fide* owner paid to acquire the object, this price could reach the actual market price of the time of the restitution of the object, or even higher than that if costs of preservation and restitution are to be included.[194] Neither is it mentioned how much control on regulating that compensation the *bona fide* possessor

possessor . . . [but] would be obliged to compensate the *bona fide* possessor only if compensation could not be obtained from another source', Acts 183.

[192] Especially if the goods at issue are a bargain. The compensation which will be paid might exceed the actual price of the good when it was bought.

[193] It is also possible that the *bona fide* purchaser might not be compensated for the return of the artefact to the claimant if the Contracting State applies any rules that are more favourable to the restitution or the return of a stolen object than provided in this Convention, and that do not provide for any compensation (article 9(1)). Thus, the grant of compensation to the *bona fide* possessor will depend upon the legal system where the claim is heard. If this is the case, of course, the State in which this judgment is to be enforced is under no obligation according to article 9(2) of the Convention to recognise and enforce this decision. In reality no State will be willing to do so if it does not want to jeopardise the return of the cultural object at issue.

[194] There is no provision on costs in the chapter on stolen cultural objects, contrary to the position adopted in relation to illegally exported artefacts. In the latter case the Convention stipulates that the cost of returning an illegally exported cultural object will be borne by the requesting State, without prejudice to the right of that State to recover costs from any other person (art. 6(4)). In the case of stolen artefacts it was thought wiser to leave the issue to the national judge to decide in view of the circumstances of the case that had come before him.

has.[195] This gap in the Convention will allow for varying State interpretations, and in fact for a manipulation of the provision according not only to every State's approach to title, but also according to its attitude towards protecting personal property. Generalising to some extent, 'importing States' are more likely to grant a full compensation consistent with their attitude that a person having made a significant investment in purchasing a cultural object should not stand a loss, while 'exporting States' will probably interpret the provision strictly since their main concern will be the return of the cultural object to its country of origin. Consequently, when a claim is made against an 'importing' State it is very likely that the other party, which more often than not will be an economically weak State,[196] will have to pay full compensation and, in fact, pay back the full price of the object that has been stolen from it. In this case it is clear what conflicting results the concepts 'fair' and 'reasonable' might have. What might be reasonable, for example, for the *bona fide* possessor might not be reasonable for the poor dispossessed owner and *vice versa*. The notion of 'reasonable' depends in every case on someone's reason which might differ substantially from State to State when it comes to the restitution of culture.[197]

The option of market price compensation being paid to the purchaser of the cultural good essentially puts a burden on the States and especially on the poor States. It is basically the heritage of the poor States that is usually plundered and spoliated and these States will by this policy be obliged, though they are economically weak, to compensate the economically powerful and wealthy owner, who is already protected by the law of his State against his predecessor who sold him the object illegally.[198] But even

---

[195] By finding, for example, a buyer for the artefact who offers him a very high price. Interesting in this respect is the case of *Webb v. A-G for Ireland* [1988] 8 ILRM (Irish Law Reports Monthly) 565, where a dealer of a northern Kwakiutl Thunderbird headdress, which was refused export permission in Canada, used the period before all court proceedings were completed for extensive 'restoration' work. This restoration had the effect of very substantially increasing the price offered by a United States client for that artefact. In this context, and though questions concerning the integrity of the object so 'restored' were raised, the dealer could require a higher remuneration for the return of the object. However, no Canadian museum was prepared to pay the asking price.

[196] As previously explained, these States are the ones that suffer the most from plundering.

[197] This may also prompt us to think that the provisions for compensation might be 'more' enforceable in certain countries compared to others.

[198] In most cases where objects are bought from serious and reputable owners, an insurance or warranty of title accompanies them. N. Palmer pointed out at the Conference on 'Law and Art: the free movement of cultural property', held in

in cases where the dispossessed owner is not the State, the claim for return will be brought and supported by the State if the owner him or herself is not in a position to sue[199].[200]

According to article 4(5) 'the possessor shall not be in a more favourable position than the person from whom it acquired the cultural object by inheritance or otherwise gratuitously'. This is an important provision because it covers situations where a bad faith purchaser decides to donate an object to a museum in order to gain tax advantages. The transfer of the object to a museum does not 'clear' the object. According to this provision the museum is not in a more favourable position than its transferor/ donator. This provision also prevents museums from circumventing their own acquisition policies by accepting undocumented antiquities from donors. In this case a cultural object will have to be returned to its original owner without the payment of compensation.

2.2.5 Return of Illegally Exported Cultural Objects

2.2.5.1 Return

Cultural objects, which have been illegally exported from the territory of a Contracting State, also come under the scope of the Unidroit Convention. They form one more category of cultural objects meriting protection.[201]

Illegally exported objects have, in the same sense as stolen cultural objects, to be returned upon the request of a Contracting State. Two factors have to be borne in mind. First, not anyone is entitled to request the return of an illegally exported object; only the deprived State is.[202] Second, the return of an object illegally exported from the territory of a

Maastricht, 6–7 March 1997, that if the Unidroit Convention is implemented in any country, the implied warranty for quiet possession of an art object sold by a professional in England will imply a liability of the seller for claims which result in the return of the item, whether for theft or illegal export.

199 The examples L. Prott gives in this respect are an indigenous community or an impoverished temple. Prott, L.V. (1997), *Commentary on the Unidroit Convention*, n. 102 above, 43.

200 The second point, where article 4 seems to break new ground, relating to the reversion of the burden of proof in favour of the claimant, is thought to be a decisive point towards the protection of the restitution of cultural property, and is therefore not separately discussed in this chapter.

201 However, it was thought that there was a considerable difference in the demerit of stealing compared to illegally exporting a cultural object. Doc. 10 § 33.

202 In the case of stolen cultural objects, both private parties and States can require the return of the stolen object.

Contracting State,[203] is not unconditional, even if article 5(1) provides, as article 3 does, for the return of stolen objects in principle. The requesting State has to establish, as a prerequisite, that the removal of the object from its territory significantly impairs one or more of the interests enshrined in article 5(3)(a)–(d)[204] or that the object is somehow of significant cultural importance to it.[205].[206]

That brings us back to almost the same problem as that of the lack of any provision providing for the competence of the requesting State to designate its own cultural property, or else the cultural property which is of significance to it. An important margin of discretion is left to the courts that will examine the claim brought before them. These courts will in most cases be the courts of an 'importing' State, since this is where illegally exported cultural objects are usually found. Under these circumstances it will not be easy for one to establish before these courts the significance of a cultural object, which for the tradition of an 'importing' State is no more than a common trading commodity. This judicial control over the importance of a particular cultural object for a State contradicts the aim of the Convention, which is to protect the stolen or illegally exported cultural heritage of the State, since the Convention does not recognise a State's competence to define for itself what is important to its culture.

Allegations that one State is unable to enforce the public laws of another State are no more than an excuse at this stage.[207].[208] First, in so

---

[203] In the case of illegally exported objects, it is from the territory of a contracting State only that the object should have been exported, otherwise the Unidroit Convention does not apply. In the case of stolen objects what matters is that the stolen object is located in a Contracting State, although its theft might have taken place in a non-Contracting State.

[204] The physical preservation of the object or of its context; the integrity of a complex object; the preservation of information of, for example, a scientific or historical character; the traditional or ritual use of the object by a tribal or indigenous community.

[205] One may, of course, wonder at this point why a State would have export limitation on a particular object, let alone bring a claim before a court for it which in most cases results in expensive litigation, if it did not consider it as being of importance to its cultural heritage.

[206] This list is not strictly exhaustive since a State may decide to apply more favourable rules compared to those of the Convention. See, for example, Australia, Canada and Greece who provide in their legislation (implementing the 1970 UNESCO Convention) for the return of all cultural objects which are illegally exported from their States. See also the Explanatory Report § 35.

[207] The same allegations can also be used with regard to enforcing another State's export regulations, as is required by article 5 of the Convention.

[208] See also the discussion in section 6.2.1.1

far as a State has undertaken the obligations provided in the Convention (which have also been reciprocally accepted by the other Contracting Parties), it is perfectly conscious of the fact that it has also accepted the obligation of applying another State's public law to the extent that this law concerns the enforcement and effective application of the rules of the Convention. And second, the recognition of a third State's law is nowadays widely accepted, not only regarding cultural property (i.e. article 3 of the Resolution of the Institute of International Law of 3 September 1991),[209] but also regarding generally the application of foreign public law, on which the extraterritorial application of a State's export regulations can be based[210] (e.g. article 7(1) of the EEC Rome Convention on the Law Applicable to Contractual Obligations[211] and article 19

---

[209] 'The provisions of the law of the country of origin governing the export of works of art shall apply.'

[210] 'There is no reason for the prima facie exclusion of foreign rules, relating to cultural heritage protection', Prott, L.V. (1989), 'Problems of Private International Law for the Protection of Cultural Heritage', *Recueil des Cours*, 235, at 299–300; and at p.267 'comity and common sense suggest a policy of reciprocal recognition of such laws'. See also, Nott, S. (1984), 'Title to Illegally Exported Items of Historic or Artistic Worth', *International Comparative Law Quarterly*, 206. The case law of the national courts is also significant. See e.g. the decision of the House of Lords on 21.10.1957 in the case *Regazzoni / K.C. Sethia Clunet* 1961, 1140 ff.; Hoge Raad 13.5.1966 (*van Nievelt, Goudriaan et Co's Stoomvaartmij N.V. / N.V. Hollandsche Assurantie Societeit et autres*) Rev. Crit. 1967, 522–3 (and note A.V.M. Struycken); Trib. d'arrondissement de la Haye 17.9.1982 (*Compagnie Europeenne des petroles s.a. / Sensor Nederland B.V.*), Rev. Crit. 1983, 473 ff. (479). Also, the legal basis and widely accepted principle of public order and common interest can be used to render invalid agreements which offend cultural property, e.g. the famous case of the German Federal Supreme Court, where an insurance agreement for the transfer of goods, whose object was the export of cultural goods from Nigeria, in violation of Nigeria's legislation for the protection of its cultural heritage, was invalid, because the violation of such legislation was contrary to the interest of all nations for the preservation of their cultural heritage. In this case it is also obvious that, although Germany has not ratified the 1970 UNESCO Convention, the Court recognised and applied the principles deriving from it as international customary law. And, Tribunale of Torino in *Repubblica dell'Ecuador c. Danusso*, Trib. Torino, 22 February 1982, Riv. dir. priv. e proc. (1982) at 625 ff., where the Italian court found it to be in Italy's interest to enforce Ecuador's export controls.

[211] Article 7: 'When applying under this Convention the law of a country, effect may be given to the mandatory rules of the law of another country with which the situation has a close connection, if and in so far as, under the law of the latter country, those rules must be applied whatever the law applicable to the contract'.

of the Swiss Law of 18 December 1987, concerning private international law[212]).[213]

The different treatment of illegally exported cultural objects in comparison to that of stolen ones significantly restricts the scope of the Convention's application without any apparent good reason. If the difference in treatment at this point has been made by reason of the crime involved, it remains a difference which is unjustifiable. It should be made clear so far that it is not the seriousness of the offence which is at issue but the protection of the cultural property. In both cases the same good is affected and to the same degree. Thus, in so far as the aim of the Convention is the protection and the restitution of that particular good, it follows that the conduct required and the sanction imposed must be the same.

Additionally, the limitations set out in article 5 for the return of an illegally exported object are not the only ones provided in the Unidroit Convention. Even when these requirements are satisfied, the prerequisites of article 7 have to be satisfied as well: 'The provisions of th[e] chapter [on illegally exported cultural objects] shall not apply where: (a) the export of a cultural object is no longer illegal at the time at which the return is requested; or (b) the object was exported during the lifetime of the person who created it or within a period of fifty years following the death of that person'.[214]

The second requirement of this article seems to be a sweeping one. As long as the creator of the object is alive nobody can interfere, even indirectly, with his rights. This provision has been put there to allow the free sale and movement of someone's creative work as part of his or her copyright in it. This is also the reason why this provision coincides with the term of copyright protection as this term is found in the relevant

---

212 Article 19(1): '[L]orsque des intérêts légitimes et manifestements prépondérants au regard de la conception suisse du droit l'exigent, une disposition impérative d'un droit autre que celui désigné par la présente loi peut être prise en consideration, si la situation visée présente un lien étroit avec ce droit'.

213 It could also be argued at this point that the export regulations of a State do not consist of that kind of public law, which if applied by another State, impinges on its sovereignty, as would be the case, for example, with rules on public order, ethics, etc.

214 According to article 7(2): 'Notwithstanding the provisions of sub-paragraph (b) of the preceding paragraph, the provisions of this Chapter shall apply where a cultural object was made by a member or members of a tribal or indigenous community for traditional or ritual use by that community and the object will be returned to that community'. In other words, these objects can be claimed back under article 5 of the Convention.

international Conventions.[215] However, this provision does not take into account the fact that the creator is not given the right to disagree with the treatment of his work as a commodity, or simply not to be interested in international marketability.[216] After his death, his inheritors will enjoy the same regime of protection for 50 more years.[217] But, what if no inheritors exist? This absolute time ban will result in putting cultural objects of enhanced significance for the State in danger.[218] The same applies for works whose creators are not known (orphan works) or works of religious art whose creators prefer to stay unidentified.[219] This view is consistent with the fact that art movements and trends change very quickly, sometimes within periods of ten or twenty years (for example abstract art, pop art, contemporary art and so on), and their need for protection demands a rapid reaction before these objects become a target for the illicit trade.[220]

2.2.5.2 'Illegally exported' cultural objects

Illegally exported cultural objects are objects which have left the territory of a State without its authorization, which in most instances is proven by an export certificate. Thus, it is the requesting State that decides which objects have been illegally exported from its territory. As explained above, this does not suffice in order to have them returned. Also considered to be illegally exported are the cultural objects which have been temporarily exported from the territory of the requesting State, for purposes such as exhibition, research or restoration, under a permit issued according to the law regulating export for the purpose of protecting its cultural heritage and not returned in accordance with the terms of that permit (article 5(2)).

---

[215] Note the parallel with the provisions of the term of copyright in the Berne Convention for the Protection of Literary and Artistic Works (1886).

[216] Especially in the case of spiritual or religious articles. See Prott, L.V. (1997), *Commentary on the Unidroit Convention*, n. 102 above, 70.

[217] In the European Union and the US copyright protection is extended to 70 years after the death of the author.

[218] It is interesting to note that the Convention is more generous at this point than the British provisions. In 1994 the British authorities refused an export licence for a painting by Lucien Freud: 'Export of Works of Art 1994–1995: Forty-first Report of the Reviewing Committee (UK)' HMSO Cm 3008 October 1995, at 22–23, as referred to in Prott, L.V. (1997), *Commentary on the Unidroit Convention*, n. 102 above, 69.

[219] This issue with regard to tribal and indigenous communities has been solved on the basis of article 7(2) of the Convention.

[220] We should note here that when a cultural object is both stolen and illegally exported it can be claimed back on either the basis of Chapter II or Chapter III of the Convention.

2.2.5.3 Time limitations

Time limitations for a claim concerning the return of illegally exported cultural objects have been aligned with those for stolen objects. However, there are no special provisions for particular objects such as objects belonging to public collections. The absolute 50-year period is calculated from the date of the export or from the date on which the object under a permit should have been returned to the State issuing the permit.[221]

2.2.5.4 Compensation

Compensation should also be paid by the requesting State to the *bona fide* possessor of an illegally exported object that has to be returned to the country from which it has been illegally exported (article 6(1)).[222] The compensation paid should be 'fair and reasonable' as was explained in relation to stolen objects. This compensation may include the costs of the return of the cultural object to the requesting State. This is also the reason why a separate provision to this end was not necessary.[223]

It was argued that, in order for the stigma attached to theft not to be transposed to illegally exported cultural objects,[224] the obligation for compensating the *bona fide* possessor will be subject to only one requirement, and that is for the possessor to prove that he did not know nor could reasonably have been expected to know at the time of the acquisition of the object that it had been illegally exported.[225]

Yet, the omission of the 'due diligence'[226] requirement in the third chapter of the Convention is unfortunate. It puts the *bona fide* possessor

---

221 Article 5(5): 'Any request for return shall be brought within a period of three years from the time when the requesting State knew the location of the cultural object and the identity of its possessor, and in any case within a period of fifty years from the date of the export or from the date on which the object should have been returned under a permit referred to in paragraph 2 of this article.'

222 It goes without saying that an owner who illegally exports a cultural artefact from the territory of the requesting State is not entitled to compensation.

223 Article 6(4): 'The cost of returning the cultural object in accordance with this article shall be borne by the requesting State, without prejudice to the right of that State to recover costs from any other person.'

224 Schneider, M. (1995), 'The UNIDROIT Convention on Stolen or Illegally Exported Cultural Objects', www.city.ac.uk/artspol/schneider.html.

225 Article 6(2): 'In determining whether the possessor knew or ought reasonably to have known that the cultural object had been illegally exported, regard shall be had to the circumstances of the acquisition including the absence of an export certificate required under the law of the requesting State'.

226 Which already in article 4(2) forms the minimum standard of diligence among reputable dealers and collectors. von Plehwe, T. (1995), 'European Union and the Free Movement of Cultural Goods', *European Law Review*, 431, at 447.

in a more favourable position compared to the purchaser of a stolen cultural object. It seems again that the Convention, in its attempt to reconcile the diverging interests, loses sight of its goal and 'punishes' the possessor according to his predecessor's crime. However, it is the retrieval of the missing cultural object which is at issue and not the punishment of the possessor. Thus, there is no reason for the Convention to facilitate the granting of compensation to a possessor who was lucky enough, in all his unawareness, to be dealing with a seller who had not stolen the object but 'just' illegally exported it. In any case, the purchaser is invited to take the risk as long as his obligation to prove his good faith is not too difficult to fulfil.

However, the fact that the term 'due diligence' is not there does not preclude the possibility that a judge will take into account all circumstances mentioned in article 4(4) in relation to stolen objects. The absence of an export certificate required under the law of the requesting State is an issue that should also be taken into account by the judge. On most occasions the absence of such a certificate would equal bad faith, especially if the purchaser is a knowledgeable person in the field,[227] given also the fact that information on national export regulations is readily available in UNESCO and on the relevant sites of many countries.[228]

The increasing need of the State to protect its heritage is also undermined by paragraph (3) of the same article. The possessor of the object, instead of being compensated, has, subject to an agreement with the requesting State, the following choices. Either he can retain ownership of the object, or he can transfer ownership against payment or gratuitously to a person of his choice residing in the requesting State, who provides the necessary guarantees. This provision was said to introduce a valuable alternative for States which cannot afford to pay a high amount in compensation to the possessor in order to reacquire their missing cultural objects. However, closer to truth and to the real intention of the parties is the fact that some States, especially those with a common-law background and an 'art market' tradition, would not accept a provision which, strictly speaking, could be thought to constitute a confiscation of private property, and which would therefore encroach on private interests.[229] They

---

[227] See for example, *R. v. Yorke*, Supreme Court of Nova Scotia, 20 June 1996, CR 11741 (nyr).

[228] As Prott, L. mentions all countries once included within the boundaries of the Roman Empire have export control on antiquities, Prott, L.V. (1997), *Commentary on the Unidroit Convention*, n. 102 above, 65.

[229] The UK interest in the proposals for the control of national treasures differs in a number of ways from that of the other Member States: (i) the number

would undertake such an obligation only if and in so far as it is the result of an agreement between the parties (i.e. the *bona fide* possessor and the requesting State).

It is common sense to observe at this point that since the requesting State has gone as far as litigation, it will be willing in most cases to take back its lost object at any expense. So, the choice of how the cultural object is returned will mainly be left to the possessor. At this stage the possessor may use the power afforded to him by the Convention and create obstacles or delay the conclusion of an agreement trying to push for the alternatives. Yet, the Convention makes it clear that the option to replace the payment of compensation by any of the two alternatives offered in article 6(3) can only be used if the requesting State agrees to the alternative that is suggested by the possessor of the cultural good.

The mention, also, of the word 'ownership' in paragraph (3)(a)–(b) demonstrates that the return of illegally exported cultural objects has nothing to do with the transfer of ownership. The reality, of course, is that it has to do with restrictions on ownership, since the possessor of the object is deemed to choose between certain ways[230] of disposing of the cultural object.[231] The possessor can retain ownership upon the return of the cultural good, or make use of it by selling the object to a person of his choice, whether or not he holds the nationality of the requesting State, as long as that person resides within the requesting State's territory. In the latter case, it is interesting to mention that subparagraph (b) provides for

---

of national heritage objects in private hands is very much larger than the number of national treasures privately owned in any other Member State (Report of the Reviewing Committee on the Export of Works of Art, October 1991, paragraph 30); (ii) the market in objects of cultural value or interest is much larger than any other Member State [it is estimated that Britain is handling about 75% of the European export trade, see Goyder, J. (1993), 'European Community Free Movement of Cultural Goods and European Community Law Part III: Two New Legislative Proposals', *International Journal of Cultural Property*]; (iii) there is in the UK no system of listing national treasures in order to prohibit their export [. . .]; (iv) the UK appears to have a less protective approach to its national treasures in that if they have gone abroad – whether lawfully or unlawfully – little public effort has been made to seek restitution.

House of Lords Select Committee on the European Communities, Control of National Treasures, session 1992–93 6th Report, HL Paper 17, 1992, at 8. (Comments in brackets added).

230 As these ways were referred to in article 6(3).

231 Restrictions on ownership are not always a vice, if they are weighed against such principles as the protection of cultural property.

payment instead of compensation, which gives the possessor the chance to acquire the market price of the object[232].

Article 6(3)(b) requires that the person who is chosen to buy or be given the artefact at issue, has to provide the necessary guarantees. Yet, what these guarantees are is totally unclear. Are they to include conservation, preservation, security or public access? Who is going to decide if and for how long these guarantees will be offered? And lastly, will there be any legal consequences if the third party that acquired the object under these conditions is found to be in breach of his obligations or no longer offers these guarantees in the future? The provision on guarantees in particular seems to be more wishful thinking than any sort of legally enforceable rule. It is true that vague legal provisions leave a great margin of discretion to the national judge, which, however, in most of the cases, is a discretion, which can be highly undesirable for many national courts.[233]

2.2.6 Private International Law Matters

The Unidroit Convention provides for provisions which facilitate the promotion of claims for restitution or return of cultural objects. In other words it regulates private international law matters within the purpose of the Convention.

2.2.6.1 Jurisdiction and enforcement of judgments

Article 8 deals with jurisdictional matters and provides for a new ground of jurisdiction on top of the ones provided by other legislation. Specifically, it provides that a claim may be brought before the courts or other competent authorities of the Contracting State where the cultural object is located, in addition to the courts or other competent authorities otherwise having jurisdiction under the rules in force in Contracting States. In practice it is not common in Europe to apply the jurisdiction of the court (or other competent authority) of the location of the object in cases of recovery of moveable property. According to the 1968 Brussels Convention on Jurisdiction and the Enforcement of Judgments in Civil and Commercial Matters, which applies between European Union Member States (and has been replaced by

---

232 Nothing precludes the situation where the State itself may be willing to buy the object, which means that the possessor can still receive the full market price, or even make a profit from it.

233 Article 6(5): 'The possessor shall not be in a more favourable position than the person from whom he acquired the cultural object by inheritance or otherwise gratuitously' is parallel to article 4(5) in relation to stolen cultural objects and therefore serves the same purpose.

Council Regulation 44/2001 of 22 December 2000 on jurisdiction and the recognition of enforcement of judgments in civil and commercial matters), persons domiciled in a Member State will be sued in the courts of that Member State whatever their nationality (article 2(1) of the Regulation); alternatively they can be sued according to special jurisdiction in the courts of the place where the harmful event occurred or may occur in matters relating to tort, delict or quasi-delict (article 5(3) of the Regulation).[234] The same is provided by the 1988 Lugano Convention on jurisdiction and the enforcement of judgments in civil and commercial matters which was replaced by the New Lugano Convention (2007) that is applicable between the EU Member States and certain EFTA Member States (Denmark, Norway, Iceland and Switzerland), and is based on Regulation 44/2001.

These bases of jurisdiction are not precluded by the Unidroit Convention. However, the new basis of jurisdiction introduced by the Unidroit Convention is an alternative basis and has been introduced to facilitate the procedure of restitution or return. Cultural objects may be located when they are offered for sale by an auction house or dealer in a State which is not the same as the one where the vendor is domiciled. The State of location may be bound by the Unidroit Convention. The State where the vendor is domiciled may not. In this respect (by being able to bring a claim before the courts of the State of location) the dispossessed owner is put in a more favourable position. This provision is also likely to improve enforcement since the State of location will not have to impose another State's judgment ordering return but the judgment of its own courts.

The parties to a dispute may choose, if they wish, to submit to another forum or submit the dispute to arbitration.[235] This is also consistent with the relevant aforementioned legislation. Yet, even if an action is brought in another State, the dispossessed owner or State may apply for provisional measures in the courts of the State of location of the cultural object in order to secure quickly and effectively that the object is withdrawn from an auction, is not sold or does not disappear. They can also ensure the integrity and safety of the object, its proper handling or prevent its further export.[236] If that were not possible, it is very likely that by the time one had a judgment for the restitution or return of a cultural object, the object could no longer be found for the judgment to be enforced.

Judgments given in EU Member States are almost always automatically

---

[234] The latter basis of jurisdiction was clarified by an ECJ judgment, *Bier BV v. Mines de Potace d'Alsace SA* (1976) ECR 1735.

[235] Article 8(2).

[236] Article 8(3).

applicable between those States. The same applies in relation to EU Member States and certain EFTA States, as was mentioned above. This is so according to the relevant aforementioned legislation. However, there are exceptions to such recognition in certain specific cases, for example if a judgment is manifestly contrary to public policy (see articles 34 *et seq.* of Regulation 44/2001). If a judgment is produced by a third country then national law applies unless there are bilateral agreements in this respect. In the US there are special provisions for recognition and enforcement of foreign judgments which differ from state to state.

2.2.6.2 Applicable law

The provisions of the Unidroit Convention in relation to stolen cultural objects apply only where the object is stolen after the Convention entered into force in the State where the claim is brought and provided that (a) the object was stolen from the territory of a Contracting State after the entry into force of this Convention for that State or (b) the object is located in a Contracting State after the entry into force of the Convention for that State.[237] This means that on the basis of the Convention, a claim may be brought before a Contracting State, which is other than the State of location (for example the State of domicile of the possessor). If the State of location is not a Contracting Party to the Convention, the judgment can still be enforced. However, its enforcement will depend on that State's laws including the treaties by which the State is bound. The Convention also applies irrespective of the nationality or the place of domicile of the possessor of the object and whether this place/State is a Party to the Convention. If the object is auctioned in a Contracting State and the requesting State is also a Contracting State to the Convention, the Convention applies irrespective of the fact that the vendor is domiciled in a non-Contracting State.

A cultural object can also be claimed back if it is stolen in a State which is not a Party to the Convention (on the basis of article 10(1)(b)) if that object was in that State while on temporary loan.

In relation to illegally exported cultural objects the Convention applies only in cases where the object was illegally exported after the Convention entered into force for the requesting State as well as the State where the request is brought.[238].[239] If the claim is brought in a State other than the State of location, the status of the Convention in the State of location is irrelevant.

---

237 Article 10(1).

238 Artice 10(2).

239 According to Article 12, no claim can be brought before 1998 (the first day of the sixth month following the date of deposit of the fifth instrument of ratification, acceptance, approval or accession) and on the first day of the sixth month

The Unidroit Convention does not prevent a Contracting State from applying rules which are more favourable to the restitution or the return of stolen or illegally exported cultural objects than those provided for by the Convention.[240] The aim of the Convention is to provide for minimum uniform rules and not for a general uniform law applicable in the area. This article enables States to retain more favourable rules in their laws, if these rules are already there, or adopt more favourable rules for the protection of cultural property. However, this does not mean that if a judgment is delivered by a court or competent authority on this basis, a Contracting State is under an obligation to recognise or enforce it. In fact a Contracting State is under no obligation to recognise or enforce a decision which departs from the provisions of this Convention.[241] This provision was put there as a safety valve for those States who feared that more favourable rules may require the return of a cultural object by a *bona fide* possessor without him being entitled to compensation.[242] This fear, however, is rather unjustified since it might be an outcome any court could reach in any country, if this court were to apply another State's law. A characteristic example in this respect was given by the Irish Law Reform Commission in their Consultation Paper[243] which noted that if the applicable law was determined by a French court to be that of a country which would order return without requiring compensation, then it would have to apply it, just as the English court applied Italian law in *Winkworth v. Christie's Ltd.*[244]

In relation to States to which the Unidroit Convention does not apply there are the private international rules of these States unless they are bound by an international Treaty or a bilateral agreement. In relation to the EU Member States Regulation 864/2007 applies.[245]

---

following the date of deposit of its instrument of ratification, acceptance, approval or accession for the State which claims the applicability of the Convention.

240 Article 9(1).

241 Article 9(2).

242 It was particularly France who put forward this proposal.

243 As this is referred to in Prott, L.V. (1997), *Commentary on the Unidroit Convention*, n. 102 above, 77, n. 32.

244 [1980] 1 Ch. 496 (England). In this case the applicable law did not lead to the return of the stolen material. See also *Autocephalous Greek-Orthodox Church of Cyprus v. Goldberg & Feldman Fine Arts Inc.* 917 F.2d 278 (1990) where Indiana law applied and it recognised Cyprus's replevin action to recover the stolen mosaics from the Kanakaria church in Cyprus in 1979.

245 Council Regulation 864/2007 of 11 July 2007 on the law applicable to non-contractual obligations (Rome II) L 199/40 which entered into force on 11 January 2009.

2.2.7 The *Ex Nunc* Application of the Unidroit Convention

The retroactive effect of the Unidroit Convention was an issue of great concern to the representatives of the various States. It was feared that if a retroactive effect was provided for in the Convention, many States would find it impossible to ratify it, as in this way their museum collections and a great part of their art trade could be exposed to challenge.[246] In the end the Unidroit Convention followed the 1970 UNESCO Convention's paradigm. Article 10(1) and (2) provides that '[t]he provisions of chapters II and III shall apply only in respect of a cultural object that is stolen or illegally exported *after* this Convention enters into force' (emphasis added).

Although the insertion of this provision is consistent with the 1969 Vienna Convention on the Law of Treaties,[247] the view of those States which allege that a vast number of their significant cultural objects have already been stolen and illegally exported to other countries is also interesting to take into account. Therefore the emerging need for restitution should primarily concern those objects that have already been lost, whilst future protection and control could only be of little interest. If we consider that the illicit trade and trafficking of cultural objects was the scourge of the 1920s, 30s and 40s, in other words during and after the two World Wars, we realise that indeed little is left to restore.

However, the States whose art markets are considered to be strong would not jeopardise the legal status of cultural objects within their territory, even if these objects were held to be of vital importance to the requesting State and if their return would contribute a lot to the preservation of the world's cultural heritage. These cases will either be dealt with on political frontiers, under national laws, or artefacts will be used once more as 'sweeteners and bargaining chips in political negotiations that have nothing whatever to do with preservation of works of art or archaeological sites'.[248]

However, the Convention does not impinge on the right of a State to have recourse, with regard to the return of an artefact that has been stolen

---

[246] See Unidroit, Conf. 8/C.1/S.R, 1–19, 13–23 June 1995, at 2–7; see also the Unidroit Diplomatic Conference for the adoption of the Draft Unidroit Convention on the return of stolen or illegally exported cultural objects: text of the draft Convention with Explanatory Report, Conf8/3, 20 December 1994, at 33.

[247] Vienna Convention on the Law of Treaties, 23 May 1969, 1155 U.N.T.S. 331, articles 28 and 100.

[248] P. Marks, n. 102 above, at 121. Yet this article argues for the free movement of cultural goods.

or illegally exported before the Convention entered into force, to the legislation of a country that is more expansive and favourable towards the protection of cultural property. This right of the States is confirmed by article 10(3) of the Convention.[249]

2.2.8 Other Matters

The Unidroit Convention deals with a number of other issues, which are found in its final clauses. Most of them are issues of usual practice in international conventions. We shall only have a quick glance at some of them.

According to article 13(1) the Unidroit Convention does not affect any international instrument by which any Contracting State is legally bound and which contains provisions on matters governed by this Convention, unless a contrary declaration is made by the States bound by such instrument. In addition to this, any Contracting States may enter into agreements with one or more Contracting States, with a view to improving the application of this Convention in their mutual relations (article 13(2)).[250] This is so since the Unidroit Convention does not aim to attain general uniform rules in the area. It aims to attain minimum uniform rules. In other words, it aims to increase protection towards cultural property in those States where such protection is less than that provided in the Convention. At the same time, any State may, if it wishes, be more protective towards cultural property, either by retaining such laws in its legislation or by amending or introducing more laws in this respect.

Article 13(3) provides that Contracting States which are members of organisations of economic integration or regional bodies may declare that they will apply the internal rules of these organisations or bodies between themselves and not the provisions of the Unidroit Convention. The Unidroit Convention shall apply between those States and the Contracting States which are not members of the aforementioned organisations or regional bodies. Such declaration was made on behalf of the European Union by France on the signing of the Final Act of the Diplomatic

---

[249] Article 10(3) of the Convention reads as follows: 'This Convention does not in any way legitimise any illegal transaction of whatever nature which has taken place before the entry into force of this Convention or which is excluded under paragraphs (1) and (2) of this article, nor limit any right of a State or other person to make a claim under remedies available outside the framework of this Convention for the restitution or return of a cultural object stolen or illegally exported before the entry into force of this Convention.'

[250] The States which have concluded such an agreement shall transmit a copy to the depositary.

Conference. Fifty-three States of the English-speaking Commonwealth have also adopted model legislation concerning illicit export.[251] However, any declaration made in this respect upon signing should also be confirmed upon ratification, acceptance or approval of the Convention.[252]

Claims for restitution or requests for return of cultural treasures will be submitted to a State under a procedure designated by it, which needs to have been declared by the time of signature, ratification, acceptance, approval or accession to the Unidroit Convention. This procedure may involve the courts or other competent authorities, diplomatic or consular channels and so on (article 16(1)–(3)). In any case this provision does not affect bilateral or multilateral agreements on judicial assistance in respect of civil and commercial matters that may exist between Contracting States (article 16(4)).

What is most welcome in this Convention is that no reservations are permitted. Article 18 provides that 'no reservations are permitted except those expressly authorised in this Convention', but since no reservations are authorised in the Convention, none are permitted. This provision has been put there rather cursorily and has no substantial effect. The reason for not allowing acceding States to make reservations is that all provisions in the Convention are closely linked with each other, forming part of a compromise package. That means that provisions favouring, for example, the dispossessed owner seeking return of an artefact are given in exchange for other provisions less favourable to him (for example payment of compensation upon return). If reservations were allowed, this balance attained through negotiations would be disturbed.

2.2.9 Final Remarks

The area the Unidroit Convention sought to regulate has so far been a blank area in terms of regulation. And as happens with any blank area, any regulatory step in that direction is considered to be a progressive step. This does not mean, of course, that the existence of rules that are retrogressive and fail to consolidate the struggle against the illicit trafficking in cultural objects are eliminated in the Convention. There are, however, some important innovative points, such as the unequivocal return of stolen and illegally exported cultural objects to the disposessed owner or the dispossessed State, the reversal of the burden of proof in order to

---

[251] Prott, L.V. (1997), *Commentary on the Unidroit Convention*, n. 102 above, 83, 117.

[252] Article 15(1).

demonstrate due diligence, the establishment of special jurisdiction, and encouragement to Contracting Parties to provide for more favourable rules, always on the basis of reciprocity. The Unidroit drafting committee clearly had to make concessions. But, as shown, the concessions it made in the end aimed more at obtaining the widest consensus possible amongst 'importing' States, especially those which had been reluctant to ratify the 1970 UNESCO Convention. It placed less importance on the design of an effective legal and procedural framework favourable to the protection of the States' cultural property and the battle against the illicit trade in artefacts.[253] Since the Unidroit Convention was an attempt to convince the 'market' States, which had not ratified the 1970 UNESCO Convention[254] (because they found it 'extremely' protective towards cultural property), to agree to another international instrument with a similar aim, but revised in such a way as to accommodate their interests, this effort could only have been successful if the new obligations the States had to undertake were as minimalist as possible. However, the line drawn between 'minimal' protection and 'least' protection possible is a very delicate one;[255] and the Unidroit committee in its attempt to draft as successful a Convention as possible, focused its attention on adopting restrictions, involving concessions and achieving compromises, rather than on substantially protecting the States' cultural property.

The most important problem, perhaps, is that when one looks at the Convention's provisions which incorporate those concessions, one has the

---

253 'Faced with a very real prospect of failure, an informal group came into existence to negotiate a compromise text away from the glare of publicity on the Conference floor. The United Kingdom worked closely with those in this informal group which succeeded in producing a compromise text in the very last moments of the Conference. It is this text which was adopted by the Conference'. Jenkins, P. (1995), n. 169 above. Yet only 30 States have ratified the Unidroit Convention up to now, http://www.unidroit.org/english/implement/i-main.htm. The UK, France, Germany, the Netherlands, Denmark, Austria, Sweden and the US are not amongst them. However, France and the Netherlands are signatories to the Convention.

254 120 States have ratified the 1970 UNESCO Convention. Entered into force: 24 April 1972. From the European Union Member States, Greece, Italy, Cyprus, Spain, Portugal, Slovakia, Slovenia, France, Finland, UK, Sweden, Denmark, Germany, Poland, Romania, Bulgaria, Estonia, Hungary and Lithuania have ratified the1970 UNESCO Convention (19 out of 27 States).

255 By 'minimalist' protection we mean a protection which offers the basic rules in order for an aim to be effective, without, however, impinging on the effectiveness of the aim itself; whilst the 'least' protection possible is such a 'basic' protection, that it necessarily has to impinge on the aim which is to be attained.

impression that some of them[256] can easily be manipulated and adjusted to the primary attitudes of the States, to an 'extreme' or to a 'loose' protection of cultural property. It seems that the time has not yet arrived for some States to realise that the protection of the world's heritage is of vital importance, and a duty which has to be fulfilled even at the expense of the market. The marketing of legitimate art treasures is not affected. It is argued here that art dealers and purchasers of art really should be made to be more attentive when they are buying artefacts. Why does pleasure, entertainment or education derived from artefacts have to be obtained at the expense of certain States only, the very States whose culture has been plundered for centuries? Why should States that own great collections be fearful of exposing them to litigation, especially when nothing of that kind has happened since the enactment of the EU Directive or since, for example, the US,[257] which is the number one market for art, ratified the 1970 UNESCO Convention? Perhaps too much fuss has been made for nothing. 'Judges and academics have been too preoccupied with ex post dispute resolution to see the ex ante impact of their rules upon future behaviour.'[258] Even if a legal instrument is not used often, it might play a valuable role in formulating future behaviour and establishing positive attitudes in the area.

The States arguing for a totally free art market, condemning anything else as a blatant retentionist ethnocentric approach, are hiding behind excuses of a political or legal nature, presented as obstacles to their goodwill to protect cultural property, which all in fact aim at supporting a maximum marketability in the area of culture. Yet it should not be the maximum marketability we are aiming at, but the optimum one. What we do should not only be legitimised by the financial gain it brings with it, but it should always be seen in balance with other values and interests, such as the protection of cultural property, which in turn is a protection of identity, history and social cohesion. The protection of cultural property is a human rights issue. Cultural goods are not the same as any other good. Sometimes they bring with them values and virtues that can be incomprehensible to other people.

As long as the most 'influential' States remain steady in their beliefs, progress in the area of protection of the world's heritage can only be slow. It is, perhaps, high time we realised that the growing problem in

---

[256] Discussed previously extensively, i.e. compensation to the *bona fide* possessor, prerequisites for the return of illegally exported cultural objects.

[257] The US ratified the UNESCO Convention in 1972.

[258] Bibas, St. n. 156 above, 74.

the area of culture can no longer afford mediocre solutions. The Unidroit Convention, although not a mediocre solution, is still a very timid and reserved step forward, despite the fact that it has heightened awareness and stimulated more willingness and determination on the part of all nations[259] to prevent the illicit trade in art[260].[261]

Thirty States up to now have ratified the Unidroit Convention. This is a sign that attitudes in this area are maturing, if slowly. The 1970 UNESCO Convention has helped in this respect. In a Swiss case[262] where France sought judicial assistance for the return of a painting, the Federal Court of Public Law noted the public international interest in the return of stolen cultural property and, citing the 1970 UNESCO Convention to which France was a party and the 1995 Unidroit Convention, which France, Italy and Switzerland had all signed, stated that these represent a common inspiration and thus constitute the expression of international public order either in force or in formation.[263] Perhaps, the most important role performed by this Convention at this stage is not the establishment of minimal uniform rules for all Parties to the Convention but the transformation of the mindsets of those involved in the art trade (so that they are more diligent and careful when they acquire art) as well as the raising of awareness among members of the public.

---

259 Some, obviously, more than others.

260 The strongest advocate of the views opposing the ones presented in this chapter is Merryman, J.H. (1996), 'The UNIDROIT Convention: Three Significant Departures from the Urtext', *International Journal of Cultural Property*, 11.

261 The States that have ratified the Unidroit Convention are the following: Afghanistan, Argentina, Azerbaijan, Bolivia, Brazil, Cambodia, China, Croatia, Cyprus, Ecuador, El Salvador, Finland, Gabon, Greece, Guatemala, Hungary, Iran, Italy, Lithuania, New Zealand, Nigeria, Norway, Paraguay, Peru, Portugal, Romania, Slovakia, Slovenia, Spain. Entry into force: 1.7.1998.

262 Desportes Still-Life case, Chambre d'accusation de Genève, Cour de Droit Public, 1 April 1997.

263 Prott, L.V. (1997), *Commentary on the Unidroit Convention*, n. 102 above, 87.

3. European Union law

3.1 FREE MOVEMENT OF GOODS AND THE 'NATIONAL TREASURES' EXCEPTION

3.1.1 The Provisions on the Free Movement of Goods

3.1.1.1 Free movement of goods

The principle of the free movement of goods is one of the fundamental principles and constituent elements of the Single Market and of European Union law. The Member States' national markets should be seen as parts of an integrated whole, a Common Market, which functions in the same way as a national market and where any kind of restrictions on the free movement of goods are prohibited. Restrictions, imposed by national laws on trade relating to cultural goods, run the risk of being considered restrictions within the meaning of articles 34 and 35 of the Treaty on the Functioning of the European Union (TFEU) given, of course, the fact that cultural treasures fall within the notion of 'goods' according to article 28(1) TFEU[1] and there is no express exception for them.

Article 34 TFEU provides that 'Quantitative restrictions on imports and all measures having equivalent effect shall be prohibited between Member States'. Equivalent to article 34 TFEU is article 35 in relation to exports: 'Quantitative restrictions on exports, and all measures having equivalent effect, shall be prohibited between Member States'.

In 1968, in *Commission v. Italy,*[2] the Court of Justice of the European Union clarified that even unique works of art are 'goods' within the meaning of the TFEU. More specifically it was provided that even unique works of art should be held to be goods within the meaning of article 28(1),

---

[1] Article 28(1) (ex article 23): 'The Union shall comprise a customs union which shall cover all trade in goods and which shall involve the prohibition between Member States of customs duties on imports and exports and of all charges having equivalent effect, and the adoption of a common customs tariff in their relations with third countries'.

[2] Case 7/68, *Commission v. Italy,* [1968] ECR 618. See also 48/71, *Commission v. Italy,* [1072] ECR 85; 18/71, *Eunomia di Porro e C v. Italian Ministry of Education* [1971] ECR 941.

because they are 'products which can be valued in money and which are capable, as such, of forming the subject of commercial transactions'.[3] Yet the special character of these goods, meaning that they cannot be put in the same basket as any good, derives from the fact that they form part of the exception found in article 36 TFEU.[4]

3.1.1.2 The article 36 TFEU exception

Article 36 provides for an exception to the rule of articles 34 *et seq.* for the free movement of goods.[5] 'The provisions of Articles 34 and 35 shall not preclude prohibitions or restrictions on imports, exports or goods in transit justified on grounds of . . . the protection of national treasures possessing artistic, historic or archaeological value. . . . Such prohibitions or restrictions shall not, however, constitute a means of arbitrary discrimination or a disguised restriction on trade between Member States'. Consequently, prohibitions or restrictions on the free movement of national treasures possessing artistic, historic or archaeological value, which are introduced

---

[3] However, two points are of interest in this case. First, the fact that all objects which can be valued in money, irrespective of their artistic, historic or archaeological value, constitute 'goods' within the meaning of article 28(1), jeopardises the structure of European Union cultural policy. Second, this case does not distinguish between 'cultural goods' and 'works of art'. 'Cultural goods' come closer to the notion of cultural heritage and they are linked to the public interest of their state of origin, whilst works of art essentially refer to modern or contemporary works of art whose commercialisation and free movement is taken for granted. The notions of a 'cultural good' and a 'work of art' do not always coincide. A cultural good may not be a work of art and *vice versa*. There may, of course, be cases where a cultural good is a work of art, without this applying necessarily to all situations. According to the spirit of the TFEU, works of art do not come within the notion of 'national treasures', since the former are goods whose movement within the Single Market should be free and without reservations. National treasures are goods which are subject to certain national regulation according to their particular characteristics and the national values they incorporate. This case, of course, was decided in a period when the economic targets of the Treaty had to be attained.

[4] Voudouri, D. (1994), 'Circulation et protection des biens culturels dans l'Europe sans frontières', *Revue du Droit Public*, 483.

[5] The exception found in article 36 TFEU is similar to the exception found in article XX of the 1994 General Agreement on Tariffs and Trade (GATT) concerning '[measures] (f) imposed on the protection of national treasures of artistic, historic or archaeological value'. Article XX introduces exceptions to article XI which prohibits quantitative restrictions (quotas) on both the export and the import of goods. GATT is one of the agreements of the general 1995 Agreement Establishing the World Trade Organization that governs the movement of goods in international trade.

by national law, are justified only and to the extent that they do not constitute a means of 'arbitrary discrimination' or 'a disguised restriction' on trade between Member States.

The notions of 'arbitrary discrimination' and 'disguised restriction' have not been tested so far with regard to the protection of national treasures before the Court of Justice. They have been tested, however, in relation to other exceptions found in article 36 TFEU but always with regard to the particular facts pertaining to each case. Some conclusions can, nevertheless, be drawn by analogy. The conduct which discriminates between two or more equivalent situations without any objective justification for doing so can be considered 'arbitrary discrimination'. A 'disguised restriction' is held to be the exercise of a legal right with the intention of restricting trade within the Union rather than serving the purpose it was originally designed to serve (that is serving a purpose which is alien to the aim of protecting a State's national heritage).

In *Cinéthèque*[6] it was explicitly stated that 'cultural aims may justify certain restrictions on the free movement of goods', subject to the principle of non-discrimination and proportionality, while in the *Tourist Guides*[7] case and *Collectieve Antennevoorziening Gouda*,[8] it was stated that '[g]eneral interest in the proper appreciation of the artistic and archaeological heritage of a country . . . can constitute an *overriding reason* (or *overriding requirement*, according to the wording of the second case) justifying a restriction on the freedom to provide services' (emphasis added).[9]

However, these statements do not necessarily imply a choice in favour of a wider definition or interpretation of article 36 TFEU. In none of these cases was any 'overriding principle' found which would justify the derogatory measure adopted. The exception has been interpreted narrowly, in line with the interpretation given to the other exceptions in article 36 TFEU.

The exception found in article 36 paragraph 1, as is the case with all other exceptions in the same paragraph,[10] is due to the fact that there are considerable differences between Member States in terms of their legal

6 Cases 60 and 61/84 [1985] ECR 2605.

7 Case C-198/89, *Commission v. Greece* [1991] ECR I-727.

8 Case 288/89 *Stichting Collectieve Antennevoorziening Gouda and others v. Commissariaat voor de Media* [1991] ECR I-4007.

9 *Ibid.* at para 13. See also C-169/91 *B & Q* [1992] ECR I-6635 and 379/87 [1989] ECR 3967.

10 The other exceptions found in article 36 TFEU are public morality, public policy or public security; the protection of health and life of humans, animals or plants; or the protection of industrial and commercial property.

systems, their social values and their traditions.[11,12] However, the rule is that exceptions to the general principle of the free movement of goods should be interpreted narrowly so that the principal aim of the proper functioning of the Single Market is preserved. Any measure dictated or allowed by article 36 should be subject to the principle of proportionality, as this is provided for in article 5 TEU. According to this principle, the measure should a) be appropriate for the accomplishment of the intended purpose (that is the protection of national treasures possessing an artistic, historic or archaeological value) and b) enable the purpose to be achieved by the means least restrictive to trade between Member States. Therefore the principle of proportionality restricts even further the interpretation of the exceptions found in article 36 TFEU in favour of the free movement of goods within the European Union.

The principle of subsidiarity (article 5(2) TEU) should also be taken into account.[13] According to this

> in areas which do not fall within its exclusive competence, the Union shall act only if and insofar as the objectives of the proposed action cannot be

---

[11] Stamatoudi, I. (1998), 'The National Treasures Exception in Article 36 EC: How Many of them Fit the Bill?', *Art, Antiquity and Law*, 39. Stamatoudi, I. (2004), 'National Cultural Treasures and Free Movement of Goods in the Single Market', in E. Trova (ed.), *Cultural Heritage and the Law*, Athens – Thessaloniki: ed. Sakkoulas, 261.

[12] In *Cassis de Dijon* (Case 120/78, *Rewe v. Bundesmonopolverwaltung für Branntwein* [1979] ECR 649) the Court pointed out that there can be 'values or interests of sufficient importance to outrank the principles of free movement'. The Court in this case was referring to interests that were not restricted to those provided for in article 36 paragraph 1. Until then, there had been the view that the interests found in article 36 paragraph 1 were referred to exhaustively. Now the 'mandatory requirements' ('Obstacles to movement within the Community resulting from disparities between the national laws relating to the marketing of the products in question must be accepted in so far as those provisions may be recognized as being necessary in order to satisfy mandatory requirements relating in particular to the effectiveness of fiscal supervision, the protection of public health, the fairness of commercial transactions and the defence of the consumer'. Ibid., para 8) of *Cassis de Dijon* were added to them.

[13] See also Protocol 2 to the Lisbon Treaty on the application of the principles of subsidiarity and proportionality. See also the principle of conferral (Art. 5 TEU, ex Article 5 TEC) according to which the Union shall act within the limits of the competences conferred upon it by the Member States in the Treaties to attain the objectives set out therein. All other competences remain with the Member States. Member States – and they alone – may confer to the Union parts of their sovereign powers, if and when they consider that their interests are better served by common action.

> sufficiently achieved by the Member States, either at central level or at regional and local level, but can rather, by reason of the scale or effects of the proposed action, be better achieved at Union level. The institutions of the Union shall apply the principle of subsidiarity as laid down in the Protocol on the application of the principles of subsidiarity and proportionality. National Parliaments shall ensure compliance with that principle in accordance with the procedure set out in that Protocol.

The exception to national treasures should work within the prescribed limits set by paragraph 2 of article 36 TFEU. If these limits are not respected and restrictions or prohibitions based on national legislation in these areas are exercised abusively, then the general rule of the free movement of goods applies. In other words, paragraph 2 of article 36 works as an exception to the exception, where the general rule applies.

The exceptions found in article 36 TFEU serve as a vehicle to recognise the Member States' right to continue legislating and applying their national laws in these areas, which are held to be sensitive areas of public interest.[14] However, as M. Ross[15] points out, 'by putting cultural heritage along with other recognised interests such as protection of the environment, consumers and workers, the Court of Justice has isolated cultural heritage as a concern which is protectable by virtue of it being compatible with the goals of the European Community'.

In view of the absence of any precise legislation, the consistency of national legislation with European Union law will, as a last resort, be based on the Court of Justice's interpretation. It is very likely that this interpretation will not only reflect the strict legal points of European Union law but also the attitude of the Union and its policy on cultural property issues. Taking the aforementioned into account, G. Karydis has

---

[14] In the area of 'public morality', which also forms one of the exceptions of article 36 TFEU, the Court in *Henn & Darby* 34/1979, [1979] ECR 3795 has followed a rather broad interpretation of the term. It has also accepted that the term 'public morality' should be defined according to each Member State's value system. If this approach is transposed to national treasures, one can easily reach the conclusion that each Member State can attempt its own definition of national treasures according to its own set of values and beliefs. Papagiannis, D. (2004), 'The Notion of Cultural Goods under Community Law', in E. Trova (ed.), *Cultural Heritage and the Law*, Athens – Thessaloniki: Ed. Sakkoulas, 607, at 608–9. See also Weatherill, St. and P. Beaumont (1995), *EC Law*, 2nd edition, London, New York: Penguin Books, 476–7.

[15] Ross, M. (1995), 'Cultural Protection: A Matter of Union Citizenship or Human Rights?', in N. Neuwahl and A. Rosas (eds), *The European Union and Human Rights*, The Hague/Boston/London: Martinus Nijhoff Publishers, 235, at 238.

attempted to set out what the role of the Court of Justice should be in relation to cultural property:

> the margin for manoeuvre by the Member States has to be very wide. The Community judicial control should not interfere but only to condemn manifest abuses (as for example when a State designates as 'national treasures' cultural goods that are found licitly and by the free will of the parties on its territory, after they have been legally exported from another Member State). In any other case the principle of judicial security will suffer.[16]

3.1.2 The Notion of National Treasures in the TFEU

3.1.2.1 National treasures possessing artistic, historic or archaeological value

In order to define the notion of 'national treasures', we must first examine what is generally meant by the word 'treasures'. Its primary meaning was initially something precious or very valuable. Later, this word took on a metaphorical meaning, encompassing not only objects of high monetary value, but also objects whose value consists in their importance for humanity, history and art.[17] In other words, treasures are objects which represent, or are in fact, elements essential and basic to a nation's heritage and history, although they may not necessarily be precious. These objects have to meet a test of 'quality', which implies that it is not the level of their value (quantity) that is being judged, but their significance to the nation. The outcome of this test is, however, subject to further objectively conceived criteria, in order for the object to be considered a 'treasure'. These objective criteria are less to do with monetary value than the cultural importance of the object. In some cases, the object may not have any monetary value simply because this has not been evaluated or because it is priceless.

Not all treasures qualify for the exception in article 36 TFEU. Only those which are of national importance to the state do so. Problems of attribution arise since the typical rules of origin, which apply to ordinary commercial goods, do not apply to artefacts. No guidelines are offered in the text of the Treaty as to what will be decisive in order for a treasure to qualify as 'national'. It is evident that the object has to be closely linked

---

16 See Karydis, G. (1994), 'Le juge communautaire et la préservation de l'identité culturelle nationale', *Revue Trimestrielle de Droit Européen*, 4.

17 See e.g. *Charrier v. Bell* 496 So.2d 601 (1986), where burial goods excavated from a site in Louisiana, without being of any great financial value, were, nevertheless, thought to be 'priceless', as they formed an association of cultural material from which scholars could learn.

to the art, history and archaeology of a state, but what exactly this link is, is not defined. Is it the birthplace of the creator, the country in which the object was created, the place where it was found or the place where the artefact has remained for the longest period? Questions of great practical significance may arise from these considerations. Would, for example, the UK be entitled to invoke article 36 in order to prevent the export of the Parthenon Marbles, or is Greece alone entitled to that right? Is a Matisse smuggled from Italy to London an Italian artistic treasure? The criteria for a cultural object to qualify as a national treasure differ from state to state. Some consider its attachment to the nation's tradition, culture and patrimony to be crucial; others, the place where the object was created, or the place where the building from which the object was detached is situated. According to Plehwe,[18] complex problems of attribution can be avoided by each state applying its own 'closest connection test'. This, however, does not preclude problems of overlap or of classification of the same object in the laws of more than one state.[19]

Given the conflicting results concerning origin that one may reach by applying different criteria, the determination of the notion 'national' treasure in any national or European Union legal instrument has to be one

---

[18] von Plehwe, T. (1995), 'European Union and the Free Movement of Cultural Goods', *European Law Review*, 431, at 434.

[19] See the various views expressed by Pescatore, P. (1985), 'Le commerce de l'art et le Marché Commun', *Revue Trimestrielle de Droit Européen*, a.XXI (1), 451; Biondi, A. (1997), 'The Merchant, the Thief and the Citizen: The Circulation of Works of Art within the European Union', *Common Market Law Review*, 1173; Stagos, P. (1986), 'The Free Movement of Artistic Goods in the Community and the Cultural Dimension of European Integration', *Greek European Law Review*, 683 (in Greek); Ferrer-Correia, A., 'La vente national d'objets d'art sous l'angle de la protection patrimoine culturel', *Annuaire de l'Institut de Droit International* (64-I), 1991, session de Bâle, 90, at 90–121 and 140–192; Rigaux, F. (1995), 'Libre circulation des biens culturels et protection des trésors nationaux', *European Review of Private Law*, 95; See also Weatherill, St. and P. Beaumont, n. 14 above, at 476–7 and Voudouri, D., n. 4 above, 479, as they are all referred to in Grammatikaki-Alexiou, A. (2002), *International Trade of Cultural Property and Private International Law*, Thessaloniki: Sakkoulas Publications, XV, 52–4. However, there is no leading view in the area as to the criteria to be followed in order for the link between the cultural treasure and the Member State to be established. Given also the fact that a lot of subjectivity is involved in the definition of the term 'national treasures' the European Council has rightfully mentioned that there will also be a lack of transparency with regard to those criteria. See Decision of 13.12.1990, EEC C 19/28.1.1991 and De Ceuster, J. (1993), 'Les règles communautaires en matière de restitution de biens culturels ayant quitté illicitement le territoire d'un état membre', *Revue du Marché Unique Européen*, 43.

of quality.[20] Irrespective of any other characteristics, a national treasure is an object which is not geographically but mainly historically[21] linked with the place. This, in a sense, solves problems of attribution for cultural objects of dubious or unknown origin, which are otherwise very likely to be outside the scope of article 36 TFEU. The notion 'national' should also include treasures which are of significance to certain territorial parts of a country, in other words regional treasures. These treasures are not mentioned separately since they can be considered as being included in the wider notion of 'national treasures'.[22]

'National treasures' is a term found in the English language version of the TFEU and its equivalent appears in a number of other language versions. However, this terminology is not uniform all over Europe. Italy, Spain, Portugal and the Netherlands provide instead for 'national patrimony'; while Germany provides for 'cultural goods'. This diverging terminology reflects the different national approaches to cultural heritage. Seen from a literal point of view, some of these terms are broader ('patrimony'), while others are narrower ('treasures', and even narrower, 'goods'). Yet this is of little significance for European Union law. Since the interpretation of this notion should be uniform all over the European Union, the different terms can apply interchangeably. The question of which term will be the one that prevails and which term, the broader or the narrower, corresponds better to the European philosophy, are issues which have to be interpreted in line with the objectives of the TFEU.

The notion of 'national treasures' has been partly defined by two basic European Union legal instruments in the area, for the purpose of these instruments only: a Regulation (1992, codified in 2009) on the export of cultural goods out of the territory of the European Union[23] and a

---

20 The Resolution of the Institute of International Law of 3.9.1991 provides in its first article that the country of origin of an artefact is that which, from a cultural point of view, presents the closest link to this object.

21 Works of local or regional significance are included.

22 Grammatikaki-Alexiou, A., n. 19 above, 51. See also Weatherill, St. and P. Beaumont, n. 14 above 476–7.

23 Council Regulation 3911/92 of 9 December, 1992 on the export of cultural goods, OJ L 395/1 (Corrigendum OJ L267/30, 19/10/1996), as amended by Council Regulation 2469/96 of 16 December, 1996 OJ L 335/9, Council Regulation 974/2001 of 14 May, 2001 OJ L 137/10 and Council Regulation 806/2003 of 14 April, 2003 OJ L 122/1. Council Regulation (EC) No 116/2009 of 18 December, 2008 on the export of cultural goods (codified version). See also Commission Regulation 752/93 of 30 March, 1993 laying down provisions for the implementation of Council Regulation 3911/92 on the export of cultural goods, as amended by Commission Regulation (EC) 1526/98 of 16 July, 1998, OJ L

Directive (1993) on the return of cultural objects illegally exported from the territory of a Member State.[24] Although the Regulation refers to 'cultural goods' and the Directive to 'cultural objects', they are both considered to have defined 'national treasures', whereby a derogation from the rules for the free movement of goods would be subject to their 'protective regime'. Both legal instruments refer to Member States' competence in the area. However, the degree to which this competence is determinative differs in each case. On the one hand, the Member States' competence in the Regulation is mentioned[25] not in connection with the definition of cultural goods, but as a reminder that Member States can designate a higher or lower number of goods as cultural, although these will not be subject to the Regulation's regime if they do not correspond to one of the items listed in the Annex. On the other hand, designation by the Member States of cultural objects as national treasures has a decisive role in relation to the Directive. In fact, it is one of the conditions for an object to qualify as protectable under the Directive. Only when both conditions are met (an object is defined by the Member State as a national treasure and is included in the list of the Directive) can the object be the subject of restitution. These two pieces of legislation were designed to be able to work together.[26] However, the definitions deriving from these two legal instruments appear to conflict, due mainly to the absence of Member States' competence as a decisive factor in the provisions of the Regulation, which may lead to various objects being caught every time under the regime of the Regulation and the Directive.[27]

3.1.2.2 Competence to define 'national treasures'

Member States The area of the free movement of goods comes under the European Union's exclusive competence. The Regulation and the Directive have only dealt with a limited area with regard to the free

---

201/47 and Commission Regulation (EC) 656/2004 of 7 April, 2004, OJ L104/50 (Corrigendum, OJ L 203, 8.6.2004, p.14 (656/2004)).

[24] Directive 93/7/EEC of 15 March, 1993 on the return of cultural objects unlawfully removed from the territory of a Member State (OJ L 74/74, 27.3.1993), amended by Directive 96/100/EC of 17 February, 1997 (L 60/59 1.3.1997) and Directive 2001/38/EC of 5 June, 2001 (L 187/43 10.7.2001).

[25] Article 1 of the Regulation: 'Without prejudice to Member States' powers under Article [36] of the Treaty, the term "cultural goods" shall refer, for the purposes of this Regulation, to the items listed in Annex I.'

[26] See the Opinion of the European Parliament and the Council in the proposal for the Directive, [1993] OJ No C72.

[27] See a detailed analysis under sections 3.2 and 2.3.

movement of cultural goods. Thus they have not defined the concept of 'national treasures' exhaustively, nor have they explained fully the article 36 exception.[28] As a result they have left unaffected the Member States' competence to choose the means appropriate for the protection of their cultural heritage, apart, of course, from the areas[29] within the limited ambit of the Regulation and Directive themselves. Consequently, Member States still retain their competence to define their national treasures.[30] Nevertheless, this competence is neither exclusive[31] nor

---

28 See in this respect article 1 of Regulation 116/2004 where it is stated that the term 'cultural goods' refers, for the purposes of the Regulation, to the items listed in the Annex and it is without prejudice to Member States' powers under article 36 of the Treaty. See also the preamble to Directive 7/1993 where it is referred that Member States retain the right to define their national treasures and to take the necessary measures to protect them in the internal market.

29 If the European Union has provided the necessary measures, i.e. enacted directives, Member States can have no more recourse to article 36 with regard to the area that has been regulated by these Directives. Case 72/83, *Campus Oil* [1984] ECR 2727, at para 27; case 251/78, *Denkavit* [1979] ECR 3369, at para 14; case 227/82, *Leendert* [1983] ECR 3883, at para 35; case 29/87, *Denkavit* [1988] ECR 2965; case 190/87, *Moormann BV* [1988] ECR 4689; case C-304/88, *Commission v. Belgium* [1990] ECRI-2801; case 35/76, *Simmenthal v. Italian Minister of Finance* [1976] ECR 1871; *Ratti* case 148/78 [1979] ECR 1629; *Tedeschi v. Denkavit* case 5/77 [1977] ECR 1555.

30 This can be derived also from the Court of Justice of the European Union's stance in the case of 'public morality' which forms another exception found in article 36 TFEU as is discussed earlier in this chapter. See Case 34/79, *Regina v. Henn & Darby* [1979] ECR 3795; 121/85, *Conegate Ltd v. Commissioners of Customs and Excise*, [1986] ECR 1007; C-23/89, *Quitlynn Ltd And Richards v. Southend Borough Council* [1990] ECR I-3059; C-350/89, *Sheptonehurst Ltd v. Newham Borough Council* [1991] ECR I-2387. The Member States' responsibility in the area of culture and protection of national treasures was also emphasised in the Interim Report of the EP Committee on Youth, Culture, Education, the Media and Sports of 28 November 1990 on the circulation of cultural goods in the Single Market, EP Document No A3-0324/90. See, also, the Ministers of Culture meeting on 19 November 1990 (Revue du Marché Commun, 1991, at 65) and in Europe, No 5508 of 8 June 1991, at 7. Indicative in this respect is also the European Court of Human Rights' jurisprudence with regard to public morality. See *Handyside*, 7.12.1976, Series A, vol. 24; *Müller*, 24.5.1988, Series A, vol. 133, and *Dudgeon*, 22.10.1981, Series A, vol. 45.

31 According to the Court of Justice's case law, 'article 36's aim is not to reserve certain issues for the exclusive competence of the Member States, but only to recognise that national laws may exempt something from the principles of the free movement of goods only to the extent that this exemption is justified for the attainment of the objectives aimed' [translation from the French text]. See particularly, *Tedeschi v. Denkavit* 5/77 [1977] ECR 1555, case 251/78, *Denkavit*

unlimited.[32] Given the different approaches to cultural property in the European Union, basically those of the northern and southern states, the outcome of any unilateral designation of such objects is bound to be very different by virtue of the different traditions and interests.[33] These designations, however, will be called into question, to the extent that they exceed certain limits that are set by fundamental European principles, including

---

Futtermittel v. Minister of Agriculture [1979] ECR 3369, and *Campus Oil,* case 72/83 [1984] ECR 2727.

32 [I]t is for each Member State to determine its own criteria for identifying cultural objects that can be regarded as 'national treasures'; nevertheless, the concept of 'national treasures possessing artistic, historic or archaeological value' *cannot be defined unilaterally by the Member States without verification by the Community institutions* . . . Moreover, Article 36 of the EEC Treaty – which should be interpreted restrictively since it derogates from the fundamental rules of the free movement of goods – cannot be relied upon to justify laws, procedures or practices that lead to discrimination or restrictions which are disproportionate with respect to the aim in view. [Emphasis added].

Communication by the Commission to the Council on 22 November 1989 COM (89) 594 final on the protection of national treasures possessing artistic, historic or archaeological value: needs arising from the abolition of frontiers in 1992, at para 5.

This Communication points out that it is important to establish between the need to protect national treasures and the principle of the free movement of goods. See, also, the Commission's answer to written question No 1962/88 by MEP Mr Raftery, [1989] OJ 1989, C 180/39.

33 For a wide interpretation of the notion of cultural treasures see, for example, the judgment of the French Conseil d'État, 7 October 1987, Ministre de la Culture/Consorts Genty, Dallox 1988, jurisprudence p.269. This judgment found that an export licence that was denied by the French Ministry of Culture in relation to certain medieval Chinese jars was compatible with articles 30–36 TFEU. See also *Beyeler v. Italy*, 28 May 2002 [2002] ECHR 462, where a violation of article 1 of the First Protocol to the European Convention for the Protection of Human Rights and Fundamental Freedoms was found. (Article 1 provides that 'every natural or legal person is entitled to the peaceful enjoyment of his possessions. No one shall be deprived of his possessions except in the public interest and subject to the conditions provided for by the law and by the general principles of international law'). In this case Italy exercised its right of preemption in relation to a Van Gogh painting called *Portrait of a Young Peasant* and bought it at a considerably lower price compared to the one the Peggy Guggenheim Foundation intended to buy it at, based on the fact that the Swiss owner of the painting (Beyeler) had not informed the Italian State that he was the real purchaser of it when he first bought the painting in 1977. See Hoffman, B.T. (2006), 'European Union Legislation Pertaining to Cultural Goods', in Hoffman, B.T. (ed.) (2006), *Art and Cultural Heritage. Law, Policy and Practice*, Cambridge University Press, 191.

that of the free movement of goods.[34] Consequently, the following questions emerge: to what extent do Member States have discretion to define their national treasures, and where is the boundary drawn, in order for the European Union to take over?

Given that this borderline is unclear, many views have been put forward. An interesting, though heretical one, would be that cultural objects, being considered as a special category of objects and not ordinary goods,[35] are generally excluded from the scope of the Treaty and that they consequently do not constitute a simple exception to the free movement of goods. In such a case, it is the Treaty restrictions in relation to those treasures that constitute an exception to the States' general protection of their culture, and not *vice versa*. According to this view, the free movement of goods and the protection of national heritage should not be seen as conflicting interests but rather as interests deserving equal respect from the European Union. This, of course, argues for a balancing of interests instead of a 'rule and exception' approach. This approach is less of a threat to the national sovereignty of Member States and is also more consistent with the general principle of subsidiarity contained in the TFEU.[36]

Such a view is likely to be considered rather optimistic, given the approach that the European Union institutions are apt to take. The most widespread view is that, since article 36 TFEU is a provision that derogates from the rules of the free movement of goods, it must be interpreted as narrowly as possible. Still, it is not clear how a narrow interpretation is defined. Is it the definition given in one of the international legal instruments, the interpretation adopted by the Regulation and Directive, or the one that the 'art market' states are more likely to adopt, encompassing only the national treasures which are of great importance to a state

---

34 'By reason of the absence of any Community regulation, the Member States can define their national treasures according to their own scale of values and in the form they choose, as long as these values and these forms are reasonable and meet the imperatives of the European Community as to the free movement of goods.' Case 34/79, *Henn & Darby* [1979] ECR 3795. Yet the Court of Justice of the European Union won't be able to draw any conclusions as to the criteria to be applied in order to define the concept of 'national treasures'. It will only be able to indicate which are those cultural treasures (limiting its judgment to the case at issue) that do not fall within the concept of national treasures as these are referred to in the TFEU.

35 Resolution of the European Parliament of 13.12.1990.

36 According to Bekemans, L. (1993), 'Le traité de Maastricht et l'éducation, la formation professionnelle et la culture', *Revue du Marché Unique Européen*, 99, at 108, we must distinguish 'subsidiarity *generalis*', deriving from article 5 from 'subsidiarity *specialis*', found for example in article 167 TFEU.

in terms of monetary evaluations?[37] A more modest view holds that the definition of national treasures is essentially subject to two legal considerations, set by article 36 itself: the principle of proportionality,[38] and the fact that national measures enacted for the protection of a State's cultural heritage should not amount to a 'means of arbitrary discrimination or disguised restriction on trade between Member States' (both subject to judicial review). Trade in the European Union still remains the principal aim, and is at the same time a yardstick for non-economic policies.

Nevertheless, this approach leaves open various questions. Is the European Union allowed to intervene only in cases where protective restrictions by Member States amount to discrimination and exceed certain minimal limits set by the Treaty, or is it the restriction itself which, in most cases, is held as discrimination?[39] Generalising to some extent, one could argue that a restriction in intra-community trade will not be held to be legal by the mere fact that it has as its objective the protection of national treasures. It has also to be subject to the following rules: 1) Article 36, being identified as a provision which derogates from the fundamental principle of the free movement of goods, must be interpreted narrowly and as an exception.[40] 2) The derogating measure must be

---

[37] This approach taken by the EU Regulation and Directive ignores the fact that treasures do not necessarily involve a high monetary value. Their monetary value necessarily reflects a European Union philosophy as partly reflected in Regulation 116/2009 and Directive 93/7 which approach (as amended) cultural goods as simple commodities. This, however, should not be the intended approach. It is clear that monetary value is not always a safe criterion to follow because a cultural object may be valued differently between states depending on its significance for each state as well as on the market rules. That means that there may be Member States where the cultural object may not be subject to the special Regulation and Directive regimes. Interesting in this respect was also the European Parliament's view that cultural objects which are the result of a crime (theft, misappropriation and so on) should not be subject to monetary values. However, this view was not adopted in the end (European Parliament, Proceedings PE 161.272, p.6). See Papagiannis, D., n. 14 above, at 623–4.

[38] Deriving from the first paragraph of article 36 TFEU.

[39] The tests of non-discrimination and proportionality may overlap and therefore should not be considered in isolation. See Wyatt, D. and A. Dashwood (1993), *European Community Law*, London: Sweet & Maxwell, 3rd edn., at 228 and case 272/80, *Fraus-Nerlandse* [1981] ECR 3277, at paras 13, 14; cases 2–4/82, *Le Lion* [1983] ECR 2973, at para 12.

[40] This has been confirmed by the ECJ in *Bauhuis v. Netherlands*, case 46/76 [1977] ECR 5; *Eggers v. Freie Hansestadt Bremen* case 13/78 [1978] ECR 1935; *Salgoil v. Italian Ministry for Foreign Trade*, case 33/68 [1968] ECR 453; case 7/68, *Commission v. Italy* [1968] ECR 618; case 113/80, *Commission v Ireland* [1981] ECR 1625; case 95/81, *Commission v. Italy* [1982] ECR 2187.

justified[41] with regard to the protection of national treasures possessing artistic, historic or archaeological value. In order for that principle to be justified there are three further tests that have to be satisfied: a) the test of 'causality' or 'causal link', where the cause of the measure must be directly linked to the result of protecting the national treasures of a state;[42] b) the test of proportionality,[43] where the measure must be appropriate and not exceed the necessary limits within which the intended result can be achieved; and lastly, c) the test of substitution, where no other means, less burdensome, are available for the attainment of the same objective.[44] The final confirmation of the legitimacy of the measure, as a *deuxième filet de securité*, will be made on the premise that it does not result in abuse. This abuse is defined as a means of arbitrary discrimination or disguised restriction on trade between Member States.

There remains a third view, arguing that Member States are allowed to establish their own definitions, which, although different, will reflect diversity, that is both desirable and specifically respected in the area of culture. The European Union will interfere only where Member States are in breach of paragraph 2 of article 36 TFEU. Any proportionality test will not be assessed in isolation, but will be seen in conjunction with

---

41 See 1989 Commission Communication, n. 32 above. According to Goyder, J. (1992), 'Free Movement of Cultural Goods and European Community Law', *International Journal of Cultural Property*, 219, at 222–3, although the Commission's view in this Communication has no direct legal force, '[h]owever, if Community legislation is to be introduced, the Commission has responsibility for drafting a proposal and putting it before the Member States. Its view is therefore significant'. Case 5/77, *Tedeschi* [1977] ECR 1556; case 251/78, *Denkavit* [1979] ECR 3327. The Court has, also, pointed out in its case law that 'justified' is to be understood as 'necessary', case 153/78, *Commission v. Germany* [1979] ECR 2555, at para 8; case 251/78, *Denkavit* [1979] ECR 3327, at para 21.

42 Mattera, A. (1993), 'La libre circulation des œuvres d'art à l'intérieur de la Communauté et la protection des trésors nationaux ayant une valeur artistique, historique ou archéologique', *Revue du Marché Unique Européen*, 9, at 16.

43 'However [public health] measures are justified only if it is established that they are necessary in order to attain the objective of protection referred to in Article 36 and that such protection cannot be achieved by means which place less of a restriction on the free movement of goods within the Community', *Commission v. Belgium*, case 155/82 [1983] ECR 531; case 97/83, *Melkunil* [1984] ECR 2367, at para 12.

44 This test can also be viewed as another aspect of the proportionality test. At this point, it is suggested that one more test should be set, that of finding means which, though less appropriate for the protective purpose, are less restrictive to the free movement of goods, and so less objectionable where there is a balancing of interests. *De Peijper* case 104/75 [1976] ECR 613; *Eggers v. Freie Hansestadt Bremen* case 13/78 [1978] ECR 1935.

this paragraph so that the measure at issue will not result in a means of arbitrary discrimination or disguised restriction on trade between Member States.[45] If the measure at issue satisfies the test, Member States can apply it without any additional requirements.

European Union institutions and the role of the Court of Justice of the European Union The European Union has been given the right by the TFEU[46] to legislate directly on issues concerning the free movement of goods. Thus, it can also attempt an autonomous definition of 'national treasures', as it has already partly done in the case of the Directive and Regulation. The European Union can interfere with national measures only in cases where they are discriminatory and disproportionately restrictive to their aim, as long as a general definition, which will determine the limits of the derogation in article 36 relating to cultural protection, does not yet exist. There is, however, a view that the European Union should not autonomously define 'national treasures'. According to this view the concept can be defined only according to a national scale of values, given that the artistic or historic value of 'national treasures' depends entirely on the ideological attachment to them of the Member State concerned[47].[48]

3.1.3 Other Provisions in the TFEU Relevant to Culture

A new title (Title IX) in the EC Treaty, which refers to culture, was introduced by the Maastricht Treaty. This title has undergone some changes since then and became Title XIII in the revision of the EC Treaty in Lisbon (now Treaty on the Functioning of the European Union). According to

---

45 Discrimination has been defined in case 34/79, *Henn & Darby* [1979] ECR 3795, at para 21, and in case 40/82, *Commission v. UK* [1984] ECR 283, at para 36, as to 'prevent restrictions on trade based on the grounds mentioned in the first sentence of art. 36 from being diverted from their proper purpose and used in such a way as either to create discrimination in respect of goods originating in other Member States or indirectly to protect certain national products'. Yet, such discrimination is very unlikely to be found in the area of protection of national treasures. As Goyder points out, '[discrimination] could occur, if a Member State were to have a rule which prevented the release of an object for sale to a buyer in one Member State, but not to a buyer in a different Member State. However, such a difference in treatment at the level of the rule itself is very unlikely, since national cultural export controls aim to retain objects and are not generally concerned with the destination of the object once it leaves the State's territory.' n. 41 above, at 222.

46 Article 3 TFEU.

47 Karydis, G., n. 16 above, at 556.

48 See above section 3.1.1.2.

article 167,[49] cultural policy is a European Union competence, although a concurrent one, and is considered as an equally appreciable aim, carrying the same weight as that of the free movement of goods. This prompts us to think that there has been a shift in European Union policy in this area, and that instead of regarding the protection of national treasures as an exception to articles 34 to 36, it may be considered as one more task to be fulfilled. The 'derogation approach' or the economic-orientated hierarchy of values might be substituted by that of the balancing of interests.

Article 167 requires, *inter alia*, the European Union to respect the national and regional diversity of the Member States while at the same time bringing the common cultural heritage to the fore.[50] Article 167 does not define national treasures for the European Union nor does it circumscribe a precise European Union culture. One may, therefore, question

---

[49] Article 167 (ex 151 EC):

1. The Union shall contribute to the flowering of the cultures of the Member States, while respecting their national and regional diversity and at the same time bringing the common cultural heritage to the fore.
2. Action by the Union shall be aimed at encouraging cooperation between Member States and, if necessary, supporting and supplementing their action in the following areas:
   —improvement of the knowledge and dissemination of the culture and history of the European peoples,
   —conservation and safeguarding of cultural heritage of European significance,
   —non-commercial cultural exchanges,
   —artistic and literary creation, including the audiovisual sector.
3. The Union and the Member States shall foster cooperation with third countries and the competent international organisations in the sphere of culture, in particular the Council of Europe.
4. The Union shall take cultural aspects into account in its action under other provisions of the Treaties, in particular in order to respect and to promote the diversity of its cultures.
5. In order to contribute to the achievement of the objectives referred to in this Article:
   —the European Parliament and the Council acting in accordance with the ordinary legislative procedure and after consulting the Committee of the Regions, shall adopt incentive measures, excluding any harmonisation of the laws and regulations of the Member States,
   —the Council, on a proposal from the Commission, shall adopt recommendations.

[50] That does not necessarily mean a common heritage: Lomans, A., K. Mortelmans, H. Post and Watson (1992), *Culture and Community Law – Before and after Maastricht*, Netherlands: Kluwer Law and Taxation Publishers, as quoted in Plehwe, n. 18 above, at 433, footnote 12.

whether that is really a recognition of the importance of the different national treasures and their contribution to a Euro-culture. It might be argued on the one hand that even if it is not so directly, it is nevertheless an important guarantee of respect for Member States' cultural heritage, as an indispensable element of a global European culture.[51] On the other hand we are not in a position to determine exactly how much it promises. Respect can vary from positive action to mere tolerance. It can only be argued that since culture has explicitly been included among the European Union's concerns, it will stop playing merely a residual role and will cease to be treated as adjunct to economic policy.

The European Union also has the task of the 'conservation and safeguarding of cultural heritage of European significance'.[52] This conservation and safeguarding of cultural heritage can only begin with effective protection of Member States' national treasures in an otherwise completely open market. Anything else will just pay lip service to the protection afforded by article 167, while at the same time emptying the provision of its substance and rendering it only a declaratory aspiration. The European Union shall also 'take cultural aspects into account in its action under the provisions of the Treaty',[53] and it will 'exclude any harmonisation of the laws and regulations of the Member States'.[54] Does this provision foretell a respect of national legislation in the area of culture?[55] Can it, perhaps, be considered as a strengthening of the heretical view, previously set out, that culture will be held as an equally important aim of the European Union's strategy? It has been pointed out[56] that article 167, paragraph 4 outweighs paragraph 5 since it confirms the option of the European Union to justify

---

[51] The concept of 'European culture' can be considered as forming part of the world's culture. In that sense even the concept of the 'world's culture' should not be held to jeopardise the notion of national cultural property since it necessarily passes through it.

[52] 'Cultural heritage of European significance' is not defined, but it cannot be unrelated to the heritage of the Member States.

[53] Article 167(4).

[54] Article 167(5). Coupled with the principle of subsidiarity (article 5(2) TEU), they reinforce Member States' responsibility in the protection of national treasures.

[55] 'The place of cultural heritage in existing EC law has been to perform a legitimising role for Member State activity, rather than a specific goal for Community level action and protection', M. Ross, n. 15 above, at 237. This also derives from the EP Report on the Commission proposal for the amendment of the Annex to the Council Directive 93/7/EEC, 16.4.1996, PE 216.643/fin., at 5. 'Member States [are] authorised to determine which of their cultural goods are to be exempted from the general rule of free trade'.

[56] Ross, n. 15 above, at 243.

measures in the area of culture under the provisions of the free movement of goods. Yet the conflict, if there is any, between those two provisions is not obvious. According to the spirit and aim of article 167, one could argue that paragraph 4 is no more than a reassurance of the aim of paragraph 5. In fact it stresses that the free movement of goods and protection of culture are not contradictory aims, but that they can co-exist. Even if a contradiction surfaces, as von Plehwe also points out,[57] the free movement provisions do not necessarily take precedence: 'although the provisions of the new title have to be viewed in the light of European policy, by its central aim of preserving the unique and diverse nature of the differing cultures, article 167 seems to reinforce article 36 TFEU, possibly at the expense of intra-community freedom of trade'.

In this respect article 167 should not just be seen as a new provision on substance, but rather as a clause reflecting already well-established trends in the area of culture. No real Union can exist without taking cultural developments into account, especially as they are formed by international legal instruments,[58] which may in time have the validity of customary international law and which, in one way or another, will penetrate the European Union legal order as widely accepted fundamental principles. In this context, even if article 167 does not prove to be innovative or far-reaching, it has nevertheless performed a very important role, namely, the formal recognition by the European Union of the significance of culture as a basic concern of the Union.[59]

Apart from article 167 there are other provisions in the Treaty which, although they do not directly refer to culture, can be used as legitimate bases in order to support it. Article 107(3)(d)[60] may serve as a basis for

---

[57] See T. Plehwe, n. 18 above, at 433.

[58] Set in part I(2).

[59] Article 167 could also be seen in conjunction with the Preamble to the Convention which provides that 'DESIRING to deepen the solidarity between their peoples while respecting their history, their culture and their traditions' and article 6: 'The Union shall have competence to carry out actions to support, coordinate or supplement the actions of the Member States. The areas of such action shall, at European level, be: [. . .] (c) culture; [. . .]'.

[60] Article 107 (aids granted by States) (ex 87(2)(d) EC): '1. Save as otherwise provided in the Treaties, any aid granted by a Member State or through State resources in any form whatsoever which distorts or threatens to distort competition by favouring certain undertakings or the production of certain goods shall, in so far as it affects trade between Member States, be incompatible with the internal market. 2. The following shall be compatible with the internal market: [. . .]. 3. The following may be considered to be compatible with the internal market: [. . .] (d) aid to promote culture and heritage conservation where such aid does not affect

measures affecting the area of culture. Given the flexibility in interpreting some Treaty provisions, taxes or other financial burdens may in some cases be held to constitute State aids that are permitted by the relevant article. Since culture and heritage conservation are considered to be justifying reasons for rendering any State aid for this purpose compatible with the common market, we get the impression that the European Union is starting to be supportive of culture, instead of just being tolerant.

Union citizenship, human rights (as general principles of the Treaty) and social cohesion can also have an influence on cultural property. Union citizenship is an 'open-textured'[61] provision that 'constitutes a vehicle already in existence which can be used to house layers of interests, rights and duties'.[62] Articles 20–25 (ex 17–22) TFEU are not very concrete in substance. Yet article 20(2) (ex 17(2)) provides that '[c]itizens of the Union shall enjoy the rights and be subject to the duties provided for in the Treaties'.[63] Given that article 167 provides for European Union action in certain cases and, what is more, recognises the European Union's respect thereof, this right can also come under the flexible scope of article 20(2), as being one of the bundle of rights inherent in the concept of citizenship. The draft text on citizenship[64] which states that one of the rights of citizens of the Union should be the 'right to cultural expression and the obligation to respect cultural expression by others', also argues towards this end.

In addition, article 6 TEU (which offers a human rights basis)[65] and

---

trading conditions and competition in the Union to an extent that is contrary to the common interest; [. . .]'.

[61] Ross, n. 15 above, at 246.

[62] *Ibid.*

[63] Interesting in this respect is also article 20 (ex article 17) paragraph 1: '1. Citizenship of the Union is hereby established. Every person holding the nationality of a Member State shall be a citizen of the Union. Citizenship of the Union shall be additional to and not replace national citizenship'.

[64] Supplement 2/91 – Bull. EC.

[65] Article 6:

'1. The Union recognises the rights, freedoms and principles set out in the Charter of Fundamental Rights of the European Union of 7 December 2000, as adopted at Strasbourg, on 12 December 2007, which shall have the same legal value as the Treaties.

The provisions of the Charter shall not extend in any way the competences of the Union as defined in the Treaties.

The rights, freedoms and principles in the Charter shall be interpreted in accordance with the general provisions in Title VII of the Charter governing its interpretation and application and with due regard to the explanations referred to in the Charter, that set out the sources of those provisions.

the Preamble[66] and article 22[67] of the Charter of Fundamental Rights of the European Union, which expressly refer to the diversity of cultures, coupled with the general principle of maintaining and respecting the *acquis communautaire*, can lead to similar results. These references argue in favour of a policy which will fully take into account both the right of people to conserve cultural heritage as an expression of personality and national identity as well as national duties, such as the preservation of patrimony, enshrined in the Constitutions of many Member States. Principles and duties inherent in the Treaty can still be used as grounds for judgments by the Court of Justice, as in earlier cases, even where these duties are not based on human rights or citizenship.[68]

Finally, the principle of social cohesion, which strives for a more socially integrated Europe, one that is sensitive to people's problems, more democratic and transparent and which allows and respects diversity, reflects the post-Single Market period, when economics are no longer the sole consideration. In weighing up the various interests involved in the interpretation of the concept of 'national treasures',[69] a balance is sought through the adoption of an evolutionary and flexible approach.

It can be concluded from the above that culture as well as cultural concerns have come to the forefront of the European Union policy. The fact, however, that culture has been given greater weight does not diminish the importance of the free movement of goods in the Single Market. It will probably take one or more test cases in order for us to

---

2. The Union shall accede to the European Convention for the Protection of Human Rights and Fundamental Freedoms. Such accession shall not affect the Union's competences as defined in the Treaties.
3. Fundamental rights, as guaranteed by the European Convention for the Protection of Human Rights and Fundamental Freedoms and as they result from the constitutional traditions common to the Member States, shall constitute general principles of the Union's law'.

[66] Preamble to the Charter of Fundamental Rights of the European Union: 'The Union contributes to the preservation and to the development of these common values while respecting the diversity of the cultures and traditions of the peoples of Europe as well as the national identities of the Member States [. . .]'.

[67] Article 22 (Cultural, religious and linguistic diversity): 'The Union shall respect cultural, religious and linguistic diversity'. This Article is based on Articles 6 and 167(1) and (4) TFEU.

[68] See the arguments developed in Joined Cases C-6/90 and C-9/90, *Francovich and Others* [1991] ECR I-5357, at 5403.

[69] 'Although the list of exceptions of art. 36 is exhaustive, there is still ground for an interpretation consistent with the evolutionary character of European Community law, for the protection of the "national patrimony", which is a concept wider than that of "national treasures"'. Karydis, n. 16 above, at 557.

ascertain whether this shift in interests is substantial, rather than just a shift on paper.

3.1.4 Conclusions

So far it has been shown that the definition of 'national treasures' raises a number of judicial problems which argue for either a broad or narrow interpretation,[70] according to the approach taken. Changes to the Treaty during recent years have thrown new light on the concept of culture. The explicit recognition of culture as one of the European Union competences and the vague concepts of citizenship and human rights can be comprehensive enough to cover a liberal interpretation of 'national treasures', and considerably affect the European Union's evaluation regarding the compatibility of national law with the free movement of goods.

However, this approach to 'national treasures' is still rather contentious. Numerous factors may inhibit the Court of Justice from being very protective towards cultural treasures: the strict attitude of the Court regarding exceptions such as those contained in article 36 TFEU; the ratification of the international Conventions on culture by only very few European Union Member States (with the exception of the 1970 UNESCO Convention), and their debate and diverging views thereon; the Council's approach towards cultural property as reflected in the definitions attempted in the Directive and Regulation concerning cultural objects;[71] the hazy concepts of citizenship and general principles derived from human rights conventions and national constitutions and the unexplored and generalised content of article 167 TFEU; and the fact that any action may be undermined by the various interests involved in the area of culture and the trade in art. Culture and the Single Market still represent conflicting interests. Thus, the approach to 'national treasures' is very likely to be restricted to a certain core of cultural goods, while all the rest will be caught by the rules on the free movement of goods.

---

[70] This also concerns the interpretation of the concepts 'artistic, historic or archaeological value'.

[71] It is worth mentioning the European Union's restrictive approach towards culture and towards the Member States' discretion thereon, as this stems from the rejection (on 18 May 1992) of the Draft proposal of Directive 92/280 on the return of cultural objects unlawfully removed from the territory of a Member State [OJ C 172, 7], because it would have allowed each State to define its protected cultural heritage as it considered appropriate. Another reason was the broader list of cultural objects it had compared to the lists of the Regulation and Directive.

As a result, part of national cultural heritage, though perhaps no longer a substantial part, will remain outside the scope of 'national treasures', and Member States' cultural interests will be afforded only minimal protection, certainly not enough to protect them from the results of the 'all-consuming appetite' of an open market with no custom controls.[72] Perhaps the emergence of the concepts of 'common European heritage' and 'diversity of cultures' could reconcile the conflicting interests of the free movement of goods and the protection of cultural treasures.[73] No real Union can exist without taking into account the cultural developments and the cultural concerns of the Member States. And these concerns must not only be tolerated but satisfied fully. A 'two-tiered' culture, one culture for the Member States and only half of it covered by the Treaty, cannot be easily sustained.

3.2 EXPORT CONTROLS FOR CULTURAL PROPERTY GOODS: REGULATIONS 116/09 AND 752/93

3.2.1 Scope and Aim of the Regulations

European Union measures in the field of protection of cultural goods (i.e. the Regulations and the Directive) have been adopted because of the abolition of internal frontiers between Member States (1 January 1993). Member States can no longer apply national measures of border control for goods transferred from one Member State to another.

Regulation 3911/92, which came into force in 1993, established a common export policy for cultural goods exported to countries outside the European Union.[74] This Regulation has been substantially amended

---

72 The general rule is that exports are unrestricted. See article 1 of the Council Regulation (EEC) 2603/69, 20.12.1969 (OJ 1969 L324/25) as amended on several occasions and repealed by Council Regulation 1061/2009 of 19 October, 2009 establishing common rules for exports (OJ 2009 L291/1). The situation became even more difficult for the protection of national treasures after 1 January 1993, when the Single European Market was completed and States lost the opportunity to carry out checks at national frontiers. States, of course, can still rely on article 36 TFEU for export controls (article 10 of Council Regulation 1061/2009), but practice has proved them to be rather ineffective.

73 See Commission Communication, n. 32 above, at para 2.

74 Council Regulation 3911/92 of 9 December 1992 on the export of cultural goods, OJ L 395/I (Corrigendum OJ L267/30, 19/10/1996), as amended by Council regulation 2468/96 of 16 December 1996 OJ L 335/9, Council Regulation

several times and recently codified by Regulation 116/09[75]. This policy is based on legal provisions and administrative co-operation[76] between Member States[77] and a Committee assists in the implementation of the Regulation.[78] Member States are also responsible for determining penalties for the infringement of the obligations deriving from the Regulation.[79]

In order for the European Union to achieve uniform export controls at its external borders, it first defined the categories of cultural goods that come within the scope of the Regulation. Secondly, it ensured that the export of cultural goods outside the customs territory of the European Union was subject to the presentation of an export licence.

3.2.2 The Notion of 'Cultural Goods'

For the purposes of the Regulation, the notion of 'cultural goods' is defined in article 1 and refers to all the items listed in Annex I to the Regulation. The Annex provides for categories of goods, whilst at the

---

974/2001 of 14 May 2001 OJ L 137/10 and Council Regulation 806/2003 of 14 April 2003 OJ L 122/1. Council Regulation 116/09 of 18 December 2008 on the export of cultural goods, OJL 39/1, 10.2.2009, has repealed Regulation 3911/92 as amended by the aformentioned Regulations. See also First Report from the Commission to the Council, the European Parliament and the Economic and Social Committee on the Implementation of Council Regulation (EEC) No 3911/92 on the export of cultural goods and Council Directive 93/7/EEC on the return of cultural objects unlawfully removed from the territory of a Member State (COM (2000) 325 final).

[75] Documents preceding the Regulation are the following: the proposal from the Commission (OJ No C 6, 11.1.1996, p.14), the opinion of the European Parliament (OJ No C 166, 10.6.1996, p.39) and the opinion of the Economic and Social Committee (OJ No C 97, 1.4.1996, p.28). See also Commission Communication, n. 32 above.

[76] Article 6 of the Regulation. See also Commission Communication, n.32 above.

[77] Council Regulation (EC) No 515/97 of 13 March 1997 on mutual assistance between the administrative authorities of the Member States and cooperation between the latter and the Commission to ensure the correct application of the law on customs and agricultural matters [Official Journal L 82 of 22.3.1997]. (Corrigendum, OJ L 288, 27.10.1998, p.55 (515/97), as amended by Council Regulation (EC) No 807/2003 of 14 April, 2003 (L 122/36, 16.5.2003) and Regulation (EC) No 766/2008 of the European Parliament and of the Council of 9 July, 2008 (L 218/48, 13.8.2008).

[78] Article 8 of the Regulation.

[79] Article 9 of the Regulation.

same time sets chronological and monetary bases.[80,81] As will be seen later, this listing is subject to certain exceptions when it comes to the issuing of licences. According to these exceptions, some of the goods listed in the Annex are excluded in certain instances from part of the Regulation's system (article 2(2)), whilst export of 'national treasures having artistic, historic or archaeological value', which do not come within the notion of 'cultural goods' as set out in the Regulation, are subject to the national law of the Member State of export (art. 2(4)). In other words national export controls apply.

If any of the cultural goods listed in the Regulation are also covered by a Member State's national legislation with regard to the protection of its cultural heritage (within the meaning of national treasures possessing artistic, historic or archaeological value in article 36 TFEU), the Member State at issue may refuse the export licence (art. 2(2)).

It is important to note that the definition of 'cultural goods' does not correspond exactly with the definition of 'national treasures' as this is enshrined in article 36 TFEU. As is set out in the Preamble to the Regulation (and repeated in article 1)[82] 'Annex I to this Regulation is aimed at making clear the categories of cultural goods which should be given particular protection in trade with third countries, but is not intended to prejudice the definition, by Member States, of national treasures within the meaning of article [36] of the Treaty'.

3.2.3 Export Licences

There is a uniform export licensing system for the aforementioned cultural goods, when they are to be exported to third countries. The export of such goods outside the customs territory of the European Union is subject to

---

[80] The criteria depending on the value of cultural objects, as these are found in the Annex to the Regulation, have been put there as a compromise between the 'exporting States' of the south and the 'importing States' of the north of Europe. Carducci, G. (1997), *La restitution internationale des biens culturels et des objets d'art volés ou illicitement exportés*, Paris: Librairie Générale de Droit et de Jurisprudence, 101.

[81] It is not certain who will assess these criteria. They will either be derived from the declaration of the possessor of the cultural object (which will more often be the case) or will be assessed by the issuing State. In the former case the issuing State will be in a position to make at least a posteriori examination in order to detect any cases of fraud.

[82] Article 1 provides that the term 'cultural goods' as this is defined in the Regulation is 'without prejudice to Member States' powers under article [36] of the Treaty'.

the presentation of an export licence (article 2(1)). This export licence is issued at the request of the person concerned (article 2(2))[83] and is valid throughout the European Union (article 2(3)).

A question which arises at this point is which Member State is competent to issue the export licence. The Regulation has tried to solve this problem by providing that the export licence is issued a) by the competent authority of the Member State in whose territory the cultural object in question *was lawfully and definitely located* on 1 January 1993, or b) thereafter, by the competent authority of the Member State in whose territory it is *located* following either i) lawful and definitive dispatch from another Member State, or ii) importation from a third country, or iii) re-importation from a third country after lawful dispatch from a Member State to that country.[84] The issuance of export certificates by the competent authorities of the Member State of the location of the cultural object should take into account the interests of other Member States and in particular those of the Member State of origin.[85]

---

[83] The 'person concerned' is rather a vague notion. It may be the proprietor of the object or its possessor. However, there is nothing in the Regulation to exclude a request made by a person interested in acquiring the object, exhibiting it and so on.

[84] It is interesting to note that the Regulation makes no reference to a 'State of origin'. This is a term that is highly charged in international law when it comes to the protection of cultural goods. It sets out specific (neutral) requirements which should be met for the issuing of a licence by a Member State linking the presence of the object to its territory.

[85] In the First Report from the Commission to the Council, the European Parliament and the Economic and Social Committee on the Implementation of Council Regulation (EEC) No 3911/92 on the export of cultural goods and Council Directive 93/7/EEC on the return of cultural objects unlawfully removed from the territory of a Member State (COM (2000) 325 final) it was stated that

> It is extremely rare for the Member State in question to actually carry out checks or request information from the Member State of origin of the object. Generally speaking, the authorities confine themselves to issuing the export licence, on the basis of documentation which is incomplete or has no connection whatsoever with the object and do not carry out detailed checks as to its provenance and legality. It should be noted that, to overcome the difficulties described above, two Member States – France and Italy – have introduced respectively the following arrangements:
>
> —A system of prior application to the competent authorities of the other Member States in order to ensure, before an export licence is issued, that the object was lawfully removed from another Member State;
>
> —The introduction of an accompanying document which allows the object in question to freely circulate, once the origin of the object and the credibility

Although the Regulation's system was set to apply to all cultural goods listed in the Annex, there is an exception introduced by article 2(2). In the aforementioned cases the Member State which is to issue the export licence need not do so (on the basis that an export licence is not required) for archaeological objects more than 100 years old which are of limited archaeological or scientific interest, and provided that they are not the direct product of excavations, finds or archaeological sites within a Member State, and that their presence on the market is lawful. This exception is the result of pressure exercised by the UK, which calculated that, by reason of its flourishing market in art, any other provision would cost it the issuance of about 200,000 export licences each year.[86]

Regulation 752/93[87] sets out in detail the uniform export licensing system for the cultural goods provided in Regulation 116/09 including rules governing the drawing up, issuing and use of the necessary forms.[88] It also provides for specimen licences to this end.[89] There are three types of licences for the export of cultural goods:[90] a) the standard licence, b) the specific open licence and c) the general open licence.[91]

The standard licence is normally used for each export subject to

---

of the requester have been checked; this also improves the national administration's ability to react when it subsequently receives an application for an export licence (First Report, pp.8–9).

It is also interesting to note that only the Netherlands and the UK have rejected export licence applications on the grounds that no proof of the legality of the transfer of the cultural object from another Member State has been forthcoming (First Report, p.12).

86 Margue, T. (1993), 'L'exportation des biens culturels dans le cadre du Grande Marché', *Revue du Marché Unique Européen*, 2, 93, note 107.

87 Commission Regulation 752/93 of 30 March, 1993 laying down provisions for the implementation of Council Regulation 3911/92 on the export of cultural goods, as amended by Commission Regulation (EC) 1526/98 of 16 July 1998, OJ L 201/ 47 and Commission Regulation (EC) 656/2004 of 7 April 2004, OJ L104/50 (Corrigendum, OJ L 203, 8.6.2004, p.14 (656/2004)). These Regulations (as all regulations) are binding in their entirety and directly applicable in all Member States.

88 The export licence must be accompanied by an export declaration which needs to be presented to the customs offices authorised to complete the formalities for the export of cultural goods.

89 See Annex to the Regulation.

90 The open licences have been introduced by EC Regulation 1526/98, OJ L 201/47 of 17 July 1998.

91 The system of 'open licences' was introduced by Commission Regulation 1526/98 of 16 July 1998, OJ L 201/47.

Regulation 116/09.[92] However, it is up to each Member State concerned to decide whether or not to issue a standard licence or a specific or general open licence, in cases where the conditions for all three licences are met.[93] In other words, the standard licence applies to all exports of cultural goods, whilst Member States may choose to issue a specific or general open licence instead to the cases provided for specifically in the 752/93 Regulation.

Standard licences are issued for each consignment of cultural goods, which may vary from a single cultural object to a number of cultural objects. But yet again it is up to the Member State concerned to determine whether one or more export licences are required for consignments which comprise more than one cultural object.[94]

Standard licences should not be issued for more than twelve (12) months from their date of issue. If they refer to temporary exportation, they may specify the time limit within which the cultural goods must be re-imported into the issuing Member State. If a licence expires without having been used, the holder must immediately return the sheets in his possession to the issuing authority.[95]

A specific open licence is used in cases of repeated temporary export of a particular cultural good by a person or organisation,[96] whilst a general open licence is issued in cases of temporary export of cultural goods that form part of the permanent collection of a museum or other institution.[97] These licences are usually valid for a period of five years. The

---

[92] Regulation 116/2009 (former Regulation 3911/92) is referred to in the 753/93 Regulation (as amended) as the 'Basic Regulation'.

[93] As these conditions are set out in Articles 10 and 13 of the Regulation.

[94] Article 4 of the Regulation.

[95] Article 9 of the Regulation.

[96] Article 10 (Specific open licences): '1. Specific open licences may be issued for a specific cultural good which is liable to be temporarily exported from the Community on a regular basis for use and/or exhibition in a third country. The cultural good must be owned by, or be in the legitimate possession of, the particular person or organisation that uses and or exhibits the good.

2. A licence may only be issued provided the authorities are convinced that the person or organisation concerned offers all the guarantees considered necessary for the good to be returned in good condition to the Community and that the good can be so described or marked that there will be no doubt at the moment of temporary export that the good being exported is that described in the specific open licence.

3. A licence may not be valid for a period that exceeds five years.'

[97] Article 13 (General open licences): '1. General open licences may be issued to museums or other institutions to cover the temporary export of any of the goods that belong to their permanent collection that are liable to be temporar-

open licences may be revoked at any time if the conditions under which they were issued are no longer met. In this case the Commission shall be informed immediately in order for it to inform the other Member States. Member States may introduce whatever reasonable measures they deem necessary in their national territory to monitor the use of their own open licences[98].[99]

3.2.4 Critical Points

The Regulations enacted for the establishment of a uniform export licensing system of cultural goods to third countries do not affect (even after the abolition of internal frontiers, 1.1.1993) national measures for the protection of 'national treasures' within the meaning of article 36 TFEU, put in place both for the export of those treasures to other Member States as well as to third countries.

The export licences will be issued by the country of location of the cultural object even if the object originates from another Member State, provided that it was lawfully dispatched by that Member State. The Regulation, as seen above, has set some rules in this respect.[100] Although it is not expressly provided, it is however assumed that in this case the applicable law will be the law of the State issuing the export licence. This State will decide whether it should issue a licence or not for a particular cultural object. In fact it will have to decide whether an object a) falls within the scope of the Regulation (and is listed in Annex I), or b) whether or not it belongs to that category of objects for which an export licence is not required by reason of the fact that they are of limited archaeological

---

ily exported from the Community on a regular basis for exhibition in a third country.

2. A licence may only be issued if the authorities are convinced that the institution offers all the guarantees considered necessary for the good to be returned in good condition to the Community. The licence may be used to cover any combination of goods in the permanent collection on any one occasion of temporary export. It can be used to cover a series of different combinations of goods either consecutively or concurrently.

3. A licence may not be valid for a period that exceeds five years'.

[98] Article 2 of the Regulation.

[99] Council Regulation 515/97 (OJ L82/1 of 22.3.1997) applies with regard to mutual assistance in customs matters. (Corrigendum, OJ L 288, 27.10.1998, p.55 (515/97), as amended by Council Regulation (EC) No 807/2003 of 14 April, 2003 (L 122/36, 16.5.2003) and Regulation (EC) No 766/2008 of the European Parliament and of the Council of 9 July, 2008 (L 218/48, 13.8.2008)).

[100] Article 2(2) of Regulation 116/09.

or scientific interest (and they are not the direct product of excavations, finds and archaeological sites within a Member State and that their presence on the market is lawful),[101] or c) that though listed in Annex I (or not listed at all but coming under the 'national treasures' definition as the State itself understands it) an export licence could be refused altogether. In this latter category Member States shall apply their own export policies according to their national laws or international conventions to which they are parties.[102]

According to the above, the Member State concerned should apply its own export policies with regard to the particular cultural good, the result of which will be binding for all Member States of the European Union. It is, however, possible that some cultural objects are transferred to 'export paradises' where their export to third countries will be easier. Of course in order to do that they need at least to prove that the object was permanently ('definitively' to use the wording of the Regulation) and lawfully located in that State before 1 January 1993. This requirement will not be hard to prove since in most cases it will only be on the basis of a declaration of the possessor of the object (i.e.'the person concerned'). It is easy to imagine that 'source States' and 'import States' will not share the same views on the conditions for issuing export licences, no matter how uniform the system aims to be.

When it comes to cultural objects falling within its scope which do not require an export licence, the Regulation is not very helpful either. Three cumulative conditions have to be met in this respect: a) the object must be of limited archaeological or scientific interest, b) it must not be the direct product of excavations, finds and archaeological sites within a Member State, and c) its presence on the market must be lawful. To begin with it is not entirely clear when an archaeological object (more than 100 years old) is the indirect rather than direct product of excavations, finds and archaeological sites. Furthermore, when an object is found lawfully on the market, it is not clear what the relevant market is and how a judgment as to the 'lawfulness' of the object has been arrived at. Lastly, it seems that it will be up to the issuing State to decide all three criteria. That means that

---

101 All these conditions (three in number) should be met cumulatively.

102 It seems that Member States cannot invoke this provision (article 2(2)) in order to refuse an export licence and allow the export of the cultural good to third countries but only in cases where such refusal is accompanied by stricter national measures for the protection of the cultural object at issue.

interested parties are very likely to choose 'export paradises' in order to secure the export of a cultural object.[103]

In the next section we shall examine the extent to which the EU Regulations on export of cultural goods to third countries are compatible with Directive 7/93/EEC on the return of cultural objects unlawfully removed from the territory of a Member State.

3.3 DIRECTIVE 7/93 ON THE RETURN OF CULTURAL OBJECTS UNLAWFULLY REMOVED FROM THE TERRITORY OF A MEMBER STATE

3.3.1 Scope and Aim of the Directive

Directive 7/93[104] forms part of the measures that the European Union adopted with regard to the protection of cultural treasures in view of

---

[103] In the First Report from the Commission to the Council, the European Parliament and the Economic and Social Committee on the Implementation of Council Regulation (EEC) No 3911/92 on the export of cultural goods and Council Directive 93/7/EEC on the return of cultural objects unlawfully removed from the territory of a Member State (COM (2000) 325 final) it was stated that most Member States took the view that the Regulation had a positive impact on the protection of cultural goods, if only by virtue of raising awareness among the various parties and a growing realisation of the importance of protecting national cultural heritage (First Report, p.7).

[104] Council Directive 93/7/EEC of 15 March 1993 on the return of cultural objects unlawfully removed from the territory of a Member State (OJ L 74/74, 27.3.1993), amended by Directive 96/100/EC of the European Parliament and of the Council of 17 February 1997 amending the Annex to Directive 93/7/EEC on the return of cultural objects unlawfully removed from the territory of a Member State (L 60/59, 1.3.1997) and Directive 2001/38/EC of the European Parliament and of the Council of 5 June 2001 amending Council Directive 93/7/EEC on the return of cultural objects unlawfully removed from the territory of a Member State (L 187/43, 10.7.2001). See also First Report from the Commission to the Council, the European Parliament and the Economic and Social Committee on the Implementation of Council Regulation (EEC) No 3911/92 on the export of cultural goods and Council Directive 93/7/EEC on the return of cultural objects unlawfully removed from the territory of a Member State (COM (2000) 325 final) and Second Report from the Commission to the Council, the European Parliament and the Economic and Social Committee on the application of Council Directive 93/7/EEC on the return of cultural objects unlawfully removed from the territory of a Member State (COM (2005) 675 final). Third Report from the Commission to the Council, the European Parliament and the European Economic and Social

the abolition (since 1 January 1993) of physical checks at the European Union's internal borders[105].[106] This protection was drafted on two levels. First, a system was created according to which uniform controls at the external borders of the European Union would prevent the export of cultural goods. This would be done on the basis of the issuance of export certificates by the competent authorities of the Member State of the location of the cultural object, which would take into account the interests of other Member States, in particular of the Member State of origin. In order for such a system to work effectively, the scope of cultural objects coming under Regulation 116/09 had been defined on the basis of a list of objects annexed to the Regulation. Second, a complementary system was created under Directive 7/93, which provides for mechanisms and procedures for the restoration of cultural objects unlawfully removed from a Member State. Thus, on the one hand the Regulation sets up a mechanism which prevents cultural goods from being taken out of the European Union without export controls, whilst on the other hand the Directive sets up a mechanism according to which, when a cultural object has been unlawfully removed from its country of origin (which is also a European Union Member State), it can be restored.

These measures were deemed necessary because of the fact that, at least at that stage, not many Member States had ratified the 1970 UNESCO Convention on the Means of Prohibiting and Preventing the Illicit Import, Export and Transfer of Ownership of Cultural Property, whilst no Member State had ratified the 1985 Convention of the Council of Europe on offences relating to cultural property.[107] However, even the ratification of those Conventions was not regarded as adequate in order to protect Member States' national treasures.[108] In addition to that, international conventions

---

Committee on the application of Council Directive 93/7/EEC on the return of cultural objects unlawfully removed from the territory of a Member State (COM (2009) 408 final), http://ec.europa.eu/enterprise/policies/single-market-goods/files/resolution-cultural-goods_en.pdf.

105 See in this respect Communication from the Commission on the protection of national treasures possessing artistic, historic or archaeological value: needs arising from the abolition of frontiers in 1992, COM (89) 594 final (22 November 1989).

106 The Directive is also applicable in the Member States of the European Free Trade Association that are parties to the Agreement on the European Economic Area.

107 There are six signatories (no ratifications) to the Convention of the Council of Europe 1985 on offences relating to cultural property: Greece, Italy, Cyprus, Turkey, Portugal and Liechtenstein.

108 See First Report, n. 104 above, p.3.

in the area of protection of cultural property, which would follow the enactment of the Regulation and the Directive, could allow grounds for the application of the relative European Union legislation. Indeed, the 1995 Unidroit Convention on Stolen or Illegally Exported Cultural Objects provides for such a disconnection clause, whereby European Union Member States that ratify the Convention can give precedence to the European Union legislation in their relations with other Member States.

The Directive does not apply to the import, export or transfer of cultural goods between Member States. It only enables Member States to secure the return to their territory of cultural goods that have been removed from their territory in breach of national or European Union law. The role of the Commission is vital in the application of the Directive and is set out in articles 16 and 17.[109]

Before we go any further we need to clarify that the Directive does not in itself protect national treasures. It only introduces the extraterritorial enforcement of national protection measures between member states. It does not preclude civil or criminal proceedings for the restitution and return of cultural objects (article 15), nor does it change national rules on movable property whether these are substantive rules or conflicts provisions (article 12).[110]

---

[109] Article 16:

'1. Member States shall send the Commission every three years, and for the first time in February 1996, a report on the application of this Directive.
2. The Commission shall send the European Parliament, the Council and the Economic and Social Committee, every three years, a report reviewing the application of this Directive.
3. The Council shall review the effectiveness of this Directive after a period of application of three years and, acting on a proposal from the Commission, make any necessary adaptations.
4. In any event, the Council acting on a proposal from the Commission shall examine every three years and, where appropriate, update the amounts indicated in the Annex, on the basis of economic and monetary indicators in the Community'.

Article 17: 'The Commission shall be assisted by the Committee set up by Article 8 of Regulation (EEC) No 3911/92. The Committee shall examine any question arising from the application of the Annex to this Directive which may be tabled by the chairman either on his own initiative or at the request of the representative of a Member State'.

[110] K Siehr, 'The Protection of Cultural Heritage and International Commerce', (1997) 6 *IJCP* 304, at 313–14.

3.3.2 The Notion of 'Cultural Objects'

There does not seem to exist any particular reason why the Regulation refers to 'cultural goods' whilst the Directive refers to 'cultural objects'. Both 'cultural goods' and 'cultural objects' seem to be interchangeable terms and form part of the wider term found in article 36 TFEU 'national treasures possessing artistic, historic or archaeological value'.[111] The reason for that is that the two former terms found in the Regulation and Directive do not exhaust the notion of 'national treasures', whilst they leave Member States' discretion to define their own national treasures intact.[112] Yet, there may be cases where a cultural good qualifying under the Regulation or Directive may not qualify under a Member State's national legislation. For that very reason, although the two legal instruments (the Regulation and the Directive) were designed to work together and contain the same list of qualifying cultural objects (i.e. the same Annex), the definition of 'cultural objects' found in the Directive is considered to be wider when compared to that of the Regulation. In fact, for the purposes of the Regulation, it suffices for a cultural good to be included in one of the categories of the Annex. According to the Directive, 'cultural objects' are the objects a) classified under national law or administrative procedures[113] (before or after their unlawful removal

[111] The adjective 'national' does not imply that the treasures belong to the State. Rather it refers to the special connection (cultural, historical or other) of the cultural good to that particular State. This is also derived by article 15 of the Directive which provides that the owner of a cultural good may also bring proceedings (other than the special proceedings provided in the Directive) for cultural goods that are stolen. The Directive places the emphasis on the 'national treasures' themselves and not on their ownership status since it distinguishes between cultural goods that belong to the State and cultural goods that belong to private parties or institutions. See S. Vrellis, 'The drafts of Unidroit and the EC Directive: a parallel set back?' in *Archaeological Heritage: Current trends in its Legal Protection*, international conference (Athens, 26–27 November 1992), Athens: P. Sakkoulas, 1995, 171, at 180.

[112] This is expressly provided for in both legal instruments.

[113] There are various definitions of the concepts involved. To give but one example, the concept of a collection is defined in a footnote in the Annex of the Directive by reference to the Court of Justice's judgment in Case 252/84 (*Collector Guns v. Hauptzallamt Koblenz* [1985] E.C.R. 3387). There, the Court said that 'collectors' pieces within the meaning of heading No. 99.05 of the Common Customs Tariff are articles which possess the requisite characteristics for inclusion in a collection, that is to say, articles which are relatively rare, are not normally used for their original purpose, are the subject of special transactions outside the normal trade in similar utility articles and are of high value'.

from the territory of a Member State) as 'national treasures possessing artistic, historic or archaeological value' (within the meaning of article 36 TFEU) and b) either belonging to one of the categories listed in the Annex to the Directive or forming an integral part of public collections listed in the inventories of museums, archives or libraries' conservation collections or the inventories of ecclesiastical institutions. Member States may extend their obligation to return cultural objects to cover additional categories of objects to those listed in the Annex (article 14(1)).

The notion of 'public collections' is defined in the Directive as collections that are the property of a Member State, local or regional authority within a Member State or an institution situated in the territory of a Member State and defined as public in accordance with the law of that Member State, and that are the property of, or are significantly financed by, that Member State or a local or regional authority.[114]

According to the above, if an object does not qualify as a national treasure, even if this object belongs to one of the categories of the Annex or forms an integral part of a public collection, it cannot be claimed back by its country of origin because the underlying purpose, which is the protection of the Member States' cultural heritage, is missing. In any case it would be illogical to return to a Member State a cultural object that could then be freely exported from it.[115]

---

[114] Article 1(1): 'For the purposes of this Directive: 1. "Cultural object" shall mean an object which:

—is classified, before or after its unlawful removal from the territory of a Member State, among the "national treasures possessing artistic, historic or archaeological value" under national legislation or administrative procedures within the meaning of Article [36] of the Treaty, and

—belongs to one of the categories listed in the Annex or does not belong to one of these categories but forms an integral part of:

—public collections listed in the inventories of museums, archives or libraries' conservation collection.

For the purposes of this Directive, "public collections" shall mean collections which are the property of a Member State, local or regional authority within a Member States or an institution situated in the territory of a Member State and defined as public in accordance with the legislation of that Member State, such institution being the property of, or significantly financed by, that Member State or a local or regional authority;

—the inventories of ecclesiastical institutions'.

[115] A study by the Commission on the traceability of cultural objects, finalised at the end of 2004, has shown that 'the system of cultural heritage protection in each country consisted of a core of national treasures which could not permanently leave the national territory, a second category comprising cultural objects that required national authorisation in order to be transferred abroad and a third category consisting of all the objects which could move freely without controls because

The same could not apply in relation to the Regulation by reason of the fact that no uniform export system could exist if the notion of cultural objects were not common for all Member States. As we saw in the relevant chapter, there may be cases where this uniformity is not absolute (i.e. where archaeological objects more than 100 years old are of limited archaeological or scientific interest, provided that they are not the direct product of excavations, finds or archaeological sites within a Member State and their presence on the market is lawful).

If one compares the two definitions, one can easily reach the conclusion that there may be instances where a cultural object may be accompanied by an export certificate, whilst at the same time the export can be prevented on the basis of article 4(4) of the Directive as having been unlawfully removed from the territory of a Member State.

It is not all cultural objects which can be claimed back by their countries of origin (if these countries are European Union Member States). It is only cultural objects that have been *unlawfully removed* from the territory of a Member State (article 2)[116] on or after 1 January 1993 (article 13).

A cultural object is unlawfully removed from a Member State if its removal was in breach a) of this State's laws on the protection of national treasures, or b) Regulation 116/2009, or c) was not returned at the end of a period of lawful temporary removal or any breach of any other condition governing such temporary removal.[117] That means that it is both national and European Union law that is taken into account. This translates into the fact that the Directive adopts a system of return which is based on the Member States' public law provisions regarding both the protection and export of cultural goods (to the extent that these provisions are compatible with article 36 TFEU).

It is interesting to note at this point that the Directive does not dis-

---

of their relative lack of importance in cultural terms. The study concluded that traceability was possible only for cultural objects belonging to the core category and, to a lesser extent, the second category which could be removed on the basis of a licence' (Second Report, n. 105 above, 5–6).

[116] Article 2: 'Cultural objects which have been unlawfully removed from the territory of a Member State shall be returned in accordance with the procedure and in the circumstances provided for in this Directive'.

[117] Article 2(2): '"Unlawfully removed from the territory of a Member State" shall mean:

—removed from the territory of a Member State in breach of its rules on the protection of national treasures or in breach of Regulation (EEC) No 3911/92, or

—not returned at the end of a period of lawful temporary removal or any breach of another condition governing such temporary removal.'

tinguish between stolen and illegally exported cultural objects (as international legal instruments do) since in both instances there is a clear provision for the return of these objects to their country of origin. Theft and illegal export, as well as other cases, all form a breach of a Member State's rules on the protection of its national treasures. In that sense the emphasis is placed on the protection of treasures without delving into the unlawful act in question[118].[119]

3.3.3 Return

Article 2 of the Directive is unequivocal. 'Cultural objects which have been unlawfully removed from the territory of a Member State shall be returned in accordance with the procedure and in the circumstances provided for in this Directive'.

No other form of restitution is provided for in the Directive but return, i.e. the physical return of the cultural object to the territory of the requesting Member State (article 2(5)). This provision is very important in the sense that the European Union recognises the fact that no other form of restitution can serve the purpose of an efficient protection of a Member State's cultural heritage but physical return to that Member State. This is a concept which has been adopted and promoted both by the 1954 Hague Convention and its Protocols as well as by the 1970 UNESCO Convention. It is also a vital principle of the 1995 Unidroit Convention and underlies all international instruments in the field of protection of cultural property. The values inherent in a cultural object cannot be met or substituted by a monetary sum or an equivalent object. On top of that, taking away the object from the bad faith possessor can also work as a deterrent to illegal practice. That is not always the case, though, with the paying of compensation.

Return can take place only under the circumstances which are specifically provided for in the Directive. The system followed for the return is a blend of administrative co-operation and judicial proceedings and is initiated at the application of the requesting Member State. 'Requesting Member State' means the Member State from whose territory the cultural object has been unlawfully removed (article 2(3)). 'Requested Member

---

[118] In this way the Directive avoids problems of defining theft and illegal export.

[119] The cultural goods coming under the scope of the Regulation and the Directive can be considered as constituting a form of *res extra commercium europeum*. Siehr, K. (1995), 'Vereinheitlichung des Mobiliarsachenrechts in Europa, insbedondere im Hinblick auf Kulturgueter', *RABELSZ*, 454, at 464.

State' is the Member State in whose territory the cultural object (which was unlawfully removed from the territory of the requesting Member State) is located (article 2(3)).

The aforementioned proceedings are proceedings which can be brought only by Member States and not by individuals or institutions. However, these proceedings are without prejudice to any civil or criminal proceedings that may be brought, under the national laws of the Member States, by the requesting Member State and/or the owner of the cultural object that has been stolen (article 15). According to the Directive there may be cases where parallel proceedings are initiated. That means proceedings brought both by the requesting Member State and by the dispossessed owner against the possessor or holder of the cultural object in question. The latter proceedings (those by the dispossessed owner) may be brought before the court of a Member State other than the Member State where the former proceedings (those by the requesting Member State) are brought. Although in theory the two legal suits have a different petition (i.e. the former aims at the return of the cultural object to the territory of the requesting Member State, whilst the latter aims at the recognition of the claimant's ownership and the return of the cultural object to him/her irrespective of the place he/she intends to keep the object), this in practice may create problems (which, however, the *lex fori* may solve).[120]

3.3.3.1 Administrative co-operation

Member States should appoint the central authorities to carry out the tasks provided for in the Directive.[121] These authorities shall in particular:

1. seek, upon application by the requesting Member State, the specific cultural object, which has been unlawfully removed from its territory,

---

[120] De Ceuster, J. (1993), 'Les règles communautaires en matière de restitution de biens culturels ayant quitté illicitement le territoire d'un état membre', *Revue du Marché Unique Européen*, 2, 33, at 51, note 49.

[121] Article 3: 'Each Member State shall appoint one or more central authorities to carry out the tasks provided for in this Directive. Member States shall inform the Commission of all the central authorities they appoint pursuant to this Article. The Commission shall publish a list of these central authorities and any changes concerning them in the C series of the Official Journal of the European Communities'.

List of the central authorities nominated by the Member States to deal with the return of cultural objects unlawfully removed from a Member State, published pursuant to Article 3 of Council Directive 93/7/EEC. Official Journal C 180 of 26.06.2001; Official Journal C 130 of 04.06.2003; Official Journal C 212 of 21.08.2004; Official Journal C123 of 24.05.2006.

identifying the possessor and/or holder. The application must include all information needed to facilitate this search, with particular reference to the actual or presumed location of the object;

2. notify the Member State concerned, where the cultural object is found in their own territory and there are reasonable grounds for believing that it has been unlawfully removed from the territory of another Member State;[122]
3. enable the competent authorities of the requesting Member State to check that the object in question is a cultural object, provided that the check is made within 2 months of the notification referred to above;
4. take any necessary measures, in co-operation with the Member State concerned, for the physical preservation of the cultural object;
5. prevent, by the necessary interim measures, any action to evade the return procedure;
6. act as an intermediary between the possessor and the requesting Member State with regard to return. In fact, they can facilitate the implementation of an arbitration procedure, in accordance with the national legislation of the requested State, provided that the requesting State and the possessor or holder give their formal approval. The arbitration will not impinge on the requesting Member State's right to turn to the Courts, as this right is provided in article 5 of the Directive.

If the check under point 3 is not made within the stipulated period (two months of the notification), the requesting Member State cannot claim from the requested Member State to carry out the obligations under points 4 and 5 (article 4).[123]

3.3.3.2 Judicial proceedings

The Directive also provides (articles 5 to 12) for the initiation of return proceedings and their implementation. Administrative co-operation is

---

[122] As regards notification of discoveries, in the First Report, n. 105 above, it is stated that 'legal problems may arise when a Member State, following the receipt of a notification, announces that the object has been unlawfully removed from its territory but does not avail itself of the return procedure, allowing the statutory period to elapse. In such cases, it is impossible for the notifying State to grant a licence for export to a third country' (First Report, p.15).

[123] Between 1993 and 2003 only ten cases were dealt with successfully on the basis of administrative co-operation between Member States without recourse to legal proceedings. See First Report, *ibid*, p.22; and Second Report, n. 105 above, p.11; and Third Report, n. 105 above, p.8 (according to which only eight legal actions for the return of cultural objects pursuant to article 5 of the Directive were instituted during the period 2004–2007).

without prejudice to these return proceedings. According to the former, Member States must provide in their implementing legislation that the requesting Member State may initiate, before the competent court in the Member State in which the cultural object unlawfully removed from the requesting Member State is located, proceedings against the possessor (or the holder, if the possessor is not known or cannot be found) with the aim of securing the return of the object. These proceedings may only be brought, however, where the document initiating them is accompanied by a) a document describing the requested object and stating that it is a cultural object and b) a declaration by the competent authorities of the requesting Member State that the cultural object has been unlawfully removed from its territory (article 5).

According to the Directive, proceedings may be initiated against the 'possessor' or 'holder' of the cultural object. The 'owner' is not mentioned. If, however, one reads the definitions provided for in the Directive, one realises that the notions of 'possessor' and 'holder' do not always correspond to the terms known in the various Member States' legal traditions. In fact, these notions blur to a certain extent the triptych 'owner-possessor-holder'. According to the definitions found in the Directive, 'possessor' is the person who is physically holding the cultural object on his own account (article 2(6)), whilst 'holder' is the person who is physically holding the cultural object for third parties (article 2(7)). In other words, the notion of 'possessor' comes very close to that of 'owner'. The reason for that is that it is irrelevant for the purposes of the Directive whether the possessor of a cultural good also qualifies as its owner. On the contrary, this could create obstacles as to the effective application of the Directive in the sense that a considerable number of the cultural objects that are claimed back are considered to be the requesting Member State's property, whilst the legal status of the person possessing them is not clear. Therefore what is of importance is that proceedings are initiated against the person (or institution) which possesses (either on his own account or for third parties)[124] the object and for that very reason it is easier for that person to be located and brought to the court. That means that proceedings can start as soon as one finds out where the object is located without needing to establish the legal relation between that person and the object. Ownership issues are addressed by the Directive once return has taken place. Specifically it is provided that ownership of the cultural object after return is governed by the law of the requesting Member State (article 12).

---

124 In the latter case he/she would be referred to as 'holder'.

The Directive provides to a certain extent for both a rule on conflict of jurisdictions and a rule on conflict of laws. According to the first rule (article 5), the court of the requested Member State is competent, whilst matters of recognition and enforcement of judgments are left to the law of the State where the judgment is to be executed. The applicable law is provided for only in relation to matters of ownership of the cultural object after it is returned to the requesting State. In this case the *lex originis* applies, i.e. the law of the requesting Member State (article 12). Yet, the Directive does not make clear whether it is the substantive law of the requesting State that applies or its private international law. If it is the latter, it is not certain that it is the substantive law of the requesting State which is applicable in the case at issue. For the purpose of deciding the validity of an illegal transaction, the law of the country where the object was situated may also be applicable.[125]

Once the preconditions set by the Directive[126] are met, the court has to order the return of the cultural object in question (article 8).[127]

3.3.4 Time Limitations

The return proceedings provided for in the Directive may not be brought more than *one year* after the requesting Member State became aware of the location of the cultural object and of the identity of its possessor (or holder). And they cannot be brought under any circumstances more than *30 years* after the object was unlawfully removed from the territory of the requesting Member State, except in the case of objects forming part of public collections and ecclesiastical goods where these goods are subject to special protection arrangements under national law (article 7(1)). In this case there is a longer time limit of *75 years*, except in Member States where

---

125 Carducci, G., n. 80 above, 150. See also Siehr, K. (1996), 'Kultursgüterschutz innerhalb der Europäischen Union', *ZvglRWiss,* 170, at 186.

126 Including the ones provided in articles 7 and 13 as well as the fact that it is a cultural object within the meaning of Article 1(1) and has been removed unlawfully from national territory.

127 Between 1993 and 1998 the judicial proceedings of article 5 of the Directive were made use of in one case only. Finland brought a case before the High Court in London. In the end the return was not effected by a court order but as a result of an amicable settlement reached between the good faith possessor and the Finnish authorities before the British Court delivered its judgment. Between 1999 and 2003 there were three cases of legal return proceedings (two cases between Greece and Germany and one between France and Belgium. Greece and France were the requesting States). First Report, p.14, and Second Report, and Third Report, n. 105 above, p.11.

proceedings are not subject to a time limit or in the case of bilateral agreements between Member States laying down a period exceeding 75 years. If such proceedings have been initiated the requesting Member State has to inform the requested Member State.[128] If at the time of initiation of the return proceedings the cultural object's removal (from the national territory of the requesting Member State) is no longer unlawful, such return proceedings cannot be brought (article 7(2)).

The Directive was met with criticism by many countries because of its short time limitations, especially the time limitation of one year, calculated from the moment one becomes aware of the location of the cultural object and of the identity of its possessor. Time limitations in the Directive look particularly short when compared to the 1995 Unidroit Convention.[129] In the Third Report on the application of the Directive (2009) almost all Member States were in favour of extending the period of one year during which return proceedings can be initiated. Some Member States, including Italy, had requested a lengthening of this time limit to three years[130] in order for it to meet the 1995 Unidroit Convention provisions.[131].[132] It seems that the time is now ripe for such an amendment and that the European Union is heading towards this direction.

---

[128] Article 6: 'The central authority of the requesting Member State shall forthwith inform the central authority of the requested Member State that proceedings have been initiated with the aim of securing the return of the object in question. The central authority of the requested Member State shall forthwith inform the central authorities of the other Member States'.

[129] The 1995 Unidroit Convention provides for three years in comparison to the one year of the Directive and for 50 years in comparison to the 30 years of the Directive.

[130] See also European Parliament Resolution, n. 131 below, p.3.

[131] See First Report, p.15 and Second Report, p.9, and Third Report, n. 105, above, p.4. See also the European Parliament Resolution of 12 June 2001 on the First Report (OJ C 53 E of 28 February 2002, p.125, at 7), which states that the European Union should, within its sphere of jurisdiction, attach greater importance to combating illegal trade in cultural objects and that the Commission had a central role to play. Parliament therefore called for: a) a change in the one-year time limit laid down in Directive 93/7/EEC, b) a campaign in the 15 Member States and the 10 candidate countries, aimed at raising public awareness of the adverse effects of the illegal trade in cultural objects, c) comprehensive, public catalogues of all such objects in the possession of public or private institutions, foundations or bodies, and d) a Green Paper on illegal trade in cultural objects and specific proposals at Community level to combat it.' (Second Report, n. 104 above, Section 3.2). And the Third Report, n. 105 above, p.5.

[132] Italy and France took also the view that the starting point of this corresponding period should also be clarified. Third Report, p.5, n. 104 above.

The Directive applies only to cultural objects unlawfully removed from the territory of a Member State on or after 1 January 1993 (article 13). This cut-off date is rather unfortunate given the fact that the illegal trade in art was flourishing during the decades that preceded it. However, Member States may, if they wish, accept requests for the return of cultural objects unlawfully removed from the territory of other Member States prior to 1 January 1993 (article 14(2)). So far it is only Greece that has made use of this provision.

3.3.5 Compensation

According to the Directive, in cases where the competent court orders the return of a cultural object, it should also award compensation as it deems fair in relation to the circumstances of the case, to the possessor,[133] if it is satisfied that he/she exercised due care and attention in acquiring the object. In the case of a donation or succession, the possessor shall not be in a more favourable position than the person from whom he acquired the object by that means. This compensation should be paid by the requesting Member State upon the return of the object (article 9).

The wording of this provision is rather vague and raises a number of issues: a) how will this compensation be calculated? Would it be the price paid for the acquisition of the object, the market price, its real value or part of it, and so on? Is it also equivalent to the 'just compensation' and/or the 'fair and reasonable compensation' provided for in the Unidroit Convention? The word 'fair' in the Directive is not used as a description of the compensation (or a definition of it) but rather as a term denoting a reasonable payment made subject to the circumstances of the case. b) In order for the possessor to be awarded compensation, he/she should have exercised 'due care and attention'. It is clear that the term 'due care' is not a legal term recognisable by the legal traditions of Member States. In fact it is a term which is not equivalent to 'good faith' or 'due diligence'. It is rather an empirical term which needs to be approached by the dictates of common sense. c) In order for the court to award damages it has to be 'satisfied' as to the due care exercised by the possessor. The Directive does not seem to require proof of this.[134]

---

133 The holder is not entitled to compensation. So, if the possessor is unknown and cannot be located the holder will have to return the object to the requesting State without receiving any compensation.

134 It should be noted here that according to article 9 of the Directive the burden of proof is governed by the law of the requested Member State.

'*Fair compensation*': Although it is not expressly provided in the Directive, the compensation due should be fair. That means that it is for the national court to decide what constitutes fair compensation, bearing in mind at all times the particular circumstances. Questions to be considered include: how he/she acquired the object, from whom (a reputed dealer or other), in what conditions (auction, proper sale or other), what was the expertise of the possessor, what was the price paid and how did that compare to its real value and so on. In this respect, the discussion on fair compensation in the chapter on the 1995 Unidroit Convention is relevant.[135] The assumption that the Directive means 'fair compensation' is also indicated by the fact that article 11 makes direct reference to it,[136] distinguishing it from the expenses provided in article 10 (expenses incurred in implementing a decision ordering the return of the cultural object). These expenses, together with any costs of measures taken by the requested Member State (in co-operation with the Member State concerned) (article 4(4)) for the physical preservation of the cultural object, are to be borne by the requesting Member State.

Payment of fair compensation and of the aforementioned expenses does not prejudice the requesting Member State's right to take action with a view to recovering those amounts from the persons responsible for the unlawful removal of the cultural object from its territory (article 11).

'*Due care*': This derives from the First Report of the Commission to the Council that the use by some Member States of the expression 'good faith' in implementing their laws as a precondition for compensating the possessor, was used wrongly since the Directive makes reference only to 'due care and attention'.[137] However, neither in the Directive nor in the Report is the content of this term defined. It can, however, be inferred that this term finds itself one step short of the requirement of good faith acquisition. In other words, the former requirement is more lenient compared to the latter. This becomes even clearer when it is coupled with the fact that the court needs only to be 'satisfied' of the existence of due care and attention and there is no direct reference to any proof. The national courts will have difficulties in applying this requirement (as is also proven by the Report) since there exists no reference to what they already know in their laws. Even if this is not spelt out expressly, it is very likely that, in practice, national courts will look for good faith acquisition in order to

135 See 2.2.4.4 and 2.2.5.4.
136 It also mentions article 9 as such.
137 First Report, n. 104 above, p.13.

award compensation. It is unfortunate that the Directive has not taken these difficulties into account, as well as the fact that the precondition of good faith would have been received more easily by Member States, both because of their legal traditions and also by reason of the fact that these terms have been more or less adopted by international instruments in the area.[138]

'*Satisfied*': The appearance in the text of the word 'satisfied' is rather curious when it comes to a court judgment which in fact corresponds to the application of hard core law. The word 'satisfied' is again a word alien to Member States' legal traditions even when we refer to preliminary measures, where the full extent of proof is not required in order for an interim measure to be awarded. The award of compensation is by no means a preliminary measure and therefore proof should have been required. Again in this case Member States will experience difficulties in applying this requirement. It is also unfortunate that there is no provision for the reversal of the burden of proof as is the case with the 1995 Unidroit Convention. The Directive, by providing that 'the burden of proof shall be governed by the legislation of the requested Member State', in fact makes reference to classic civil law provisions of Member States according to which the burden of proof lies with the dispossessed owner. The particularities of the illegal removal of cultural goods from their place of origin have not been taken into account properly and from that point of view the Directive is retrogressive in comparison to the 1995 Unidroit Convention. In reality it will be very difficult for the dispossessed owner to prove that the possessor did not exercise due care and attention in acquiring the object. It is very likely that a standard document accompanying an antiquity bought by a dealer, certifying that it is not the outcome of an illegal transaction or export from its country of origin, would suffice for the award of compensation. That means that there will scarcely be any cases where compensation will not be awarded, and Member States, not in a position to afford this compensation, will be deprived of the cultural object at issue.

---

138 Article 7(b)(ii) UNESCO Convention 1970 provides for 'just compensation to an innocent purchaser or to a person who has valid title to that property'. Article 4 of the 1995 Unidroit Convention provides for the 'payment of fair and reasonable compensation provided that the possessor neither knew nor ought reasonably to have known that the object was stolen and can prove that it exercised due diligence when acquiring the object'.

3.3.6 Final Remarks

The Directive is, without doubt, a step in the right direction. It has a preventive effect and discourages the unlawful removal of objects within the EU.[139] However, it has proven to be a rather timid step, which has not reflected the trends of the time, as incorporated in various legal instruments.[140] Also in practice it is rarely applied either in the context of administrative co-operation or in the exercise of return proceedings. In fact only eight legal actions for the return of cultural objects (pursuant to article 5) have been launched between 2004 and 2007. The reason for that seems to be the administrative complexity, the cost of applying the Directive, the limited scope of the cultural objects covered by it and those covered only from 1st January 1993 afterwards as well as the short one year deadline for initiating recovery proceedings. In practice Member States prefer to use civil or criminal proceedings, whilst proposals have been submitted to the Commission with regard to including new categories of goods such as certain contemporary works of art and amending the current financial thresholds.[141]

The 1995 Unidroit Convention followed the Directive chronologically but it came quite soon afterwards. Since then the Directive has not been updated to accommodate developments in the area. From that point of view, it is not a very bold legal instrument with short time limitations and with limited scope as regards the cut-off date for cultural objects coming within its remit. It is positive, however, that it leaves to Member States the discretion to extend both the scope of the cultural objects covered as well as the cut-off date of 1 January 1993. Presently the Commission has undertaken to consider the amendment of the Directive. It has noted

---

[139] See European Parliament Resolution, n. 104 above, p.2.

[140] In the First Report, n. 104 above, it was stated that 'several States have noted that the Directive has had a major impact in raising awareness among the various parties concerned about the protection of cultural goods in the various Member States. One notable result is the fact that professional circles in certain States have organised themselves more effectively and, where appropriate, adopted codes of good practice' (First Report, p.13). In the Second Report, n. 105 above it was stated that 'the Member States regard the Directive as a useful instrument for recovering national treasures removed unlawfully from their territory from 1993 onwards. However, their comments reveal that: a) the Directive is not often applied; there is insufficient co-operation between the competent authorities at Community level; and the central authorities lack data on the actual application of the Directive' (Second Report, pp.6–7). Similar conclusions are found in the Third Report, n. 104 above, p.8–9.

[141] See the Annex of the Third Report, n. 105 above, and p.6 seq.

though that although there is a consensus among Member States that the one-year period is too short and should be extended, such consensus does not exist with regard to extending the list of cultural goods in the Annex or amending the financial thresholds.[142]

The Directive was meant to work as a complementary instrument to the Regulation. Yet, this was not fully attained because, as was shown above, the definitions of cultural goods found in the two instruments are not always compatible and they may create difficulties in practice.

The Directive (as well as the Regulation) should work coherently with the 1970 UNESCO Convention and the 1995 Unidroit Convention. The 1970 UNESCO Convention, which had already been ratified by a number of Member States before the enactment of European Union legislation, was taken into account by a European Union Communication and a European Union Report[143] and it is now ratified and implemented by the majority of Member States. One could argue that it is in the light of this Convention that European Union legislation is approached. The same cannot be said for the 1995 Unidroit Convention, which follows European Union legislation chronologically, and which has not been ratified by many Member States (and also provides for a disconnection clause with regard to European Union legislation for those Member States which want to use it in their intra-community relations). This is also perhaps the reason why so many and such important differences are contained in the two legal instruments. Yet, the 1995 Unidroit Convention reflects the international trends in the area and (as was mentioned earlier in the book with regard to a Swiss case) together with the 1970 UNESCO Convention, both represent a common inspiration as well as an expression of international public order in force or in formation.[144]

---

142 Third Report, p.8–9, n. 104 above.

143 See Communication from the Commission, n. 105 above. See also First Report, n. 104 above.

144 Prott, L.V. (1997), *Commentary on the UNIDROIT Convention on Stolen and Illegally Exported Cultural Objects 1995*, Leicester: Institute of Art and Law, 87.

4. Other sources of regulation and the role of international organisations

4.1 INTRODUCTION

Apart from the legal instruments discussed in previous chapters, there are also other sources of regulation in the area of protection of cultural property, known as 'soft law'. Such sources are essentially the codes of ethics, which regulate the activities of certain professions or agents in the areas of trade in art, collection and museology (also known as codes of practice or codes of conduct),[1] the Recommendations (or Guidelines)[2] and the Memoranda of Understanding (MoUs)[3].[4] Recommendations are issued by UNESCO and other international organisations in the field, whilst MoUs are drafted between interested parties in relation to a particular subject (usually between Member States). Recommendations form an important set of guidelines with an enhanced significance due to the fact that they are adopted in intergovernmental meetings or intergovernmental conferences. Recommendations on the restitution of cultural property are usually adopted in the course of the Intergovernmental Committee for Promoting the Return of Cultural Property to its Countries of Origin or its Restitution in Case of Illicit Appropriation (ICPRCP). MoUs are, in most cases, agreed between states and have less weight when compared to an agreement, in the sense that they are not enforceable in the way contracts

[1] There is a difference between codes of ethics and codes of conduct but this difference is a slight one. The former refer to general principles underlying their practices whilst the latter refer to the practices which incorporate these principles.

[2] There can also be other forms of soft law, such as 'Declarations', 'Understandings' and so on. Their weight differs according to the circumstances of their adoption (which bodies have adopted them, how many participating States there were and so on). Yet, declarations and understanding usually take place unilaterally by one or more States. If there are more States, then we refer to common Declarations or Understandings.

[3] Bilateral agreements between States constitute hard law legal instruments, i.e. they provide for binding and enforceable legal provisions.

[4] The soft law provisions of the European Union as usually issued in the form of Communications.

or agreements are. They only form a common understanding between parties in writing, which parties can bring to an end if they wish. They work as a gentlemen's agreement.

The aforementioned documents do not contain provisions that are legally binding but they do reflect the trends and practices in the area as well as promoting and encouraging them.

UN Resolutions[5] also belong to the same category. In general they are not binding on Member States but when they are dealing with general norms of international law, acceptance by a majority vote constitutes evidence of the opinions of the governments in the widest forum of the expression of such opinions and provides a basis for the progressive

---

[5] See, for example, Resolutions 3026 A (XXVII) of 18 December, 1972, 3148 (XXVIII) of 14 December, 1973, 3187 (XXVIII) of 18 December 1973, 3391 (XXX) of 19 November, 1975, 31/40 of 30 November 1976, 32/18 of 11 November, 1977, 33/50 of 14 December, 1978, 34/64 of 29 November 1979, 35/127 and 35/128 of 11 December, 1980, 36/64 of 27 November, 1981, 38/34 of 25 November, 1983, 40/19 of 21 November 1985, 42/7 of 22 October, 1987, 44/18 of 6 November, 1989, 46/10 of 22 October, 1991, 48/15 of 2 November, 1993, 50/56 of 11 December, 1995, 52/24 of 25 November, 1997, 54/190 of 17 December, 1999, 56/8 of 21 November, 2001, in which 2002 was proclaimed as the United Nations Year for Cultural Heritage, 56/97 of 14 December, 2001, 58/17 of 3 December, 2003 and 61/52 of 4 December, 2006 on the return or restitution of cultural property to the countries of origin, 64/78 of 7 December, 2009, Resolution 2003/29 of 22 July, 2003, entitled 'Prevention of crimes that infringe on the cultural heritage of peoples in the form of movable property', Resolution 2004/34 of 21 July, 2004, entitled 'Protection against trafficking in cultural property', and the Economic and Social Council (ECOSOC) Resolution 2008/23 of 24 July 2008 on the 'Protection against trafficking in cultural property'. See also the model treaty for the prevention of crimes that infringe on the cultural heritage of peoples in the form of movable property, which was adopted by the Eighth United Nations Congress on the Prevention of Crime and the Treatment of Offenders and welcomed by the General Assembly in its Resolution 45/121 of 14 December, 1990 (Eighth United Nations Congress on the Prevention of Crime and the Treatment of Offenders, Havana, 27 August–7 September 1990: report prepared by the Secretariat (United Nations publication, Sales No. E.91.IV.2), Chapter I, section B.1) and the Report of the Secretary-General on protection against trafficking in cultural property (E/CN.15/2006/14). See also the statement of the then Greek Minister G. Voulgarakis in the UN General Assembly, Official Records, 61st session, doc. A/61/PV.65 of 4 December, 2006, p.9, who refers to the trends in the area: '[I]n recent years, a new wind of optimism has appeared on the horizon. Increasingly, museums recognize the moral obligation to conform with ethical codes in their acquisition policies. In the international scientific community, including archaeologists, voices have been raised for the protection of cultural heritage worldwide. Demands have been expressed that the looting of archaeological sites and the illicit trafficking in antiquities must stop'.

development of the law and the speedy consolidation of customary rules.[6]

The codes of ethics (or codes of conduct) set out the professional standards by which those working in the profession should operate. They are drawn up by professional associations and adhered to by their members. Agreeing to abide by a code of ethics is a way of demonstrating your commitment to acting professionally (upholding the high standards in your profession), fairly, ethically, honestly and within the law. The contents of codes of ethics vary depending on the professional body and its focus. However they all contain references to acting with due diligence and preventing the trade in illicit and stolen cultural property. Codes of ethics can also be drafted by international organisations, as is the case with UNESCO.[7]

Codes of ethics do not replace the law. Rather they complement it (particularly if they are developed because the existing law in the area is inadequate, as historically was the case), or supplement it (if the law in the area is ambiguous or unclear). They usually provide for the minimum ethical rules in the area. If these codes (like other standard-setting legal instruments such as the United Nations General Assembly Resolutions and the UNESCO Recommendations, which do not have the degree of compulsion of law, but have nonetheless an important hortatory and guidance role) are endorsed by substantial practice, they often reach a degree of moral constraint not inferior to that of law.[8] Codes of ethics may

---

[6] Brownlie, I. (2003), *Principles of Public International Law*, 6th edn., Oxford University Press, 14–15.

[7] According to Schmidt, F. (1992), 'Codes of Museum Ethics and the Financial Pressure on Museums', *Museum Management and Curatorship*, 11 (2), 257, at 259, ethical codes a) represent an ideal and are morally binding on the members of the group; b) give some professional orientation and recommendations for action, and provide guidance especially in ethically ambiguous situations; and c) clarify the ethical responsibility of the organisation. See also Gerstenblith, P. (2003), 'Acquisition and Deacquisition of Museum Collections and the Fiduciary Obligations of Museums to the Public', *Cardozo Journal of International and Comparative Law*, 11.

[8] O'Keefe, P.J. (1994), *Feasibility of an International Code of Ethics for Dealers in Cultural Property for the Purpose of More Effective Control of Illicit Traffic in Cultural Property*, UNESCO Document CLT-94/ WS/11, Paris: UNESCO, 99, http://unesdoc.UNESCO.org/images/0009/000985/098554Eo.pdf. 45–6. On page 53 O'Keefe refers to *1956 UNESCO Recommendation on International Principles Applicable to Archaeological Excavations* that has become an important international standard for the conduct of archaeological excavations and a model for national legislation in this area,<http://unesdoc.UNESCO.org/images/0009/000985/098554Eo.pdf>. See also Palmer, N. (2003), 'Litigation, the

provide sanctions against members who infringe them or do not respect them. The most important sanction is the dismissal of the member from the association.

Codes of ethics are very popular at the moment because they are considered to demonstrate high standards of operation by the associations which abide by them and it is easier and faster to draft and adopt them. This is usually done by the interested parties themselves as part of a self-regulation process, in order to reconcile the private interests of their professional group with those of the public. Also the procedures for their drafting and adoption are flexible, fast and more cost-effective compared to the bureaucracy required for the drafting, adoption and policing of legislation. In addition, codes can easily be updated to accommodate developments in the area. However, due to the fact that codes of ethics are not compulsory and enforceable in court, they are not usually respected and their influence is limited to exhortation and guidance, the content of which is rarely made public.[9] Codes are also not always respected because most of them do not contain sanctions and their language is vague and therefore subject to multiple interpretations. Even if expulsion of a member takes place, this member can continue trading outside the association. On top of that, codes do not apply to all professionals in the area but only to those that are members of the association. That means that these members are exposed to competition from outside traders who do not respect any ethical standards and in the art trade, traders who do not belong to professional associations outnumber those who do.

The drawing up of codes does not constitute a new practice. They date back many years. One of the oldest and most well-known codes of ethics is the Hippocratic Oath taken by all doctors. The first national organisation to publish a code of ethics seems to have been the German Museums Association.[10] In 1918 it published a code of behaviour concerning art dealing and the public (*Grundsätze über das Verhalten der*

Best Remedy?', in The Permanent Court of Arbitration/Peace Palace Papers, *Resolution of Cultural Property Disputes*, Kluwer Law International, 265, at 281 where he refers to the fact that 'a code may in due course set the legal standard for professional conduct within its particular field, rendering a violation of it a breach of legal duty. In time the code itself may become the source of the duty'.

[9] According to McKenzie, S.R.M. (2005), *Going, Going, Gone: Regulating the Market in Illicit Antiquities*, London: Institute of Art and Law, 106, and a sample of traders he has interviewed, it can be concluded that codes of ethics are not respected.

[10] Even before that, in 1898, there was a publication on the subject of museum ethics in the field of entomology, Bateman, J.A. et al. (1981), 'Towards a Code of Ethics in Museums', London: *Museum Professionals Group Transactions*.

Mitglieder des Deutschen Museumsbundes gegenüber dem Kunsthandel und dem Publikum[11]). Since then a number of codes have appeared. The American Association of Museums published its first code of ethics in 1925 (*Code of ethics for museum workers*). Neither code has ever been used.[12] It was not until many years later that this practice became

---

[11] Klausewitz, W. (1985), 'Museumsethik in Deutschland', *Museumskunde*, 50 (1), 2.

[12] See in this respect van Mensch, P. (1992), *Towards a methodology of museology* (Ph.D thesis, University of Zagreb), <http://www.otherspace.co.uk/students/simoncaslaw/thesis/standards/PVMethicsPhD.htm >, 'In the United States a number of controversies – mainly concerning de-accessioning practices – brought museum ethics on the agenda again in the beginning of the 1970s. A special issue of Museum News on ethics was published in 1974, containing a reprint of the 1925 code (Museum News 52, 1974, 9). In the same year a study group was set up to review and update the old code. A new code of ethics (or rather a statement on ethics) was published in 1978 (*Museum ethics*). In the same period a number of other national codes were adopted: New Zealand and the United Kingdom 1977, Canada and Israel 1979, Australia 1982. It is remarkable that apart from Africa all big English speaking countries developed a national code at the same time. It shows a rather intense circulation of ideas favoured by a common language and a common professional "culture". On an international level the most important development was the (unanimous) adoption of the *Code of professional ethics* at the 15th General Conference of the International Council of Museums in Buenos Aires, Argentina (1986). The initiative was taken at the 11th General Assembly (Copenhagen 1974). The resulting code was mainly based on the codes of the American Association of Museums (1978) and the Museums Association (1983). The leading role taken by the United States is also evident from the set of specially targeted codes for different professional specialisations within the museum. The first of such codes concerned the work of conservators. In 1963 the American Group of the International Institute for Conservation published its *Standards of practice and professional relationships for conservators*, also known as the Murray Pease Report. The code was adapted in 1967 and published by the then American Institute for Conservation as a Code of ethics for art conservators. A new version was published in 1980 as *AIC Code of ethics and standards of practice*. Other specialised codes of the American Association of Museums cover the work of the curator (adopted in 1983), the educator (adopted in 1989), the registrar (adopted in 1984), and the public relations officer (adopted in 1984). In 1982 the Museum Store Association adopted its code of ethics for museum shops. In 1991 a *Code of ethics for museum training* was proposed by the ICOM International Committee for the Training of Personnel. One activity that at an early stage attracted attention in the discussion on museum ethics is collecting. In 1971 the International Council of Museums published its *Ethical Acquisition Code*, which has since been incorporated in the *ICOM Code of Professional Ethics* of 1986. Collecting archaeological material was already the subject of certain rules formulated at the International Conference on Excavations in 1937. In 1976 a code of ethics and standard of research performance was adopted by the US Society of Professional Archaeologists. In these documents collecting policies and especially the danger

widespread. Many professional organisations or other bodies active in the field of cultural property have adopted codes of ethics.[13] Most of these codes deal with handling unprovenanced and undocumented cultural objects. However, very few of them deal with the issue of stolen artefacts. This is perhaps so because there is a belief that the law deals with this issue more adequately. All codes urge professionals to pay due diligence when

---

of destroying evidence by incompetent excavation were extensively dealt with. Collecting in the field of anthropology was dealt with in a statement on ethics issued by the American Anthropological Association (1971). Professional codes in the field of collecting are especially important since national legislation usually focuses on export of cultural property rather than transfer and import. Despite the fact that archaeology took the lead in collecting natural history, the first category of museums to formulate a specific code of ethics was art museums. In 1966 a special code of behaviour for art museums was adopted by the Association of Art Museum Directors in the United States (updated in 1972 and 1981). In 1980 an ethics code was discussed among the ICOM International Committee of Natural History Museums. In the same year ethics appeared as the central issue at the meeting of the ICOM International Committee of Ethnography Museums. Whereas the ethnography committee returned to the theme regularly, ethics seems to have disappeared from the agenda of the natural history committee. The University Museum of the University of Pennsylvania was perhaps the first to adopt an individual museum ethical policy (Boylan, P. (1976), 'The Ethics of Acquisition: The Leicestershire Code', *Museums Journal* 75 (4), 165. at 169). Its *1st April 1970 Declaration* was to be followed by policy statements of many other museums. Most of them focused on the ethics of acquisition, based on the 1970 UNESCO convention'.

[13] Amongst the societies which have adopted codes of ethics are also the following: Antiquarian Booksellers Association (ABA), The Association of Art and Antique Dealers (LAPADA), British Antique Dealers' Association (BADA), British Code of Practice for the Control of International Trading in Works of Art, Society of Fine Art Auctioneers (SOFAA), Society of London Art Dealers (SLAD), International Association of Dealers in Ancient Art (IADAA), International League of Antiquarian Booksellers (ILAB), La Confédération Internationale des Négociants en Oeuvres d'Art (CINOA), The American Association of Museums (AAM), Association of Art Museum Directors (AAMD). The AAMD on 28 June 2004 published a Report on Acquisition of Archaeological Materials and Ancient Art (http://www.aamd.org) which amongst other things provides that 'II.A.2. Member museums should make a concerted effort to obtain accurate written documentation with respect to the history of the work of art, including import and export documents. Member museums should always obtain the import documentation when the work of art is being imported into the US in connection with its acquisition by the museum'. See also the Asociación Española de Gestores de Patrimonios Culturales (AEGPC), Canadian Museums Association (CMA), Conselho Federal de Museologia (Brazil), The Museums Association (UK), Museums Australia, Inc., The Netherlands Museums Association/De Nederlandse Museumvereniging, Pacific Islands Museums Association (PIMA), South African Museums Association.

they trade or acquire cultural objects. They also play an important informative and educational role and they can raise awareness among both the public and professionals. If they also apply for a considerable length of time they may be held to reflect the legal standards in the area, which may also be taken into account by courts in deciding, for example, cases of due diligence and care, either directly by adopting the standards of the code or indirectly by deciding, for example, whether the buyer has purchased the object from a 'reputable dealer'.[14] Two of the most important codes in the area are the UNESCO International Code of Ethics for Dealers in Cultural Property (1999) and the International Council of Museums' (ICOM) Code of Professional Ethics (2004). Their respective provisions for handling illegal cultural goods will be examined.

4.2 CODES OF ETHICS

4.2.1 UNESCO International Code of Ethics for Dealers in Cultural Property (1999)

The UNESCO International Code of ethics for dealers in cultural property was a project started in 1987[15] and was considered in subsequent sessions by the UNESCO intergovernmental Committee for Promoting the Return of Cultural Property to its Country of Origin or its Restitution in Case of Illicit Appropriation. It was finally adopted by the same Committee at its 10th Session in January 1999 and endorsed by the 30th General Conference of UNESCO in November 1999.[16]

---

[14] See, for example, *Autocephalous Greek-Orthodox Church of Cyprus v. Goldberg & Feldman Fine Arts Inc.* 917 F.2d 278 (1990).

[15] It was in 1987 (the 5th Session of the UNESCO intergovernmental Committee for Promoting the Return of Cultural Property to its Countries of Origin or its Restitution in Case of Illicit Appropriation) that the Code was requested.

[16] It could be argued that this Code accords with article 5(e) of the UNESCO Convention 1970 which provides that 'to ensure the protection of their cultural property against illicit import, export and transfer of ownership, the States Parties to this Convention undertake, as appropriate for each country, to set up within their territories one or more national services, where such services do not already exist, for the protection of the cultural heritage, with a qualified staff sufficient in number for the effective carrying out of the following functions: . . . (e) establishing, for the benefit of those concerned (curators, collectors, antique dealers, etc.) rules in conformity with the ethical principles set forth in this Convention; and taking steps to ensure the observance of those rules'.

According to article 1,[17] which is a key clause in the Code, 'Professional traders in cultural property will not import, export or transfer the ownership of this property *when they have reasonable cause to believe* it has been stolen, illegally alienated, clandestinely excavated or illegally exported'.[18] The notion of 'professional traders' includes dealers and auctioneers who belong to a professional body (or association) that has adopted the Code.

The meaning of the phrase 'have reasonable cause to believe', which is also found later in other articles, is not very clear. According to UNESCO's commentary on the code[19] this phrase should be read

> as requiring traders to investigate the provenance of the material they handle. It is not sufficient to trade in material without questions and consider that the clause only comes into effect when somehow evidence of the illegality is fortuitously acquired. To satisfy this requirement, traders must *actively examine the background of the objects they are offered and question the person concerned.* They must pay attention to any circumstances likely to arouse suspicions, such as a demand for a large payment in cash or too low a price asked for a valuable object. That having been said, if there are no suspicious circumstances and questions are answered satisfactorily, traders can proceed with the transaction having no reasonable cause to believe there is any illegality.[20]

Therefore only verbal reassurances on the part of the seller do not suffice. The trader needs to examine the background of an object actively and documents from the seller concerning the provenance of the object should also be produced. If no documents are produced or the history of the object is not established in any other way, then the trader has reasonable cause to believe that the object at issue is not being offered for sale legally. Any suspicious circumstances should urge the trader to be even more diligent.[21]

---

[17] Interesting in this respect is also the Preamble to the Code which sets out that 'They acknowledge the world wide concern over the traffic in stolen, illegally alienated, clandestinely excavated and illegally exported cultural property and accept as binding the following principles of professional practice intended to distinguish cultural property being illicitly traded from that in licit trade *and they will seek to eliminate the former from their professional activities*' (emphasis added).

[18] Emphasis added.

[19] http://portal.UNESCO.org/culture/en/ev.php-URL_ID=13095&URL_DO=DO_TOPIC&URL_SECTION=201.html. See also O'Keefe, P.J. (2001), 'Unlawful traffic in cultural heritage and UNESCO', *Media & Arts Law Review*, 139–41 and McKenzie, S.R.M., n. 9 above, 106.

[20] Emphasis added.

[21] This approach is also confirmed by O'Keefe's analysis with regard to the British/CINOA Code, n. 8 above, at 36, where it is set out that 'the phrase "reasonable cause to believe" gives the dealers/auctioneers a measure of appreciation.

This article covers almost all cases of illicit trafficking of cultural objects and it can be argued that its scope is wider than that of the 1970 UNESCO or the 1995 Unidroit Conventions. In fact, it covers theft, clandestine excavation and illegal export as well as objects which have been illegally alienated in any way according to the law of their country of origin or export, depending on the case.

Article 2 provides that 'a trader, who is acting as agent for the seller, is not deemed to guarantee title to the property, provided that he makes known to the buyer the full name and address of the seller. A trader, who is himself the seller, is deemed to guarantee to the buyer the title to the goods'. This phrasing is not very helpful. One could think that it suffices for a trader, provided he only acts as an agent, to make known to the buyer the full name and address of the seller, leaving it up to the buyer to find out whether the seller has title to the goods and check this title diligently. The dealer only guarantees title if he is the seller himself. However, if this provision is coupled with article 1,[22] one comes to the conclusion that, although title may not be guaranteed in the former case, the trader should nevertheless not pursue the transaction if he has reasonable cause to believe that the good has been stolen, illegally alienated, clandestinely excavated or illegally exported. Although he does not himself import, export or transfer the ownership in the good, as provided in article 1, he is still involved in the transaction. Therefore he is under an obligation not to proceed with the transaction. If this were not the right interpretation then one could easily evade obligations under the code, if one only acted as an agent and not as a seller. That means that the code would carry no weight whatsoever since most dealers act as agents and not sellers. It is only rarely that they act in the latter capacity. Apart from that it is for this very reason that article 1 precedes article 2. Article 1 aims to set the general principle under which dealers should act in all cases of trading.

This interpretation is reinforced by articles 3 and 4, which provide that a trader who has reasonable cause to believe that an object a) has been the product of a clandestine excavation, or has been acquired illegally or dishonestly from an official excavation site or monument, or b) has been illegally exported, will not assist in any further transaction with that

It probably does not require them to see documentation and to note any blatant defects or missing documents. It is questionable, however, whether it requires a more diligent testing of these documents'.

22 Article 1: 'Professional traders in cultural property will not import, export or transfer the ownership of this property when they have reasonable cause to believe it has been stolen, illegally alienated, clandestinely excavated or illegally exported'.

object, except (in the former case) with the agreement of the country where the site or monument exists[23] or (in the latter case) the object has been exported. A trader who is in possession of the object, where that country seeks its return within a reasonable period of time, will take all legally permissible steps to co-operate in the return of that object to the country of origin or export respectively.[24] That means that dealers have to act in compliance with the laws of the country of origin of a cultural object which has been the product of a clandestine excavation or has been acquired illegally from an official excavation of a monument. They have to act in compliance with the laws of the country of export for an object which has been exported illegally from a State. Even if the trader acts as an agent and even if he knows that the seller has title to the object, he still should not pursue the transaction. Being the seller of such an object himself is, of course, out of the question. If the object is found to be illegal in the sense described above, the dealer who is in possession of it (and not necessarily the owner) has to return it. This requirement complies with the principles of the 1995 Unidroit Convention. It is important to note here that the requirement of title should not be confused with the fact that an object is the product of illicit trade according to article 1 of the Code. A trader should not attempt to evade his obligations under article 1 by reason of the existence of a title.[25] This is also the reason why a trader is not obliged to guarantee title to the property if he acts as an agent. The notion of title is not linked to a particular jurisdiction although it is thought to refer to the country concerned.

Article 5 is even wider in scope and operates in the same spirit. It provides that 'Traders in cultural property will not exhibit, describe, attribute, appraise or retain any item of cultural property with the intention of promoting or failing to prevent its illicit transfer or export. Traders will not refer the seller or other person offering the item to those who may perform such services'. Again this article requires positive action on the part of the dealer, given the fact that he should not only refrain from promoting the illicit transfer or export of an object, but he should actively prevent such transfer or export. Prevention may include notifying the authorities or the

---

23 If the country of origin cannot be known with certainty then the trader has to co-operate with all possible countries.

24 Whether compensation is payable in the case at issue is a matter to be settled between the buyer and the seller and not a matter of relevance to the dealer unless he is the seller himself. That means that the dealer cannot use this issue as an excuse for non-compliance with article 4. See O'Keefe, n. 8 above, at 61.

25 *Ibid* at 37 and 42.

State of origin or export and so on. Failure to do so constitutes a violation of the provisions of the Code.

This Code of Ethics is adopted by dealers on a voluntary basis. It does not replace the law; it complements it. If it is adhered to by a dealer, this dealer also adheres to the sanctions provided for. According to article 8, violations of the Code are rigorously investigated by a body that is nominated by the participating dealers. A person (or a government) aggrieved by the failure of a trader to adhere to the principles of this Code may lay a complaint before that body and they will investigate it. Results of the complaint and the principles applied are made public. The procedures applicable to the judging of complaints are left to the body itself to determine.

The Code complies with the basic principles found in the 1970 UNESCO Convention on the Means of Prohibiting and Preventing the Illicit Import, Export and Transfer of Ownership of Cultural Property and the 1995 Unidroit Convention on Stolen or Illegally Exported Cultural Objects. This is especially evident in the fact that if illegal cultural objects are found by the dealer, he has to co-operate in the return of those objects. No other kind of restitution is provided for in the Code. It is by means of this Code that UNESCO assists dealers to adhere to high standards, allowing them to be diligent in ascertaining the provenance of the cultural objects they trade in. These standards are under the scrutiny of their fellow dealers, who will press for compliance. Dealers abiding by this Code are usually recognisable by the public. When cultural objects are bought from such a dealer it is presumed that the dealer is reputable and has acted diligently. Therefore if a claim for return of an object arises (e.g. under the 1995 Unidroit Convention) the buyer, having purchased the object from such a dealer, will most probably be considered to be a *bona fide* buyer, entitled to compensation.

The Code also relies on other national dealers' codes (even though it is an improvement on them) including those of Switzerland, the United Kingdom, France and the Netherlands as well as the code of the World Association of Art and Antique dealer associations (CINOA).[26] It is also close to the ICOM Code of Professional Ethics. The latter, however, has been updated since then to include developments in the area.

---

[26] See UNESCO's official Commentary on the Code: http://portal.UNESCO.org/culture/en/ev.php-URL_ID=13095&URL_DO=DO_TOPIC&URL_SECTION=201.html.

4.2.2 The International Council of Museums (ICOM) Code of Professional Ethics (2004)

ICOM first published a document entitled *Ethics of Museum Acquisitions* in co-operation with UNESCO in 1971. This document later inspired a Code of Ethics. The ICOM Code of Professional Ethics was adopted for the first time on 4 November 1986 and was revised twice in 2001 and 2004. In 2001 it was also given a new title: the ICOM Code of Ethics for Museums.[27] It provides for minimum standards of professional practice and performance for museums and their staff and is obligatory for all its members. In fact it is said to reflect principles generally accepted by the international museum community, as well as reasonable public expectations of the museum profession, given that legislation in the area is variable. The Code sets out eight basic principles which are then developed.[28] However, we shall focus only on the principles and provisions which concern the illicit traffic of cultural objects.

Some of the basic provisions concerning the lawful acquisition of cultural objects are found under principle 2 of the Code (museums that maintain collections hold them in trust for the benefit of society and its development) and under the subtitle 'Acquiring Collections'. Rule 2.2 provides that 'No object or specimen should be acquired by purchase, gift, loan, bequest, or exchange unless the acquiring museum is satisfied that a valid title is held. Evidence of lawful ownership in a country is not necessarily valid title'.[29] Under this rule the onus is on museums to check and investigate not only the lawful ownership of a cultural object, but also all

---

[27] The ICOM Code of Professional Ethics was adopted unanimously by the 15th General Assembly of ICOM in Buenos Aires (Argentina) on 4 November 1986. It was amended by the 20th General Assembly in Barcelona (Spain) on 6 July 2001, retitled ICOM Code of Ethics for Museums, and revised by the 21st General Assembly in Seoul (Republic of Korea) on 8 October 2004.

[28] The eight general principles set out in the ICOM Code are the following: 1. Museums preserve, interpret and promote the natural and cultural inheritance of humanity; 2. Museums that maintain collections hold them in trust for the benefit of society and its development; 3. Museums hold primary evidence for establishing and furthering knowledge; 4. Museums provide opportunities for the appreciation, understanding and promotion of the natural and cultural heritage; 5. Museums hold resources that provide opportunities for other public services and benefits; 6. Museums work in close collaboration with the communities from which their collections originate as well as those they serve; 7. Museums operate in a legal manner; 8. Museums operate in a professional manner.

[29] According to ICOM's Code of Ethics Glossary 'Legal Title' means 'Legal right to ownership of property in the country concerned. In certain countries this may be a conferred right and insufficient to meet the requirements of a due

documentation and circumstances concerning its title, before they accept it into their collections. Verbal or written reassurances by a seller, dealer or donor do not suffice under this provision. It is also important that the requirement of title is not linked to a particular jurisdiction. That means that a legal title in general is required and not a title in any country where the transaction could be facilitated. This requirement is supported by Rule 2.3 which provides that 'Every effort must be made before acquisition to ensure that any object or specimen offered for purchase, gift, loan, bequest, or exchange has not been illegally obtained in or exported from, its country of origin or any intermediate country in which it might have been owned legally (including the museum's own country). Due diligence in this regard should establish the full history of the item from discovery or production'.[30]

The requirement of investigation is reinforced by Rule 2.4 which provides that 'Museums should not acquire objects where there is reasonable cause to believe their recovery involved the unauthorised, unscientific, or intentional destruction or damage of monuments, archaeological or geological sites, or species and natural habitats. In the same way, *acquisition should not occur if there has been a failure to disclose the finds to the owner or occupier of the land, or to the proper legal or governmental authorities*'.[31] According to the above provisions no link in the chain should be missing so that the full history of the cultural object can be documented. It is also important that a museum cannot allege a) that since destruction of a monument has taken place anyway the acquisition of the object by the museum no longer does any harm and b) an object is a gift or donation so they are under no obligation to investigate its provenance.[32] The legality required of a cultural object should be beyond any reasonable doubt. This conclusion should be drawn by the interpretation of the phrase 'reasonable cause to believe' as explained above in relation to the UNESCO Code of Ethics.

The above requirements are very stringent given the fact that with

---

diligence search' whilst 'Valid Title' means 'Indisputable right to ownership of property, supported by full provenance of the item from discovery or production'.

[30] According to the ICOM Code of Ethics Glossary 'Due Diligence' means 'The requirement that every endeavour is made to establish the facts of a case before deciding a course of action, particularly in identifying the source and history of an item offered for acquisition or use before acquiring it'.

[31] Emphasis added.

[32] According to the ICOM Code of Ethics Glossary 'Provenance' means 'The full history and ownership of an item from the time of its discovery or creation to the present day, from which authenticity and ownership is determined'.

certain objects it is very difficult to establish all the links in the chain of their provenance. There may be objects which have been in public collections for a long time, having been passed from generation to generation. Some objects may have been repeatedly exhibited in publicly accessible places, such as public institutions and museums, with no claim made for their recovery. It would be absurd to allege that such objects cannot be acquired for museums for the public benefit. This is the reason why the Code provides for reservations to the general principle applicable to those cases.

In fact Rule 2.9 provides that 'The acquisition of objects or specimens outside the museum's stated policy should only be made in exceptional circumstances. The governing body should consider the professional opinions available to them, and the views of all interested parties. Consideration will include the significance of the object or specimen including its context in the cultural or natural heritage, and the special interests of other museums collecting such material. However, even in these circumstances, objects without a valid title should not be acquired'. This provision is complemented by Rule 3.4 according to which 'In exceptional cases an item without provenance may have such an inherently outstanding contribution to knowledge that it would be in the public interest to preserve it. The acceptance of such an item into a museum collection should be the subject of a decision by specialists in the discipline concerned and without national or international prejudice'. According to these provisions acquisition of a cultural object which breaches the museum's policy can only take place in 'exceptional circumstances'. Precisely what these circumstances are, is not defined in the Code but it is made clear they should form the exception rather than the rule. Given the fact that only the least/minimum requirements are provided for in the Rule, the requirements for such an acquisition are at least the following: a) exceptional circumstances apply, b) there is valid title to the object, c) the significance of the object is taken into account, including its context in cultural or natural heritage and the special interests of other museums collecting such material. If it is not a significant object, which complements a collection particular to the museum, then this object should not be considered for acquisition. It should also not be considered for acquisition if, though a significant object, it complements another museum's collection. The museum should always try to establish the provenance of an object. An unprovenanced object may be acquired in 'exceptional cases' (wording which differs from that of 'exceptional circumstances' though not in a clear way) if it offers such an inherently outstanding contribution to knowledge that it would be in the public interest to preserve it. There is a danger that this provision could work as a Trojan horse to the general principle of non-acquisition of unprovenanced cultural objects. However, it is clear from the wording of the Code that the provision does not apply to all objects but to such objects in exceptional cases only. It seems that the Code provides that any acquisition should be without prejudice to national or international law (it would be hard to imagine any other sort of national or international prejudice). It is not clear why paragraphs 2.9 and 3.4 use a different wording ('exceptional circumstances' – 'exceptional cases' and 'significance of the object' – 'an item with an inherently outstanding contribution to knowledge'). It may indicate that the case of unprovenanced objects (those referred to in paragraph 3.4) is even more 'exceptional' compared to the objects indicated in paragraph 2.9. In both cases, however, the notion of objects with valid title but without a documented history and unprovenanced objects should not be confused with objects forming the subject of an illegal movement or transaction according to their country of origin or any intermediate country. Cultural objects should be considered unprovenanced when a thorough examination of their provenance has proved fruitless.[33] Such objects should never be acquired by museums, no matter how exceptional the circumstances. The question, of course, is how one can assess whether an object has turned up as a result of such a movement or transaction. There again the test of 'reasonable cause to believe' (or more practically 'reasonable doubt') applies. If the museum has thoroughly investigated the cultural object and there is no reason to doubt its legal provenance (i.e. its legal provenance is established beyond any reasonable doubt), it can proceed with its acquisition only if the object at issue is a particularly significant object and there are exceptional circumstances, which call for its acquisition. In any case, a thorough examination of the history of the object is required on all occasions.[34]

The ICOM Code provides for the return of cultural objects to their countries or peoples of origin on scientific, professional and humanitarian grounds as well as on the grounds of applicable local, national and

---

[33] See also in this respect Rule 2.20 according to which 'Museum collections should be documented according to accepted professional standards. Such documentation should include a full identification and description of each item, its associations, provenance, condition, treatment and present location. Such data should be kept in a secure environment and be supported by retrieval systems providing access to the information by the museum personnel and other legitimate users.'

[34] Interesting in this respect is also Rule 2.11 'Nothing in this Code of Ethics should prevent a museum from acting as an authorised repository for unprovenanced, illicitly collected or recovered specimens and objects from the territory over which it has lawful responsibility'.

international law (Rule 6.2).[35] This principle is reiterated in Rules 6.3 and 6.4 which provide that 'When a country or people of origin seeks the restitution of an object or specimen that can be demonstrated to have been exported or otherwise transferred *in violation of the principles of international and national conventions, and shown to be part of that country's or people's cultural or natural heritage, the museum concerned should, if legally free to do so, take prompt and responsible steps to co-operate in its return*' (Rule 6.3) and 'Museums should abstain from purchasing or acquiring cultural objects from an occupied territory and *respect fully all laws and conventions that regulate the import, export and transfer of cultural or natural materials*' (Rule 6.4).[36] These three provisions a) provide for the return of cultural objects to their countries of origin in compliance with the UNESCO and Unidroit Conventions (to which they refer with the use of a general clause) and b) such a return is not subject either to compensation or to time limitations and it may take place on a number of grounds expressly provided in the Code, without being limited only to situations of violations of national or international law. There is one reservation though. The museum only has to co-operate in the return of a cultural object if it is legally free to do so. Many museums use this clause to evade both their ethical and legal obligations. They allege that they are obliged, according to the statutes of operation, to keep their collections in trust and not return or otherwise divest themselves of any part of their collections, because such an act would run contrary to the higher aims and obligations of a museum. Yet this argument seems to carry little weight because a) one cannot invoke a museum's statutes in order to deny return in cases of illicit import, export or transfer of cultural property when this is in violation of international law, b) statutes which prohibit such acts under any circumstances are outdated, do not reflect public expectations and should be changed, c) there have been instances where the existence of such statutes has not prevented museums from acting on the basis of codes of ethics. It has just been a question of finding the right legal formula (e.g. extended repeated loans), which would allow them to act accordingly. The return of the Kwakwaka'wakw mask in 2005 as a long-term loan by the British Museum in London to Alert Bay, British Columbia, Canada from where

[35] Paragraph 6.2 of the ICOM Code: 'Museums should be prepared to initiate dialogues for the return of cultural property to a country or people of origin. This should be undertaken in an impartial manner, based on scientific, professional and humanitarian principles as well as applicable local, national and international legislation, in preference to action at a governmental or political level'.

[36] Emphasis added.

it was removed in 1921 is a case in point.[37] In any case it would be hard to think of museum statutes that would not allow the unethical acquisition of a cultural object but would allow the museum to keep the object once it had been acquired. On top of that, statutes are not cast in stone. They should be updated to respond to modern ethics as well as to public interest and expectations.

Principles 7 and 8 of the Code are also particularly important. According to these two principles, museums should operate in a legal manner (Pr. 7) and in a professional manner (Pr. 8). This is further elaborated as 'Museums *must conform fully to international, regional, national, or local legislation and treaty obligations.* In addition, the governing body should comply with any legally binding trusts or conditions relating to any aspect of the museum, its collections and operations' (Pr. 7). And 'Members of the museum profession should observe accepted standards and laws and uphold the dignity and honour of their profession. They should safeguard the public against illegal or unethical professional conduct. Every opportunity should be used to inform and educate the public about the aims, purposes, and aspirations of the profession to develop a better public understanding of the contributions of museums to society' (Pr. 8).[38]

The ICOM Code elaborates on principle 7. In paragraph 7.1 it sets out that 'Museums should conform to all national and local laws and respect the legislation of other states as they affect their operation'. Paragraph 7.2 lists the international conventions it acknowledges.[39]

Under Principle 8 paragraphs 8.5, 8.6 and 8.8 are relevant to the illicit

---

[37] Sanborn, A. (2009), 'The Reunification of the Kwakwaka' wakw mask with its Cultural Soul', *Museum International*, 6 (1–2). Other cultural objects were also repatriated to this region by the Smithsonian's National Museum of the American Indian in New York, from the André Breton Collection in Paris, France, and so on.

[38] Emphasis added.

[39] Paragraph 7.2 (International Legislation): 'Museum policy should acknowledge the following international legislation which is taken as a standard in interpreting the ICOM Code of Ethics:

- UNESCO Convention for the Protection of Cultural Property in the Event of Armed Conflict (The Hague Convention, First Protocol, 1954 and Second Protocol, 1999);
- UNESCO Convention on the Means of Prohibiting and Preventing the Illicit Import, Export and Transfer of Ownership of Cultural Property (1970);
- Convention on International Trade in Endangered Species of Wild Fauna and Flora (1973);
- UN Convention on Biological Diversity (1992);

trade in art. More specifically paragraph 8.5 provides that 'Members of the museum profession should not support the illicit traffic or market in natural and cultural property, directly or indirectly'. In addition, although museums must protect confidential information obtained during their work (paragraph 8.6),[40] '[c]onfidentiality is subject to a legal obligation to assist the police or other proper authorities in investigating possible stolen, illicitly acquired, or illegally transferred property' (paragraph 8.8).

4.2.3 Other International Codes of Ethics

As was explained in the introductory chapter, there are quite a few national, regional and international codes of ethics. However, discussion of all of them would merit a separate study. For that reason we shall limit ourselves to discussion of the basic principles underlying two more international codes of ethics, on earlier drafts of which the UNESCO Code of Ethics was based: a) the Code of Ethics of the World Association of Antique Dealer Associations (Confédération internationale des Négociants d'Oeuvres d'Art (CINOA)), (2005)[41] and b) the International Association of Dealers in Ancient Art (IADAA) Code of Ethics and Practice (2007).[42] Because of regular updating these two codes form some of the most recent examples in their area and they both deal with the issue of illegal trafficking in art.[43]

- Unidroit Convention on Stolen and Illegally Exported Cultural Objects (1995);
- UNESCO Convention on the protection of Underwater Cultural Heritage (2001);
- UNESCO Convention for the Safeguarding of Intangible Cultural Heritage (2003).'

40 Paragraph 8.6 (Confidentiality): 'Members of the museum profession must protect confidential information obtained during their work. In addition, information about items brought to the museum for identification is confidential and should not be published or passed to any other institution or person without specific authorisation from the owner'.

41 This Code was resolved at the General Meeting in Florence in 1987, amended in Stockholm on 26 June 1998 and in New York on 11 May 2005.

42 It seems that this Code was last updated on 2 April 2007.

43 Interesting in this respect is also the European Association of Archaeologists (EAA) Code of Practice and in particular paragraphs 1.6 'Archaeologists will not engage in, or allow their names to be associated with, any form of activity relating to the illicit trade in antiquities and works of art, covered by the 1970 UNESCO Convention on the means of prohibiting and preventing the illicit import, export, and transfer of ownership of cultural property' and 1.8 'It is the responsibility of

The CINOA Code provides that:[44]

2. The affiliated members of CINOA who happen to possess an object about which there are *serious suspicions* that it was illegally imported *and of which the country of origin demands that it is returned within a reasonable amount of time*, shall have to do everything that is possible to them *according to the current laws* to cooperate in returning the object to its country of origin. *In the case of a purchase in good faith by the antique dealer, an amicable refund may be agreed to.*
4. The members will have to *take all the necessary measures to detect stolen objects and refer, among others, to registers that are published to this effect and to use these judiciously.*[45]

The IADAA Code provides that: [46]

1. The members of the IADAA undertake *to the best of their ability to make their purchases in good faith.*
2. The members of the IADAA undertake not to purchase or sell objects *until they have established to the best of their ability that such objects were not stolen from excavations, architectural monuments, public institutions or private property.*
7. The Members of the IADAA undertake to the best of their ability to *inform the Administrative Board about stolen goods and thefts*. They also undertake to *co-operate with international and national agencies involved in the recovery of stolen goods.*
8. All members undertake to check objects with a purchase value of *Euro 3000 or over (or local currency equivalent) with the Art Loss Register unless the item has already been checked.*[47]

It is interesting to note that neither Code is as extensive as the UNESCO and ICOM Codes, nor are they as detailed. Although at certain points the language is similar, many loopholes can be found, which can be subject to multiple interpretations and therefore jeopardise their effectiveness in the combat of illicit trade. In both cases it seems that the interests of the profession prevail whilst ethical issues are taken into account in a rather

---

archaeologists to draw the attention of the competent authorities to threats to the archaeological heritage, including the plundering of sites and monuments and illicit trade in antiquities, and to use all the means at their disposal to ensure that action is taken in such cases by the competent authorities'.

[44] The numbering followed is that in the Code.

[45] Emphasis added. See also para 5 of the Code which provides that 'the member cannot under any circumstance participate in transactions which to the best of their knowledge can result in money-laundering operations'.

[46] The numbering followed is that in the Code.

[47] Emphasis added.

more flexible manner. In any event a code of ethics or conduct is only considered effective and influential if it is applied and enforced in a rigid way. If it simply forms a list of statements, no matter how strict or loose these statements are, its scope of application is, by definition and practice, limited.[48,49]

---

[48] Interesting in this respect is also the Museums and Galleries Commission (United Kingdom): Excerpts from 'Restitution and Repatriation – Guidelines for Good Practice' 2000, which in section 2.2.2 states the 'Arguments that Favour Return':

> Arguments in favour of return generally acknowledge prior rights, derived from customary and/or western property rights, and the changing significance of objects. These include:
>
> - New approaches to professional practice in scientific research, archaeological excavation and museum activities which recognise others' rights to control cultural material and knowledge;
> - Consideration for the spiritual beliefs and cultural imperatives of relatives and descendants;
> - Acknowledgement of rights of indigenous people to regain control of their cultural heritage;
> - Acknowledgement of past wrongful taking and/or misunderstandings of complex customary ownership concepts, and attempt to redress;
> - Establishment of constructive relationships with previously under-acknowledged stakeholders;
> - Recognition that it is easier for westerners to travel to consult with requesting parties than for culturally affiliated indigenous peoples to travel to the United Kingdom;
> - Recognition that a particular object would benefit from being in a different context;
> - Information technology enabling easier access to research information;
> - Continuing ability to carry out research while objects are in the care of the requesting party;
> - Opportunity to build new relationships important to the museum and potential to add new, more accurate information, and even new accessions, to museum collections.

[49] Brodie, N., 'An Archaeological View of the Trade in Unprovenanced Antiquities' in B.T. Hoffman (ed.) (2006), *Art and Cultural Heritage. Law, Policy and Practice*, New York, p.61, 'several associations have been established to represent the interests of the trade, and they state publicly that their members are required to adhere to certain standards of behaviour, which are sometimes formulated as codes of ethics or practice. The existence of these codes allows the trade to argue that it is self-regulating and that therefore statutory control is unnecessary, an argument with political resonance in the ostensively free-trade jurisdictions of North America and Europe, where most of the end trading goes on. Unfortunately, it is questionable to what extent the codes are respected or enforced'.

4.3 THE ROLE OF INTERNATIONAL ORGANISATIONS

The issues of restitution of cultural property would not have been dealt with effectively at international level if it were not for international organisations, associations and other institutions. These organisations have been very successful in bringing together diametrically opposed views in the area and achieving consensus and agreement on issues. The result has been either international conventions or soft law (UN Resolutions, UNESCO Recommendations, Codes of Ethics and so on), as has been discussed above. In addition to that, international organisations have set up administering bodies and funds to promote greater co-operation and facilitate negotiations and agreements between States. They have helped to raise awareness and public consciousness, developed expert advice, enhanced education and set standards and operating norms in the area. In this chapter we shall look briefly into some of these organisations and their role in the restitution of cultural property.[50]

4.3.1 UNESCO

The United Nations Educational, Scientific and Cultural Organization (UNESCO) is the most important organisation in the area of culture. It is a specialised United Nations agency which was founded on 16 November 1945. UNESCO's goal is to promote international co-operation among its 193 Member States and six Associate Members in the fields of education, science, culture and communication.[51]

UNESCO has been very active in the field of culture and in particular in the area of combating the illicit trade in art and the restitution of cultural property to its countries of origin. To this end UNESCO has undertaken action in four main areas: a) normative action, b) diplomatic action, c) the

---

[50] Not all institutions and organizations active in the field of restitution and return of cultural property to its countries of origin are referred to in this book since this would require a separate treatise. Other institutions and organizations active in this area are Unidroit, the United Nations Office for Drugs and Crime (UNODC), the Italian Carabinieri, the French Office Central de Lutte contre le Traffic des Biens Culturels (OCBC), the Greek Police Department on the Illicit Trafficking of Antiquities, the FBI Art Theft Program (USA), the Art and Antiquities Unit of Scotland Yard – Metropolitan Police (UK), the Instituto do Patrimônio Histórico e Artístico Nacional (IPHAN) (Brazil), the Instituto Superior de policía judiciária e ciências criminais (Portugal) and so on.

[51] The number of Member States as of October 2007.

development of practical and ethical tools and d) the organisation of training and awareness-raising events.

In the course of its *normative action*, UNESCO has helped in the impementation of a number of international (multilateral) conventions (i.e. the Hague Convention for the Protection of Cultural Property in the Event of Armed Conflict (1954) and its two protocols (1954 and 1999), the UNESCO Convention on the Means of Prohibiting and Preventing the Illicit Import, Export and Transfer of Ownership of Cultural Property (1970), the Unidroit Convention on Stolen or Illegally Exported Cultural Objects (1995), the Convention on the Protection of the Underwater Cultural Heritage (2001), the Convention for the Safeguarding of Intangible Cultural Heritage (2003), and the Convention on the Protection and Promotion of the Diversity of Cultural Expressions (2005)).

In the course of its *diplomatic actions*, UNESCO has been actively involved in the return and restitution of cultural property for many years. However, this has been institutionalised by the establishment of the 'Intergovernmental Committee for Promoting the Return of Cultural Property to its Countries of Origin or its Restitution in Case of Illicit Appropriation'. This Committee is an intergovernmental body with an advisory role which meets biennially and provides a platform for discussion and negotiation between Member States. It promotes co-operation towards the restitution or return of cultural property and deals with cases where Member States have lost cultural objects of fundamental significance and cannot claim them back by means of an international convention. Lately, however, it has also been involved with issues directly affecting the illicit trade in art and provided for in international conventions. The Committee was set up in 1978[52] and comprises 22 Member States. It usually meets every two years but it can also meet yearly and organise extraordinary sessions. The first extraordinary session was organised in Seoul, Republic of Korea, from 25 to 28 November 2008. The role of the Committee has been rather limited and has so far lacked authority. This is the reason why during the Athens Conference 2008[53] and the extraordinary session in Seoul 2008, it was agreed to find ways to strengthen its role. Proposals were discussed in the 15th session of the Committee in May 2009 and included discussion of alternative dispute resolution methods.

This Committee has set up a Fund (Fund of the Intergovernmental

---

[52] It was set up by Resolution 20 C4/7.6/5 at the 20th Session of the UNESCO General Conference of UNESCO.

[53] Athens International Conference on the Return of Cultural Objects to their Countries of Origin (co-organised by the Greek Ministry of Culture and UNESCO), Athens, 17–18 March 2008.

Committee for Promoting the Return of Cultural Property to its Countries of Origin or its Restitution in case of Illicit Appropriation), which accepts voluntary contributions from states and private donors and aims to support Member States in their efforts to pursue the return or restitution of cultural property.[54]

UNESCO has taken some *practical steps* in combating the illicit trade in art. It has collaborated with INTERPOL and ICOM over the publication of documents such as 'Basic Actions concerning Cultural Objects being offered for Sale over the Internet'. It has also set up the 'Object ID Standard', the 'UNESCO-OMD Model export certificate for cultural objects', the UNESCO Cultural Heritage Laws Database,[55] and has drafted the UNESCO International Code of Ethics for Dealers in Cultural Property (1999). It has also recently adopted Rules of Procedure for Mediation and Conciliation.[56] In addition it has commissioned reports, organised meetings, conferences, workshops, training and awareness-raising events.

4.3.2 ICOM

One of UNESCO's important partners in combating the illicit trade in cultural property is the International Council of Museums (ICOM). ICOM is a non-profit-making, non-governmental, international organisation of museums and museum professionals, which aims at the conservation, continuation and communication to society of the world's natural and cultural heritage. It maintains formal relations with UNESCO and has a consultative status with the United Nations Economic and Social Council.

---

[54] See also the 'Information Kit on the Restitution of Cultural Property', a UNESCO publication trying to clarify issues of restitution and return, http://portal.UNESCO.org/culture/en/ev.php-URL_ID=35252&URL_DO=DO_TOPIC&URL_SECTION=201.html.

[55] The Cultural Heritage Laws Database is a collection of national laws on the protection of cultural heritage currently in force. It also includes official or unofficial translations of national laws, import/export certificates for cultural property, contact details for the national authorities responsible for the protection of cultural heritage and addresses of the official national websites relating to the protection of cultural heritage.

[56] During its 16th Session (Paris, 21–23 September, 2010) the ICPRCP has adopted 'Rules of Procedure for Mediation and Conciliation in Accordance with Article 4, Paragraph 1, of the Statutes of the Intergovernmental Committee for Promoting the Return of Cultural Property to its Countries of Origin or Its Restitution in Case of Illicit Appropriation'. See also Recommendation 4 adopted during the 16th session of ICPRCP. Chairman of the Sub-committee was Prof. Constantin Economidès.

It was created in 1946 and today numbers approximately 26,000 members in 139 countries.

Its main missions include fighting against the illicit trade in cultural property and in order to do this it focuses on a) preventive measures, such as promoting professional ethics and ensuring the security of collections, and b) concrete initiatives directly involving international networks of professionals. In order to help it promote professional ethics, ICOM published its Code of Ethics for museum professionals in 1986. This was last revised in 2004.

As a preventive measure it also invests in the security of collections. Its International Committee for the Training of Personnel (ICTOP) trains museum staff and its International Documentation Committee (CIDOC) helps museums draw up inventories and keep them up to date. The ICOM International Committee for Museum Security (ICMS) publishes international directives on security, and trains senior security staff. ICOM's International Committee for Education and Cultural Action (CECA) is made up of museum staff who specialise in presenting and explaining artworks to members of the public and try to make them aware of the importance of heritage and its role in preserving cultural identity. In addition ICOM's National Committees draw up national plans of action to combat illicit trade in cultural goods.

ICOM produces publications which help raise awareness and identify cultural property in jeopardy. It has published a series of four volumes entitled *One Hundred Missing Objects*.[57] ICOM also publishes a selection of objects reported stolen to Interpol in its quarterly journal, ICOM News, which is circulated free to ICOM's 17,000 members worldwide. Since April 2000 the ICOM Red List has come into existence.[58] This lists the types of objects which are prohibited by law from being exported and therefore cannot be legally offered for sale but which are most frequently removed from sites or stolen. This publication exhorts museums, dealers and collectors not to buy these objects. In an effort to raise public aware-

---

[57] These publications are respectively devoted to the Angkor archaeological site (*Looting in Angkor*), African heritage (*Looting in Africa*), Latin American heritage (*Looting in Latin America*) and European religious heritage (*Looting in Europe*) (information obtained from ICOM's site).

[58] The first *ICOM Red List* is devoted to African archaeological heritage, and was drawn up by African, European and North American museum professionals. The second Red List is devoted to the cultural heritage in Latin America and the third one, entitled 'Emergency Red List of Iraqi Antiquities at Risk' was published to help customs and officials recognise objects that could originate from Iraq (information obtained from ICOM's site).

ness, ICOM also devoted International Museum Day 1997–1998 to 'the fight against illicit traffic of cultural property'.

Since 1993, ICOM has held a number of workshops in co-operation with Interpol and UNESCO on effective regional measures against thefts and looting.[59] In 2000 ICOM signed agreements with both the World Customs Organization (WCO) and Interpol on their role in the fight against illicit trade in cultural goods and particularly thefts from museums and looting of archaeological sites. It co-operates closely not only with these organisations but also with UNESCO especially with regard to the promotion of the 1970 UNESCO Convention and the 1995 Unidroit Convention to countries that have still not ratified them.

Last but not least, it promotes object ID. Object ID is an international standard for describing cultural objects and is the result of years of research in collaboration with museums, Interpol, customs agencies, the art trade, the insurance industry and valuers of art and antiques. Object ID can prove very helpful for the tracing and recovery of a missing cultural object.[60]

4.3.3 ICCROM

The decision to found the International Centre for the Study of the Preservation and Restoration of Cultural Property (ICCROM) was

---

[59] In Africa and Latin America and in Southeast Asia, these workshops have resulted in the setting-up of operational teams of people directly involved in heritage protection, and have facilitated regional and international co-operation (Tanzania, 1993; Mali, 1994; Ecuador, 1995; Rep. Dem. of Congo, 1996; Tunisia, 1998; Vietnam, 2001; Colombia, 2002; Sri Lanka, 2003) (information obtained from ICOM's site).

[60] 'The Object ID project was initiated by the J. Paul Getty Trust in 1993 and the standard was launched in 1997. It is promoted by major law enforcement agencies, including the FBI, Scotland Yard and Interpol, UNESCO, museums, cultural heritage organisations, art trade and art appraisal organisations, and insurance companies. Having established the descriptive standard, the Object ID project now helps combat the illegal appropriation of art objects by facilitating documentation of cultural property and by bringing together organisations around the world that can encourage its implementation. From 1999 to 2004, the Object ID project was housed at the Council for the Prevention of Art Theft (CoPAT). In October 2004, the International Council of Museums (ICOM) signed an agreement with the J. Paul Getty Trust for ICOM's non-exclusive worldwide use of the Getty's Object ID standard. ICOM, in close collaboration with UNESCO and other organisations fighting illicit trade, will actively disseminate information about Object ID and also organise workshops on its implementation. New translation initiatives are constantly being promoted and undertaken' (Text taken from ICOM's site).

made at the 9th UNESCO General Conference in New Delhi in 1956 as a response to an increased interest in the protection and preservation of cultural heritage. The Centre was established in Rome in 1959 at the invitation of the Government of Italy.[61]

ICCROM is an intergovernmental organisation which seeks to conserve cultural heritage.[62] In fact it aims at improving the quality of conservation practice as well as raising awareness about the importance of preserving cultural heritage. It numbers more than 126 States. There are five main areas of activity: training, information, research, co-operation and public awareness. ICCROM is not active in the area of the illicit traffic in art. This issue is affected only indirectly by actions which fall within its general aims and goals.

4.3.4 ICOMOS

The International Council on Monuments and Sites (ICOMOS) is an international non-governmental organisation of professionals, which aims at the conservation of the world's historic monuments and sites. ICOMOS co-operates with other organisations in the field of culture. It only deals indirectly with matters of illicit trade in art and to the extent that these activities fall within its general aim of conservation of cultural heritage. An area of ICOMOS activity that indirectly serves the needs of the combat of illicit trade in cultural heritage is the 'Heritage at Risk' programme. This programme was endorsed by ICOMOS members at the General Assembly in Mexico in 1999 and tries to identify threatened heritage places, monuments and sites, present typical case studies and trends, and share suggestions for solving individual or global threats to cultural heritage.

4.3.5 INTERPOL

INTERPOL was created in 1923 and is the world's largest international police organisation with 187 member countries. It facilitates cross-border police co-operation, and supports and assists all organisations, authorities and services whose mission is to prevent or combat international

---

[61] It used to be a subsidiary of UNESCO. Today it is an independent organisation, which acts as a scientific consultant to the UNESCO World Heritage Committee, drafting and implementing projects for the restoration and protection of the sites enrolled on the World Heritage List, in addition to its primary activities as these were explained above.

[62] It is dedicated to the promotion of all kinds of cultural heritage, movable and immovable, tangible and intangible.

crime.[63] Part of international crime is cultural property crime and INTERPOL has a special division to deal with it.[64] INTERPOL, UNESCO and the WCO all co-operate with each other by using each other's expertise and co-organising conferences and training workshops. INTERPOL has also created a database on stolen works of art, which will be discussed later on.

4.3.6 WCO

The movement of stolen cultural objects is a crime which involves borders. Borders offer the best opportunity to intercept stolen cultural artefacts, and therefore customs play a fundamental role in the fight against the unauthorised export of cultural property. The World Customs Organization (WCO) in partnership with other international organisations and law enforcement agencies, such as ICOM, UNESCO and INTERPOL, aim at exchanging information to help combat this illegal activity. To this end WCO and UNESCO have signed a Memorandum of Understanding and have jointly developed a UNESCO-WCO Model Export Certificate for Cultural Objects and explanatory notes to the model.[65]

4.4 REGISTERS OF STOLEN AND ILLEGALLY EXPORTED CULTURAL OBJECTS

National, regional and international registers of stolen and illegally exported cultural objects help considerably in the recovery of those objects. The tracing of these objects would otherwise be difficult if not impossible. Documenting an object and listing it in a database considerably improves the chances of locating and recovering it since it renders trafficking very difficult. The consultation of registers is a practice which is followed by most reputable dealers. Dealers know that if they trade in a

---

[63] INTERPOL aims to facilitate international police co-operation even where diplomatic relations do not exist between particular countries. Action is taken within the limits of existing laws in different countries and in the spirit of the Universal Declaration of Human Rights, http://www.Interpol.int.

[64] It co-operates with Europol and national police forces if needed. Europol does not have a special unit for cultural property claims. These claims are dealt with by its property crime unit.

[65] For the combat of illicit trade the WCO relies to a great extent on member customs, administrations, as well as on its Regional Intelligence Liaison Offices – RILO Network.

listed object, they run the risk of having to give up the object without the payment of any compensation, since it would be difficult for them to prove their good faith. They also run the risk of incurring legal and other costs, losing their reputation and their trustworthiness in the eyes of clients, and acquiring an object whose value is considerably diminished if its illegal provenance is proven.

Registries with an international reputation are the following:

- *Art Loss Register* The Art Loss Register (ALR), a private database of stolen art and antiques, was established in 1991 through a partnership between auction houses, trade associations, the insurance industry and the International Foundation for Art Research (IFAR). ALR routinely screens catalogues of national losses and auction house catalogues for stolen items and responds to provenance enquiries. It has a specialised service for those tracing items looted, stolen or forcibly removed from families between 1933 and 1945, the Nazi and Holocaust Era. The Art Loss Register issues certificates to dealers and auction houses to confirm that they have searched the database with regard to a specific item.[66]
- *The International Foundation for Art Research (IFAR)*: A not-for-profit educational and research organization which offers information on authenticity, ownership issues, legal, and ethical matters concerning art objects.
- *Trace* Trace is a database, which was launched in 2006 under the name 'Swift Find', and contains objects that are lost, stolen or looted and have been reported to the police as well as items lost in the Nazi and Holocaust era.
- *Salvo* This is an on-line database of stolen items of architectural salvage and antiques such as doors, fireplaces, garden furniture and statuary.[67]
- *INTERPOL Database about stolen works of art* This database began in 1947 and it contains a considerable number of stolen works of art.
- *ICOM Red Lists of cultural objects at risk* These are ICOM publications of examples of cultural objects originating from various parts

---

66 http://www.artloss.com. In the same area see also the Central Registry of Information on Looted Cultural Property, 1933–1945, the Commission for Looted Art in Europe (CLAE), the Documentation Project, the Frick Art Reference Library, the Lost Art Internet Database, Musées Nationaux Recupération, the National Archives and Records Administration (NARA) and the New York State Holocaust Claims Office.

67 ALR, Trace and Salvo are all commercial databases.

of the world, which are particularly at risk and most likely to be stolen. The lists aim to promote public awareness and help customs and police officers, art dealers and collectors identify these objects and protect them.[68]

- *Carabinieri National Stolen Cultural Property Database* (Italy) This is a database composed of items of stolen cultural property which relate not only to Italy but to the whole of the world.
- *Find Stolen Art Database(UK)* This is the Metropolitan Police Art and Antiques Unit's database, which lists 51,000 items of stolen property. Objects are included in the database if they are properly documented, unique and identifiable.[69]
- *The Lost Art Internet Database* (Germany) This database is the result of a partnership between the German Government and the *Länder* to register cultural objects relocated, moved or seized during the Nazi and Holocaust Era.[70]
- *The Central Registry of Information on Looted Cultural Property 1933–1945* This database was set up as a charity in 2001. It is a non-commercial database which allows people to search it for free. It contains over 25,000 missing and looted objects and has expert staff on Nazi looting.
- Many countries maintain their own *national databases*.[71]

4.5 CONCLUSIONS

From the above it is clear that as well as the law there is also soft law, which, though not legally binding, nevertheless affects the law either by

---

[68] The Red Lists published on the ICOM website (http://icom.museum/redlist) are the following: Red List of African Archaeological Cultural Objects at Risk, Red List of Latin American Cultural Objects at Risk, Emergency Red List of Iraqi Antiquities at Risk, Red List of Afghanistan Antiquities at Risk and Red List of Peruvian Antiquities at Risk.

[69] Other databases are: *Invaluable – Art Market Intelligence*: a database, police liaison team and magazine, http://www.thesaurus.co.uk/protect/theft_default.asp and for museums http://www.thesaurus.co.uk/protect/museums/ and *Stolen Art Databases:* a website containing information on Stolen Art Databases, Private Stolen Art Listings, Police Listings and so on, http://www.saztv.com/page9.html.

[70] The INTERPOL Database on stolen works of art, the Carabinieri National Stolen Cultural Property Database, the London Stolen Art Database and the Lost Art Internet Database are government-funded databases.

[71] See, for example, the database of the Greek Ministry of Culture and Tourism with regard to stolen and illegally exported cultural objects.

way of interpretation or as a complementary tool. This is especially true if it is widely accepted and has constituted the practice in the area for a considerable length of time. The most important soft law instruments are the UN General Assembly Resolutions, the UNESCO Recommendations and Codes of ethics or conduct. There are also Guidelines[72] and Memoranda of Understanding which do the same thing. However, these carry less weight if they are adopted by a limited number of states or form the content of a bilateral non-binding 'agreement'. Codes of ethics play a very important role in the area of culture and in particular in the combat of illicit trade although their implementation has not proven entirely successful so far. Usually codes of ethics should be combined with public awareness and information campaigns and have to be built into educational programmes and workshops. Their drafting and adoption are important steps in the right direction. However, the manner of their implementation is crucial to their success. It is also important that their results are publicised. Codes of ethics are important for one additional reason. They apply to an area where national laws vary or present considerable gaps and loopholes. That, in conjunction with the fact that the illicit trade in art is a borderless area with worldwide effects, makes their application (as a method of self-regulation) imperative and renders them the second best solution after law.

The combat of the illicit trade in art cannot be dealt with efficiently at national level. It needs international co-operation, exchange of information and expertise, co-ordination of various agencies, fast action and effective enforcement. This is particularly so because crime in art moves through chains and routes, which are common in many cases, whilst the same people or 'teams of people' are involved again and again. Exchange of information and expertise can therefore be of considerable value and that is one of the reasons why a number of international organisations and enforcement agencies co-operate with each other. Their role is fundamental to the effective combat of the illicit trade in art. Problems still remain. Those problems centre primarily on the different national approaches to cultural property (as explained in the first chapter of this book). Some states take a minimalist approach towards protection, whilst others take a maximalist approach. Co-operation in these cases can be problematic. In

---

[72] In 2000 the UK Museums and Galleries Commission published guidelines to encourage museums to become proactive in the development of institutional policies for the handling of restitution requests. See Vrdoljak, A.F. (2008), *International Law, Museums and the Return of Cultural Objects*, Cambridge University Press, 288 and Legget, J. (2000), *Restitution and Repatriation: Guidelines for Good Practice*, London: Museums and Galleries Commission.

the area of stolen cultural property the interest is common and unequivocal. UNESCO, though promoting the combat of the illicit trade in art, offers services which are mostly neutral and rather modest in this respect. This was the reason that at the Athens and Seoul Conferences (2008) it was agreed that its role, and in particular the role of the ICPRCP, should be strengthened in various ways.

Practical tools, such as the UNESCO database of national laws, the ICOM database of cultural items at risk and databases of stolen and illegally exported objects, play a significant role in the combat of the illicit trade in art. It seems that the databases covering only stolen objects outnumber those which also contain illegally exported items, probably because it is very difficult to locate and identify the latter. These tools do help detect and recover such cultural objects. National, regional and international co-operation coupled with expertise in the area is particularly important. Public awareness campaigns, training seminars and workshops, educational activities, publicity, information kits, publications, research and reports, as well as cultural diplomacy, are all valuable tools. Their effectiveness, however, depends directly on how important the protection of cultural heritage is considered to be by the interested parties (including states) and other agents in the international trade in art (such as collectors, dealers, auctioneers) and how motivated all are to ameliorate the current situation.

5. Dispute resolution in cultural property cases

5.1 JUDICIAL RECOURSE

Cultural property claims, especially those involving the return of cultural objects to their countries of origin, are usually international claims. Either they involve more than one state or, even where states are not involved, they are trans-border claims where one party in one state is required to return a cultural object to another party in another state.[1] International conventions apply in both inter-state and private disputes, depending on the scope of the convention. Sometimes, the application of the convention to the case will take the form of general principles derived from it.

Up to now experience has shown that recourse to the courts usually takes place if a) the claim is crystal clear in terms of its facts (e.g. how the object has been alienated from the claimant, where it is found, who owns or possesses it) and its legal bases (the law applicable in the case at issue clearly provides for its return/restitution, the claim is not statute barred and so on), and b) there are private parties involved where the influence of a state cannot be used for the out-of-court settlement of the case.

Litigation is usually expensive and takes time. However, it also gives claimants the opportunity to act swiftly in order not to have their claim statute-barred (the filing of a suit interrupts the running of any time limitations and one can also file for provisional measures/injunction in order to 'freeze a situation'[2] until a final decision is reached). On top of that, the filing of a suit (or worse still, recourse to the penal courts) can exert pressure for the resolution of the issue. In fact, the reason why so many cultural property cases for which a lawsuit has been filed have not been pursued further is that the parties have reached a mutually acceptable out-

---

1 International claims may also be considered the claims where parties of a different nationality residing in the same country are involved. However, in these instances it would be difficult to have claims for 'return' of an object to its country of origin if the object is also found in the territory of the same country.

2 That means that there may be a prohibition on transfer or sale of the cultural object until a final judgment is delivered by the competent court.

of-court settlement.[3] There are other benefits of recourse to the courts. For one thing litigation is capable of gathering strong evidence (e.g. through orders for disclosure) on the case, which can be helpful, not only for the fair resolution of the matter brought before the court, but also for the resolution of other matters linked to the case (e.g. if more cultural objects are missing from the same museum or archaeological site, whilst the case refers to only some of them). Compliance with the judgment is mandatory and non-compliance is followed by sanctions. Also the resolution of the matter is definitive and there is no risk of further litigation (especially if the case is heard and decided at all levels). Finally, recourse to the courts does not preclude recourse to other modes of dispute resolution even during court proceedings.

On the other hand recourse to the courts also presents some disadvantages[4]:

- First, there are very different legal traditions and attitudes amongst the various states. The outcome of a court decision cannot be predicted and the parties are not always willing to enter into a process with uncertain results. This may prove detrimental not only to the case at issue but also set a precedent for the future.
- Second, litigation is a very costly process. If the party claiming a cultural object is a poor state or a developing country, it is not easy for that country to bear the costs of legal proceedings. The same applies to private parties who do not possess adequate financial resources.
- Third, when one has a court judgment, one needs to enforce it. It is not always easy to enforce court judgments in other states on various legal grounds, including sometimes the grounds of public order.
- Fourth, private international law issues may also cause difficulties. In order for one to bring a case before a national court, matters of jurisdiction and applicable law should be decided. It is not always

---

[3] See, for example, the return of the Aidonia Treasure (originating from Nemea), presented in an auction in New York, to Greece in 1996. For further information, see Demakopoulou K. and N. Divari-Valakou 1997, *The Aidonia Treasure*, Athens: Greek Ministry of Culture, Archaeological Receipts Fund.

[4] A case which demonstrates the deficiencies of legal recourse is the Sevso Treasure case. See Kurzweil, H., L.V. Gagion and L. De Walden (2005), 'The Trial of the Sevso Treasure: What a Nation Will Do in the Name of Its Heritage', in K. Fitz Gibbon (ed.), *Who Owns the Past? Cultural Policy, Cultural Property and the Law*, New Brunswick, New Jersey and London: Rutgers University Press in association with American Council for Cultural Policy. See also Meyer, K.E. (1973), *The Plundered Past*, New York: Atheneum, 41.

certain whether the court chosen by the claimant is competent to decide (issues of jurisdiction) or which law is applicable in the case at issue (the law of the state that claims the object, the law of the state where the object is situated and so on). Even when the applicable law is sorted out, this law may contain loopholes or may be incomplete. This is because the issue of the restitution of cultural property is an area which is not fully (if at all) developed in all countries. One may therefore run the risk of having the case dealt with as any case of illegally alienated objects[5] and not cultural objects in particular. This would mean risking short time limitations as well as risking the possibility that the claim will not be dealt with in the context of specially drawn legal or other provisions.

- Fifth, even if issues of jurisdiction and applicable law are overcome, it is not always easy for the parties to produce the necessary proof needed to establish that a cultural object has been illegally alienated. This is especially true for cultural objects that have been the product of an illegal excavation or have never been documented or listed in a database as missing. Proof is not easy to find when it relates to the circumstances of the alienation of an object from a particular country. In ancient times many neighbouring countries had trading relations with each other and therefore objects could have travelled or been exchanged between them and ended up in the soil of different countries. It is also difficult to prove the date of such an alienation, even though that is crucial in order for a claim to be filed admissibly.
- Sixth, law is not retroactive. It therefore leaves out a considerable number of cases. On top of that, many claims for return have been statute barred because of time limitations. At least in some states, and most likely in the states where the object is situated, time limitations are short. This, however, does not mean that the claim is not sound on ethical, scientific, historical, humanitarian or other grounds. These grounds, however, are not grounds that are judiciable by courts, which have to follow the rigid legal approach.
- Seventh, judicial recourse cannot take into account other interests of the parties, which might require them to be flexible. These interests are closely linked to the smooth conclusion of a case without attracting any bad publicity or harming good relations with the other party. States, museums or collectors, for example, wish to preserve their

[5] 'Illegally alienated objects' may be considered any objects which have been taken away from their owner contrary to law. The terminology may differ from state to state.

> good reputation, co-operate with reputable museums and care for art and archaeology. These parties would in some cases be in favour of assisting in the repatriation of an object that perhaps left its place of origin many years ago in an illegal or even a legal manner. The restitution of an object may help foster good relations between two or more countries and may open the door for future co-operation. This can also work well for museums if they choose to exchange loans, exhibitions, make annexes in other countries and so on.[6]

All the above reasons might contribute to an out-of-court settlement of the case. This settlement may be judicial (i.e. arbitration as an alternative to a dispute brought to courts) or non-judicial (alternative dispute resolution). This will form the subject of the sections to follow. At this point, however, we need to note that cultural property claims, depending on whether they constitute disputes between states or between private parties, can be taken (in the case of states) to the International Court of Justice[7] and (in the case of private parties) to national courts. To give but one hypothetical example, the Parthenon Marbles case could be brought before the courts either as a case of private law or as a case of public international law. If the Greek Government decides to sue the Trustees of the

---

[6] See Stamatoudi, I. (2009), 'Mediation and Cultural Diplomacy', *Museum International*, 61 (1–2), 110, at 112.

[7] The International Court of Justice was created in 1945 by its Statute, which forms part of the Charter of the United Nations. Only states may by parties in cases before the Court (article 34(1)). Certain international organisations may request advisory opinions from the Court (article 65). They cannot, however, be parties to contentious cases (states, on the other hand, may not request advisory opinions). Article 36 of the Statute provides for the methods of conferring jurisdiction to the Court. Article 36(1) provides that 'The jurisdiction of the Court comprises all cases which the parties refer to it and all matters specially provided for in the Charter of the United Nations or in treaties and conventions in force'. Article 36(2) provides for states to make unilateral declarations accepting the compulsory jurisdiction of the Court over future disputes known as the 'Optional Clause'. There are in fact four ways (a fifth is also discussed in Collier and Lowe, below) in which jurisdiction can be conferred. Two of these confer jurisdiction before any dispute has arisen, that is (i) where a treaty or convention in force between the states in question provides for it, and (ii) where there are declarations under article 36(2); and two do so after a dispute has arisen, that is (iii) where the states in question specially agree to refer their dispute to the Court, and (iv) where the doctrine of *forum propagatum* (a kind of implied submission) applies. The fundamental rule with regard to the jurisdiction of the Court is that submission to it depends on the consent of the states. Collier, J. and V. Lowe (1999), *The Settlement of Disputes in International Law: Institutions and Procedures*, Oxford University Press, 124 *et seq* and in particular 125, 132 and 133.

British Museum in the British courts (where the defendant is resident)[8] this is then clearly a case of private law. Alternatively the Greek State could bring an action against Britain before the International Court of Justice. Both Greece and the United Kingdom are members of the United Nations and according to article 36(2) of the Statute of the International Court of Justice they 'may at any time declare that they recognise as compulsory . . . the jurisdiction of the Court in all legal disputes concerning . . . any question of international law'. In this case public international law applies. That means that the Court will refer to international treaties in the area as well as to customary law.

5.2 ALTERNATIVE DISPUTE RESOLUTION

Alternative dispute resolution seems to be the trend these days, especially in relation to cultural property cases where the law continues to be vague and confusing. That has meant that courts are not well equipped and confident to deal with these sorts of cases and the outcome can be uncertain and inflexible. As a result the particularities of cultural property cases, for example the ethical and public policy concerns, are often not taken into account. Alternative (to courts) dispute resolution may therefore be preferable, and welcomed by both (or more) sides because on most occasions

---

[8] Article 2 of the Brussels Convention 1968, as amended. See also Regulation (EC) no 864/2007 of the European Parliament and of the Council of 11 July 2007 on the law applicable to non-contractual obligations (Rome II) Article 4 (General rule):

> 1. Unless otherwise provided for in this Regulation, the law applicable to a non-contractual obligation arising out of a tort/delict shall be the law of the country in which the damage occurs irrespective of the country in which the event giving rise to the damage occurred and irrespective of the country or countries in which the indirect consequences of that event occur. . . . 3. Where it is clear from all the circumstances of the case that the tort/delict is manifestly more closely connected with a country other than that indicated in paragraphs 1 or 2, the law of that other country shall apply. A manifestly closer connection with another country might be based in particular on a preexisting relationship between the parties, such as a contract, that is closely connected with the tort/delict in question.

According to Article 31 'This Regulation shall apply to events giving rise to damage which occur after its entry into force'. According to Article 32 'This Regulation shall apply from 11 January 2009, except for Article 29, which shall apply from 11 July 2008'. See also I. Stamatoudi (2002), 'Legal grounds for the return of the Parthenon Marbles' Revue Hellénique de droit International, 2, 513.

it is flexible enough to take into account not just the legal but also ethical, social, scientific and humanitarian aspects.[9]

Alternative dispute resolution (ADR) encompasses many well-known (as well as less well-known) forms of dispute resolution. In particular, it includes arbitration (which is a more rigid quasi-legal form of dispute resolution), mediation or facilitation, conciliation, good offices and inquiry (fact finding). There are also other forms of ADR, which do not necessarily amount to a resolution of the dispute but work as consultation tools. These include local panels set up by City Councils, Advisory Panels set up by Ministries, specialist non-profit dispute resolution services and inter-professional agreements. Of course, there is also the practice of negotiations directly between the parties themselves, including the use of lawyers and experts in the field.

Alternative dispute resolution is promoted by the UN Charter as well as by international conventions in the area. Specifically, article 33(1) of Chapter IV of the Charter, which deals with the powers of the Security Council and the General Assembly in respect of the Pacific Settlement of Disputes, provides that 'the parties to any dispute, the continuance of which is likely to endanger the maintenance of international peace and security, shall, first, seek a solution by negotiation, enquiry, mediation, conciliation, arbitration, judicial settlement, resort to regional agencies or arrangements, or other peaceful means of their own choice'.[10] The same spirit is reflected in the specialised international conventions on the return of cultural objects. Article 17(5) of the 1970 UNESCO Convention on the Means of Prohibiting and Preventing the Illicit Import, Export and Transfer of Ownership in Cultural Property provides that 'at the request of at least two States Parties to this Convention which are engaged in a dispute over its implementation, UNESCO may extend its good offices to reach a settlement between them'. According to Article 8(2) of the 1995 Unidroit Convention on Stolen and Illegally Exported Cultural Objects, parties to a dispute under Part II or Part III of the Convention 'may agree to submit the dispute to any court or other competent authority or to arbitration'.[11]

---

[9] Stamatoudi, n. 6 above, 110. See also Byrne-Sutton, Q. (1998), 'Resolution 273 methods for art-related disputes', IJCP 249; Cornu, M. and M.-A. Renold (2010), 'New developments in the restitution of cultural property: alternative means of dispute resolution, IJCP, **17**, 1–31.

[10] Alternative dispute resolution has been promoted at the European Union level. See the Green Paper on alternative dispute resolution in civil and commercial low (COM (2002)) 196 final, 19.4.2002) and Directive 2008/52/EC of 21 May 2008 on certain aspects of mediation in civil and commercial matters. This Directive applies in cross-border disputes to civil and commercial matters.

[11] 'Alternative dispute resolution is specifically advocated in the case of Holocaust-related claims to cultural property by the Eleventh Principle of the

The UNESCO Intergovernmental Committee for Promoting the Return of Cultural Property to its Countries of Origin or its Restitution in Case of Illicit Appropriation (ICPRCP) has adopted during its 16th session (Paris, 21–23 September, 2010) rules on mediation and conciliation in order to facilitate cultural property dispute resolution within the ambit of its activities and role. This was done in order to strengthen the Committee's role and enhance it in comparison to the mere offering of its good offices with regard to cases that appear on its agenda. These rules are rather flexible and give the parties that wish to submit to them on an *ad hoc* basis, the opportunity, upon agreement, to change a number of these terms on the basis of which a pending case shall be decided.

5.2.1 Arbitration

The notion of judicial settlement is not entirely alien to arbitration. This is because the award in arbitration, as is the case with judgments following court litigation, is based on strict legal doctrine, usually drawn from the law of a particular national legal system.[12]

Initiation of arbitration depends on consent, so in cases of looted or illegally possessed cultural objects, an *ad hoc* agreement between the parties is required.[13] The process followed is usually confidential (even the award can be confidential if the parties agree for it to be so)[14] and relies on a formal procedure, which resembles court litigation in many respects. If this procedure is not followed there are usually sanctions. The award is binding on the parties and can be enforced internationally.

Applicable law can either be public international law (if it is international

Washington Principles of 1998, endorsed by the Vilnius *International Forum on Holocaust Era Looted Cultural Assets* in October 2000, and by the Resolution of the Parliamentary Assembly of the Council of Europe of November 4, 1999, as well as by museum groups in the United States. The establishment of the French Holocaust Restitution Committee in September 1999 and of the UK Spoliation Advisory Panel in May 2000 accords with these enjoinders', see Palmer, N. (2003), 'Litigation, the Best Remedy?', in The Permanent Court of Arbitration/Peace Palace Papers (ed.), *Resolution of Cultural Property Disputes*, Kluwer Law International, 265, at 283 and the corresponding footnotes.

12 Palmer, N. (2003), 'Litigation the Best Remedy?', in The Permanent Court of Arbitration/Peace Palace Papers (ed.), *Resolution of Cultural Property Disputes*, Kluwer Law International, 265, at 279. See also Palmer, N. (2003), 'Arbitration and the Applicable Law', in *ibid.*

13 There can be no original agreement before the claim arises since the dispute is not in itself, or based on, a contractual agreement.

14 The process before the courts is public.

arbitration between states which is at issue) or national law. The procedural law should be defined accordingly. The parties may also agree for the application of extra-legal principles.[15] International arbitration (arbitration under public international law) usually refers to disputes between states. If it is not states that are involved on both sides then we refer to 'mixed arbitration'. A classic example of international arbitration between states is the *Cambodia v. Thailand case* (1962 I.C.J., p.109, known as the Preah-Vihear dispute), which was conducted by the International Court of Justice. In this case Cambodia sought and recovered from Thailand statues and other carvings, which had been removed from the Preah-Vihear Temple by the Thai authorities since the date of the occupation of the Temple by Thailand in 1954.

This case is interesting because it highlights the use that could be made of the Permanent Court of Arbitration (PCA).[16] The PCA was created within the scope of article 33(1) of the UN Charter and was set up by the 1899 Hague Convention I for the Pacific Settlement of Disputes. It was amended by the 1907 Hague Convention.[17] The PCA is not a court. Its

---

[15] This can be derived by article 36(2) of the Statute of the International Court of Justice which permits the Court to decide the case *ex aequo et bono* if the parties agree, but this has never been done. Collier, J. and V. Lowe, n. 7 above, 33. However, such an agreement between private parties may cause problems with regard to the enforcement of the award in a state.

[16] See the examples of two arbitration tribunals established by the Peace Agreement signed in Algiers on 12 December 2000 between the Governments of the State of Eritrea and the Federal Democratic Republic of Ethiopia (The Eritrea–Ethiopia Claims Commission and Eritrea–Ethiopia Boundary Commission). One of the claims the First Commission considered was the deliberate destruction by the Ethiopian military of the Stela of Matara which is considered to be the most famous and historically significant archaeological site in Eritrea. The Commission found that Ethiopia was liable for the destruction and that it should pay monetary damages to Eritrea for this destruction. It is interesting to note that article 5(13) of the Peace Agreement provides that 'in considering claims, the Commission shall apply relevant rules of international law'. Article 19 of the Claims Commission's Rules of Procedure directs the Claims Commission to look to 'international conventions, whether general or particular, in establishing rules expressly recognized by the parties; international custom, as evidence of a general practice accepted as law; the general principles of law recognized by civilized nations; judicial and arbitral decisions and the teaching of the most highly qualified publicists of the various nations, as subsidiary means for the determination of rules of law'. Dally, B.W. (2006), 'Arbitration of International Cultural Property Disputes: the Experience and Initiatives of the Permanent Court of Arbitration', in Hoffman, B.T. (ed), *Art and Cultural Heritage: Law, Policy and Practice*, Cambridge University Press, 465, at 467.

[17] Interesting in this respect are also the Model Rules on Arbitral Procedure, which were adopted by the UN General Assembly in 1958. They have no binding

only permanent organ is an International Bureau, which functions as a registry for the arbitration tribunals that are created on an *ad hoc* basis by the parties to the dispute in order to hear particular cases.[18]

An example of arbitration between an individual and a State is the case of *Maria V. Altmann v. The Republic of Austria* concerning six paintings by Klimt which were seized by the Nazis and given by the Austrian government to a state museum after World War II. In fact the six paintings were housed at the Austrian National Gallery for more than fifty years.[19] The parties agreed to submit to arbitration in Austria after a court ruling was delivered by the US Supreme Court providing that an individual can bring an action against a foreign state for looted art in breach of public international law.[20] In the arbitration which followed this court ruling (and the parties had agreed that it would be final and that they would not have a right to appeal) it was found that Altmann was the sole descendant of Adèle Bloch-Bauer who was the owner of the paintings that were looted from her husband during the Nazi period in Austria. The five paintings were returned to her. A second arbitral award was delivered a few months later concerning the sixth painting.[21] This time the arbitral court found against Altmann due to the fact that the history of ownership relating to this sixth painting was different compared to the other five.

---

force and the parties are free to adopt them if they wish. However their impact seems to be very slight.

[18] Collier, J. and V. Lowe, n. 7 above, 35–6. See also Barker I. (2006), 'Thoughts of an Alternative Dispute Resolution Practitioner on an International ADR Regime for Repatriation of Cultural Property and Works of Art', in B.T. Hoffman n. 15 above, at 483–4, where he refers to the benefits of arbitration: a) enforceability of arbitral awards (see the 1958 Convention on the Recognition and Enforcement of Foreign Arbitral Awards in contrast with judgments of national courts which encounter severe problems in being enforced in the courts of other jurisdictions (the 'New York Convention') to which 144 states have acceded. According to this Convention an award of an Arbitral Tribunal in one country can be enforced in any other country party to the Convention by registering the award in a court in that country), and b) confidentiality. He also refers to useful precedents such as the International Centre for the Settlement of Investment Disputes and the ICANN policy for domain names (at 486–7).

[19] *Maria V. Altmann, Francis Gutmann, Trevor Mantle, George Bentley v. The Republic of Austria*, arbitral award of January 15, 2006, http://bslaw.com/altmann/Klimt/award.pdf.

[20] *Republic of Austria v. Maria V. Altmann*, 541 U.S. 677 (2004) 327 F.3d 1246, affirmed, http://www.law.cornell.edu/supct/html/03-13.ZO.html.

[21] *Maria V. Altmann, Francis Gutmann, Trevor Mantle, George Bentley v. The Republic of Austria*, arbitral award of May 7, 2006, http://bslaw.com/altmann/Zuckerkadndl/Decisions/decision.pdf.

5.2.2 Mediation

Mediation is another form of alternative dispute resolution. As with arbitration, the consent and co-operation of the parties is needed. It is usually not conducted on the basis of law (in the sense of strict legal doctrine) although on most occasions law is taken into account. The mediator is a person who has the approval and mutual consent of the parties to act as a facilitator (or else a diplomat) in the negotiations between them. The mediator usually acts confidentially (if the parties agree) and is not bound by any procedural rules. That means that he/she can meet any party as he/she wishes, on its own, without disclosing details of their discussion (unless an agreement to the contrary is made before the commencement of the process).[22] Also he/she does not need to be a lawyer, although a lawyer is usually needed at the end of the process if an agreement is reached, in order to draft the final agreement. The claim submitted to mediation may change (expand or diminish) during the process or new elements may be added to it. Furthermore, it need not be strictly a legal claim. The outcome of the mediation will be enforceable as a contract but will not be enforceable in the sense that a judicial judgment or an arbitration award are.

The main benefit of mediation is that it is a very flexible procedure. It allows parties to submit wider claims that are of interest to them, following a procedure that is mutually acceptable. Also the resolution is not something which is imposed on them by a third party. Rather, it is an agreement that is reached by the free will of the parties and is mutually acceptable to them. In mediation, other interests apart from law are taken into account. These include ethics, codes of conduct, national policies, public feeling, etc. Mediation permits alternatives that are not possible under law, such as exchanges of objects, forms of co-operation and so on. It may be free, which is another thing that can make it an attractive option. One drawback is that its outcome is not enforceable. The protection offered only equals that of a binding contract.

In public international law mediation is defined as the intervention of a third party who assumes the task of 'reconciling the opposing claims and appeasing the feelings of resentment which may have arisen between the States at variance' (article 4 of the 1899 Hague Convention). It seems that, to a large extent, the literature uses the terms 'mediation' and 'good offices' interchangeably.[23] However, these two notions may be distinguished on the

---

[22] The parties can change any agreement between them as to the process to be followed if there is mutual agreement.

[23] The Hague Conventions 1899 and 1907 do not differentiate between them. Article 33(1) of the UN Charter does not specifically mention good offices. Yet, other instruments do differentiate, such as the Pact of Bogota 1948. Good offices

basis that in mediation the third party involved in facilitating a mutually acceptable solution (who can be either a third state, or a neutral third party such as an interested individual or an Organ of the United States) takes active steps of his own in order for a compromise to be reached. 'Good offices' consists of action taken by a third party to bring about, or initiate, or cause to be continued, negotiations without the third party actively participating in the discussion of the dispute.[24] Good offices include services offered by the UNESCO Intergovernmental Committee for Promoting the Return of Cultural Property to its Countries of Origin or its Restitution in Case of Illicit Appropriation. It can offer assistance in cases of return requests that have been put on its agenda for cultural objects falling outside the 1970 UNESCO Convention. Such cases currently on its agenda[25] are the Parthenon Marbles (currently on display in the British Museum) between the Greek and British Governments and the Sphinx of Boğazköy (currently on display in the Berlin Museum) between the Turkish and German Governments.

This last case has been referred to (informal) mediation under the aegis of the ICPRCP and with the Swiss authorities acting as facilitators.

During its 16th Session (Paris, 21–23 September 2010) the ICPRCP has adopted 'Rules of Procedure for Mediation and Conciliation in Accordance with Article 4, Paragraph 1, of the Statutes of the Intergovernmental Committee for Promoting the Return of Cultural Property to its Countries of Origin or Its Restitution in Case of Illicit Appropriation'. According to them, any request for the return or restitution of cultural property submitted to the Committee may also be dealt with under a mediation or conciliation procedure as these are provided under these rules and if the parties agree to submit to it. These rules define the content of mediation and conciliation for the purposes of the Rules. 'Mediation' is 'a process whereby, with the prior consent of the parties concerned, an outside party intervenes to bring them together and to assist them in reaching an amicable solution of their dispute with respect to the restitution or return of cultural property'. 'Conciliation' is 'a process whereby, subject to their prior consent, the parties concerned submit their dispute with respect to restitution or return of cultural property to a constituted organ for investigation and for efforts to effect an amicable settlement of their dispute'. Only UNESCO Member States and Associate Members of UNESCO may have recourse to these procedures and may represent either their own interests or the interests of public or

---

are specifically mentioned in relation to cultural property claims in article 17(5) of the 1970 UNESCO Convention on the Means of Prohibiting and Preventing the Illicit Import, Export and Transfer of Ownership in Cultural Property.

24 Collier, J. and V. Lowe, n. 7 above, 27.

25 As of September 2010.

private institutions located in their territory or the interests of their nationals. A request to initiate mediation or conciliation may also be addressed to a public or private institution instead of a Member or Associate Member State only if the State in whose territory this is found has been immediately informed of the request by the initiating Member State and does not object.

Mediation and conciliation require the consent of the parties, are to be conducted in conditions of confidentiality and in accordance with the general principles of fairness, impartiality and good faith whilst due regard should be given to international law and recognized principles. It is interesting to note that these procedures are extremely flexible, do not prejudice any other procedure or other means of dispute solving or dispute settlement that the parties have already undertaken and wish to undertake in the future, including legal proceedings. Also the parties may amend the rules of these procedures before their commencement. The procedure is deemed to have been concluded only when a) the parties agree that a settlement has been reached; b) consent in writing that the procedure is concluded; c) at the expiry of a time limit that the parties have set without a settlement having been reached and; d) when one of the parties has notified in writing its withdrawal from the procedure. The outcome of the procedure is binding on the parties only when the parties reach a binding agreement.

5.2.3 Other Modes of ADR

Apart from arbitration, mediation and good offices, there are also other forms of ADR, such as conciliation, inquiry and fact finding, negotiation, not-for-profit dispute resolution services, inter-professional agreements (which facilitate dispute resolution), and local or governmental panels working towards this aim.[26]

Inquiry or fact finding is a mode used in public international law disputes and does not involve the application of legal rules. It is used in disputes that are factual in order to shed light on the true facts. Article 9 of the Hague Convention for the Pacific Settlement of Disputes 1907 defines inquiry as the means 'to facilitate a solution of . . . disputes by elucidating the facts by means of an impartial and conscientious investigation'. This inquiry is usually carried out by a third party and the facts deriving from it should be accepted by both parties. If legal aspects arise during the course of the inquiry, they can be solved by means of negotiation, mediation, good offices and conciliation.[27]

---

[26] For cases settled on the basis of mediation, see Chapter 6, fn.96.

[27] Fact finding is also defined in the UN Declaration on Fact-Finding (9 December 1991) in relation to international peace and and security: 'any activ-

Conciliation is a mode of ADR, which combines the characteristics of inquiry and mediation. That means that the person or commission to which the dispute is referred has to make an impartial elucidation of the facts and to put forward proposals for settlement. Such proposals are not binding on the parties.[28] J.P. Cot describes it as 'intervention in the settlement of an international dispute by a body having no political authority of its own, but enjoying the confidence of the parties to the dispute, with the task of investigating every aspect of the dispute and of proposing a solution which is not binding on the parties'.[29] Although conciliation is not based on rules of law since the aim is to reach an equitable solution, such rules are taken into account together with state practices. There are multilateral treaties which provide for conciliation, though not in the area of culture.[30] Also the General Assembly of the United Nations may appoint commissions to effect conciliation. For that reason, in 1990 the UN circulated Draft Rules for the Conciliation of Disputes between States, which provide for procedural points.[31] In 1996 the Permanent Court of Arbitration adopted Optional Rules for Conciliation for States making use of its facilities.[32]

In the UNESCO ICPRCP Rules of Procedure for Mediation and Conciliation (2010) conciliation is defined as 'a process whereby, subject to their prior consent, the parties concerned submit their dispute with respect to restitution or return of cultural property to a constituted organ for investigation and for efforts to effect an amicable settlement of their dispute'.[33] UNESCO Member States and Associate Members of UNESCO only have recourse to this procedure (or to mediation) and they may represent the interests of public or private institutions located in their territory or the interests of their nationals. They can also amend the rules

---

ity designed to obtain detailed knowledge of the relevant facts of any dispute or situation which the competent United Nations organs need in order to exercise effectively their functions in relation to the maintenance of international peace and security'.

[28] *United Nations Handbook on the Peaceful Settlement of Disputes* (1992), New York: United Nations, 45–5, and Merrills, J.G. (1987), 'The Role and Limits of International Adjudication,' in Butler, W.E. (ed.), *International Law and the International System*, Dordrecht: M. Nijhoff, chapter 4, as they are referred to in Collier, J. and V. Lowe, n. 7 above, 29.

[29] Cot, J.P. (1972), *International Conciliation*, London: Europa, p.9.

[30] Such is the French-Swiss Agreement of 6 April 1925.

[31] (1991) *International Legal Materials* 229, adopted as UN GA res. /50/50 (1996).

[32] Permanent Court of Arbitration, Basic Documents: conventions, rules, model clauses and guidelines, The Hague, 1998, http://www.law.cornell.edu/icj/pca/eng/home.htm. There are also the UNCITRAL Conciliation Rules adopted in 1980 for international commercial disputes.

[33] Article 2(3) of the Rules of Procedure for Mediation and Conciliation.

before the commencement of the procedure (art.1(2)).[34] As mentioned above with regard to the ICPRCP Rules of Mediation and Conciliation, conciliation is defined in these Rules in a very flexible way whilst clear priority is given to how Member States of UNESCO and UNESCO Associate Member States want to form it given the fact that they have the right to amend the rules before the commencement of the procedure (article 1(2)).[35] A request to initiate a mediation or conciliation procedure may be submitted by a Member State or Associate Member of UNESCO with regard to a public or private institution or an individual if they are in possession of the cultural property concerned (article 4(2)).

Negotiation (or else *consultation*) constitutes *par excellence* the means by which the majority of disputes are resolved and settled. It is a direct process which involves only the parties in the dispute and prior consultation is variously referred to in treaties as an obligation, a means of settlement[36] or even as a preliminary resort to other means of settlement[37]

---

[34] For more details, see above section 5.2.2 on 'mediation'.

[35] See also article 2(3)–(6):

'3. For purposes of these Rules, 'Conciliation' means a process whereby, subject to their prior consent, the parties concerned submit their dispute with respect to restitution or return of cultural property to a constituted organ for investigation and for efforts to effect an amicable settlement of their dispute.

4. A conciliation commission shall be composed of conciliators who are preferably independent experts on restitution and return of cultural properties whose number shall be mutually agreed upon by the parties concerned.

5. Each party to the dispute shall appoint one or two conciliators. An additional conciliator, which shall be of a nationality different from that of the parties involved, shall be chosen jointly by the parties and will be the President of the conciliation commission. If the parties cannot agree on that person within 60 days the procedure provided under Article 7.2 below will be followed.

6. A list of potential mediators and conciliators shall be drawn up and maintained by the Secretariat for the information of, and possible use by, the Parties in appointing mediators or conciliators. To that end, each Member State of UNESCO shall be invited to nominate two individuals who could fulfil the role of mediator or conciliator in international cultural property disputes. The list shall be reviewed at two-year intervals when Member States may confirm existing nominations or submit new nominations. The Parties to a mediation or conciliation procedure shall remain free to appoint mediators or conciliators not included in this list'.

[36] See for example the Mexico – US Convention for the Recovery and Return of Stolen Vehicles and Aircraft 1981, art. VIII, (1981) 20 *International Legal Materials* 711. As referred to in Collier, J. and V. Lowe, n. 7 above, 21.

[37] See for example the Treaty Concerning the Establishment of the Republic of Cyprus 1960, art. 10, 382 United Nations Treaty Series 10. As referred to in Collier, J. and V. Lowe (1999), n. 7 above, 21.

before action is taken.[38] It goes without saying that it does not preclude resort to other settlement procedures including recourse to the courts.

'Negotiations' is rather a flexible term. Given the fact that cultural property disputes can be solved either at an international level or a private level, 'negotiations' need not signify a particular format or weight. Most cultural property disputes are solved by negotiations between the interested parties in the format they find convenient. They also sometimes run parallel to court action as court action may exert pressure for their conclusion. Some cases that were recently settled through negotiations were disputes concerning the return of Greek and Italian antiquities from the J.P. Getty Museum in California (Los Angeles) to the Greek and Italian States, as well as the return of two antiquities from the Shelby White and Leon Levy collection (famous collectors residing in New York) to the Greek Government.[39,40] Other recent cases that were resolved on the basis of talks

---

[38] See for example the NATO Agreement, 4 Paris 1949, art. 4, 34 United Nations Treaty Series 243 and Kirgis, F.L. (1983), *Prior Consultation in International Law*, Charlottesville: University of Virginia Press. As referred to in Collier, J. and V. Lowe (1999), n. 7 above, 21.

[39] There are also a series of other cases concerning the return of antiquities to Greece, such as the return of a fragment from the Parthenon's sculptural decoration from the University of Heidelberg (2006), the return of four antiquities from the Getty Museum (2006), a collection of 48 ancient Greek coins from Sweden (2006), the return of a fragment of an ancient Greek marble relief portraying Athens from a Danish citizen after 110 years (2007), six ceramic oinochoe from a British professor of archaeology (2007), a stolen statue of Apollonas Lykeios from Gortyna, Crete from Switzerland (2007), 94 stolen antiquities from the Theodoropoulos collection in Germany (2007), the upper part of a grave stele dated to the early part of 4th century B.C. originating from Porto Rafti and a bronze calyx krater dated approximately to 340 B.C. originating from Pieria, Northern Greece, were returned from the Shelby White and Leon Levy collection to Greece (2008), the voluntary return of a fragment coming from the Acropolis site found in Sweden to Greece (2008), an icon dated to 14th century AD stolen from a monastery in Serres, Northern Greece, spotted in London and returned to Greece on the basis of legal proceedings (2008), 116 shells and 7 coins dated from 5th century BC to 2nd century BC originating from Thoriko in Attika were returned to Greece from the University of Gent in Belgium (2009), 96 bronze and pottery dated to the late classic period originating from Thessalia were returned from Germany (where they were confiscated) to Greece (2009), a fragment of a byzantine stele dated between 11th and 12th century AD was returned from a British collector to Greece (2009), five rare Byzantine hagiography frescoes stolen in 1978 from the Palaiopanagia Church in Steni, Evia, were returned to Greece from Basle, Switzerland (2010), and so on.

[40] Negotiations usually result in the conclusion of Agreements which occasionally take place between states and public or private institutions or private parties. Such examples are the agreements between Peru with Yale University in the

and negotiations between the parties are the return of the Axum Obelisk from Italy to Ethiopia, the return of the Stone Birds from Germany to Zimbabwe and their reunification, the return of ancestral human remains from the Royal College of Surgeons to South Australia and the return of the ceremonial mask of the Kwakwaka'wakw people of Vancouver Island from the British Museum to Canada. They were all success stories in the sense that they have promoted co-operation, collaboration and good relations between the parties. The same applies to the reunification of the neo-Sumerian alabaster figure, which was divided between the Louvre and the Metropolitan Museum and to the very successful 'Utimut' Project for the return of cultural objects from Denmark to Greenland.[41]

There have been panels or advisory bodies in certain countries, which have dealt with the issue of restitution of cultural property with the aim of either resolving it, or at least making proposals to set the process in motion. One local panel, well known because of the publicity it attracted, is the Repatriation Committee set up by the Glasgow City Council. In 1998 it decided to return the Lakota Ghost Dance Shirt to the Wounded Knee Survivors Association from one of the museums that was under the control of Glasgow City Council. This decision was reached on the basis of public opinion (expressed at a public hearing and via invited correspondence) and the fulfilment of five criteria put forward by the Committee. The five criteria were: a) the status of those making the request, i.e. their right to represent the community to which the object originally belonged, b) the continuity between the community which created the object and the current community on whose behalf the request was being made, c) the cultural and religious importance of the object to the community, d) how the object had been acquired by the museum and its subsequent and future use, and e) the fate of the object if it were to be returned. This case was an exemplary one in the sense that the Committee constituted a very flexible and equitable way to deal with such a dispute, and, as the Head of the Glasgow Museums and Galleries mentioned while giving evidence to the House of Commons Culture, Media and Sport Committee on 18 May 2000, legislative constraints should not be used to discourage broader public policy arguments and informed public debate.[42]

United States, Italy with Metropolitan Museum of Art of New York, Princeton University Art Museum, the Paul Getty Museum of Los Angeles and the Museum of Fine Arts of Boston, and Greece with the Paul Getty Museum of Los Angeles and Shelby White (a famous New York collector).

41 See the proceedings of the 2008 Athens Conference (Return and Restitution of Cultural Objects) as published in the May 2009 *Museum International*, vol. 61, No.1–2.

42 See the oral and written evidence given by representatives of the Council

Another Panel with a very similar role was set up in 2000 by the UK Minister of Arts.[43] This panel had an advisory role and dealt with claims against UK public museums by persons who lost possession of cultural objects during the Nazi period, specifically between 1933 and 1945.[44] This panel was called the Spoliation Advisory Panel and examined the claims submitted to it on legal and moral grounds. Legal grounds were examined on the basis of specific findings by an independent legal advisor, whilst moral grounds were examined on the basis of the conditions under which the object was lost, the circumstances under which it was acquired by the museum, the acts of the parties involved, whether they were sufficiently diligent and so on. The Panel could make recommendations as to the response to be made to a particular claim as well as to more general issues pertaining to legislative or other changes which should be made in order to deal more appropriately with existing and future claims. The Panel recommended the return of cultural objects as well as the payment of compensation or other measures such as mentioning the original provenance of a work once retained in the museum collection. This Panel, though it was not a legal body, took into account both the legal and moral aspects of each case in order to achieve a solution which was fair and just to the parties involved. It worked on particular rules of procedure.[45] Up to 2008 it considered about eight cases of objects looted during the Nazi period.[46]

---

to the House of Commons Culture, Media and Sport Committee in May 2000 in Seventh Report, vol. II, at pp.137–50, Commendation by the Committee, vol. I, paragraphs 136 and 199(x), and Memorandum submitted by Glasgow City Council to the Select Committee on Culture, Media and Sport in (2000) *Art, Antiquity & Law* 371, as referred to in Palmer, N, n. 11 above, 265, at 284.

[43] The then UK Minister of Arts was Alan Howarth.

[44] See N. Palmer, *Museums and the Holocaust: Law, Principle & Practice*, Leicester: Institute of Art and Law, 2000.

[45] http://www.culture.gov.uk/what_we_do/cultural_property/3296.aspx.

[46] The reports that have been produced so far are the following: Spoliation Advisory Panel rules that two fine pieces of porcelain, acquired in good faith by the British Museum and the Fitzwilliam Museum, were looted during the Nazi era (2008); Report of the Spoliation Advisory Panel in respect of three Rubens Paintings now in the possession of the Courtauld Institute of Art, London (2007); Report of the Spoliation Advisory Panel in Respect of three Drawings now in the Possession of the Courtauld Institute of Art (2007); Report of the Spoliation Advisory Panel in respect of four drawings now in the possession of the British Museum (2006); Report of the Spoliation Advisory Panel in respect of a painting held by the Ashmolean Museum in Oxford (2006); Report of the Spoliation Advisory Panel in respect of a 12th century manuscript now in the possession of the British Library (2005); Report of the Spoliation Advisory Panel in respect of a painting now in possession of Glasgow City Council (2004); Report of the Spoliation Advisory Panel in respect of a painting now in the possession of the

It is interesting to note that, although in some of these cases the Panel recommended the return of the objects, such return has been difficult to accomplish because of the legal restrictions on museums concerning the release of such objects. In 2006 the (UK) Department for Culture, Media and Sport conducted a consultation[47] on whether the current statutory and other legal restrictions preventing national museums from de-accessioning works of art in their collections should be lifted to allow restitution of items lost during the Nazi era. This consultation resulted in a Report (Restitution of Objects Spoliated in the Nazi-Era: A Consultation Document, July 2006),[48] which proposed that legislation should be introduced to permit restitution of such objects.[49] Similar panels were set up in other countries such as France, the Netherlands, Austria and Germany.

In May 2001 the then Minister for the Arts, Alan Howarth, set up a Working Group on Human Remains in order to examine the law and practice relating to the current legal status of human remains in publicly funded museums and galleries in the UK. The Working Group's Report was published in November 2003 and amongst its suggestions was the setting up of a Human Remains Advisory Panel, which would comprise independent government-appointed experts and would consider 'references relating to claims and controversies regarding the retention and treatment of human remains by national institutions'.[50] A change in

---

Tate Gallery (2001). These reports can be found at http://www.culture.gov.uk/what_we_do/cultural_property/3296.aspx.

47 The consultation period was 10 July–10 November 2006.

48 http://www.culture.gov.uk/reference_library/consultations/1116.aspx.

49 Up to 2006, the Panel had completed reports on five claims for objects held by respectively the Tate, the British Library, Glasgow City Council (as part of the Burrell Collection), the Ashmolean Museum and the British Museum. In four of the five cases it found that the claim was a valid one, and in two cases – a painting previously attributed to Chardin in the Burrell Collection, and a 12th-century manuscript (the Beneventan Missal) held in the British Library, the Panel recommended that the object concerned should be returned to the claimant. In both these cases, there were legal restrictions on the release of the objects concerned from the collections. In its report relating to the Beneventan Missal, the Spoliation Advisory Panel recommended that legislation should be introduced to permit restitution of objects falling within the Panel's terms of reference.

50 Palmer, N., n. 10 above, at 286. 'The Working Group recommended that the HRAP shall be accessible to all relevant parties with a sufficient interest in the treatment and condition of human remains held in public museum collections and shall have the power to make recommendations on all issues relating to the return, retention, treatment, handling, use, safekeeping and control of human remains', Report, of the Working Group on Human Remains, Department of Culture, Media and Sport (DCMS) of the British Government, 14 November 2003, http://webarchive.nationalarchives.gov.uk/+/http://www.culture.gov.uk/

the law was regarded as necessary, in order to enable museums to release human remains from their collections. Section 47 of the Human Tissue Act 2004 came into force in the UK enabling museums to return items, such as Aboriginal remains, to their place of origin, without being prevented from doing so by the Museums Act 1964.[51] [52]

Although these panels could be considered to offer services akin to mediation they do not constitute mediation *stricto sensu* by reason of the fact that (though having consulted the parties) they have not been set up by mutual agreement of the parties involved and their final recommendation (based on equity rather than strict law) does not necessarily constitute a solution mutually acceptable to the parties but rather an independent recommendation concluded by a body which has been set up unilaterally.

Other modes of ADR are specialist, not-for-profit dispute resolution services (such as *ArtResolve*, inaugurated in June 2000), which in fact play the role of a private mediator. Their aim is to achieve equity solutions which do not rely solely on legal doctrine. There are also private agreements between the parties that bind them to the resolution of claims which may arise in the future between them. These agreements provide for recourse to arbitration or mediation rather than to the courts. Usually if such a resolution is not achieved within a particular period of time then the claim is taken to the courts on the basis of the provisions enshrined in the contract. Such agreements usually exist between parties that have already agreed the return or restitution of one or more cultural objects and this deal has been struck as a result of the negotiations. There are also agreements between European countries and their former colonies for the return and repatriation of cultural objects.[53]

---

reference_library/publications/4553.aspx, chapter 12, Recommendation V(ii) as referred to in N. Palmer, n. 10 above, 286.

51 Human remains were returned (on 16 November 2006) from the Natural History Museum, which acted on advice from its Human Remains Advisory Panel concerning a claim lodged by the Australian Government in November 2005, which was based on a request to it from the Tasmanian Aboriginal Centre.

52 There have also been other cases where legislation was required in order for museums to return artefacts to their countries of origin. A law was passed in France in order to regulate the exchange of works between France and Spain in 1941 (Law of 19 July, 1941) and another one in 1956 for the return of sixty Japanese items by the Guimet Museum to the National Museum in Tokyo by exchange (Law No. 56–631 of 29 June, 1956). Another example is the return to South Africa of the human remains of Hottentot Venus, i.e. the remains of the person known as Saartjie Baartman (Law No. 2002–323 of 6 March, 2002).

53 Simpson, M. (1997), *Museums and Repatriation: An Account of Contested Items in Museum Collections in the UK, with Comparative Material from Other Countries*, London: Museums Association, 57 *et seq.*

An example of an agreement within the ambit of the ones described in the previous paragraph is that between the Rare Books Group of the Libraries Association and the Antiquarian Book Dealers' Association, which was concluded in 1996, and concerns the resolution of claims relating to antiquarian books stolen from libraries and acquired by book dealers.[54] There have been some problems under UK law with regard to the enforcement of such a resolution. However, such agreements should be welcomed particularly on the basis that they deal with objects whose economic value does not always justify legal action.[55]

5.3 CULTURAL DIPLOMACY

Cultural diplomacy is a wider term that covers any kind of cultural exchange and co-operation between states, such as exhibitions, loans, exchange of know-how and expertise, co-organised and co-operated excavations, combined research, coordination of cultural politics and policies and so on. These exchanges can be used as a bargaining tool to put pressure on the resolution of cultural property claims or as a basis for the creation of a positive friendly spirit within which such claims can be solved. Culture is the currency of our days and in an era of globalisation, it has been proven on many occasions that state interests in culture can be co-accommodated and served in a mutually acceptable way. Claims for the return of cultural objects to their countries of origin should be approached in this spirit of mutual understanding and benefit to world culture. In this climate, the return of an object may form the basis of co-operation and cultural exchanges between states.

5.4 CONCLUSIONS

More than ever it seems that the trend lies towards an out-of-court resolution of cultural claims concerning the return of cultural objects to their countries of origin. That, of course, does not mean that resort to court litigation will not remain an important way to request the return of objects that have been stolen, or are illegally exported from their country

---

[54] Feather, J. (1997), 'Disputed Titles in Antiquarian Books', *Art, Antiquity & Law, 373.*

[55] Palmer, N. n. 10 above, 282. N. Palmer contends that modern English Law is now willing to uphold non-curial resolutions on non-legal principles.

of origin and for which time limitations have not expired and considerable proof is available. However, most cultural property cases lie in the grey area with regard to time limitations and proof because of the particularities the black market in art presents.[56] On top of everything else, cultural property claims present ethical, moral or humanitarian aspects, which on many occasions are at least as important as the legal ones. Court litigation, by its nature, is not sufficiently equipped to take such aspects into account. Therefore the judgments delivered by the courts do not always amount to equitable solutions that are well suited to cultural property claims. In addition they do not always correspond to public feeling. Alternative dispute resolution and especially modes other than arbitration (which comes particularly close to court litigation), provide for flexibility in the sense that they take into account various aspects and trends, put the matter in a wider context and work on parties' mentalities through proposals, discussions and the possible offer of cultural exchanges. Such modes of resolution of disputes may occasionally be hindered by law and public policy when it comes to the enforcement of their outcome. Yet such problems can be overcome since the final result will usually take the form of a contract and will be enforced as such to the extent that it does not impinge on a state's public policy provisions.[57]

The fact that a considerable body of soft law has been developed in the field of cultural property restitution is another indication of the fact that the law seems inadequate to deal with these issues. Soft law starts transforming wider equitable principles into legal principles by practice and consistent application. These principles can easily be taken into account in ADR.

ADR has been encouraged by many national legal systems as well as international law, because on most occasions it is cost-effective, flexible, can be conducted in a positive and friendly spirit, and helps towards the attainment of mutually acceptable solutions. The most recent example is that of the UNESCO ICPRCP Rules of Procedure for Mediation and Conciliation adopted in Paris in 2010, as explained above.

---

56 Difficulty in finding prior possessors because of the confidentiality in the area, which covers the in-between illegal transactions, covert routes of trafficking of these objects, the fact that they are hidden in bank vaults or other places for years until claims become statute-barred, and so on.

57 Decisive in this respect will be the law of the state where the contract is to be enforced.

6. Evolution and basic trends

6.1 FACTS AND INDICATIONS

Cultural property found in museums and private collections has been acquired through the years on the basis of different factual circumstances. Some of these were illegal or of an ambiguous/unethical nature. War, hostilities or occupation (which are not the subject of this book), penury, turbulent political circumstances, colonisation or a mixture of all, form some of those circumstances.[1] In fact, they could be summarised as the result of power, oppression and necessity combined with an appetite for money or love of art or a habit of collecting. Theft, illegal export, import and transfer of ownership of cultural objects are also included.

The states where most of this property has ended up are western states. The reason for that is that these states had the financial means to acquire such art, to build museums and house it as well as to allow world famous collectors to flourish. It was these same states that had established colonies and turned collecting into a noble pastime, clearly demonstrating wealth, prestige and superiority. After museums in the West had built up and were exhibiting their magnificent collections of artefacts, states of origin (some of them newly independent and trying to restore their assaulted dignity or create their national myths) requested the return of their objects, arguing that they were indispensable to their national identity – an identity over which they had fought wars. Museums and collectors (public or private) have tried to find an ideology that would legitimise these collections and permit them to refuse restitution and return. The ideology has changed and evolved over time and has varied from theories (such as the 'primacy of the object',[2] 'internationalism', 'cosmopolitan-

---

[1] See more recently the looting of Iraq's cultural treasures. Bogdanos, M. and William P. (2005), *Thieves of Baghdad: One Marine's Passion for Ancient Civilizations and the Journey to Recover the World's Greatest Stolen Treasures*, New York: Bloomsbury.

[2] Wyss, M.Ph. (1992), *Kultur als eine Dimension der Völkerrechtsordnung, Von Kulturgüterschutz zur internationalen kulturellen Kooperation*, Zurich: Schultthess Polygraphischer Verlag, 171, and Merryman, J.H. (1994) 'The Nation and the Object', *International Journal of Cultural Property*, 61, at 74.

ism') to the concept of the 'universal museum'. It has been distressing for the source states (or communities) to realise that the destination states, which did not appear to respect them in war, occupation or for some other reason, nevertheless respected and valued their culture, as if culture was something distinct and different from the people who created it. More than ever these people needed this part of their heritage back, to prove their worthiness, their history, their continuation in time and their cultural identity. A series of requests was made in the late nineteenth and early twentieth centuries. The dispossessed states, because of their earlier suffering, had considerable arguments about the return of their cultural treasures at a time when cultural property law was still very much under formation.

There is common agreement that in the last decades, and especially since the adoption of the 1970 UNESCO Convention on the Means of Prohibiting and Preventing the Illicit Import, Export and Transfer of Ownership in Cultural Property, cultural property law and sentiment have developed and progressed considerably towards more humanitarian approaches. They no longer assess the worth of an artefact purely in terms of its decorative or aesthetic value, but relate it to its cultural, archaeological, ethnographic, religious, humanitarian or other context. In other words, they relate it to its living or surviving environment in which people, their principles, beliefs and ethics have an important role to play.

6.1.1 Law

It would have been very difficult in the 1970s for one to imagine that an international legal instrument, such as the 1970 UNESCO Convention, would become a standard-setting instrument in the area of protection of cultural property. It would also have been hard to imagine that this Convention would be adopted by market states and that these states would enact laws protective of other countries' national heritage. The negotiations during its drafting pointed in the opposite direction. The different views and mentalities in the area looked insurmountable. Yet, the 1970 UNESCO Convention was signed and (much) later adopted by a large number of states. Although its provisions are quite vague (thus subject to multiple interpretations) and sanctions are almost non-existent, it still constituted a decisive step in the area of protection of cultural property in the sense that it a) raised awareness and performed an educative role, b) created the basis and paved the way (by setting minimum standards of protection) for the adoption of other instruments in the area at national, regional and international level, and c) linked the protection of cultural property to the protection of national cultural heritage and to the fact that a cultural object's value can best be appreciated in its original context.[3]

Today 120 states have ratified the 1970 UNESCO Convention. Amongst these states are major market states such as the United States, the United Kingdom, Switzerland, Japan and others. These states have enacted (or amended) their national laws in order to conform with the Convention and no devastating changes – as they feared – have taken place. In other words, offering protection to other countries' cultural heritage and co-operating with them to this end has not, apparently, undermined their cultural policies, has not killed their art trade, has not jeopardised the status of their museums, public or private collections nor has it emptied their collections.[4] It has merely taught states and the agents of trade to be more vigilant and more respectful towards other peoples' cultures and operate in a climate of good faith, transparency and co-operation.

The 1970 UNESCO Convention has also helped attitudes mature and therefore paved the way towards the drafting of the 1995 Unidroit Convention on Stolen or Illegally Exported Cultural Objects. The Unidroit Convention provides for common minimal rules on the good faith acquisition of cultural objects that have been stolen or illegally exported from their countries of origin. The Convention was an attempt to eliminate the obstacles placed in the way of the restitution and return of cultural objects to their countries of origin by reason of the disparities between the various national systems. So far this Convention has only been ratified by 30 states; not as many states as ratified the 1970 UNESCO Convention. However, it is considered to be a standard-setting instrument in the area (by reason of the fact that it is the sole international legal instrument in its regulating field) and the principles it reflects can be taken into account by the courts. In a Swiss case[5] where France sought judicial assistance

---

[3] 'Considering that cultural property constitutes one of the basic elements of civilisation and national culture, and that its true value can be appreciated only in relation to the fullest possible information regarding its origin, history and traditional setting.' The Preamble to the 1970 UNESCO Convention.

[4] Both Switzerland and Britain have enacted legislation in this respect. In particular Britain has enacted the Dealing in Cultural Objects (Offences) Act 2003, http://www.culture.gov.uk, which makes it illegal to knowingly deal in stolen artefacts. Zainab Bahrani (2004), 'British and Swiss get tough about smuggling in the fray', *Wall Street Journal*, 18 February. See also Parkhouse, A. (2006), 'The Illicit Trade in Cultural Objects: Recent Developments in the United Kingdom', in B.T. Hoffman (ed), *Art and Cultural Heritage. Law, Policy and Practice*, Cambridge University Press, 178, at 180 *et seq*.

[5] *Desportes Still-Life case*, Chambre d'accusation de Genève, Cour de Droit Public, 1 April 1997. See also the *Republic of Ecuador v. Danusso* case (Tribunale

for the return of a painting, 'the Federal Court of Public Law noted the public international interest in the return of stolen cultural property and, citing the UNESCO Convention of 1970 to which France is a party and the Unidroit Convention, which France, Italy and Switzerland have all signed, stated that these represent a common inspiration and thus constitute the expression of international public order either in force or in formation'.[6]

It is also worth noting that the international legal instruments that follow in the area (such as the 2001 UNESCO Convention on the Protection of Underwater Cultural Heritage and the 2005 UNESCO Convention on the Protection and Promotion of the Diversity of Cultural

---

di Torino, 25 March 1982, RDIPP 1982, 625) in relation to a collection of archaeological objects illicitly removed and exported from Ecuador into Italy where the judge made reference to the 1970 UNESCO Convention, although it was not applicable to the dispute. The Convention served as a threshold to measure the compatibility of Ecuadorian law to the forum's fundamental public policy. As referred to in Carducci, G. (2006), 'The Growing Complexity of International Art Law: Conflict of Laws, Uniform Law, Mandatory Rules, UNSC Resolutions and EU Regulations', in Hoffman (ed), *Art and Cultural Heritage* n. 5 above, 68, at 80. See also Francioni, Fr. and Lenzerini, F. (2006) 'The Obligation to Prevent and Avoid Destruction of Cultural Heritage: From Bamiyan to Iraq', in Hoffman (ed), *ibid*, 28, at 34 where they mention the importance of customary international law which, unlike treaty law, is *ex se* of binding character for all the countries of the world because it needs no formal acceptance by governments, whereas treaties must be ratified or acceded to by the state concerned in order to produce any binding effect for such a state. Later on they provide the example of the US Supreme Court which 'has proclaimed since 1815 that courts are 'bound by the laws of nations, which is part of the law of the land' [See *The Neriede*, 13 U.S. 388, 423 (1815) and *The Paquete Habana*, 175 U.S. 677, 700 (1900)], thus instructing national judges to routinely enforce customary international law. In a recent judgment, a District Court of New York applied such a principle by stating that 'Congress's failure to ratify [an international treaty is not sufficient to exempt the United States from the obligation to respect] the customary international law principles contained in and underlying [such a] treaty' [*Befarry v. Reno*, 183 F. Supp. 2d 584 (E.D.N.Y. 2002), p.29], thus confirming the assumption that, when a customary norm actually exists, states are bound to respect it irrespective of whether or not they have ratified the existing international conventions proclaiming the rule that corresponds to the content of the customary norm itself' (at 34). In order to create a customary norm, it is important that a Convention has been ratified by a large number of states, that it is of an authoritative character (such as the UNESCO Conventions where a general *opinion iuris* is supposed to exist because it represents nearly all of the nations of the world that participate in the General Conference) and that the protection of cultural heritage is a matter of public interest recognised in most national legal systems of the world (at 35).

6 Prott, L. (1995), *Commentary on the Unidroit Convention on stolen and Illegaly Exported Cultural Objects 1995*, Leicester: Institute of Art and Law, p.87.

Expressions), though not specific to the prevention and combat of the illicit trade in cultural objects, are nevertheless underpinned by some of the same substantial principles, for example *in situ* preservation of underwater cultural heritage and respect for cultural diversity, respectively.[7]

National and regional law should also be added. During recent decades a number of national legal instruments have been enacted, largely as a result of the countries' accession to international conventions, but also as a result of sensitisation, co-operation and interest in the area. A substantial exchange of information has taken place on the basis of bilateral or multilateral agreements and co-operation through international organisations. One such example is UNESCO and its legal database, which contains substantial amounts of information about national cultural property laws, administrative procedures and export certificates. In addition the ICPRCP currently promotes model legislation, which would allow states that have not already done so, to adopt laws recognising state proprietary rights to their cultural property, in order to facilitate restitution and return of their missing cultural property.[8] Even the European Union, with a clear trade-oriented background, has recognised through legislation the need for the protection of its Member States' cultural property. Similar provisions exist in relation to the Commonwealth Scheme.[9]

---

7 See also Preamble 18 to the 2005 UNESCO Convention on the Protection and Promotion of the Diversity of Cultural Expressions: '*Being convinced* that cultural activities, goods and services have both an economic and a cultural nature, because they convey identities, values and meanings, and must therefore not be treated as solely having commercial value'.

8 UNESCO, Report on the 2008–2009 activities and the fifteenth session of the intergovernmental committee for promoting the return of cultural property to its countries of origin or its restitution in case of illicit appropriation, General Conference (35th Session, Paris, 2009), 35 C/REP/14, 24 August 2009 <http://unesdoc.unesco.org/images/0018/001837/183741e.pdf>.

9 The Commonwealth Scheme was initiated on the basis of the problems that had arisen in 1973 by the *Ortiz* case (*Attorney-General of New Zealand v. Ortiz* [1982] 2 W.L.R. 10. See also Cater, R. R. (1982), 'The Taranaki Panels – A case-study in the recovery of cultural heritage', *Museum*, 34, 256). In 1973 a London dealer in primitive art took a Maori carving from New Zealand without a permit (according to New Zealand law). The House of Lords decided (1983) that New Zealand had no standing in the English Courts to recover the carving. After a series of meetings and discussions the Law Ministers of the Commonwealth agreed in Mauritius in November 1993 to a 'Scheme for the Protection of the Material Cultural Heritage'. The Scheme deals with illegally exported cultural treasures and provides a simplified procedure for the return of those objects to their country of origin (which is party to the Scheme). For a more detailed analysis see O' Keefe, P. (1995), 'Protection of the Material Cultural Heritage:

6.1.2 Ethics, Morality and Public Feeling

Apart from the legal instruments, a number of soft law instruments (such as codes of ethics, declarations, recommendations, guidelines and so on), which were discussed in the relevant chapter,[10] point in the direction of using the protection of national cultural heritage as a vehicle for the protection of the world's cultural heritage. Although the above do not constitute law *stricto sensu*, they are still capable of creating and conveying law-making principles, which may become law by consistent practice and application.[11] These soft law instruments, along with public feeling, have educated, sensitised and formed mentalities which were favourable towards the return of cultural objects to their countries of origin, in order for these objects to be put back into their original context, where they can reflect their full meaning. Their alienation from such a context is in itself a wrongful act, irrespective of time limitations, good faith acquisition or any other actual infringement of law. Ethics have a dual role to play: a) a *preventive* one requiring the agents of the art trade (traders, dealers, auctioneers, museums, collectors, purchasers and so on) to be more vigilant, acquire the full documentation and history of the artefact, gain permission by the state(s) of origin and conduct their purchase in a transparent and overt manner, and b) a *co-operative* one in order for the *return* of the object that has been detached from its cultural environment to be effected as soon as possible and with the least possible expense incurred by the requesting party.

---

the Commonwealth Scheme', *International and Comparative Law Quarterly*, 44, 147. Currently the Commonwealth numbers 54 countries: 19 from Africa, 8 from Asia, 2 from the Americas, 12 from the Caribbean, 3 from Europe and 10 from the South Pacific.

[10] Chapter 4.

[11]

'While it is probably premature to speak of the formation of an international custom making some form of return or restitution of cultural property mandatory, we can, however, observe a practice emerging coupled with a sense of obligation, based on precisely those ethical considerations that come close to the *opinion necessitatis*, the condition required for a custom to come into being. In the area of cultural property, as in many others, ethical considerations precede the formation of a rule of law'.

See Cornu, M. and M.-A. Renold (2010), 'New Developments in the Restitution of Cultural Property: Alternative Means of Dispute Resolution', *International Journal of Cultural Property*, **17**(1), 23.

6.2 PRINCIPLES AND TRENDS

Various conclusions can be drawn from the above. These conclusions can be considered as principles or trends in the area in the sense that some of them are well established, whilst others, corresponding more to morality and public feeling and less to law, are still under formation.[12]

6.2.1 Protection of the Cultural Heritage of the Country of Origin

The first principle is the protection of the national cultural heritage of the country of origin.[13] Under particular circumstances this also covers the protection of the cultural heritage of a community or a group.[14] This principle has been consistently recognised in all international and European Union legal instruments concerning the illicit trade in art. In particular the main aim of the 1970 UNESCO Convention is set out as the non-impoverishment of the cultural heritage of the countries of origin (article 2). It is specifically provided in the same Convention that the trade in cultural objects exported contrary to the law of the country of origin is 'illicit' (article 3) and that the States Parties agree to prevent the importation of such objects and facilitate their return to source nations (articles 7, 9 and 13). The forerunners to the Convention and the instruments that follow it (law or soft law instruments) share the same spirit.[15] The 1995

---

[12] Morality and public feeling are subject to socioeconomic and political changes which are considered here, however, to have limited impact in the area of return of cultural treasures to their countries of origin.

[13] See also in this respect Moustakas, J. (1988–1989), 'Group Rights in Cultural Property: Justifying Strict Inalienability', *Cornell Law Review*, 74.

[14] For the requirements of the existence of such a community or group (e.g. an indigenous community) see Moustakas, *ibid.*

[15] The forerunners to the 1970 UNESCO Convention include Resolution XIV; Protection of Moveable Monuments of the Seventh International Conference of American States of 1933 (Report of the Delegates of the International Conference of American States, Montevideo, Uruguay, 3–26 December 1933, US Department of State Conference Series No. 19, at 208 (1934)); three draft international conventions prepared by the League of Nations in 1933, 1936 and 1939 (the latter also known as Draft International Convention for the Protection of National Collections of Art and History) all published in 1 US Department of State, Documents and State Papers 865 (1949), and the UNESCO Recommendation on the Means of Prohibiting and Preventing the Illicit Export, Import and Transfer of Ownership of Cultural Property of 1964 (UNESCO, The Protection of Cultural Property: Compendium of Legislative Texts 382 (1984)). See also (as relevant texts and not necessarily as forerunners) UNESCO Recommendation on International Principles Applicable to Archaeological Excavations 1956;

Unidroit Convention unequivocally provides for the return of stolen or illegally exported cultural objects to the territories from which they have been removed (articles 1 and 3). The Preamble to the same Convention refers to the cultural heritage of national, tribal, indigenous or other communities.[16]

On the basis of this principle it is recognised that states should co-operate for the non-impoverishment of the national cultural heritage. They should take measures to do this either by law or by practice. The protection of national cultural heritage works as a vehicle for the protection of the world heritage. The latter cannot exist *in abstracto* but only as the sum of each country's national heritage.[17]

This basic principle can be divided into two sub-principles:

6.2.1.1 Respect for the cultural heritage laws of the countries of origin

Although such a principle may be considered to give rise to public policy issues, this is not always the case. First, because it has already been applied

---

UNESCO Recommendation concerning the International Exchange of Cultural Property 1976; UNESCO Recommendation for the Protection of Movable Cultural Property 1978. Later instruments include the Convention on the Protection of Archaeological, Historical, and Artistic Heritage of the American Nations (Convention of San Salvador) of 1976, *ibid.* at 370; and the UNESCO Recommendation for the Protection of Movable Cultural Property of 1978, *ibid.* at 386; the 1985 European Convention on Offences Relating to Cultural Property, ETS No. 119 (Council of Europe). Merryman, J.H. (1986), 'Two ways of thinking about cultural property', *American Journal of International Law*, 80, 831, at 842. J.H. Merryman in the same article argues that a different perspective is followed in the 1954 Hague Convention, which focuses on the cultural heritage of all mankind (Preamble) rather than on national cultural heritage, at 833 *et seq.* However, this is not entirely true because the ultimate aim of the Convention as well as its two Protocols (Protocol I to the Hague Convention of 1954 for the Protection of Cultural Property in the Event of Armed Conflict 1954 and Protocol II to the Hague Convention of 1954 for the Protection of Cultural Property in the Event of Armed Conflict 1999) is the protection of the cultural property of the territory where the armed conflict is taking place and where possible its *in situ* protection.

16 See also more recent legal instruments such as the 2005 UNESCO Convention on the protection and promotion of the diversity of cultural expressions and the 2001 UNESCO Convention on the Protection of Underwater Cultural Heritage.

17 In an ICOM statement on reclaiming cultural property made by Udo Gößwald in the Athens Conference 2008, it was stated that 'cultural heritage is an integral component of identity for a given community': Gößwald, Udo (2009), 'ICOM Statement on Reclaiming Cultural Property', *Museum International*, 61 (1–2), 87, at p.89.

in other cases[18] and second, because without such a recognition, there can be no effective protection of a country's cultural heritage (in other words the basic principle becomes inoperative). This translates into two main issues: a) *States should accept that the countries of origin are the only competent bodies to define the content and scope of their cultural treasures.*[19] It is these treasures that should be protected by states of destination or transit states. This is provided for explicitly in the 1970 UNESCO Convention (article 1), the Council Directive 93/7 on the return of cultural objects unlawfully removed from the territory of a Member State[20] and Council Regulation 116/2009 on the export of cultural goods.[21] b) *The countries of origin should be the ones to define when their cultural objects have been illegally exported from their territories, are stolen or otherwise illegally removed* (see e.g. articles 3(2)[22] and 5[23] of the 1995 Unidroit Convention concerning the enforcement of other states' export regulations). The

---

18 Allegations concerning the inability of the states to enforce the public law of other countries are no more than an excuse at this point. First, because as far as a state has undertaken the obligations provided in the Convention, and which have been reciprocally accepted by the other Contracting Parties, it is perfectly conscious of the fact that it has also accepted the obligation of applying another state's public law to the extent that this law concerns the enforcement and effective application of the rules of the Convention. And secondly, the recognition of a third state's law is nowadays widely accepted, not only regarding cultural property (i.e. article 3 of the Resolution of the Institute of International Law of 3.9.1991), but also regarding the application of foreign public law in general, on which the extraterritorial application of a state's export regulations can be based (e.g. article 7(1) of the EEC Rome Convention on the Law Applicable to Contractual Obligations and article 19 of the new Swiss Law of 18.12.1987, concerning private international law).

19 This is also dictated by reason of efficiency and it is in line with the principle of subsidiarity. According to this principle, if a measure can be taken efficiently at a low level (e.g. be resolved by local administration), it should not be decided by the upper level (e.g. a state or an international organisation). See Fechner, F. (1998), 'The Fundamental Aims of Cultural Property Law', *International Journal of Cultural Property*, 7, 376, at 379, 380.

20 Council Directive 93/7/EEC of 15 March 1993 on the return of cultural objects unlawfully removed from the territory of a Member State.

21 Council Regulation (EEC) No 116/2009 of 18 December 2008 on the export of cultural goods.

22 Article 3(2): 'For the purposes of this Convention, a cultural object which has been unlawfully excavated or lawfully excavated but unlawfully retained shall be considered stolen, *when consistent with the law of the State where the excavation took place*' (Emphasis added).

23 Article 5: '(1) A Contracting State may request the court or other competent authority of another Contracting State to order the return of a cultural object *illegally exported from the territory of the requesting State.*

Commonwealth Scheme also operates in the same spirit. According to the Scheme, a commonwealth country should return to another commonwealth country (party to the Scheme) a cultural object that is found in its territory, which has been unlawfully exported from the first. 'Unlawful export' is considered to be the export that has taken place in breach of the laws of the country of export.

Theft (and acts akin to it)[24] are acts which are internationally recognised as a crime. It should be noted that when no concrete national legislation is in place, there may be difficulties for these states in claiming back and recovering their treasures, even if these treasures are considered by them to be illegally exported or stolen.

Two examples are indicative in this respect. In the case *Iran v. Barakat*[25] where Iran sued the Barakat Gallery in the English courts in order to recover antiquities originating in the Jiroft region (south-east Iran) that were unlicensed and unlawful under the law of Iran, the views of the English Courts diverged. The High Court decided in favour of the gallery because there was no law in Iran specifically indicating that Iran was the

---

(2) A cultural object which has been temporarily exported from the territory of the requesting State, for purposes such as exhibition, research or restoration, under a permit issued according to its law regulating its export for the purpose of protecting its cultural heritage and not returned in accordance with the terms of that permit shall be deemed to have been illegally exported.

(3) The court or other competent authority of the State addressed shall order the return of an illegally exported cultural object if the requesting State establishes that the removal of the object from its territory significantly impairs one or more of the following interests:

(a) the physical Preservation of the object or of its context;

(b) the integrity of a complex object;

(c) the preservation of information of, for example, a scientific or historical character;

(d) the traditional or ritual use of the object by a tribal or indigenous community, or establishes that the object is of significant cultural importance for the requesting State.

(4) Any request made under paragraph 1 of this article shall contain or be accompanied by such information of a factual or legal nature as may assist the court or other competent authority of the State addressed in determining whether the requirements of paragraphs 1 to 3 have been met.

(5) Any request for return shall be brought within a period of three years from the time when the requesting State knew the location of the cultural object and the identity of its possessor, and in any case within a period of fifty years from the date of the export or from the date on which the object should have been returned under a permit referred to in paragraph 2 of this article' (Emphasis added).

24 Such as fraud, conversion and so on.

25 *Republic of Iran v. Barakat Galleries* [2007] EWCA Civ 1374.

owner of these antiquities. The Court of Appeal, however, came to a different conclusion: 'it is important to bear in mind that it is not the label which foreign law gives to the legal relationship, but its substance, which is relevant. If the rights given by Iranian law are equivalent to ownership in English law, then English law would treat that as ownership for the purposes of the conflict of laws'.[26] Another relevant case is *United States v. Schultz*.[27] In this case again, the US court had difficulties in accepting Egypt's state ownership of the antiquities at issue. In the end it was convinced of such ownership when Egypt proved[28] that the government was active in enforcing its ownership rights in antiquities.[29]

Because of the difficulties that countries may encounter in relation to the recovery of their antiquities, the ICPRCP currently promotes model legislation for states,[30] which allows them to provide clearly and unambiguously for the state ownership of (at least)[31] undiscovered cultural objects. Such legislation facilitates the courts of the requested state (in case they apply the law of the requesting state) to find for the recovery of the cultural object, if this object is removed after the enactment of the

---

[26] In relation to state ownership of antiquities and whether this right is judiciable in another country the Court referred to the case *King of Italy v. de Medici* (1918) 34 TLR 623. According to this case, when a state owns property, in the same way as a private citizen, there is no impediment to recovery.

[27] 178 F. Supp 2d 45 (2002); 333 F.3d 393 (2003).

[28] This was evidence produced by the Secretary General of the Egyptian Supreme Council of Antiquities.

[29] The relevant provision of the Egyptian law of 1983 was article 117 which provided that 'all antiquities are considered to be public property – except for charitable and religious endowments'. In a similar case the US Court recognised that under Guatemalan law, upon illegal export, cultural property becomes the property of the Republic of Guatemala (*United States of America v. Pre-Columbian Artifacts and the Republic of Guatemala*, United States District Court, N.D. Illinois, E.D., 14 October 1993, 845 F. Supp. 544).

[30] A draft was submitted by P. O'Keefe at the 15th session of the ICPRCP on 13 May 2009 (Joint presentation with J. Sanchez-Cordero). UNESCO and UNIDROIT formed a committee of experts in order to prepare model legislation defining the property of the State, including archaeological heritage. This model legislation could be used as the basis for the drafting of national laws and promote the standardization of terminology. Its aim is to ensure that all governments have introduced sufficiently explicit legal principles on the matter. A first report on the efforts of the committee was presented during the 16th session of the ICPRCP (Paris, 21–23 September 2010. See also Recommendation 3 adopted during the 16th session of ICPRCP).

[31] The draft characteristically mentions that 'nowhere is this more important than when an unknown object is removed from the ground and taken out of the country'.

aforementioned law. This is so because according to private international law, many states consider an object to be stolen if it is determined as such by the law of the state where the crime was committed. Usually this state is the state of origin of the cultural object at issue. If this state's law does not unequivocally provide that the unauthorised removal of undiscovered cultural objects is considered to be theft (even if its law applies), it will not help the state to recover its cultural objects.

In relation to illegally exported/imported cultural objects and the argument that certain countries will not enforce foreign public law relating to the administrative control of imports and exports,[32] it can be noted that a) this stance has been called into question by the literature in the area and by some institutions, such as the Institute of International Law in 1975,[33] b) many countries such as Canada, Australia, New Zealand, and South Africa have legislation that reverses this situation[34] and c) a number

---

[32] Other arguments are also used, such as that the law prohibiting export may be considered penal, public, running counter to the territoriality and nationality principles (the two generally acceptable bases of jurisdiction under international law) and thus not enforceable.

[33] A Report by Lalive, P. (1975), 'L'application du droit public étranger', Institut de droit International, Annuaire, Session de Wiesbaden, Paris: Karger, p.157, with regard to the application of foreign public laws came to the conclusion that there was no general principle that foreign public laws should not apply and that such a principle was not appropriate to the needs of modern society. To this end the Institute adopted one Resolution in 1976 ((1976) Revue Critique de Droit International Privé 423) and one in 1977. For further details see Prott, L. (1989), 'Problems of Private International Law for the Protection of Cultural Heritage', *Recueil des Cours*, 217, (V), 215, at 293 *et seq*. See also Schultz, J.C. (1983) 'Dutch Antecedents and Parallels to Article 7 of the EEC Contracts Convention of 1980', *Rabels Zeitschrift für ausländisches und internationales Privatrecht*, 47, 267, and Verheul, J.P. (1984), 'Foreign Export Prohibition: Cultural Treasures and Minerals', *Netherlands International Law Review*, 31, 419. See also Campos, J., Gonzales D. and Virgos Soriano, M. (1988), 'Le commerce international d'art en droit espagnol', in P. Lalive (ed), *International Sales in Works of Art*, Paris: Institute of International Business Law and Practice, and Faculté de Droit de Genève, 341, at 356.

[34] See the International Law Association Draft Report on National Controls over the Export of Cultural Material, The Hague, 2010, http://www.ila-hq.org/en/committees/index.cfm/cid/13, where it is mentioned that

> this reversal is usually based on the understanding that such recognition and enforcement conforms with the 1970 UNESCO Convention and UNIDROIT. In Canada, for example, federal law provides that a foreign State Party to the 1970 UNESCO Convention can request the Canadian Minister of Canadian Heritage to assist it to recover cultural material that has been illegally exported from its territory. The action can only be commenced by the Attorney General

of national judicial decisions have come to the conclusion that the 1970 UNESCO Convention provisions amount to international public policy, which is applicable by courts even in cases where the country has not ratified the Convention.[35] Even so, the enforcement in one state of another state's export regulations, though acceptable in some cases if common interests are served by it,[36] is still a trend under formation, where international conventions and regional legislation (for example European Union or Commonwealth legislation and bilateral treaties between the various countries) play a significant role.[37] As L. Prott mentions 'a further way of

---

of Canada on behalf of a foreign state that is party to the 1970 UNESCO Convention. The court ordering the return of the material can also order monetary compensation to a *bona fide* purchaser for value or to someone who otherwise has legal title to the property and was unaware of its illegal export.

Whether a state's ratification of either or both the 1970 UNESCO Convention and UNIDROIT results in a reversal of the traditional rule against recognition will depend on two factors: (1) the effect of accession to treaties under the legal system of the importing state, and (2) state accession to the treaties subject to reservations. An example of the latter is the United States, which has signed the 1970 UNESCO Convention with a reservation whereby it will recognize foreign export controls only when a separate bilateral agreement is in place between the United States and a foreign state. Over a period of more than twenty years, the United States has entered into eleven such bilateral agreements – many with developing countries facing particularly egregious situations affecting the vulnerability of their cultural heritage (such as Guatemala, Mali, China, Italy, and Cyprus). This approach is based on Article 9 of the 1970 UNESCO Convention.

Overall, the 1970 UNESCO Convention and UNIDROIT have spurred the recognition by many countries of the cultural material export controls of other countries. The scope of such recognition, however, is subject to considerable variation based on constitutional, legislative, and other factors.

See also the discussion in chapter 2.2.5.1

[35] *Allegemeine Versicherungsgesellschaft v. E.K.BGHZ* 59.83 (German Federal Court in Civil Matters) 1972.

[36] Such a common interest is the protection of cultural property, especially within the ambit of the 1970 UNESCO Convention. Verheul, n. 34 above, at 419.

[37] See, for example, *Attorney-General of New Zealand v. Ortiz* [1982] 2 W.L.R. 10, where New Zealand was unsuccessful in the British Courts in recovering illegally exported Maori carvings; *Kingdom of Spain v. Christie, Manson & Woods Ltd.*, [1986] 1 W.L.R. 1120, where Spain did not sue in the British Courts for the return of a Goya painting but asked instead for a declaratory judgment that the Spanish export documents were forged; Tribunale di Roma of 27 June 1987 (Stato francese c. Ministero per I beni culturali e ambientali e De Contessini), (1988) 71 Rivista di Diritto Internazionale 920, confirmed by Corte di Cassazione of 24 November 1995, n. 12166, (1997) 33 Rivista di Diritto Internazionale Privato e Processuale 427, where France was unsuccessful in the Italian Courts with regard to the return of stolen and illegally exported tapestries; Bundesgerichtshof of 22

dealing with state claims of ownership over items not in their possession but alienated or exported contrary to the rights of the state was for a court to recognise the rights of the state of origin because of the need of reciprocity and comity of nations in their efforts to preserve their respective national heritages'[39].[38]

6.2.1.2 Reinforcement of due diligence checks/reversion of burden of proof for the establishment of good faith

The circumstances under which cultural objects are transferred are not always entirely transparent and the reasons for this vary. One of them is the fact that some jurisdictions regard cultural objects as any other chattel from a legal point of view. Another reason is the fact that cultural artefacts constitute the object of a lucrative illicit trade, which is comparable to the one in drugs,[40] and for which there seems to be constant demand. That by itself accounts for the undercover movement of artefacts as well as their long-term storage in bank vaults or other secret places so that the possessor can benefit from time limitations or launder provenance details.

In jurisdictions which treat cultural objects as any other chattel (movable property), the general provisions for the transfer of title apply. According to these provisions, there is a presumption in most cases that the possessor of the object is also the object's owner.[41] A thorough check of title is generally not required, whilst a simple declaration (even an oral one) by the transferor

---

June 1972, (1972) 59 Entscheidungen des Bundesgerichtshofes in Zivilsachen 82, where the case was decided on the basis that the Nigerian artefacts at issue were covered by an insurance contract which was considered to be immoral and therefore invalid. See also the analysis in Siehr, K. (1997), 'The Protection of Cultural Heritage and International Commerce', *International Journal of Cultural Property*, 304, at 311 *et seq*. See, however, the American case *US v. McClain* 545 F. 2d 988 (1977) where it was decided that goods illegally exported from a foreign country are considered stolen within the meaning of the National Stolen Property Act, if the state of origin has declared that the class of goods concerned are owned by the state.

[38] *Republic of Ecuador v. Danusso*, Court of Appeal, Turin (Italy), 2nd Civil Section 593/82. Based on principles and practice developed on the basis of the Convention concerning the Laws and Customs of War on Land 1907, the Declaration of London 1943 and the Hague Convention for the Protection of Cultural Property in the Event of Armed Conflict 1954.

[39] Prott, L.V. (2009), 'The Ethics and Law of Returns', *Museum International*, 61 (1–2), 101, at p.102.

[40] Brodie, N., Doole, J. and Watson, P. (2000), 'Stealing History: The Illicit Trade in Cultural Material', Cambridge: ICOM UK and Museums Association, The McDonald Institute for Archaeological Research, 16.

[41] See, for example, article 1110 of the Greek Civil Code.

himself as to his ownership will generally suffice to establish the purchaser's good faith. Bad faith is usually established if the third party proves that the purchaser had knowledge of the lack of valid title or such knowledge is presumed by the circumstances (for example a purchase outside a shop, during the hours of darkness, or at a very low price which does not correspond to the object's actual price). In these cases the burden of proof lies with the third party asserting rights to the object. Special laws exist for stolen objects, which differ, however, between common law and civil law systems. Whilst the former seem to favour the dispossessed owner (*nemo dat quod non habet* – no one can transfer title to stolen property), the latter favour the good faith purchaser in the sense that if the purchaser is found to be in good faith, he acquires title to a stolen object under certain additional circumstances.[42]

Cultural objects forming a state's cultural heritage are not, however, comparable to other chattels. This is not only because of their irrefutable significance for the states of origin, but also because of the particular circumstances of their movement. The illicit trade in artefacts has increased considerably during recent decades. It is thought to be the third largest (after weapons and drugs). It has developed its own illegal trafficking routes and it also includes cultural objects which are unknown to the state of origin. That means either that cultural objects are the product of illicit and unauthorised excavations or that the state finds it impossible to list and document all its cultural treasures. A great number of antiquities on the market are found to be illegal. There are also antiquities for which there is a presumption that they could not have been legitimately offered for sale (Apulian vases and Cycladic figurines, for example).[43] This alone should alert purchasers, dealers and other agents involved in the art trade

[42] See also Renold, M. (2004), 'Stolen Art: The Ubiquitous Question of Good Faith', in The Permanent Court of Arbitration/Peace Palace Papers (ed.), *Resolution of Cultural Property Disputes*, The Hague: Kluwer Law International, 251.

[43] See Brodie, N. (2001), 'Britannia Waives the Rules? The Licensing of Archaeological Material for Export from the UK', in N. Brodie and K. Walker Tubb (eds), *Illicit Antiquities: The Theft of Culture and the Extinction of Archaeology*, London: Routledge, at 197 *et seq.*, where it is mentioned with reference to R. Elia that any Apulian vase appearing on the market today without provenance has almost certainly been looted. (Elia, R.J. (2001), 'Analysis of the looting, selling, and collecting of Apulian red-figure vases: a quantitative approach', in N. Brodie, J. Doole and C. Renfrew (eds), *Trade in Illicit Antiquities: The Destruction of the World's Archaeological Heritage*, Cambridge: McDonald Institute for Archaeological Research, 145). In relation to Cycladic white marble figurines, some 1,600 of these found in Bronze Age graves in the Cycladic Islands, Greece are known, but only about 150 were found during archaeological excavations. The rest appeared on the market with no context or provenance. It is impossible to date them by scientific means, so unless they have an archaeological

to be more diligent and suspicious as to what they buy. Good faith in these circumstances should be difficult to establish. Therefore more issues, incidents, factors and circumstances should be taken into account in order for a dealer's or purchaser's good faith to be proven. An open-ended provision with this aim is provided for in the 1995 Unidroit Convention. According to article 4(4):

> In determining whether the possessor exercised due diligence, regard shall be had to all the circumstances of the acquisition, including the character of the parties, the price paid, whether the possessor consulted any reasonably accessible register of stolen cultural objects, and any other relevant information and documentation which it could reasonably have obtained, and whether the possessor consulted accessible agencies or took any other step that a reasonable person would have taken in the circumstances.

According to the above there should be complete transparency in the purchase of artefacts. This means that all available databases should be checked and possible countries of origin, experts, and available publications should be consulted. Transactions should be overt and made public and there should be no justifying reason (such as the evasion of taxes or fear of theft) for the non-disclosure of the seller's details during auctions or other transactions. Furthermore, cultural objects should be fully documented. This means that their documentation should go back all the way to their original ownership and/or finding whilst the necessary export licences should accompany the object. In other words there should be a reinforcement of due diligence checks since a simple check applying to any chattel does not suffice. Legal practice and international instruments in the area point towards this direction,[44] though they are not very explicit as to the exact scope of such a due diligence test.

In addition to the above, a reversion of the burden of proof in favour of the original owner (state or private owner) is required in order for good faith to be established.[45] This is the only way, in practice, for a legal system to work effectively because it would be extremely difficult for a state to produce all the necessary evidence in order to prove that an object has been illegally excavated or exported from its territory.[46] It would also be

---

context one cannot tell if they are genuine or not. See <http://www.mcdonald.cam.ac.uk/projects/iarc/illicit-antiquities/whyarch.htm>.

44 As was shown in the relevant sections on good faith acquisition and codes of conduct for dealers.

45 Article 4(4) of the 1995 Unidroit Convention.

46 See, for example, the Canadian case *R. v. Heller* (1983) 27 Alta.L.R. (2d) 346 where the court concluded that there was no evidence that the Nok sculpture

impossible for a state to control the finding, movement and export of all its cultural treasures.[47] Particularly in cases where no export of artefacts is allowed without the state's authorisation, it should be presumed that the absence of such an authorisation is tantamount to illegal movement. The reversion of the burden of proof also works in an educational manner. Purchasers are made more prudent and diligent because of the fear of losing the cultural object they have acquired, without being paid any compensation. This is a trend under formation rather than actual practice, particularly for those countries that treat cultural objects as any other chattel and have not ratified the 1995 Unidroit Convention (article 4(4)).[48]

6.2.2 International Co-operation for the Prevention of Illegal Movements of Cultural Property

Prevention of illegal movements of cultural property is as important as restitution and indeed on many occasions is the most effective tool for the protection of cultural property. It means that one does not have to undergo all the procedures for its recovery, which can be costly and prolonged and do not always yield a guaranteed outcome. Therefore the second principle is that states should co-operate towards the prevention of illegal movements of cultural property. It is not sufficient for states to allege that they have laws in place that provide for the restitution and return of illegally removed cultural property. They should co-operate energetically by all practical means possible, but especially through legal and institutionalised procedures, such as the co-operation of police forces,

---

concerned had been exported from Nigeria after Nigeria had enacted legislation on export control. It is interesting to note that Nigeria had such legislation in place already in 1924, whilst the first remains of the Nok culture had only been discovered in 1943. See also the US case *Government of Peru v. Benjamin Johnson, Lawrence Wendt, David Swetnam, Jacqueline Swetman, George Gelesbach, Oman Gaspar, Ronald Stanman and 352 Peruvian Artifacts*, 720 F. Supp. 810 (CD Cal. 1989), where Peru lost its suit for the recovery of certain artefacts because it could not prove that they originated from Peruvian territory. Similar artefacts were also found in Ecuador, Colombia, Mexico and Polynesia.

[47] Fechner, 'The Fundamental Aims of Cultural Property Law', n. 20 above, 389.

[48] This is in fact happening in the US with regard to civil forfeiture statutes on the basis of which the US government, at the discretion of federal prosecutors, is acting to seize property that is alleged to be the subject of criminal activity. The burden of proof is on the current owner (and not on the US government) to show that the property was not stolen. See Hoffman, B.T. (2006), 'International Art Transactions and the Resolution of Art and Cultural Property Disputes: A United States Perspective', in B.T. Hoffman (ed), *Art and Cultural Heritage. Law, Policy and Practice*, Cambridge University Press, 159, at 163.

customs authorities, judicial services, diplomatic services, courts, ministries, museums and so on. Co-operation is a basic principle deriving both from law[49] and ethics in the area.

6.2.3 Return as a Prerequisite for the Preservation of the Integrity of Cultural Contexts

As we have seen, the terms 'restitution' and 'return' are used interchangeably in the area of cultural property law although they frequently mean different things or refer to different circumstances. The term 'restitution' refers to any sort of restitution in the case of illegally alienated cultural objects, in order for the 'wrong' committed to be rectified. This even takes place in cases where the object no longer exists. Restitution in this sense includes return, compensation or any other sort of rectification which a court may consider appropriate in the circumstances. It is, however, only *restitutio in integrum*, which directly refers to the return of a cultural object to the place from which it has been illegally alienated, or else the re-establishment of the situation as it was before the removal of the cultural good. This type of restitution comes close to the notion of 'compensation *in natura*', which means that instead of the dispossessed owner being paid compensation, he is entitled to the actual return of the object. This constitutes compensation in kind and is a notion which is borrowed from civil law.[50] It applies to those cases where such restitution is possible where it corresponds to what the claimant wants and requests from the court, and where it constitutes what the court considers most appropriate in the circumstances. *Restitutio in integrum* is recognised under international customary law.

An example of a wrong is specifically described in national and international law and would include a theft (or similar crime) or an illegal import/export. Yet, return in cultural property law is not an act initiated only under circumstances of commitment of a wrong in the narrow sense of the word. It may be initiated in other cases too, where a 'wrongful' act in the wider sense of the word has been committed without necessarily constituting an unlawful act in the circumstances. The displacement of cultural property from its country of origin could have taken place for many reasons. It could be the result of acts of war, hostilities, occupation, colonisation, punitive raids (where a country cannot retain control of its

---

[49] References throughout the UNESCO Convention 1970 and the Unidroit Convention 1995. This co-operation has been institutionalized between EU Member States on the basis of EU Directive 7/92 and EU Regulation 116/2009 (which is a codification of EU Regulation 3911/92 as amended).

[50] In fact in civil law it is referred to as compensation *in natura*.

heritage as was the case with Benin (Nigeria)[51] and Ethiopia[52]), or due to the exploitation of political, social or other circumstances (for example the weakness of a state or arrangements between other states, which the state of origin could not prevent in the given circumstances).[53] It could be argued that in these cases one concentrates on the damage done to the dispossessed state, rather than on the 'fault' by reason of the breakage of the link between the object and the state of origin.[54] In these cases the physical return[55] of the object (or its preservation *in situ*)[56] is initiated on the basis of ethical, scientific, humanitarian or other grounds and not necessarily for the rectification of a legal wrong. Here the notion of 'wrong' is generally linked to the displacement of an object from its cultural context

---

51 See the British Punitive Expedition against Benin in 1897 during which the famous Benin bronzes were plundered from the royal palace of the Kingdom of Benin.

52 During the Second Italo-Ethiopian War (1935–1936) and after that during Ethiopia's annexation to the newly created colony of Italian East Africa.

53 Prott, 'The Ethics and Law of Returns', n. 40 above, 102. See also Scovazzi, T. (2009), 'Diviser c'est détruire: ethical principles and legal rules in the field of return of cultural properties', Paper presented in the 16th Session of the Intergovernmental Committee for Promoting the Return of Cultural Property to Its Countries of Origin or Its Restitution in Case of Illicit Appropriation (21–23.9.2010), Paris: UNESCO, at 21 seq. and 45, where he argues for the existence of the 'principle of non exploitation of the weakness of another subject for cultural gain' which applies to situations of war, colonial domination, foreign occupation or to indigenous people.

54 See Cornu, M. and M.-A. Renold (2010), 'New Developments in the Restitution of Cultural Property: Alternative Means of Dispute Resolution', *International Journal of Cultural Property*, **17**(1), 15, as they also refer in their footnote 111 to the fact that in 1987 'the United Nations recalled the arguments of claimant countries, in particular to "recognize the moral right to the recovery of vital tokens of cultural identity, removed in the context of colonialism"'.

55 See also the 34th UNESCO General Conference Recommendation 44 (2007) according to which digital access to cultural heritage cannot replace the enjoyment of the original in its authentic form. Korka, Elena (2009), 'Final Synthesis and Conclusions of the Athens Conference', *Museum International*, 61 (1–2), 153, at 157.

56 Relevant in this respect is the Convention on the Protection of the Underwater Cultural Heritage, which was concluded in Paris in 2001 and is another international instrument which includes provisions concerning preservation *in situ*. The Convention provides that States Parties must take measures for the seizure of underwater cultural heritage in their territory that has been recovered in a manner not conforming to the Convention (Art. 18 para 1). The seized cultural properties are subject to a special regime, based on the concept of public benefit, and the interests of states having 'a verifiable link' with the object taken. See also Fechner, 'The fundamental aims of cultural property law', n. 20 above, 383 and Merryman, 'Cultural Property Export Controls', n. 15 above, 843.

without the country of origin's authorisation or consent.[57] And it is this 'wrong' which, in many instances, has been turned into a legal wrong.

The preservation of the integrity of a single monument or a cultural site is an aim which holds value in itself, without the need to be linked to the methods or circumstances under which a cultural object has been detached from this cultural context[58].[59] Once a cultural object is removed

---

[57] Cornu M. and M.-A. Renold go even further and disassociate the right of repatriation from the unlawfulness of the object's initial removal. In fact they refer to the United Nations Declaration on the Rights of Indigenous People (article 11(2) of the Resolution adopted on 2nd October, 2007) where a right of repatriation is acknowledged for cultural, intellectual, religious and spiritual objects taken *with or without* the consent of the population concerned. Cornu, M. and M.-A. Renold (2010), 'New Developments in the Restitution of Cultural Property: Alternative Means of Dispute Resolution', *International Journal of Cultural Property*, **17**(1), 15.

[58] In 1796 a booklet was published by the French scholar Antoine-Chrysostome Quatremère de Quincy (1755–1849) containing seven letters on the prejudice that would be caused to arts and science by the removal of monuments of art from Italy. In this work (republished in Rome in 1803 and 1815) Quatremère took a clear position against the spoliation of the Italian territories (Quatremère de Quincy, Lettres sur le préjudice qu'occasionneraient aux Arts et à la Science, le déplacement des monuments de l'art de l'Italie, le démembrement de ses Ecoles, et la spoliation de ses Collections, Galeries, Musées, etc., Rome, 1815, published for the first time in 1796). For the French scholar, to divide cultural properties by removing them from the places where they had been created was to destroy them (*diviser c'est détruire*) (at p.25, all references are to the 1815 edition). Quatremère's thoughts did apply not only to cultural properties taken as war booty, but also to the traffic in such properties in time of peace. For the same reason that a State cannot remove the cultural properties from other States, it cannot trade its own cultural properties for an economic gain (at p.82). Cultural properties have a special status and cannot be treated as commercial goods (at p.65). This booklet (the 1815 edition) Antonio Canova, the sculptor (1757–1822) took with him to Paris in 1815, after the fall of Napoleon, when Pope Pius VII sent him as his special envoy to king Louis XVIII in an attempt to recover the one hundred works of art and five hundred manuscripts delivered by the Papal State to France under the Treaty of Tolentino. The thoughts of Quatremère clearly reflect the idea of a collective interest, which is shared by all human beings and aims at the protection of cultural heritage and its preservation in the context where it has been created. Scovazzi, T. (2009), 'Diviser c'est détruire: ethical principles and legal rules in the field of return of cultural properties', Paper presented in the 16th Session of the Intergovernmental Committee for Promoting the Return of Cultural Property to Its Countries of Origin or Its Restitution in Case of Illicit Appropriation (21–23.9.2010), Paris: UNESCO, at 4ff.

[59] See Resolution 1483 of 22 May, 2003 of the United Nations Security Council. It is interesting to note that according to this Resolution cultural goods taken after 6 August, 1990, irrespective of whether this was a period of war, peace or military occupation of Iraq, have to be returned. See also Scovazzi, T. (2009), 'Diviser c'est détruire: ethical principles and legal rules in the field of return of

from its context it can provide little information about the territory, history, culture or civilisation it belongs to[60].[61] This is the reason why archaeological evidence should be preserved *in situ*[62] (and – if not possible – in context) and it was stated in the conclusions of the International

cultural properties', Paper presented in the 16th Session of the Intergovernmental Committee for Promoting the Return of Cultural Property to Its Countries of Origin or Its Restitution in Case of Illicit Appropriation (21–23.9.2010), Paris: UNESCO, at 42–43, who argues that the manifestation of the principle of preservation of the integrity of cultural contexts is deeply rooted in the nature of cultural properties and refers to the fact that 'integrity, intended as a measure of the wholeness and intactness of the heritage, is a condition for a property to be inscribed on the World Heritage List, as established under the Convention concerning the protection of the world cultural and natural heritage. The UNIDROIT Convention provides that a court or other competent authority of the State addressed shall order the return of an illegally exported cultural object if the requesting State establishes that the removal of the object from its territory significantly impairs, inter alia, the interest in "the integrity of a complex object" (Art.5, para.3). The Annex to the Convention on the protection of the underwater cultural heritage provides that "the protection of underwater cultural heritage through in situ preservation shall be considered as the first option" (Rule 1) and that "the commercial exploitation of underwater cultural heritage for trade or speculation or its irretrievable dispersal is fundamentally incompatible with the protection and proper management of underwater cultural heritage" (Rule 2)'.

60 A characteristic example of this is provided by St Clair W. (2006) in relation to the Parthenon Marbles exhibited in the British Museum, 'Imperial Appropriations of the Parthenon', in J.H. Merryman (ed), (2006) *Imperialism, Art and Restitution*, Cambridge University Press, 65, at 82. He mentions that 'the Elgin Marbles were shown not only divorced from their Athenian geographical, climatic, historical, religious, and architectural context, and displayed as "works of art" in accordance with European post-romantic aesthetics, but incorporated into a metropolitan, "universal" museum that, by the sheer extent and miscelaneity of its collections, celebrated British national and imperial success'.

61 See Elia, Ricardo J. (2009), 'Preventing Looting through the Return of Looted Archaeological Objects', *Museum International*, 61 (1–2), 130. Rosenbaum, Lee (2009), 'Art History Meets Archaeology: Considering Cultural Context in American Museums', *Museum International*, 61 (1–2), 132. Brodie, N. (2006), *An Archaeologist's View of the Trade in Unprovenanced Antiquities*, in B.T. Hoffman (ed.), *Art and Cultural Heritage. Law, Policy and Practice*, Cambridge University Press, 52, Fechner (1998), 'The fundamental aims of cultural property law', n. 20 above, 379.

62 'Integrity, intended as a measure of the wholeness and intactness of the heritage, is a condition for a property to be inscribed on the World Heritage List, as established under the Convention concerning the protection of the world cultural and natural heritage. The Unidroit Convention provides that a court or other competent authority of the State addressed shall order the return of an illegally exported cultural object if the requesting State establishes that the removal of the object from its territory significantly impairs, *inter alia*, the interest in "the integrity of a complex object" (Art. 5, para 3)'.

Conference on the Return of Cultural Objects to their Countries of Origin (Athens, 17–18 March 2008)[63] and reaffirmed in the Recommendation adopted by the extraordinary session of the ICPRCP commemorating its 30th anniversary in Seoul (25–28 November 2008)[64].[65]

6.2.3.1 On the basis of law and international customary rules

By 'law' we mean national and regional law and international conventions. It is widely known that there are several national laws – especially those of source states – which provide for the inalienability of significant cultural objects and their return if they are removed from the country.[66]

In the international conventions in the area, there is a clear reference to the fact that restitution should mean return, since this is the most appropriate way of rectifying a situation where an object has been illegally removed (for example by illegal export or theft) from its country of origin. It is clear, furthermore, that it is not so much the rectification of the wrong which is at issue as the return of the object to the country of origin in order for it to be re-integrated into its original cultural context.

---

63 'Certain categories of cultural property are irrevocably identified by reference to the cultural context in which they were created (unique and exceptional artworks and monuments, ritual objects, national symbols, ancestral remains, dismembered pieces of outstanding works of art). It is their original context that gives them their authenticity and unique value.' Conclusions of the Athens International Conference on the Return of Cultural Objects to their Countries of Origin, *Museum International*, 61, (1–2), 158.

64 'Certain categories of cultural property fully reveal their authenticity and unique value only in the cultural context in which they were created.' See also the conclusions of the non-governmental expert Meeting held in commemoration of the 30th anniversary of the ICPRCP (Seoul, 26 November 2008), where it was stated that 'it is an indissociable attribute of the sovereignty of every people that it should have access to, and enjoyment of, the irreplaceable symbols of its heritage'.

65 'The preservation of the integrity of cultural contexts can also be seen as a means to ensure cultural diversity. The parties to the Convention on the protection and promotion of the diversity of cultural expressions (Paris, 2005) recognise "*the need to take measures to protect the diversity of cultural expressions, including their contents, especially in situations where cultural expressions may be threatened by the possibility of extinction or serious impairment*" (Preamble). They reaffirm "*the sovereign rights of States to maintain, adopt and implement policies and measures that they deem appropriate for the protection and promotion of the diversity of cultural expressions in their territory*" (Art. 1, *h*)'. Scovazzi, T. (2009), 'Diviser c'est détruire: Ethical Principles and Legal Rules in the Field of Return of Cultural Properties', paper presented in the 15th Session of the Intergovernmental Committee for Promoting the Return of Cultural Property to Its Countries of Origin or Its Restitution in Case of Illicit Appropriation (11–13 May 2009), Paris: UNESCO, at 31.

66 Such examples are Greece, Italy, Egypt, Peru, Bolivia, China and so on.

This 'return' in relation to stolen and illegally exported/imported cultural objects is particularly mentioned (in relation to the notion of restitution) throughout the 1995 Unidroit Convention both in relation to stolen, as well as to illegally exported, cultural objects (see, for example, the Preamble to the Convention, articles 3, 4, 5, etc.) and the 1970 UNESCO Convention (for example, article 7). Also a number of regional, sub-regional and bilateral treaties or agreements (as well as Memoranda of Understanding), which have been concluded on the basis of article 15 of the 1970 UNESCO Convention or article 13 para 1 of the 1995 Unidroit Convention, operate in the same spirit. Examples of regional and sub-regional agreements are the Convention on the Protection of the Archaeological, Historical and Artistic Heritage of the American Nations (San Salvador, 1976) (in particular articles 11 and 12) and the Centro-American Convention for the Restitution and the Return of Archaeological, Historical and Artistic objects (Guatemala City, 1995) (in particular article 1).[67] The Council Directive 93/7/EEC of 15 March 1993 on the return of cultural objects unlawfully removed from the territory of a Member State can also be added as a regional legal instrument which provides for return and though not enacted within the scope of the 1970 UNESCO Convention, has been largely influenced by it.[68] The Council Regulation 116/2009 of 18 December 2008 on the export of cultural goods [69] operates in the same spirit since it establishes a common export policy for cultural goods leaving the European Union in order to secure their return to it. Some examples of bilateral agreements are the agreements between the US and Bolivia, Cambodia, China, Colombia, Cyprus, El Salvador, Guatemala, Honduras, Italy, Mali, Nicaragua, and Peru as well as between Switzerland and Italy

---

[67] See also the Convention on the Protection of the Archaeological, Historical and Artistic Heritage of the American Nations, 16 June 1976 (known as the Convention of San Salvador) which aims, amongst other issues, to prevent the unlawful export of the cultural heritage of the American Nations http://www.oas.org.jurdico/english/treaties/c16.html.

[68] OJ l 74, 27.3.1993, p.74.

[69] Council Regulation 3911/92 of 9 December 1992 on the export of cultural goods, OJ L 395/1 (Corrigendum OJ L267/30, 19/10/1996), as amended by Council Regulation 2469/96 of 16 December 1996 OJ L 335/9, Council Regulation 974/2001 of 14 May 2001 OJ L 137/10 and Council Regulation 806/2003 of 14 April 2003 OJ L 122/1, Council Regulation 116/09 of 18 December 2008 on the export of cultural goods, OJ 39/1, 10.2.2009, has repealed Regulation 3911/92 as amended by the aforementioned Regulations. See also First Report from the Commission to the Council, the European Parliament and the Economic and Social Committee on the Implementation of Council Regulation (EEC) No 3911/92 on the export of cultural goods and Council Directive 93/7/EEC on the return of cultural objects unlawfully removed from the territory of a Member State (COM (2000) 325 final).

and Switzerland and Greece and between Greece and China.[70] They all provide for the prevention of importation of designated objects from the aforementioned countries and co-operation for their immediate return. They also contain provisions on cultural collaboration. The provisions of

---

[70] The US case *United States of America v. Frederick Schultz*, 333 F.3d 393 (2nd Cir. 2003, cert. denied, *Schultz v. US*, 157 L. Ed. 2d. 891 (2004) is relevant in this respect. It sets a precedent with regard to the enforcement by US courts of foreign cultural property laws. In the case at issue the court enforced the 1983 Egyptian Law 117 which provides that 'all antiquities are considered to be public property [. . .]. It is impermissible to own, possess or dispose of antiquities except pursuant to the conditions set forth in this law and its implementing regulations.' See also *US v. McClain*, 545 F.2d 988 (5th Cir. 1977), rehearing denied, 551 F.2d (5th Cir. 1977), and appeal after remand, 593 F.2d 658 (5th Cir. 1979) and *US v. Hollinshead*, 495 F.2d 1154 (9th Cir. 1974). All these cases, including the following, involved the enforcement of the National Stolen Property Act of 1948 (18 USC §§2314–2315) *Peru v. Johnson*, 720 F. Supp. 10 (C.D. Cal 1989), aff'd sub nom; *Peru v. Wendt*, 933 F.2d 1013 (9th Cir. 1991); *United States v. Pre-Columbian Artifacts*, 845 F. Supp. 544 (N. Dist. III. Lexis 14656, 1993); *United States v. Portrait of Wally*, 99 Civ. 9940 (MBM) (11 April 2002). See also Hughes, J. (2000), 'The Trend Toward Liberal Enforcement of Repatriation Claims in Cultural Property Disputes' *George Washington International Law Review*, 33, 131. See also Hoffman, B.T. (2006), 'International Art Transactions and the Resolution of Art and Cultural Property Disputes: A United States Perspective', in B.T. Hoffman (ed), *Art and Cultural Heritage*. n. 49 above, 159 where she mentions that US courts have become more sympathetic to foreign governments' claims for the return of stolen antiquities, whilst the US government has aggressively and successfully brought forfeiture actions under the National Stolen Property Act, customs statutes and directives (at 159). See also pages 164 *et seq.* where she refers to a number of US cases based on different legal bases for the return of cultural treasures to their original owners as well as to the legal issues these cases set: *United States v. An Antique Platter of Gold*, 991 F. Supp. 222, 1997 US Dist. Lexis 18899; *United States v. Hollinshead,* 495 F. 2d 1154 (9th Cir. 1974); *United States v. McClain*, 545 F. 2d 998 (5th Cir.) [McClain I], rehearing denied, 551 F. 2d 52 (5th Cir. 1977) (*per curiam*) ; *US v. McClain*, 593 F. 2d 658 (5th Cir.) [*McClain II*], crt. denied, 444 US 918 (1979); *McClain III*, 593 F. 2d, 658 (5th Cir. 1979); *United States v. Pre-Columbian Artifacts*, 845 F. Supp. 544 (N. Dist. II. Lexis 14656, 1993; *United States of America v. Frederick Schultz*, 178 F. Supp. 2d 445, 2002 US Dist. Lexis 15; *United States of America v. Portrait Wally*, 99 Civ. 9940 (MBM) (11 April 2002); *Kunstsammlung zu Weimer v. Elicofon*, 536 F. Supp. 829 (E.D.N.Y. 1981) aff'd 678 F.2d 1150 (2d. Cir 1982); *Autocephalous Greek-Orthodox Church of Cyprus and The Republic of Cyprus v. Goldberg & Feldman Fine Arts, Inc.*, 717 F. Supp. 1374 (S.D. Ind. 1985), aff'd, 917 F. 2d 278(7th Cir. 1990); *Republic of Croatia v. The Trustee of the Marquess of Northampton* 1987, Settlement 203 AD 2d 167, NYS 2d 263 (Dept. 1994); *Solomon R. Guggenheim Foundation v. Lubell*, 153 A.D.2d 143, 149, 550 N.Y.S.2d 618, 621–22 (1st Dept. 1990), aff'd, 77 N.Y.2d 311, 567 N.Y.S.2d 623, 569 N.E.2d 426 (1999); *O'Keefe v. Snyder* 416A. 2d 862 870 (NJ 1980); *Greek Orthodox Patriarchate of Jerusalem v. Christie's, Inc.*, 1999

the Commonwealth Scheme are also relevant. According to this Scheme, a commonwealth country can seek the return of unlawfully exported cultural objects that are found in another commonwealth country that is part of the Scheme. Although the Scheme refers to unlawfully exported cultural objects only, in practice it covers stolen artefacts too, in the sense that an artefact that is stolen will hardly ever be given a formal permission to leave the country if its possessor ever applied for one.

In relation to cultural objects which were removed *in times of war*,[71] a number of international instruments provide for their return (without any time limitations)[72] and since these instruments are widely recognised, accepted and ratified (depending on the instrument) they are also thought to constitute international customary rules.[73] Such instruments are the Westphalia Treaties of 1648 concluded by 194 European states, providing

---

US Dist. Lexis 13257; *Warin v. Wildenstein & Co.*, 740 N.Y.S. 2d 331, 2002 N.Y. App. Div. Lexis 3835 (App. Div. 1st Dept. 2002); *Republic of Austria et al. v. Maria Altmann*, 124 S. Ct 2240 (2004); *Bennigson v. Alsdorf*, (Cal. Supr. Ct. June 16, 2003) (unreported), aff'd, No. B168200, 2004 WL 803616 (Cal. Ct. App. Apr. 15, 2004) (affirming that the defendant's contacts with California were insufficient to justify assertion of personal jurisdiction), *review granted*, S124828, 2004 Cal. Lexis 6903 (Cal. July 28, 2004), *dismissed*, S124828, 2005 Cal. Lexis 13370 (Cal. Nov. 30, 2005) (dismissing the case pursuant to notice of settlement); *see also United States v. One Oil Painting Entitled 'Femme En Blanc' by Pablo Picasso*, 362 F. Supp. 2d 1175 (C.D. Cal. 2005); *Alsdorf v. Bennigson*, No. 04 C 5953, 2004 WL 2806301 (N.D. III. 2004) (granting a six-month stay awaiting resolution of *Bennigson v. Alsdorf*); *Claude Cassirer et al. v. Stephen Hahn* 01158698 (Santa Barbara Supr. Ct. filed July 19, 2004); *Sarah-Rose Josepha Adler et al. v. Elizabeth Taylor* (CV 04-H472 February 2005); *Leonard Malewicz et al. v. City of Amsterdam* 362 F. Supp. 298 (D.C. March 30 2005). For more case law see the site of the International Foundation for Art Research (IFAR) <http://www.ifar.org/home.php>. See also for developments with regard to the UK law, Parkhouse 'The illicit trade in cultural objects', n. 5 above, 178. UK courts have also been sympathetic to such claims. See *Bumper Development Corporation v. Commissioner of Police of the Metropolis and others* 1 WLR 1362, CA (1991) which concerned a stone object of religious worship that was stolen from India after 1976. In this case the UK court recognised that the Hindu temple could sue in the English courts although it would not be recognised as a legal entity under English law.

[71] Although removals in times of war do not form the subject of this book, conclusions concerning such cases are relevant for the formation of customary rules in the area of cultural property law.

[72] This principle is thought to have been established at the beginning of the 19th century. See Scovazzi, 'Diviser c'est détruire' n. 60 above, 6 *et seq.*

[73] See Merryman (ed), *Imperialism, Art and Restitution*, n. 61 above, who refers to the fact that the 'seizure of works of art in the occupied countries violated an international law prohibition on the confiscation of private property by aggressive occupying powers. This was, by 1939, a customary international law norm that had

for the reciprocal restitution of 'archives, writings and other movables', the Regulations annexed to the second Hague Convention on the Laws and Customs of War on Land 1899 as well as the Regulations annexed to the fourth Hague Convention on the Laws and Customs of War on Land 1907, which prohibits the pillage of places[74] and the seizure, destruction and willful damage to institutions, monuments and works of art.[75] Return as *restitution in integrum* was followed in the Franco-German war of 1870–1871 and the Peace Treaties that were concluded after the First and Second World Wars.[76] The Hague Convention for the Protection of Cultural Property in the Event of Armed Conflict 1954 and the First Protocol to it are considered to constitute customary international law, by reason of the high number of ratifications (123 States Parties to the Convention and 100 Parties to the Protocol). The Convention dictates (apart from the prohibition of seizure of cultural properties) an obligation for the return of cultural property to the country from which it was taken. The same applies to the Second Protocol to the 1954 Hague Convention.[77]

The fact that these rules constitute customary law was also affirmed in an Italian judgment of 28 February 2007 concerning the return of the statue of Venus of Cyrene to Libya, which was displaced from Libya by the Italians in 1915. In this decision and although there was a joint declaration signed on 4 July 1998 between Italy and Libya according to which Italy undertook to return 'all manuscripts, artifacts, documents and archaeological objects brought to Italy during and after the Italian colonization of Libya, pursuant to the 1970 UNESCO Convention on the Means of Prohibiting and Preventing the Illicit Import, Export and Transfer of Ownership of Cultural Property', the court mentioned that the return of Venus was also dictated by two customary rules of international law: the first one referred to the succession of states,[78] whilst the second rule provided that cultural

---

been formalised in art. 46 of the 1907 Hague Convention (Hague IV) on the Laws of War and in the Kellog-Briand Pact of 1928 [. . .]', at 7–8 and at footnote 21.

74 See articles 28 and 47.

75 See article 56.

76 For more details see Scovazzi, T. (2009),'Diviser c'est détruire' n. 66 above, 6 *et seq*.

77 See article 15 para 1 c and e.

78 The first rule according to the Italian court is that in the case of a newly independent state 'movable property, having belonged to the territory to which the succession of States relates and having become State property of the predecessor State during the period of dependence, shall pass to the successor State' and 'movable State property of the predecessor State [. . .] to the creation of which the dependent territory has contributed, shall pass to the successor State in proportion to the contribution of the dependent territory' (art. 15 para 1 e and f of the Vienna

heritage removed in time of war should be restored to its original situation as provided by the 1899 and 1907 Hague Conventions.

Apart from the above prohibitions of removal and obligations for return, removal in times of war is also regarded as a crime. The Charter of the International Military Tribunal of Nuremberg, established under the Agreement signed in 1945 by France, the Soviet Union, the United Kingdom and the United States, included among the crimes of war the 'plunder of public and private property' (article 6b). The same crime, this time in article 3e, is also included among the crimes of war (together with the 'seizure of, destruction or willful damage done to institutions dedicated to religion, charity and education, the arts and sciences, historic monuments and works of art and science' (article 3d)) according to the Statute of the International Criminal Tribunal for the Former Yugoslavia (Security Council Resolution 827/25.5.1993). The Statute of the International Criminal Court[79] established in Rome in 1998[80] is also equivalent.

Although the principle of return applies unequivocally in times of war, it is also considered to apply in times of occupation and colonisation, as well as during times when a state cannot have control over its cultural heritage and such weakness is exploited by another state in order to remove cultural properties from the former. In all the above instances, as is the case in times of war, force is exercised by one state over another; or a state is incapable of reacting to its exploitation and preventing the removal of its cultural property because of the particular circumstances at the time. A characteristic example of this is the 1991 Native American Graves Protection and Repatriation Act (NAGPRA) following which a large number of US museums were asked to inventory their holdings of American Indian objects and return them.[81] Another example is the

---

Convention on Succession of States in respect of State Property, Archives and Debts). This principle derived from article 15 of the 1983 Vienna Convention was found to apply even though the Convention had not entered into force.

[79] It provides for the 'extensive destruction and appropriation of property, not justified by military necessity and carried out unlawfully and wantonly' (art. 8 para 2 a iv) and for 'destroying or seizing the enemy's property unless such destruction or seizure be imperatively demanded by the necessities of war' (art. 8 para 2 b xiii).

[80] Scovazzi, 'Diviser c'est détruire' n. 65 above, 9–10.

[81] NAGPRA 'vests title to cultural objects discovered on tribal lands in the individual descendant or tribe on whose tribal land the object was discovered, not in the US government. Native American cultural objects found on federal land become the property not of the government but of the tribe which has the "closest affiliation" with the object.' *United States v. Steinhardt*, 184 F.3d 131 (2d Cir. 1999) (No. 97–6319). See also Brown, M.F. and Bruchac, M.M. (2006), 'NAGPRA from the Middle Distance: Legal Puzzles and Unintended Consequences' and Thomas,

displacement of art during the Second World War.[82] Currently a draft Declaration was being prepared by UNESCO,[83] which though a legally non-binding instrument it was 'intended to provide general guidance for bilateral or multilateral interstate negotiations in order to facilitate the conclusion of agreements related to cultural objects'. Yet, this draft Declaration was never adopted.[84]

In relation to *cultural objects displaced during colonial domination*,[85] a considerable number of soft law instruments provide for the return of those objects to their countries of origin: The United Nations General Assembly Declaration of Decolonization 1960,[86] the United Nations General Assembly Resolution 3187 (XXVIII) of 18 December 1973 (Restitution of Works of Art to Countries Victims of Expropriation),[87] the ICOM Reports in 1976 and 1980 together with the 'Plea for the Return of an Irreplaceable Cultural Heritage to Those Who Created It' by the Director General of UNESCO on 7 June 1978, which formulated an ethical basis for the return of cultural objects to their countries of origin;[88] and the 1995 Principles and Guidelines for the Protection of the Heritage of Indigenous Peoples developed by the UN Human Rights Committee.[89]

D.H. (2006), 'Finders Keepers and Deep American History: Some Lessons in Dispute Resolution' in Merryman (ed), *Imperialism, Art and Restitution*, n. 61 above, at 193 and 218 respectively.

82 See *Republic of Austria v. Altmann*, 541 U.S. 677 (2004) according to which Altmann claimed, before the federal district court in Los Angeles, six paintings by Gustav Klimt that were seized by the Nazis and found at the Austrian National Museum in Vienna. The US Supreme Court found that under a provision of the Foreign Sovereign Immunities Act, Altmann could proceed with her case in the courts of Los Angeles. In the end the case was settled before trial when the parties agreed to submit it to arbitration in Vienna.

83 UNESCO doc. 34 C/22 Add., 15 October 2007.

84 See http://unescdoc.unesco.org/images/0018/001875/187506e.pdf

85 'Seen as a sort of prolonged foreign occupation of a territory', *ibid*, 17.

86 UNGA Resolution 1514 of 14 December 1960. Declaration on the Granting of Independence to Colonial Countries and Peoples.

87 This Resolution deplored 'the wholesale removal, virtually without payment of *objets d'art*, from one country to another, frequently as a result of colonial or foreign occupation' and called for their prompt restitution. The General Assembly also recognised 'the special obligations in this connection of those countries which had access to such valuable objects only as a result of colonial or foreign occupation' (para 2) and declared itself convinced that 'the restitution of such works would make good the serious damage suffered by countries as a result of such removal'.

Scovazzi, 'Diviser c'est détruire' n. 65 above, 17.

88 Amadou-Mahtar M'Bow, (1979), 'A Plea for the Return of Irreplaceable Cultural Heritage to Those Who Created It', *Museum*, 31, 58.

89 *Ibid.*, at 104–5. The UNESCO Universal Declaration on Cultural Diversity

From the above instruments it can be deduced that the same principle applies in relation to the return of cultural objects to *indigenous communities* as applies to any sort of foreign occupation by another state, in instances where the state of origin cannot exercise control over its cultural property. The Security Council Resolution mandating the return to Iraq of cultural objects displaced from the country in 2003 is one such example.[90]

As Vrdoljak[91] mentions in a 'colonization context' the first rationale behind the restitution of cultural objects is the restoration of the 'sacred' link between people, land and cultural heritage; the second rationale behind restitution is the reversal of internationally wrongful acts, including discrimination and genocide; the third rationale is intimately tied to the broader notion of the right to self-determination that evolved following decolonisation. To this the need to re-establish or develop a cultural collective identity should be added.[92] There should be no distinction made between the various instances of the illegal movement of art. It is the movement itself which renders the artefact inoperative, depriving it of its cultural context. And this act can only be reversed by the return of the object itself. If another form of restitution was provided it would a) not constitute a sufficient disincentive for traders and purchasers of illegal objects and b) not serve the aim of the preservation of cultural contexts.

6.2.3.2 On the basis of ethics

Return is also mentioned in articles 3 and 4 of the UNESCO International Code of Ethics for Dealers in Cultural Property in relation to cultural objects which have been the product of a clandestine excavation, or have been acquired illegally or dishonestly from an official excavation site or

---

and the UNESCO Convention on the Protection and Promotion of Cultural Expressions 2005 functions in much the same spirit. See also article 12 of the Draft Declaration on the Rights of Indigenous People (1994) http://www.unhchr.ch/huridocda/huridoca.nsf/(Symbol)/E.CN.4.SUB.2.RES.1994.45.En?OpenDocument. See also the Declaration on the Rights of Indigenous Peoples adopted in 2007 by the United Nations General Assembly (Resolution 61/295).

[90] Resolution 1483 of 22 May 2003 of the United Nations Security Council. It is interesting to note that according to this Resolution cultural goods taken after 6 August 1990, irrespective of whether this was a period of war, peace or military occupation of Iraq, have to be returned.

[91] Vrdoljak, A.F. (2008), *International Law, Museums and the Return of Cultural Objects*, Cambridge University Press, 2.

[92] See Scovazzi, T. (2009), 'Diviser c'est détruire: ethical principles and legal rules in the field of return of cultural properties', paper presented in the 16th Session of the Intergovernmental Committee for Promoting the Return of Cultural Property to Its Countries of Origin or Its Restitution in Case of Illicit Appropriation (21–23.9.2010), Paris: UNESCO, at 25.

monument, or cultural objects which have been illegally exported. The ICOM Code of Ethics for Museums 2004 also refers to return. Article 6.3 of the ICOM Code provides that

> when a country or people of origin seeks the restitution of an object or specimen that can be demonstrated to have been exported or otherwise transferred in violation of the principles of international and national conventions, and shown to be part of that country's or people's cultural or natural heritage, the museum concerned should, if legally free to do so, take prompt and responsible steps to co-operate in its return.

Article 6.2 provides that

> Museums should be prepared to initiate dialogues for the return of cultural property to a country or people of origin. This should be undertaken in an impartial manner, based on scientific, professional and humanitarian principles as well as applicable local, national and international legislation, in preference to action at a governmental or political level.[93]

6.2.3.3 On the basis of practice and public feeling

The increasing number of return cases demonstrates current practice in the area and also reflects public feeling. Some examples are:

- The return to Great Zimbabwe of the lower part of the soapstone birds, a national symbol. The lower part, which came from the Museum für Völkerkunde in Berlin, was exhibited from 1997 to 1998 at the Royal Museum for Central Africa in Tervuren (Belgium) and the upper part at the National Museums and Monuments of Zimbabwe in Harare. Upon the return of the lower part to Great Zimbabwe the two parts were unified.[94]
- Between 1982 and 2001, the return from Denmark (the National Museum of Denmark) to Greenland (the Nunatta Katersugaasivia Allagaateqarfialu – the Greenland National Museum and Archives) of approximately 35,000 archaeological and ethnographic artefacts within the Utimut (meaning 'return' in Greenlandic) project.[95]

---

[93] See also Gerstenblith, P. (2003), 'Acquisition and Deacquisition of Museum Collections and the Fiduciary Obligations of Museums to the Public', *Cardozo Journal of International and Comparative Law*, 11 who argues that in the US, museum trustees by law have a fiduciary responsibility towards the institution they serve to ensure acquisitions policies and diligence procedures.

[94] Munjeri, Dawson (2009), 'The Reunification of a National Symbol', *Museum International*, 61 (1–2), 12; and Tytgat, Christiane (2009), 'The 1997 Exhibition and the Reunification Process', *Museum International*, 61 (1–2), 22.

[95] Thorleifsen, Daniel (2009), 'The Repatriation of Greenland's Cultural

- The repatriation of Ngarrindjeri Old People (human remains) from the University of Edinburgh in 1991 and from Manchester Museum in 2005 to the Ngarrindjeri country in Tasmania (South Australia). These human remains had become a subject of scientific study during the colonisation of Australia by the British in 1788.[96]
- The return of the Axum Obelisk from Italy to Ethiopia in 2005. This obelisk (the second largest stela on the site) originated from the town of Axum in Ethiopia, which appears on UNESCO's World Heritage List. The obelisk was created during the rule of the Kingdom of Axum (1st–3rd centuries AD) and was removed in 1937 following the annexation of Ethiopia by Italy (1935–36).[97]
- The return of the Kwakwaka'wakw mask in 2005 as a long-term loan from the British Museum in London to Alert Bay, British Columbia, Canada, from where it was removed in 1921.[98]
- The return of sixty-seven masterpieces to Italy (from the J. P. Getty Museum in Los Angeles (California), the Metropolitan Museum of Art in New York, the Museum of Fine Arts in Boston and the Princeton University Museum), which had left the country and were acquired under suspicious circumstances.
- The return, from France to Egypt (2009),[99] of a painted wall fragment taken from a Luxor tomb and found in the Louvre Museum.

Heritage', *Museum International*, 61 (1–2), 25; and Gabriel, Mille (2009), 'The Return of Cultural Heritage from Denmark to Greenland', *Museum International*, 61, (1–2), 30. One should note that Greenland was a Danish colony for more than 200 years (1721–1953) during which there was extensive collecting activity on the part of the Danish.

96 Wilson, Christopher (2009), 'Implications and Challenges of Repatriating and Reburying Ngarrindjeri Old People from the Edinburgh Collection', *Museum International*, 61(1–2), 37; and Fforde, Cressida (2009), 'From Edinburgh University to the Ngarrinjeri Nation, South Australia', *Museum International*, 61 (1–2), 41; and Besternam, Tristram (2009), 'Returning a Stolen Generation', *Museum International*, 61 (1–2), 107.

97 Mariam, Haile (2009), 'The Cultural Benefits of the Return of the Axum Obelisk', *Museum International*, 61 (1–2), 48; and Scovazzi, Tullio (2009), 'Legal Aspects of the Axum Obelisk Case', *Museum International*, 61 (1–2), 52; and Croci, Giorgio (2009), 'From Italy to Ethiopia: the Dismantling, Transportation and Re-erection of the Axum Obelisk', *Museum International*, 61 (1–2), 61.

98 Sanborn, Andrea (2009), 'The Reunification of the Kwakwaka'wakw mask with its Cultural Soul', *Museum International*, 61 (1–2), 81. Other cultural objects were also repatriated to this region by the Smithsonian's National Museum of the American Indian in New York, from the André Breton Collection in Paris, France, and so on.

99 http://www.google.com/hostednews/afp/article/ALeqM5gQVU1X-7yM469ItXJ3PxYfOXMnVA.

- The return of six masterpieces to Greece, four from the J. P. Getty Museum in Los Angeles (California) and two masterpieces from the L. Levy and Sh. White Private Collection in New York, which had left the country and were acquired under suspicious circumstances.
- Other cases of repatriation of cultural objects to Greece are the return of a fragment from the Parthenon's sculptural decoration from the University of Heidelberg (2006), a collection of 48 ancient Greek coins from Sweden (2006), the return of a fragment of an ancient Greek marble relief portraying Athens from a Danish citizen after 110 years (2007), six ceramic oinochoe from a British professor of archaeology (2007), a stolen statue of Apollonas Lykeios from Gortyna in Crete from Switzerland (2007), 90 stolen antiquities from the Theodoropoulos collection from Germany (2007) and so on.[100]
- Hundreds of cultural objects were repatriated to Peru from the US, Uruguay, Germany, New Zealand,[101] UK and Colombia in 2007 and 2008.[102]

The agreement between Tanzania and the Geneva Museum Barbier-Mueller on the return of the Makouda Mask which had been stolen from the National Museum of Tanzania in Dar Es Salaam in 1984. This issue was on the agenda of the ICPRCP until its resolution.[103]

The agreement between Peru and Yale University for the return to Peru of thousands of archeological pieces (Inca relics) taken from Machu Picchu between 1911–1915 when Hiram Bingham conducted excavations in the site (November 2010).[104] The aforementioned cases constitute only a fraction of all cases of return that have taken place during recent years

---

[100] Stamatoudi, Irini (2009), 'Mediation and Cultural Diplomacy', *Museum International*, 61 (1–2), 116.

[101] New Zealand has also returned artefacts on the basis of law. See the case *Tupuna Maori*, P580/88 High Court of New Zealand, Wellington, 19 May 1988 in relation to the return of a Maori head to the Maori people (the New Zealand Maori Council) and case *Department of Affairs v. The Poverty Bay Club Inc.* [1989] DCR 481 in relation to a 1776 letter written by Captain James Cook to Captain Charles Clerke, sent to Sotheby's London for auction. This letter was returned to the New Zealand government. See Barker, I. (2006), 'The Protection of Cultural Heritage Items in New Zealand', in Hoffman (ed), *Art and Cultural Heritage*, n. 5 above, 145.

[102] Guerrero, Blanca Alva (2009), 'Repatriation of Cultural Properties: the Peruvian Experience', *Museum International*, 61(1–2), 145.

[103] See http://archives.com.museum/press/MM_Presofile_eng.pdf.

[104] See http://www.bbc.co.uk/news/world_latin_america_11804937.

on the basis of law, ethics and public feeling.[105] A change in public feeling has been sensed either by states or institutions themselves and they have acted on their own initiative or after a request has been submitted to them; the current state of public feeling is also shown by opinion polls

---

[105] See http://portal.unesco.org/culture/en/ev.php-URL_ID=36505&URL_DO=DO_TOPIC&URL_SECTION=201.html:

I- Historic case studies of return and restitution under the aegis of the Intergovernmental Committee

The Intergovernmental Committee for Promoting the Return of Cultural Property to its Countries of Origin or its Restitution in case of Illicit Appropriation has assisted in several successful cases of restitution:

- In 1983, Italy returned over 12,000 pre-Columbian objects to Ecuador. The case was resolved after a seven-year litigation. The moral support expressed by the Committee was recognised by the Ecuadorian authorities as a significant factor in the success of their cause.
- Within the framework of an exchange, and following a request submitted by Jordan in 1983 to the Intergovernmental Committee, the Cincinnati Art Museum (USA) and the Department of Antiquities of Amman (Jordan) decided, in 1986, to jointly exchange moulds of the respective parts of the sandstone panel of Tyche with the zodiac in their possession, in order to be able to present the work in its entirety. This case was resolved by mediation.
- In 1987, the return of the 7,000 Bogazköy cuneiform tablets from the German Democratic Republic to Turkey. The case was resolved by direct return.
- In 1988, the return of the Phra Narai lintel to Thailand from the United States. The case was resolved by mediation.
- The Committee also supervised the return to the Museum of Corinth (Greece) of 271 objects held in the United States of America.

Another case (between Iran and Belgium about archaeological objects from the Necropolis of Khurvin) is suspended.Three other cases are still pending (regarding the Parthenon Marbles, involving Greece and the United Kingdom (before the ICPRCP since 1984), the issue of the sphinx of Bogazköy between Turkey and Germany (before the ICPRCP since 1986), and the Makondé mask case between Tanzania and Switzerland (before the ICPRCP since 1986)).

II- Recent examples of successful operations of cultural property restitutions

- *April 2008: Syria returns stolen antiquities to Iraq*

Syria has returned to Iraq around 700 pieces of antiquities, including gold coins and jewellery, which were stolen in the aftermath of the US intervention.

run by cultural institutions or non-governmental organisations or even private companies. In 1998 and 2002 opinion polls were run in Britain, which demonstrated that public opinion was in favour of the return of the Parthenon Marbles to Greece.[106] This is one of the most famous cases

---

- *April 2008: France returns more than 260 stolen archaeological items to Burkina Faso*

France has returned to Burkina Faso 262 stolen archaeological items discovered at the end of 2007 by French customs officers in the northern French port of Rouen. These items, stolen by a French couple, include: 231 fragments of pottery, 8 complete potteries, 17 stone objects and 6 bronze objects dating back to between 1,000 BC and 1,300 BC.

- *April 2008: Cultural relics illicitly exported to Denmark returned to China*

In adherence to the 1970 UNESCO Convention, the Chinese Government claimed the return of the 156 cultural relics in question through the local Danish court. The relics date back to between the Xia Dynasty (2,000 BC) and the Ming Dynasty (1368–1644). The restitution of these objects demonstrates the resolve of the Chinese Government to recover objects that were smuggled out of the country.

- *February 2008: Restitution from Greece of two statues to the Museum of Buthrote (Albania)*

Two marble statues representing Artemisia and Apollo were returned to the Museum of Buthrote where they had been stolen in the 1990s.

- *January 2008: Restitution of the bust of Marcus Aurelius from the United States to Algeria*

The U.S. Homeland Security authorities agreed to the restitution of the marble bust of a Roman Emperor that was stolen, as well as eight other archaeological objects, from the Skikda Museum (Algeria) in 1996.

- *December 2007: U.S. Court Orders German Baroness to Return Painting Stolen from Jewish Collector and Art Dealer*

The U.S. District Court in Rhode Island settled in favour of Concordia University, McGill University of Montreal and the Hebrew University of Jerusalem in their case against the baroness von Morsey Pickard. The return of the 'Girl from the Sabine Mountains', by Winterhalter, acquired by Morsey Pickard's step-father in 1937 during the forced sale of the collection of the Jewish gallery owner Max Stern, is a significant decision in the search for the possessions of the Jews stolen by the IIIth Reich.

- *October 2007: Restitution of hundred of antiques from Germany to Greece*

in the area of repatriation of cultural property to its country of origin, pending before the ICPRCP since 1984.

The Intergovernmental Committee for Promoting the Return of Cultural Property to its Countries of Origin or its Restitution in Case

---

94 objects (figurines, seals, tools and phials) from the Neolithic period that were stolen in 1985 from Larissa (Greece) were returned to Greece from Germany.

- *September 2007: Restitution by Yale University (USA) to Peru of archaeological artifacts from the Machu Picchu*

After ten years of negotiation, an agreement made between the Peruvian State and the Department of Archaeology of Yale University allowed for the return of more than 350 objects in stone, metal and ceramic and thousands of artifacts.

- *August 2007: Returned to Peru 18 pre-Hispanic archaeological pieces recovered in Germany*

Ceramics sculptures, objects made from organic material, and a funeral mask made of copper were returned to Peru. The success of the repatriation is the result of the close collaboration and coordination between the National Institute of Culture and the Ministry of Foreign Affairs, through the Peruvian Consulate in Hamburg and the Sub-Secretariat of Cultural Policy in Foreign Countries.

- *August 2007: Agreement of restitution of 40 archaeological items from the Getty Museum (USA) to Italy*

In a protocol signed between the Getty Museum Director and the Italian Minister of Cultural Property, the Getty undertook to return to Italy the Morgantina Venus and 39 other valuable archaeological items (vases, amphoras, fragments of fresco etc.), which had been taken illegally.

- *June 2007: Restitution of an antique sculpture from Switzerland to Greece*

A marble trunk from Gortyne stolen in Crete in 1991, which was featured on *Interpol*'s Database of Stolen Works of Art, was returned to Greece from Switzerland.

- *June 2007: Agreement by Italy to return hundreds of items to Pakistan*

Italy agreed to return 96 antiques to Pakistan. The vases, coins, and plates etc., dating from 3300 to 1800 B.C., had been obtained through illicit trafficking.

- *June 2007: Restitution of two statues from the USA to Kenya*

Two wooden statues, known as vigango, which were on display at the State of Illinois Museum and at the University of Hampton Museum, were returned to the Kenyan village where they were stolen in 1985.

of Illicit Appropriation, which was set up to serve claims for return not falling within the ambit and scope of the 1970 UNESCO Convention, formed and transformed the ethics in the area too. The Committee has

---

- *April 2007: Restitution of the Venus de Cyrène from Italy to Libya*

Italy agreed to return a white marble statue, in its possession for nearly a century, to Libya, which had been requesting its return since 1989.

- *March 2007: Return of 1,400 Afghan artifacts preserved in Switzerland*

Some 1,400 Afghan ethnographic and archaeological objects, preserved since 1999 at the Afghanistan Museum-in-Exile (Bubendorf, Switzerland) under the aegis of UNESCO, were repatriated to the National Museum of Afghanistan in Kabul on 16 March 2007.

- *December 2006: The Getty Museum of Los Angeles agrees to return art items to Greece.*

The Getty agreed to return a gold wreath and a marble statue of a kore (a standing young woman). In August 2006, following an amicable agreement, the Getty also returned a sixth century BC Thasian relief and a fourth century BC Boeotian stele to Greece. In response to accusations against its acquisition policy, the Getty announced a stricter policy with guidelines for bringing the Institution's procedures into line with the principles of the 1970 UNESCO Convention.

- *September 2006: The Boston Museum of Fine Arts agrees to return art items to Italy*

The Boston Museum of Fine Arts reached an amicable agreement with Italy over the return of 13 items, which included a marble statue of the Empress Sabina, dating from 136 AD, and some ancient vases.

- *September 2006: Return of a Parthenon fragment from Germany to Greece*

Through an amicable consensus, the University of Heidelberg (Germany) returned a small piece of marble portraying a man's foot to the Greek Ministry of Culture. This is the first fragment from the Parthenon sculptures to return to Greece since European collectors removed large sections from the building some 200 years ago.

- *February 2006: Agreement for restitution of the Euphronios crater from the Metropolitan Museum of Art (USA) to Italy*

Reversing its long-standing position, the Met decided to return a 2,500-year-old Greek vase that was considered to be one of the world's finest. This antique crater, made by the Greek painter Euphronios, was returned to Italy in January 2008.

been entrusted with responsibility for seeking ways and means of facilitating bilateral negotiations for the return of cultural property to its countries of origin and the promotion of multilateral and bilateral co-operation to achieve this aim (article 4, paragraphs 1 and 2, of the Statutes).

See also the cases referred to in the UNESCO's Information Kit on Restitution http://unesdoc.unesco.org/images/0013/001394/139407eb.pdf. See also the return of the Aidonia Treasure

> (In the 1980s a series of clandestine excavations at the great Mycenean site of Aidonia produced at least 312 pieces of jewelry that formed part of a magnificent funerary treasure. They were smuggled out of the country and taken to the USA. In 1993 they were put on display in a New York gallery by a certain Michael Ward as a viewing for a proposed later auction of the items, supported by a lavish catalogue. Greece filed for the repatriation of these items in May 1993, on the grounds that they were similar to pieces legitimately excavated at the site of Aidonia and likely to have come from the loot excavations from this site. Before he was forced to reveal the manner in which he had acquired the pieces, Michael Ward donated the treasure to the Society for the Preservation of Greek Heritage, who returned them to Greece in January 1996).

And the return of the Lydian Hoard

> (363 artefacts including gold and silver artefacts, marble sphinxes, jewellry and wall paintings) were acquired from 1966 – 1970 by the Metropolitan Museum of Art for $1.5 million. They were originally stolen from burial mounds in the Mansa and Usak regions of Turkey. The looters themselves were stopped in the process of stealing more, and so 100 artifacts were left behind. The looters were arrested, prosecuted and provided testimonies of what was stolen and to whom they had been sold. Minutes of the Acquisition Committee of the Metropolitan Museum show that the Museum knew that the Hoard had been stolen. They originally had plans to display the Hoard in 1970, but were put off and the hoard was not finally displayed until 1984. Immediately Turkey began an investigation aimed at recovering the Hoard. The Museum policy, once again clear from the minutes, was not to help the Turkish investigation but to return the goods if ownership could be proven. Once it became clear that the pieces were stolen, the Museum began a rearguard action. The Museum claimed that the Turkish claim was too late. The Museum then attempted to share the hoard after admitting that it came from Turkey. Eventually the Museum returned the hoard in 1993).

Text taken from http://pcwww.liv.ac.uk/~Sinclair/ALGY399_Site/return.html#examples.

Also recently an Italian court (in Pesaro) on 11 February 2010 ordered an important ancient Greek statue (the bronze 'Victorious Youth' bought by the J. Paul Getty Museum) to be seized so it can be returned to Italy. The statue dates from 300 B.C.–100 B.C. and was pulled from the sea by Italian fishermen in 1964 off the eastern town of Fano, near Pesaro.

Cases of return have also taken place on the basis of agreements between states and cultural institutions (museums or other) and individual collectors. The agreements referred to above between Italy and various

---

See also some other recent cases as they were reported by UNESCO (in document CLT-2010/CONF.203/COM.16/2, Paris, March 2010) without UNESCO's mediation or other involvement:

> '14 December 2009 : Restitution of 5 frescos (France – Egypt)
> In November 2009, France restituted five fresco fragments held by the Louvre Museum to Egypt, which had claimed them. These pieces had left Egypt illegally and, subsequently, had been acquired in good faith by the Louvre from a French gallery and at a public auction. Following the Egyptian request to return these objects, the National Scientific Commission of the Museums of France confirmed that these were from the tomb of a dignitary (Prince Tetiky) of Egypt's Eighteenth dynasty (1550–1290 BC), located in the Valley of the Kings near Luxor. The French Ministry of Culture decided to return the pieces.
>
> 19 January 2010: Restitution 139 items of cultural property (Spain – Nicaragua)
> A collection of 139 pre-Columbian archaeological objects confiscated by the *Grupo de Patrimonio Histórico* of the Spanish *Guardia Civil* was returned by the General Directorate of Fine Arts and Cultural Property of Spain's Ministry of Culture to the Government of Nicaragua. This restitution followed a letter from the Ambassador of Nicaragua, Augusto Zamora Rodriguez, in which he requested the necessary approvals to return the pieces to their country of origin. These objects will now enrich the collections of *Mi Museo*, a museum institution in the Nicaraguan city of Granada.
>
> 20 January 2010: Restitution of 2 Swords (The Netherlands – France)
> On the night of 15 to 16 November 1995, a robbery was committed at the Château de Fontainebleau. Thirteen works of art disappeared that night. Between 1996 and 2000, six objects were recovered by the Office Central de lutte contre le trafic des Biens Culturels (3 clocks, two vases and a sculpture). On 23 October, 2009, two swords recovered from a Dutch middleman arrested in the Netherlands were returned to France. These are ceremonial weapons commissioned in 1807 from the goldsmith Martin-Guillaume Biennais by Jérôme Bonaparte—Napoleon's brother and the king of Westphalia. They had been offered to Fontainebleau for the Musée Napoléon in 1979 by Louis-Napoleon Bonaparte, the great grandson of King Jerome. The official ceremony for the restitution to the Château de Fontainebleau was held in January 2010.
>
> 21 January 2010: Restitution of Sumerian Treasures (Germany – Iraq)
> Germany returned 22 artifacts thought to date from the Sumerian civilisation to Iraq. According to official authorities, these objects were looted by soldiers during the recent war and were then transported to Germany. They were finally recovered in 2007 with hundreds of other archaeological objects from other countries, during a raid on a house near Frankfurt. Archaeologists were able to geographically identify those objects that came from the ancient

American museums and between Greece and American museums and collectors are examples of such claims.

6.2.4 No Time Limitations for the Return of Cultural Objects of Particular Significance

The fourth principle (under formation), which works rather like an adjunct to the former one, is that the return of cultural objects of particular significance should not be subject to time limitations.[107] The justifying

Sumerian cities of Girsu, Isin, Larsa and Umma. Six of these items are ceramic cones used during construction to identify the owner's name, the description of the construction and the name of the god to whom the inhabitants of the city paid tribute. The restitution of these objects took place in Berlin in the presence of the Ambassador of Iraq to Germany, Mr. Alaa al-Hashimi. According to the latter, "the return of Iraqi cultural property is invaluable for Iraq".

> 3 March 2010: Restitution of 25,000 antiquities (Great Britain– Egypt)
> After lengthy negotiations between the University of London and Egyptian authorities, Great Britain decided to return to Egypt some 25,000 antiquities. Among these pieces is a 200,000 year old stone ax, as well as pottery from the seventh millennium BC. Director General of the Egyptian Supreme Council of Antiquities, Zahi Hawass, said that the coins will go to a "collection dedicated to the (pre-pharaonic) period of Nagada," named after a village in southern Egypt, which is home to "one of the oldest civilizations in the world." They will be exhibited at the Ahmed Fakhri Museum, currently under construction in the Dakhla Oasis in Egypt's Western Desert'.

Also recently in October 2010 Serbia returned to Croatia 31 icons taken during the 1991–95 war from the Serb Orthodox monasteries at Krka and Krupa and the Serb Orthodox church in Dalj. More than 20000 works of art have been returned to Croatian museums, galleries, churches and monasteries since 2001. A Croatian-Serbian commission for the restitution of cultural assets has been set up with this aim and is expected to conclude its works in 2011, http://www.croatiantimes.com/news/General_News/2010-10-29/14801/_Serbia_returns_31_icons_to_Croatia.

[106] See http://en.wikipedia.org/wiki/Elgin_Marbles.

[107] It is interesting to note that when the University of Heidelberg (then located in the State of Baden) asked the Pope for the return of thirty nine codes of the Palatine Library, that had been looted in wartime from Heidelberg in the 17th century and were donated to the Pope by Maximilian of Bavaria, Austria and Prussia, which pleaded for their return, based their request on two grounds : a) on the legal argument that the original acquisition was illegal and therefore acquisitive prescription could not apply and b) on the cultural need to ensure that unique texts of fundamental importance for the study of the origins of the German languages were returned to the country to which they were so closely linked. Return did take place. Scovazzi, T. (2009), 'Diviser c'est détruire: ethical principles and legal rules in the field of return of cultural properties', paper presented in the

reasons which dictate the putting together of the missing parts of a cultural context, site or monument, do not stop being 'justifying' by the mere lapse of time. When the international conventions in the area of illicit trade in art were adopted, this principle was regarded as a groundbreaking view which would impinge on many countries' national laws regarding time limitations for chattels. Yet law and ethics have been transformed since then and countries have become friendlier towards the concept of repatriation. The first seeds of this idea are found in international conventions, although it is true that some national laws had already fully incorporated the principle by providing for the imprescriptibility of such objects,[108] or their inalienability,[109] categorising them as *res extra commercium*,[110] or *res sacrae*. By so doing, the objects are preserved for the common interest and benefit because the only legitimate possessor is the state. The 1970 UNESCO Convention contains no provisions on time limitations, leaving States Parties free to apply the time limitations they consider appropriate. The 1995 Unidroit Convention is more specialised in the area of international claims for return of cultural objects. Apart from the general time limitations, it also provides for extended time limitations for a special category of cultural objects. Specifically article 3(4) provides that '[C]ultural object[s] forming an *integral part of an identified monument or archaeological site, or belonging to a public collection*, shall not be subject to time limitations other than a period of three years from the time when the claimant knew the location of the cultural object and the identity of the possessor'.[111] States Parties can however provide for a fixed time limitation of 75 years[112] on a reciprocal basis.[113] The Commonwealth Scheme

16th Session of the Intergovernmental Committee for Promoting the Return of Cultural Property to Its Countries of Origin or Its Restitution in Case of Illicit Appropriation (21–23.9.2010), Paris: UNESCO, at 7–8.

[108] i.e., art. 18(1) of the French law for historical monuments of 1993: 'all the movable objects listed are imprescriptible'.

[109] i.e., Mexico; Spain, in its Law on Historical Patrimony 1985 and the Law on National Patrimony 1982; Greece in its Acts 3028 of 2002 and 3658 of 2008. See also, art. 28 of the relevant Portuguese law, which does not allow for any private ownership of works of art listed in a national registry.

[110] See for example the Greek Act 3028 of 2002, which provides that 'movable ancient monuments up to 1453 belong to the State in terms of ownership and possession, are imprescriptible and *extra commercium* according to article 966 of the Civil Code'. This was also explained by Prof. Mussgnug in the 1990 Heidelberg Symposium with reference to the German administrative law and to the broadly accepted concept of *res sacrae*.

[111] Emphasis added.

[112] See also art. 3(6).

[113] Article 9(1).

provides for a five-year time limitation for making a claim for the return of an unlawfully exported cultural object, calculated from the time the country of export had knowledge of the whereabouts of the item in the country of location. No absolute time limitations are provided for, which would rule out such claims.[114]

There have been legal instruments that do not provide for any time limitations at all, especially in the area of cultural property alienated in times of armed conflict (such as the Treaty of Westphalia in 1648, the 1907 Hague Convention on the Laws of War, the post-First World War settlements, the Declaration of London of 1943 concerning the restitution of cultural property taken under the Nazi occupation, the 1954 Hague Convention on the Protection of Cultural Property in the Event of Armed Conflict, the First Protocol to the Hague Convention (1954), the Second Protocol to the Hague Convention (1999) and the Security Council Resolution mandating the return to Iraq of cultural objects displaced from the country in 2003).[115] The United Nations General Assembly Declaration on Decolonization 1960[116] and the practice of return of items from states to their former colonies (e.g. from the Netherlands to Indonesia and from Belgium to Congo)[117] reflects the same spirit with respect to cultural objects taken during colonial times.

---

[114] Interesting in this respect are the time limitations provided by some states of the United States of America. For example in New York on actions for recovery of stolen art according to the Demand and Refusal Rule developed in *Menzel v. List* in 1938 the three-year time limitation governing a cause of action for replevin against a good faith purchaser does not begin to run until the true owner makes a demand for return of the chattel and the possessor (current owner) refuses to return it. See *Solomon R. Guggenheim v. Lubell*, 153 A.D.2d 143, 149, 550 N.Y.S.2d 618, 621–22 (1st Dept. 1990), aff'd, 77 N.Y.2d 311, 567 N.Y.S.2d 623, 569 N.E.2d 426 (1999). In *O'Keefe v. Snyder* 416A. 2d 862 870 (NJ 1980) it was mentioned that the cause of action does not begin to accrue until the true owner first knew, or reasonably should have known through the exercise of due diligence, of the cause of action, including the identity of the possessor.

[115] Italy returned the Axum Obelisk to Ethiopia 68 years after its removal and the statue of Venus of Cyrene to Libya 93 years after its removal. Chile returned cultural properties to Peru 126 years after their removal (on 16 November 2007, 3788 books were returned to Peru by Chile, which had been removed in 1881 during the Pacific War (1879–83) from the National Library of Peru in Lima, when the city was occupied by Chilean troops). For this case see Hampe Martinez T. (2008), 'Cómo recuperar el patrimonio documental llevado a Chile durante la Guerra del Pacifico?' *Revista Peruana de Derecho Internacional*, 77.

[116] UNGA Resolution 1514 of 14th December 1960. Declaration on the Granting of Independence to Colonial Countries and Peoples.

[117] Prott, *Commentary on the Unidroit Convention*, n. 7 above, 36. See also L.

It seems, therefore, that there are particular categories of cultural objects, alienated under specific circumstances, for which no time limitations apply. This principle is enshrined in law, ethics and practice as derived from recent examples in the area. The objects tend to fall into the following categories: a) sacred and ritual objects, b) national symbols or emblems, c) objects detached from buildings and monuments and immovable property in general, d) objects belonging to an archaeological site, e) objects belonging to a public collection, f) human (or ancestral) remains[118] and g) objects that are inextricably linked to the identity (cultural, religious, societal or other) of a group, community or nation. In order to qualify for protection, objects should have been removed illegally or unethically. This might mean that they were removed without the authorisation or consent of the group, community or country to which they belong or that they have been acquired by exploiting the weakness of another subject during periods of war, hostilities, occupation, colonisation, poverty, etc. These circumstances of removal should form a prerequisite.[119]

6.3 OUTCOME

From the above it can be deduced that there are some general principles, which are embedded in law, ethics and practice.[120] Some of them are still under formation and are therefore called trends. Even trends, however, indicate clearly the shape cultural property law is taking and its likely future. As outlined above there are four principles: 1) protection of the cultural heritage of the country of origin, which incorporates two sub-principles: a) respect for the cultural heritage laws of the country of origin and b) reinforcement of due diligence checks in the acquisition of cultural

---

Prott (2009), 'The Ethics and Law of Returns', *Museum International*, 61, 1–2, 101, at 103–4.

[118] Article 4.4 of the ICOM Code of Professional Ethics Museums provides that 'requests for removal from public display of human remains or material of sacred significance from the originating communities must be addressed expeditiously with respect and sensitivity. Requests for the return of such material should be addressed similarly. Museum policies should clearly define the process for responding to such requests'.

[119] For example the theft of art during Nazi occupation.

[120] See Recommendation 8 adopted during the 16th session of the ICPRCP in Paris 21–23 September, 2010, referring to the Report commissioned by the Secretariat on 'Ethical Principles and Legal Rules in the Field of Return of Cultural Properties', which has identified the evolution of some basic principles on the aforementioned issues and presented to the Committee during the 14th extraordinary session, 15th and 16th sessions and their conclusions.

objects, including reversion of the burden of proof for the establishment of the possessor's good faith; 2) international co-operation for the prevention of illegal movements of cultural property; 3) return of cultural objects as a prerequisite for the preservation of the integrity of cultural contexts, irrespective of whether return takes place as a means for restitution (rectification of a 'wrong') or on the basis of ethical, scientific, humanitarian, anthropological, archaeological or other grounds; and 4) no time limitations for the return of cultural objects of a particular significance.[121] It is argued here that cultural property law should be approached, interpreted and applied in the light of the above.[122]

---

121 See also 'Conclusions of the Athens International Conference on the Return of Cultural Objects to their Countries of Origin', *Museum International*, 61, 1–2, 153, and in particular two conclusions: a) certain categories of cultural property are irrevocably identified by reference to the cultural context in which they were created (unique and exceptional artworks and monuments, ritual objects, national symbols, ancestral remains, dismembered pieces of outstanding works of art). It is their original context that gives them their authenticity and unique value, and b) in recent years a clear tendency towards the return of cultural objects to their countries of origin has been developed on legal, social and ethical grounds. The return of cultural objects is directly linked to the rights of humanity (preservation of cultural identity and preservation of world heritage).

122 Integrity and preservation form the two highest principles in cultural property law. Logic necessarily points in the same direction: is not the real (context) better than the fake and is not the whole (of the object and its cultural environment) better than the part?

Conclusion

Although the 'tale' of cultural property law is very much a 'Tale of Two Cities', the nationalist and the cosmopolitan, it is also true that the boundaries between the nationalist and the internationalist approaches have been blurred by more pragmatic views; those dictated by reality, mutual understanding and co-operation. Both sides occasionally use the same arguments to argue different points. 'Retention', for example, is used to indicate the 'retention' of cultural objects both in collections (by museums and private collectors) and in state territory (by states). 'Movement of art' is used by internationalists to argue that any home can be a good home for cultural heritage and by nationalists on the basis of cultural diplomacy and missionary art through loans. The trend, however (reflected in particular in the 1970 UNESCO Convention, the 1995 Unidroit Convention and European Union law and in general in soft law instruments) is that a nation is the most appropriate custodian of its own cultural heritage. That assumption is made on the basis of geography, historical background, cultural identity and context and does not run counter to the preservation of cultural heritage for the sake of humanity. Humanity incorporates diversity and plurality. Preservation of national cultural heritage serves exactly that.[1]

---

[1] See the Preamble to the 2005 UNESCO Convention on the Protection and Promotion of the Diversity of Cultural Expressions:

> . . . *Affirming* that cultural diversity is a defining characteristic of humanity, *Conscious* that cultural diversity forms a common heritage of humanity and should be cherished and preserved for the benefit of all, *Being aware* that cultural diversity creates a rich and varied world, which increases the range of choices and nurtures human capacities and values, and therefore is a mainspring for sustainable development for communities, peoples and nations . . .

See also the Preamble to the 2003 UNESCO Convention for the Safeguarding of Intangible Cultural Heritage:

> . . . Considering the importance of the intangible cultural heritage as a mainspring of cultural diversity and a guarantee of sustainable development, as underscored in the UNESCO Recommendation on the Safeguarding of Traditional Culture

It seems increasingly that the views of the two opposing camps are becoming less rigid and the world is becoming more humanitarian. Arguments which advocate that antiquities are best preserved in countries which have the means to preserve and exhibit them lose ground because they divide the world further into those who 'can' and those who 'cannot' instead of shifting the discussion to those who can help and those who cannot. One could compare antiquities to children. Some of them belong to poor families. Deprivation, however, is not a solution. Wealthier families could support poor families, without depriving them of their children. In that sense, the world can work together to find mutually acceptable solutions for the benefit both of culture and of those benefiting from it.

---

and Folklore of 1989, in the UNESCO Universal Declaration on Cultural Diversity of 2001, and in the Istanbul Declaration of 2002 adopted by the Third Round Table of Ministers of Culture,

Considering the deep-seated interdependence between the intangible cultural heritage and the tangible cultural and natural heritage,

Recognising that the processes of globalisation and social transformation, alongside the conditions they create for renewed dialogue among communities, also give rise, as does the phenomenon of intolerance, to grave threats of deterioration, disappearance and destruction of the intangible cultural heritage, in particular owing to a lack of resources for safeguarding such heritage,

Being aware of the universal will and the common concern to safeguard the intangible cultural heritage of humanity,

Recognising that communities, in particular indigenous communities, groups and, in some cases, individuals, play an important role in the production, safeguarding, maintenance and re-creation of the intangible cultural heritage, thus helping to enrich cultural diversity and human creativity . . . .

Appendices

APPENDIX 1 INTERNATIONAL CONVENTIONS

- The 1970 UNESCO Convention
- The 1995 Unidroit Convention

APPENDIX 2 EUROPEAN UNION LAW

- Articles 34–36, 167 TFEU
- Council Regulation (EC) 116/2009 of 18 December 2008 on the export of cultural goods (codified version)
- Commission Regulation (EC) 752/93 of 30 March 1993 laying down provisions for the implementation of Council Regulation 3911/92 on the export of cultural goods, as amended by Commission Regulation (EC) 1526/98 of 16 July 1998, OJ L201/47 and Commission Regulation (EC) 656/2004 of 7 April 2004, OJ L104/50 (Corrigendum, OJ L 203, 8.6.2004/14 (656/2004)
- Directive 93/7/EEC of 15 March 1993 on the return of cultural objects unlawfully removed from the territory of a Member State (OJ L 74/74, 27.3.1993), amended by Directive 96/100/EC of 17 February 1997 (L 60/59, 1.3.1997) and Directive 2001/38/EC of 5 June 2001 (L 187/43, 10.7.2001)

APPENDIX 3 CODES OF ETHICS

- UNESCO International Code of Ethics for Dealers in Cultural Property (1999)
- International Council of Museums (ICOM) Code of Professional Ethics (adopted in 1986, revised in 2004)

APPENDIX 4

- The 2002 Declaration on the Importance and Value of Universal Museums
- UNESCO (Intergovernmental Committee for Promoting the Return of Cultural Property to its Countries of Origin or its Restitution in case of Illicit Appropriation) Rules of Procedure on Mediation and Conciliation (2010)

APPENDIX 1

International Conventions

Convention on the Means of Prohibiting and Preventing the Illicit Import, Export and Transfer of Ownership of Cultural Property 1970

Paris, 14 November 1970

The General Conference of the United Nations Educational, Scientific and Cultural Organization, meeting in Paris from 12 October to 14 November 1970, at its sixteenth session,

Recalling the importance of the provisions contained in the Declaration of the Principles of International Cultural Co-operation, adopted by the General Conference at its fourteenth session,

Considering that the interchange of cultural property among nations for scientific, cultural and educational purposes increases the knowledge of the civilization of Man, enriches the cultural life of all peoples and inspires mutual respect and appreciation among nations,

Considering that cultural property constitutes one of the basic elements of civilization and national culture, and that its true value can be appreciated only in relation to the fullest possible information regarding is origin, history and traditional setting,

Considering that it is incumbent upon every State to protect the cultural property existing within its territory against the dangers of theft, clandestine excavation, and illicit export,

Considering that, to avert these dangers, it is essential for every State to become increasingly alive to the moral obligations to respect its own cultural heritage and that of all nations,

Considering that, as cultural institutions, museums, libraries and archives should ensure that their collections are built up in accordance with universally recognized moral principles,

Considering that the illicit import, export and transfer of ownership of cultural property is an obstacle to that understanding between nations which it is part of UNESCO's mission to promote by recommending to interested States, international conventions to this end,

Considering that the protection of cultural heritage can be effective only if organized both nationally and internationally among States working in close co-operation,

Considering that the UNESCO General Conference adopted a Recommendation to this effect in 1964,

Having before It further proposals on the means of prohibiting and preventing the illicit import, export and transfer of ownership of cultural property, a question which is on the agenda for the session as item 19,

Having decided, at its fifteenth session, that this question should be made the subject of an international convention,
Adopts this Convention on the fourteenth day of November 1970.

Article 1

For the purposes of this Convention, the term 'cultural property' means property which, on religious or secular grounds, is specifically designated by each State as being of importance for archaeology, prehistory, history, literature, art or science and which belongs to the following categories:
(a) Rare collections and specimens of fauna, flora, minerals and anatomy, and objects of palaeontological interest;
(b) property relating to history, including the history of science and technology and military and social history, to the life of national leaders, thinkers, scientists and artists and to events of national importance;
(c) products of archaeological excavations (including regular and clandestine) or of archaeological discoveries;
(d) elements of artistic or historical monuments or archaeological sites which have been dismembered;
(e) antiquities more than one hundred years old, such as inscriptions, coins and engraved seals;
(f) objects of ethnological interest;
(g) property of artistic interest, such as:
  (i) pictures, paintings and drawings produced entirely by hand on any support and in any material (excluding industrial designs and manufactured articles decorated by hand);
  (ii) original works of statuary art and sculpture in any material;
  (iii) original engravings, prints and lithographs;
  (iv) original artistic assemblages and montages in any material;
(h) rare manuscripts and incunabula, old books, documents and publications of special interest (historical, artistic, scientific, literary, etc.) singly or in collections;
(i) postage, revenue and similar stamps, singly or in collections;
(j) archives, including sound, photographic and cinematographic archives;
(k) articles of furniture more than one hundred years old and old musical instruments.

Article 2

1. The States Parties to this Convention recognize that the illicit import, export and transfer of ownership of cultural property is one of the main

causes of the impoverishment of the cultural heritage of the countries of origin of such property and that international co-operation constitutes one of the most efficient means of protecting each country's cultural property against all the dangers resulting there from.

2. To this end, the States Parties undertake to oppose such practices with the means at their disposal, and particularly by removing their causes, putting a stop to current practices, and by helping to make the necessary reparations.

Article 3

The import, export or transfer of ownership of cultural property effected contrary to the provisions adopted under this Convention by the States Parties thereto, shall be illicit.

Article 4

The States Parties to this Convention recognize that for the purpose of the Convention property which belongs to the following categories forms part of the cultural heritage of each State:

(a) Cultural property created by the individual or collective genius of nationals of the State concerned, and cultural property of importance to the State concerned created within the territory of that State by foreign nationals or stateless persons resident within such territory;

(b) cultural property found within the national territory;

(c) cultural property acquired by archaeological, ethnological or natural science missions, with the consent of the competent authorities of the country of origin of such property;

(d) cultural property which has been the subject of a freely agreed exchange;

(e) cultural property received as a gift or purchased legally with the consent of the competent authorities of the country of origin of such property.

Article 5

To ensure the protection of their cultural property against illicit import; export and transfer of ownership, the States Parties to this Convention undertake, as appropriate for each country, to set up within their territories one or more national services, where such services do not already exist, for the protection of the cultural heritage, with a qualified staff sufficient in number for the effective carrying out of the following functions:

(a) contributing to the formation of draft laws and regulations designed to

secure the protection of the cultural heritage and particularly prevention of the illicit import, export and transfer of ownership of important cultural property;
(b) establishing and keeping up to date, on the basis of a national inventory of protected property, a list of important public and private cultural property whose export would constitute an appreciable impoverishment of the national cultural heritage;
(c) promoting the development or the establishment of scientific and technical institutions (museums, libraries, archives, laboratories, workshops . . .) required to ensure the preservation and presentation of cultural property;
(d) organizing the supervision of archaeological excavations, ensuring the preservation 'in situation' of certain cultural property, and protecting certain areas reserved for future archaeological research;
(e) establishing, for the benefit of those concerned (curators, collectors, antique dealers, etc.) rules in conformity with the ethical principles set forth in this Convention; and taking steps to ensure the observance of those rules;
(f) taking educational measures to stimulate and develop respect for the cultural heritage of all States, and spreading knowledge of the provisions of this Convention;
(g) seeing that appropriate publicity is given to the disappearance of any items of cultural property.

Article 6

The States Parties to this Convention undertake:
(a) To introduce an appropriate certificate in which the exporting State would specify that the export of the cultural property in question is authorized. The certificate should accompany all items of cultural property exported in accordance with the regulations;
(b) to prohibit the exportation of cultural property from their territory unless accompanied by the above-mentioned export certificate;
(c) to publicize this prohibition by appropriate means, particularly among persons likely to export or import cultural property.

Article 7

The States Parties to this Convention undertake:
(a) To take the necessary measures, consistent with national legislation, to prevent museums and similar institutions within their territories from acquiring cultural property originating in another State Party which has

been illegally exported after entry into force of this Convention, in the States concerned. Whenever possible, to inform a State of origin Party to this Convention of an offer of such cultural property illegally removed from that State after the entry into force of this Convention in both States;

(b) (i) to prohibit the import of cultural property stolen from a museum or a religious or secular public monument or similar institution in another State Party to this Convention after the entry into force of this Convention for the States concerned, provided that such property is documented as appertaining to the inventory of that institution;

(ii) at the request of the State Party of origin, to take appropriate steps to recover and return any such cultural property imported after the entry into force of this Convention in both States concerned, provided, however, that the requesting State shall pay just compensation to an innocent purchaser or to a person who has valid title to that property. Requests for recovery and return shall be made through diplomatic offices. The requesting Party shall furnish, at its expense, the documentation and other evidence necessary to establish its claim for recovery and return. The Parties shall impose no customs duties or other charges upon cultural property returned pursuant to this Article. All expenses incident to the return and delivery of the cultural property shall be borne by the requesting Party.

Article 8

The States Parties to this Convention undertake to impose penalties or administrative sanctions on any person responsible for infringing the prohibitions referred to under Articles 6(b) and 7(b) above.

Article 9

Any State Party to this Convention whose cultural patrimony is in jeopardy from pillage of archaeological or ethnological materials may call upon other States Parties who are affected. The States Parties to this Convention undertake, in these circumstances, to participate in a concerted international effort to determine and to carry out the necessary concrete measures, including the control of exports and imports and international commerce in the specific materials concerned. Pending agreement each State concerned shall take provisional measures to the extent feasible to prevent irremediable injury to the cultural heritage of the requesting State.

Article 10

The States Parties to this Convention undertake:
(a) To restrict by education, information and vigilance, movement of cultural property illegally removed from any State Party to this Convention and, as appropriate for each country, oblige antique dealers, subject to penal or administrative sanctions, to maintain a register recording the origin of each item of cultural property, names and addresses of the supplier, description and price of each item sold and to inform the purchaser of the cultural property of the export prohibition to which such property may be subject;
(b) to endeavour by educational means to create and develop in the public mind a realization of the value of cultural property and the threat to the cultural heritage created by theft, clandestine excavations and illicit exports.

Article 11

The export and transfer of ownership of cultural property under compulsion arising directly or indirectly from the occupation of a country by a foreign power shall be regarded as illicit.

Article 12

The States Parties to this Convention shall respect the cultural heritage within the territories for the international relations of which they are responsible, and shall take all appropriate measures to prohibit and prevent the illicit import, export and transfer of ownership of cultural property in such territories.

Article 13

The States Parties to this Convention also undertake, consistent with the laws of each State:
(a) To prevent by all appropriate means transfers of ownership of cultural property likely to promote the illicit import or export of such property;
(b) to ensure that their competent services co-operate in facilitating the earliest possible restitution of illicitly exported cultural property to its rightful owner;
(c) to admit actions for recovery of lost or stolen items of cultural property brought by or on behalf of the rightful owners;
(d) to recognize the indefeasible right of each State Party to this Convention to classify and declare certain cultural property as inalienable which

should therefore ipso facto not be exported, and to facilitate recovery of such property by the State concerned in cases where it has been exported.

Article 14

In order to prevent illicit export and to meet the obligations arising from the implementation of this Convention, each State Party to the Convention should, as far as it is able, provide the national services responsible for the protection of its cultural heritage with an adequate budget and, if necessary, should set up a fund for this purpose.

Article 15

Nothing in this Convention shall prevent States Parties thereto from concluding special agreements among themselves or from continuing to implement agreements already concluded regarding the restitution of cultural property removed, whatever the reason, from its territory of origin, before the entry into force of this Convention for the States concerned.

Article 16

The States Parties to this Convention shall in their periodic reports submitted to the General Conference of the United Nations Educational, Scientific and Cultural Organization on dates and in a manner to be determined by it, give information on the legislative and administrative provisions which they have adopted and other action which they have taken for the application of this Convention, together with details of the experience acquired in this field.

Article 17

1. The States Parties to this Convention may call on the technical assistance of the United Nations Educational, Scientific and Cultural Organization, particularly as regards:
   (a) Information and education;
   (b) consultation and expert advice;
   (c) co-ordination and good offices.
2. The United Nations Educational, Scientific and Cultural Organization may, on its own initiative conduct research and publish studies on matters relevant to the illicit movement of cultural property.
3. To this end, the United Nations Educational, Scientific and Cultural

Organization may also call on the co-operation of any competent non-governmental organization.
4. The United Nations Educational, Scientific and Cultural Organization may, on its own initiative, make proposals to States Parties to this Convention for its implementation.
5. At the request of at least two States Parties to this Convention which are engaged in a dispute over its implementation, UNESCO may extend its good offices to reach a settlement between them.

Article 18

This Convention is drawn up in English, French, Russian and Spanish, the four texts being equally authoritative.

Article 19

1. This Convention shall be subject to ratification or acceptance by States members of the United Nations Educational, Scientific and Cultural Organization in accordance with their respective constitutional procedures.
2. The instruments of ratification or acceptance shall be deposited with the Director-General of the United Nations Educational, Scientific and Cultural Organization.

Article 20

1. This Convention shall be open to accession by all States not members of the United Nations Educational, Scientific and Cultural Organization which are invited to accede to it by the Executive Board of the Organization.
2. Accession shall be effected by the deposit of an instrument of accession with the Director-General of the United Nations Educational, Scientific and Cultural Organization.

Article 21

This Convention shall enter into force three months after the date of the deposit of the third instrument of ratification, acceptance or accession, but only with respect to those States which have deposited their respective instruments on or before that date. It shall enter into force with respect to any other State three months after the deposit of its instrument of ratification, acceptance or accession.

Article 22

The States Parties to this Convention recognize that the Convention is applicable not only to their metropolitan territories but also to all territories for the international relations of which they are responsible; they undertake to consult, if necessary, the governments or other competent authorities of these territories on or before ratification, acceptance or accession with a view to securing the application of the Convention to those territories, and to notify the Director-General of the United Nations Educational, Scientific and Cultural Organization of the territories to which it is applied, the notification to take effect three months after the date of its receipt.

Article 23

1. Each State Party to this Convention may denounce the Convention on its own behalf or on behalf of any territory for whose international relations it is responsible.
2. The denunciation shall be notified by an instrument in writing, deposited with the Director-General of the United Nations Educational, Scientific and Cultural Organization.
3. The denunciation shall take effect twelve months after the receipt of the instrument of denunciation.

Article 24

The Director-General of the United Nations Educational, Scientific and Cultural Organization shall inform the States members of the Organization, the States not members of the Organization which are referred to in Article 20, as well as the United Nations, of the deposit of all the instruments of ratification, acceptance and accession provided for in Articles 19 and 20, and of the notifications and denunciations provided for in Articles 22 and 23 respectively.

Article 25

1. This Convention may be revised by the General Conference of the United Nations Educational, Scientific and Cultural Organization. Any such revision shall, however, bind only the States which shall become Parties to the revising convention.
2. If the General Conference should adopt a new convention revising this Convention in whole or in part, then, unless the new convention otherwise

provides, this Convention shall cease to be open to ratification, acceptance or accession, as from the date on which the new revising convention enters into force.

Article 26

In conformity with Article 102 of the Charter of the United Nations, this Convention shall be registered with the Secretariat of the United Nations at the request of the Director-General of the United Nations Educational, Scientific and Cultural Organization.
Done in Paris this seventeenth day of November 1970, in two authentic copies bearing the signature of the President of the sixteenth session of the General Conference and of the Director-General of the United Nations Educational, Scientific and Cultural Organization, which shall be deposited in the archives of the United Nations Educational, Scientific and Cultural Organization, and certified true copies of which shall be delivered to all the States referred to in Articles 19 and 20 as well as to the United Nations.

[Declarations and Reservations are not included]

UNIDROIT Convention on Stolen or Illegally Exported Cultural Objects Rome, 24 June 1995

THE STATES PARTIES TO THIS CONVENTION,

ASSEMBLED in Rome at the invitation of the Government of the Italian Republic from 7 to 24 June 1995 for a Diplomatic Conference for the adoption of the draft Unidroit Convention on the International Return of Stolen or Illegally Exported Cultural Objects,

CONVINCED of the fundamental importance of the protection of cultural heritage and of cultural exchanges for promoting understanding between peoples, and the dissemination of culture for the well-being of humanity and the progress of civilisation,

DEEPLY CONCERNED by the illicit trade in cultural objects and the irreparable damage frequently caused by it, both to these objects themselves and to the cultural heritage of national, tribal, indigenous or other communities, and also to the heritage of all peoples, and in particular by the pillage of archaeological sites and the resulting loss of irreplaceable archaeological, historical and scientific information,

DETERMINED to contribute effectively to the fight against illicit trade in cultural objects by taking the important step of establishing common, minimal legal rules for the restitution and return of cultural objects between Contracting States, with the objective of improving the preservation and protection of the cultural heritage in the interest of all,

EMPHASISING that this Convention is intended to facilitate the restitution and return of cultural objects, and that the provision of any remedies, such as compensation, needed to effect restitution and return in some States, does not imply that such remedies should be adopted in other States,

AFFIRMING that the adoption of the provisions of this Convention for the future in no way confers any approval or legitimacy upon illegal transactions of whatever kind which may have taken place before the entry into force of the Convention,

CONSCIOUS that this Convention will not by itself provide a solution to the problems raised by illicit trade, but that it initiates a process that will enhance international cultural co-operation and maintain a proper role for legal trading and inter-State agreements for cultural exchanges,

ACKNOWLEDGING that implementation of this Convention should be accompanied by other effective measures for protecting cultural objects, such as the development and use of registers, the physical protection of archaeological sites and technical co-operation,

RECOGNISING the work of various bodies to protect cultural property, particularly the 1970 UNESCO Convention on illicit traffic and the development of codes of conduct in the private sector,

HAVE AGREED as follows:

CHAPTER I – SCOPE OF APPLICATION AND DEFINITION

Article 1

This Convention applies to claims of an international character for:
(a) the restitution of stolen cultural objects;
(b) the return of cultural objects removed from the territory of a Contracting State contrary to its law regulating the export of cultural objects for the purpose of protecting its cultural heritage (hereinafter 'illegally exported cultural objects').

Article 2

For the purposes of this Convention, cultural objects are those which, on religious or secular grounds, are of importance for archaeology, prehistory, history, literature, art or science and belong to one of the categories listed in the Annex to this Convention.

CHAPTER II – RESTITUTION OF STOLEN CULTURAL OBJECTS

Article 3

(1) The possessor of a cultural object which has been stolen shall return it.
(2) For the purposes of this Convention, a cultural object which has been unlawfully excavated or lawfully excavated but unlawfully retained shall be considered stolen, when consistent with the law of the State where the excavation took place.
(3) Any claim for restitution shall be brought within a period of three years from the time when the claimant knew the location of the cultural object and the identity of its possessor, and in any case within a period of fifty years from the time of the theft.
(4) However, a claim for restitution of a cultural object forming an integral part of an identified monument or archaeological site, or belonging to a public collection, shall not be subject to time limitations other than a period of three years from the time when the claimant knew the location of the cultural object and the identity of its possessor.
(5) Notwithstanding the provisions of the preceding paragraph, any Contracting State may declare that a claim is subject to a time limitation of 75 years or such longer period as is provided in its law. A claim made in another Contracting State for restitution of a cultural object

displaced from a monument, archaeological site or public collection in a Contracting State making such a declaration shall also be subject to that time limitation.
(6) A declaration referred to in the preceding paragraph shall be made at the time of signature, ratification, acceptance, approval or accession.
(7) For the purposes of this Convention, a 'public collection,' consists of a group of inventoried or otherwise identified cultural objects owned by:

(a) a Contracting State
(b) a regional or local authority of a Contracting State;
(c) a religious institution in a Contracting State; or
(d) an institution that is established for an essentially cultural, educational or scientific purpose in a Contracting State and is recognised in that State as serving the public interest.

(8) In addition, a claim for restitution of a sacred or communally important cultural object belonging to and used by a tribal or indigenous community in a Contracting State as part of that community's traditional or ritual use, shall be subject to the time limitation applicable to public collections.

Article 4

(1) The possessor of a stolen cultural object required to return it shall be entitled, at the time of its restitution, to payment of fair and reasonable compensation provided that the possessor neither knew nor ought reasonably to have known that the object was stolen and can prove that it exercised due diligence when acquiring the object.
(2) Without prejudice to the right of the possessor to compensation referred to in the preceding paragraph, reasonable efforts shall be made to have the person who transferred the cultural object to the possessor, or any prior transferor, pay the compensation where to do so would be consistent with the law of the State in which the claim is brought.
(3) Payment of compensation to the possessor by the claimant, when this is required, shall be without prejudice to the right of the claimant to recover it from any other person.
(4) In determining whether the possessor exercised due diligence, regard shall be had to all the circumstances of the acquisition, including the character of the parties, the price paid, whether the possessor consulted any reasonably accessible register of stolen cultural objects, and any other relevant information and documentation which it could reasonably have obtained, and whether the possessor consulted accessible agencies or took any other step that a reasonable person would have taken in the circumstances.
(5) The possessor shall not be in a more favourable position than the

person from whom it acquired the cultural object by inheritance or otherwise gratuitously.

CHAPTER III – RETURN OF ILLEGALLY EXPORTED CULTURAL OBJECTS

Article 5

(1) A Contracting State may request the court or other competent authority of another Contracting State to order the return of a cultural object illegally exported from the territory of the requesting State.
(2) A cultural object which has been temporarily exported from the territory of the requesting State, for purposes such as exhibition, research or restoration, under a permit issued according to its law regulating its export for the purpose of protecting its cultural heritage and not returned in accordance with the terms of that permit shall be deemed to have been illegally exported.
(3) The court or other competent authority of the State addressed shall order the return of an illegally exported cultural object if the requesting State establishes that the removal of the object from its territory significantly impairs one or more of the following interests:

(a) the physical Preservation of the object or of its context;
(b) the integrity of a complex object;
(c) the preservation of information of, for example, a scientific or historical character;
(d) the traditional or ritual use of the object by a tribal or indigenous community, or establishes that the object is of significant cultural importance for the requesting State.

(4) Any request made under paragraph 1 of this article shall contain or be accompanied by such information of a factual or legal nature as may assist the court or other competent authority of the State addressed in determining whether the requirements of paragraphs 1 to 3 have been met.
(5) Any request for return shall be brought within a period of three years from the time when the requesting State knew the location of the cultural object and the identity of its possessor, and in any case within a period of fifty years from the date of the export or from the date on which the object should have been returned under a permit referred to in paragraph 2 of this article.

Article 6

(1) The possessor of a cultural object who acquired the object after it was illegally exported shall be entitled, at the time of its return, to payment by

the requesting State of fair and reasonable compensation, provided that the possessor neither knew nor ought reasonably to have known at the time of acquisition that the object had been illegally exported.
(2) In determining whether the possessor knew or ought reasonably to have known that the cultural object had been illegally exported, regard shall be had to the circumstances of the acquisition, including the absence of an export certificate required under the law of the requesting State.
(3) Instead of compensation, and in agreement with the requesting State, the possessor required to return the cultural object to that State may decide:
(a) to retain ownership of the object; or
(b) to transfer ownership against payment or gratuitously to a person of its choice residing in the requesting State who provides the necessary guarantees.
(4) The cost of returning the cultural object in accordance with this article shall be borne by the requesting State, without prejudice to the right of that State to recover costs from any other person.
(5) The possessor shall not be in a more favourable position than the person from whom it acquired the cultural object by inheritance or otherwise gratuitously.

Article 7

(1) The provisions of this Chapter shall not apply where:
(a) the export of a cultural object is no longer illegal at the time at which the return is requested; or
(b) the object was exported during the lifetime of the person who created it or within a period of fifty years following the death of that person.
(2) Notwithstanding the provisions of sub-paragraph (b) of the preceding paragraph, the provisions of this Chapter shall apply where a cultural object was made by a member or members of a tribal or indigenous community for traditional or ritual use by that community and the object will be returned to that community.

CHAPTER IV – GENERAL PROVISIONS

Article 8

(1) A claim under Chapter II and a request under Chapter III may be brought before the courts or other competent authorities of the Contracting State where the cultural object is located, in addition to the courts or other competent authorities otherwise having jurisdiction under the rules in force in Contracting States.

(2) The parties may agree to submit the dispute to any court or other competent authority or to arbitration.
(3) Resort may be had to the provisional, including protective, measures available under the law of the Contracting State where the object is located even when the claim for restitution or request for return of the object is brought before the courts or other competent authorities of another Contracting State.

Article 9

(1) Nothing in this Convention shall prevent a Contracting State from applying any rules more favourable to the restitution or the return of stolen or illegally exported cultural objects than provided for by this Convention.
(2) This article shall not be interpreted as creating an obligation to recognise or enforce a decision of a court or other competent authority of another Contracting State that departs from the provisions of this Convention.

Article 10

(1) The provisions of Chapter II shall apply only in respect of a cultural object that is stolen after this Convention enters into force in respect of the State where the claim is brought, provided that:
(a) the object was stolen from the territory of a Contracting State after the entry into force of this Convention for that State; or
(b) the object is located in a Contracting State after the entry into force of the Convention for that State.
(2) The provisions of Chapter III shall apply only in respect of a cultural object that is illegally exported after this Convention enters into force for the requesting State as well as the State where the request is brought.
(3) This Convention does not in any way legitimise any illegal transaction of whatever nature which has taken place before the entry into force of this Convention or which is excluded under paragraphs (1) or (2) of this article, nor limit any right of a State or other person to make a claim under remedies available outside the framework of this Convention for the restitution or return of a cultural object stolen or illegally exported before the entry into force of this Convention.

CHAPTER V – FINAL PROVISIONS

Article 11

(1) This Convention is open for signature at the concluding meeting of the Diplomatic Conference for the adoption of the draft Unidroit Convention on the International Return of Stolen or Illegally Exported Cultural Objects and will remain open for signature by all States at Rome until June 1996.
(2) This Convention is subject to ratification, acceptance or approval by States which have signed it.
(3) This Convention is open for accession by all States which are not signatory States as from the date it is open for signature.
(4) Ratification, acceptance, approval or accession is subject to the deposit of a formal instrument to that effect with the depositary.

Article 12

(1) This Convention shall enter into force on the first day of the sixth month following the date of deposit of the fifth instrument of ratification, acceptance, approval or accession.
(2) For each State that ratifies, accepts, approves or accedes to this Convention after the deposit of the fifth instrument of ratification, acceptance, approval or accession, this Convention shall enter into force in respect of that State on the first day of the sixth month following the date of deposit of its instrument of ratification, acceptance, approval or accession.

Article 13

(1) This Convention does not affect any international instrument by which any Contracting State is legally bound and which contains provisions on matters governed by this Convention, unless a contrary declaration is made by the States bound by such instrument.
(2) Any Contracting State may enter into agreements with one or more Contracting States, with a view to improving the application of this Convention in their mutual relations. The States which have concluded such an agreement shall transmit a copy to the depositary.
(3) In their relations with each other, Contracting States which are Members of organisations of economic integration or regional bodies may declare that they will apply the internal rules of these organisations or bodies and will not therefore apply as between these States the provisions

of this Convention the scope of application of which coincides with that of those rules.

Article 14

(1) If a Contracting State has two or more territorial units, whether or not possessing different systems of law applicable in relation to the matters dealt with in this Convention, it may, at the time of signature or of the deposit of its instrument of ratification, acceptance, approval or accession, declare that this Convention is to extend to all its territorial units or only to one or more of them, and may substitute for its declaration another declaration at any time.
(2) These declarations are to be notified to the depositary and are to state expressly the territorial units to which the Convention extends.
(3) If, by virtue of a declaration under this article, this Convention extends to one or more but not all of the territorial units of a Contracting State the reference to:
(a) the territory of a Contracting State in Article 1 shall be construed as referring to the territory of a territorial unit of that State;
(b) a court or other competent authority of the Contracting State or of the State addressed shall be construed as referring to the court or other competent authority of a territorial unit of that State;
(c) the Contracting State where the cultural object is located in Article 8 (1) shall be construed as referring to the territorial unit of that State where the object is located;
(d) the law of the Contracting State where the object is located in Article 8 (3) shall be construed as referring to the law of the territorial unit of that State where the object is located; and
(e) a Contracting State in Article 9 shall be construed as referring to a territorial unit of that State.
(4) If a Contracting State makes no declaration under paragraph 1 of this article, this Convention is to extend to all territorial units of that State.

Article 15

(1) Declarations made under this Convention at the time of signature are subject to confirmation upon ratification, acceptance or approval.
(2) Declarations and confirmations of declarations are to be in writing and to be formally notified to the depositary.
(3) A declaration shall take effect simultaneously with the entry into force of this Convention in respect of the State concerned. However, a declaration of which the depositary receives formal notification after such entry

into force shall take effect on the first day of the sixth month following the date of its deposit with the depositary.
(4) Any State which makes a declaration under this Convention may withdraw it at any time by a formal notification in writing addressed to the depositary. Such withdrawal shall take effect on the first day of the sixth month following the date of the deposit of the notification.

Article 16

(1) Each Contracting State shall at the time of signature, ratification, acceptance, approval or accession, declare that claims for the restitution, or requests for the return, of cultural objects brought by a State under Article 8 may be submitted to it under one or more of the following procedures:
(a) directly to the courts or other competent authorities of the declaring State;
(b) through an authority or authorities designated by that State to receive such claims or requests and to forward them to the courts or other competent authorities of that State;
(c) through diplomatic or consular channels.
(2) Each Contracting State may also designate the courts or other authorities competent to order the restitution or return of cultural objects under the provisions of Chapters II and III.
(3) Declarations made under paragraphs 1 and 2 of this article may be modified at any time by a new declaration.
(4) The provisions of paragraphs 1 to 3 of this article do not affect bilateral or multilateral agreements on judicial assistance in respect of civil and commercial matters that may exisit between Contracting States.

Article 17

Each Contracting State shall, no later than six months following the date of deposit of its instrument of ratification, acceptance, approval or accession, provide the depositary with written information in one of the official languages of the Convention concerning the legislation regulating the export of its cultural objects. This information shall be updated from time to time as appropriate.

Article 18

No reservations are permitted except those expressly authorised in this Convention.

Article 19

(1) This Convention may be denounced by any State Party, at any time after the date on which it enters into force for that State, by the deposit of an instrument to that effect with the depositary.
(2) A denunciation shall take effect on the first day of the sixth month following the deposit of the instrument of denunciation with the depositary. Where a longer period for the denunciation to take effect is specified in the instrument of denunciation it shall take effect upon the expiration of such longer period after its deposit with the depositary.
(3) Notwithstanding such a denunciation, this Convention shall nevertheless apply to a claim for restitution or a request for return of a cultural object submitted prior to the date on which the denunciation takes effect.

Article 20

The President of the International Institute for the Unification of Private Law (Unidroit) may at regular intervals, or at any time at the request of five Contracting States, convene a special committee in order to review the practical operation of this Convention.

Article 21

(1) This Convention shall be deposited with the Government of the Italian Republic.
(2) The Government of the Italian Republic shall:
(a) inform all States which have signed or acceded to this Convention and the President of the International Institute for the Unification of Private Law (Unidroit) of:
(i) each new signature or deposit of an instrument of ratification, acceptance approval or accession, together with the date thereof;
(ii) each declaration made in accordance with this Convention;
(iii) the withdrawal of any declaration;
(iv) the date of entry into force of this Convention;
(v) the agreements referred to in Article 13;
(vi) the deposit of an instrument of denunciation of this Convention together with the date of its deposit and the date on which it takes effect;
(b) transmit certified true copies of this Convention to all signatory States, to all States acceding to the Convention and to the President of the International Institute for Unification of Private Law (Unidroit);
(c) perform such other functions customary for depositaries.

IN WITNESS WHEREOF the undersigned plenipotentiaries, being duly authorised, have signed this Convention.
DONE at Rome, this twenty-fourth day of June, one thousand nine hundred and ninety-five, in a single original, in the English and French languages, both texts being equally authentic.

ANNEX

(a) Rare collections and specimens of fauna, flora, minerals and anatomy, and objects of palaeontological interest;
(b) property relating to history, including the history of science and technology and military and social history, to the life of national leaders, thinkers, scientists and artists and to events of national importance;
(c) products of archaeological excavations (including regular and clandestine) or of archaeological discoveries;
(d) elements of artistic or historical monuments or archaeological sites which have been dismembered;
(e) antiquities more than one hundred years old, such as inscriptions, coins and engraved seals;
(f) objects of ethnological interest;
(g) property of artistic interest, such as:
- (i) pictures, paintings and drawings produced entirely by hand on any support and in any material (excluding industrial designs and manufactured articles decorated by hand);
- (ii) original works of statuary art and sculpture in any material;
- (iii) original engravings, prints and lithographs;
- (iv) original artistic assemblages and montages in any material;

(h) rare manuscripts and incunabula, old books, documents and publications of special interest (historical, artistic, scientific, literary, etc.) singly or in collections;
(i) postage, revenue and similar stamps, singly or in collections;
(j) archives, including sound, photographic and cinematographic archives;
(k) articles of furniture more than one hundred years old and old musical instruments.

APPENDIX 2

European Union law

CONSOLIDATED VERSION OF THE TREATY ON THE FUNCTIONING OF THE EUROPEAN UNION

CHAPTER 3
PROHIBITION OF QUANTITATIVE RESTRICTIONS BETWEEN MEMBER STATES

Article 34
(ex Article 28 TEC)

Quantitative restrictions on imports and all measures having equivalent effect shall be prohibited between Member States.

Article 35
(ex Article 29 TEC)

Quantitative restrictions on exports, and all measures having equivalent effect, shall be prohibited between Member States.

Article 36
(ex Article 30 TEC)

The provisions of Articles 34 and 35 shall not preclude prohibitions or restrictions on imports, exports or goods in transit justified on grounds of public morality, public policy or public security; the protection of health and life of humans, animals or plants; the protection of national treasures possessing artistic, historic or archaeological value; or the protection of industrial and commercial property. Such prohibitions or restrictions shall not, however, constitute a means of arbitrary discrimination or a disguised restriction on trade between Member States.

[....]

TITLE XIII
CULTURE

Article 167
(ex Article 151 TEC)

1. The Union shall contribute to the flowering of the cultures of the Member States, while respecting their national and regional diversity and at the same time bringing the common cultural heritage to the fore.

2. Action by the Union shall be aimed at encouraging cooperation between Member States and, if necessary, supporting and supplementing their action in the following areas:
— improvement of the knowledge and dissemination of the culture and history of the European peoples,
— conservation and safeguarding of cultural heritage of European significance,
— non-commercial cultural exchanges,
— artistic and literary creation, including in the audiovisual sector.
3. The Union and the Member States shall foster cooperation with third countries and the competent international organisations in the sphere of culture, in particular the Council of Europe.
4. The Union shall take cultural aspects into account in its action under other provisions of the Treaties, in particular in order to respect and to promote the diversity of its cultures.
5. In order to contribute to the achievement of the objectives referred to in this Article:
— the European Parliament and the Council acting in accordance with the ordinary legislative procedure and after consulting the Committee of the Regions, shall adopt incentive measures, excluding any harmonisation of the laws and regulations of the Member States,
— the Council, on a proposal from the Commission, shall adopt recommendations.

COUNCIL REGULATION (EC) No 116/2009
of 18 December 2008
on the export of cultural goods
(Codified version)
(OJ L 39/1, 10.2.2009)

THE COUNCIL OF THE EUROPEAN UNION,

Having regard to the Treaty establishing the European Community, and in particular Article 133 thereof,

Having regard to the proposal from the Commission,

Whereas:

(1) Council Regulation (EEC) No 3911/92 of 9 December 1992 on the export of cultural goods[1] has been substantially amended several times.[2] In the interests of clarity and rationality the said Regulation should be codified.

(2) In order to maintain the internal market, rules on trade with third countries are needed for the protection of cultural goods.

(3) It seems necessary to take measures in particular to ensure that exports of cultural goods are subject to uniform controls at the Community's external borders.

(4) Such a system should require the presentation of a licence issued by the competent Member State prior to the export of cultural goods covered by this Regulation. This necessitates a clear definition of the scope of such measures and the procedures for their implementation. The implementation of the system should be as simple and efficient as possible.

(5) The measures necessary for the implementation of this Regulation should be adopted in accordance with Council Decision 1999/468/EC of 28 June 1999 laying down the procedures for the exercise of implementing powers conferred on the Commission.[3]

(6) In view of the considerable experience of the Member States' authorities in the application of Council Regulation (EC) No 515/97 of 13 March 1997 on mutual assistance between the administrative authorities of the Member States and cooperation between the latter and the Commission to ensure the correct application of the law on customs and agricultural matters,[4] the said Regulation should be applied to this matter.

---

1 OJ L 395, 31.12.1992, p.1
2 See Annex II.
3 OJ L 184, 17.7.1999, p.23
4 OJ L 82, 22.3.1997, p.1

(7) Annex I to this Regulation is aimed at making clear the categories of cultural goods which should be given particular protection in trade with third countries, but is not intended to prejudice the definition, by Member States, of national treasures within the meaning of Article 30 of the Treaty,

HAS ADOPTED THIS REGULATION:

Article 1
Definition
Without prejudice to Member States' powers under Article 30 of the Treaty, the term 'cultural goods' shall refer, for the purposes of this Regulation, to the items listed in Annex I.

Article 2
Export licence
1. The export of cultural goods outside the customs territory of the Community shall be subject to the presentation of an export licence.
2. The export licence shall be issued at the request of the person concerned:
   (a) by a competent authority of the Member State in whose territory the cultural object in question was lawfully and definitively located on 1 January 1993;
   (b) or, thereafter, by a competent authority of the Member State in whose territory it is located following either lawful and definitive dispatch from another Member State, or importation from a third country, or re-importation from a third country after lawful dispatch from a Member State to that country. However, without prejudice to paragraph 4, the Member State which is competent in accordance with points (a) or (b) of the first subparagraph is authorised not to require export licences for the cultural goods specified in the first and second indents of category A.1 of Annex I where they are of limited archaeological or scientific interest, and provided that they are not the direct product of excavations, finds or archaeological sites within a Member State, and that their presence on the market is lawful. The export licence may be refused, for the purposes of this Regulation, where the cultural goods in question are covered by legislation protecting national treasures of artistic, historical or archaeological value in the Member State concerned. Where necessary, the authority referred to in point (b) of the first subparagraph shall enter into contact with the competent authorities of the Member State from which the cultural object in question came, and in particular the competent authorities within the meaning of Council Directive 93/7/EEC of 15 March 1993

on the return of cultural objects unlawfully removed from the territory of a Member State.[5]

3. The export licence shall be valid throughout the Community.

4. Without prejudice to the provisions of paragraphs 1, 2 and 3, direct export from the customs territory of the Community of national treasures having artistic, historic or archaeological value which are not cultural goods within the meaning of this Regulation is subject to the national law of the Member State of export.

Article 3
Competent authorities

1. Member States shall furnish the Commission with a list of the authorities empowered to issue export licences for cultural goods.

2. The Commission shall publish a list of the authorities and any amendment to that list in the 'C' series of the *Official Journal of the European Union.*

Article 4
Presentation of licence

The export licence shall be presented, in support of the export declaration, when the customs export formalities are carried out, at the customs office which is competent to accept that declaration.

Article 5
Limitation of competent customs offices

1. Member States may restrict the number of customs offices empowered to handle formalities for the export of cultural goods.

2. Member States availing themselves of the option afforded by paragraph 1 shall inform the Commission of the customs offices duly empowered. The Commission shall publish this information in the 'C' series of the *Official Journal of the European Union.*

Article 6
Administrative cooperation

For the purposes of implementing this Regulation, the provisions of Regulation (EC) No 515/97, and in particular the provisions on the confidentiality of information, shall apply *mutatis mutandis.* In addition to the cooperation provided for under the first paragraph, Member States shall take all necessary steps to establish, in the context of their mutual

---

[5] OJ L 74, 27.3.1993, p.74

relations, cooperation between the customs authorities and the competent authorities referred to in Article 4 of Directive 93/7/EEC.

Article 7
Implementing measures
The measures necessary for the implementation of this Regulation, in particular those concerning the form to be used (for example, the model and technical properties) shall be adopted in accordance with the procedure referred to in Article 8(2).

Article 8
Committee
1. The Commission shall be assisted by a committee.
2. Where reference is made to this paragraph, Articles 3 and 7 of Decision 1999/468/EC shall apply.

Article 9
Penalties
The Member States shall lay down the rules on penalties applicable to infringements of the provisions of this Regulation and shall take all measures necessary to ensure that they are implemented. The penalties provided for must be effective, proportionate and dissuasive.

Article 10
Reporting
1. Each Member State shall inform the Commission of the measures taken pursuant to this Regulation. The Commission shall pass on this information to the other Member States.
2. Every three years the Commission shall present a report to the European Parliament, the Council and the European Economic and Social Committee on the implementation of this Regulation. The Council, acting on a proposal from the Commission, shall examine every three years and, where appropriate, update the amounts indicated in Annex I, on the basis of economic and monetary indicators in the Community.

Article 11
Repeal
Regulation (EEC) No 3911/92, as amended by the Regulations listed in Annex II, is repealed. References to the repealed Regulation shall be construed as references to this Regulation and shall be read in accordance with the correlation table in Annex III.

Article 12
Entry into force

This Regulation shall enter into force on the 20th day following its publication in the *Official Journal of the European Union*.

This Regulation shall be binding in its entirety and directly applicable in all Member States.

Done at Brussels, 18 December 2008.

ANNEX I

Categories of cultural objects covered by Article 1

A. 1. Archaeological objects more than 100 years old which are the products of:

—excavations and finds on land or under water 9705 00 00
—archaeological sites 9706 00 00
—archaeological collections

2. Elements forming an integral part of artistic, historical or religious monuments which have been dismembered, of an age exceeding 100 years

9705 00 00
9706 00 00

3. Pictures and paintings, other than those included in categories 4 or 5, executed entirely by hand in any medium and on any material[1]

9701

4. Watercolours, gouaches and pastels executed entirely by hand on any material[1]

9701

5. Mosaics in any material executed entirely by hand, other than those falling in categories 1 or 2, and drawings in any medium executed entirely by hand on any material[1]

6914
9701

6. Original engravings, prints, serigraphs and lithographs with their respective plates and original posters[1]

Chapter 49
9702 00 00
8442 50 99

7. Original sculptures or statuary and copies produced by the same process as the original[1], other than those in category 1

9703 00 00

8. Photographs, films and negatives thereof[1] 3704
3705
3706
4911 91 80

9. Incunabula and manuscripts, including maps and musical scores, singly or in collections[1]
9702 00 00
9706 00 00
4901 10 00
4901 99 00
4904 00 00
4905 91 00
4905 99 00
4906 00 00

10. Books more than 100 years old, singly or in collections 9705 00 00
9706 00 00

11. Printed maps more than 200 years old 9706 00 00

12. Archives, and any elements thereof, of any kind or any medium which are more than 50 years old
3704
3705
3706
4901
4906
9705 00 00
9706 00 00

13. (a) Collections[2] and specimens from zoological, botanical, mineralogical or anatomical collections;
9705 00 00

(b) Collections[2] of historical, palaeontological, ethnographic or numismatic interest
9705 00 00

---

1 Which are more than 50 years old and do not belong to their originators.

2 As defined by the Court of Justice in its judgment in Case 252/84, as follows: 'Collectors' pieces within the meaning of heading No 97.05 of the Common Customs Tariff are articles which possess the requisite characteristics for inclusion in a collection, that is to say, articles which are relatively rare, are not normally used for their original purpose, are the subject of special transactions outside the normal trade in similar utility articles and are of high value'.

14. Means of transport more than 75 years old 9705 00 00
Chapters 86–89
15. Any other antique items not included in categories A.1 to A.14
(a) between 50 and 100 years old toys, games
Chapter 95
glassware 7013
articles of goldsmiths' or silversmiths' wares 7114
furniture
Chapter 94
optical, photographic or cinematographic apparatus
Chapter 90
musical instruments
Chapter 92
clocks and watches and parts thereof
Chapter 91
articles of wood
Chapter 44
pottery
Chapter 69
tapestries 5805 00 00
carpets
Chapter 57
wallpaper 4814
arms
Chapter 93
(b) more than 100 years old 9706 00 00
The cultural objects in categories A.1 to A.15 are covered by this Regulation only if their value corresponds to, or exceeds, the financial thresholds under B.
B. Financial thresholds applicable to certain categories under A (in euro)
Value:
Whatever the value
—1 (Archaeological objects)
—2 (Dismembered monuments)
—9 (Incunabula and manuscripts)
—12 (Archives)
15 000
—5 (Mosaics and drawings)
—6 (Engravings)
—8 (Photographs)
—11 (Printed maps)
30 000

—4 (Watercolours, gouaches and pastels)
50 000
—7 (Statuary)
—10 (Books)
—13 (Collections)
—14 (Means of transport)
—15 (Any other object)
150 000
—3 (Pictures)

The assessment of whether or not the conditions relating to financial value are fulfilled must be made when an application for an export licence is submitted. The financial value is that of the cultural object in the Member State referred to in Article 2(2).

For the Member States which do not have the euro as their currency, the values expressed in euro in Annex I shall be converted and expressed in national currencies at the rate of exchange on 31 December 2001 published in the *Official Journal of the European Communities*. This countervalue in national currencies shall be reviewed every two years with effect from 31 December 2001. Calculation of this countervalue shall be based on the average daily value of those currencies, expressed in euro, during the 24 months ending on the last day of August preceding the revision which takes effect on 31 December. This method of calculation shall be reviewed, on a proposal from the Commission, by the Advisory Committee on Cultural Goods, in principle two years after the first application. For each revision, the values expressed in euro and their countervalues in national currency shall be published periodically in the *Official Journal of the European Union* in the first days of the month of November preceding the date on which the revision takes effect.

ANNEX II

Repealed Regulation with its successive amendments

Council Regulation (EEC) No 3911/92
(OJ L 395, 31.12.1992, p.1)
Council Regulation (EC) No 2469/96
(OJ L 335, 24.12.1996, p.9)
Council Regulation (EC) No 974/2001
(OJ L 137, 19.5.2001, p.10)
Council Regulation (EC) No 806/2003
(OJ L 122, 16.5.2003, p.1)

Annex I, point 2 only
L 39/6 EN Official Journal of the European Union 10.2.2009

[Annex III containing the correlation table has been omitted]

COMMISSION REGULATION (EEC) No 752/93
of 30 March 1993
laying down provisions for the implementation of Council Regulation (EEC) No 3911/92 on the export of cultural goods[1]
(OJ L 77/24, 31.3.1993)

THE COMMISSION OF THE EUROPEAN COMMUNITIES,
Having regard to the Treaty establishing the European Economic Community,
Having regard to Council Regulation (EEC) No 3911/92 of 9 December 1992(1) on the export of cultural goods, and in particular Article 7 thereof,
After consulting the Advisory Committee on Cultural Goods,
Whereas it is necessary to adopt provisions for the implementation of Regulation (EEC) No 3911/92, which provides, inter alia, for the establishment of an export licensing system for certain categories of cultural goods defined in the Annex to that Regulation;
Whereas in order to ensure that the export licences provided for by the said Regulation are uniform it is necessary to lay down rules governing the drawing up, issuing and use of the form; whereas to that end a specimen licence should be drawn up;
Whereas export licences must be made out in one of the official languages of the Community,

HAS ADOPTED THIS REGULATION:

SECTION I
Form of licence
Article 1

1. There shall be three types of licences for the export of cultural goods which shall be issued and used in accordance with Council Regulation (EEC) No 3911/92, hereinafter called the 'Basic Regulation', and with this implementing Regulation:
—the standard licence,
—the specific open licence,
—the general open licence.
2. The use of export licences shall in no way affect obligations connected with export formalities or related documents.

---

[1] As ammended by Commission Regulation (EC) 1526/98 of 16 July 1998 and Commission Regulation (EC) 656/2004 (Corrigendum, OJ L 203/14, 8.6.2004 (656/2004)).

3. Export licence forms shall be provided on request by the competent authority or authorities referred to in Article 2 (2) of the basic Regulation.

Article 2

1. A standard licence shall normally be used for each export subject to the Basic Regulation. However each individual Member State concerned may decide whether or not it wishes to issue any specific or general open licences which may be used instead if the specific conditions relating to them are fulfilled as set out in Articles 10 and 13.
2. A specific open licence shall cover the repeated temporary export of a specific cultural good by a particular person or organisation as set out in Article 10.
3. A general open licence shall cover any temporary export of any of those cultural goods that form part of the permanent collection of a museum or other institution, as set out in Article 13.
4. A Member State may revoke any specific or general open licence at any time if the conditions under which it was issued are no longer met. It shall inform the Commission immediately if the licence issued is not recovered and could be used irregularly. The Commission shall immediately inform the other Member States.
5. Member States may introduce whatever reasonable measures they deem necessary in their national territory to monitor the use of their own open licences.

SECTION II

The standard licence

Article 3

1. Standard licences shall be issued on the form, a model of which is in Annex I. The form shall be printed on white paper without mechanical pulp, dressed for writing purposes and weighing not less than 55 grams per square metre.
2. Forms shall measure 210 × 297 mm.
3. Forms shall be produced in printed or electronic form and filled out in an official language of the Communities designated by the competent authorities of the issuing Member State. The competent authorities of the Member State in which the form is presented may ask for it to be translated into the language, or one of the official languages, of that Member State. In this case, the translation costs shall be met by the licence holder.
4. Member States shall be responsible:
   —for having the forms printed, bearing the printer's name and address or identifying mark,

—for taking any measure necessary in order to avoid the forging of forms. The means of identification adopted by Member States for this purpose shall be notified to the Commission, for communication to the competent authorities of the other Member States.

5. Forms shall preferably be filled in by mechanical or electronic means. However, the application may be filled in legibly by hand; in the latter case it shall be written in ink and in block capitals. Whatever the process used, forms shall not contain erasures, overwritten words or other alterations.

Article 4

1. Without prejudice to paragraph 3, a separate export licence shall be issued for each consignment of cultural goods.

2. For the purposes of paragraph 1 a consignment shall mean either a single cultural object or a number of cultural objects.

3. Where a consignment comprises of a number of cultural objects, it is for the competent authorities to determine whether one or several export licences should be issued for the consignment in question.

Article 5

The form shall comprise three sheets:

—one sheet, marked as No 1, which shall constitute the application,

—one sheet, marked as No 2, for the holder,

—one sheet, marked as No 3, which shall be returned to the issuing authority.

Article 6

1. The applicant shall complete boxes 1, 3, 6 to 21, 24 and, if necessary, 25 of the application and the other sheets except where pre-printing of the box or boxes is authorised. However, Member States may provide that only the application need be completed.

2. The application shall be accompanied by:

—documentation providing all relevant information on the cultural object(s) and its (their) legal status at the time when the application is made, by means of any supporting documents (invoices, expert appraisals etc.) where appropriate,

—a duly authenticated photograph or, where appropriate and at the discretion of the competent authorities, photographs in black and white or in colour (measuring at least 8 cm by 12 cm) of the cultural goods in question. This requirement may be replaced, where appropriate and at the discretion of the competent authorities, by a detailed list of the cultural goods.

3. The competent authorities may require, for the purposes of issuing an export licence, the physical presentation of the cultural goods to be exported.

4. Any costs incurred by the application of paragraphs 2 and 3 shall be met by the applicant requesting the export licence.
5. In order that an export licence may be granted, the duly completed form shall be presented to the competent authorities designated by the Member States pursuant to Article 2 (2) of the basic Regulation. When the authority has granted the export licence, copy 1 shall be kept by that authority and the remaining copies shall be returned to the holder of the export licence or to his authorized representative.

Article 7

The following shall be presented in support of the export declaration:
—the sheet for the holder,
—the sheet to be returned to the issuing authority.

Article 8

1. The customs office responsible for handling the export declaration shall ensure that the entries on the export declaration or, if applicable, the ATA carnet, correspond to the entries on the export licence and that a reference to the export licence is entered in box 44 of the export declaration or on the counterfoil of the ATA carnet.
It shall take suitable measures for identification purposes. The measures may consist in the affixation of a seal or stamp of the customs office. The export licence form, a copy of which is attached to sheet 3 of the single administrative document, shall be returned to the issuing authority.
2. After completing box 23 in copies 2 and 3, the customs office authorised to accept the export declaration shall return to the declarant or to his/her authorized representative the sheet intended for the holder.
3. The authorization form, which shall be returned to the issuing authority, must accompany the consignment to the customs office at the point of exit from the Community. The customs office shall affix its stamp to box 26 of the form and return it to the issuing authority.

Article 9

1. The period of validity of export licences shall not exceed twelve months from the date of issue.
2. In the case of an application for temporary exportation, the competent authorities may specify the time limit within which the cultural goods must be reimported into the issuing Member State.
3. Where an export licence expires without having been used, the holder shall immediately return to the issuing authority the sheets in his possession.

SECTION III
Open licences
CHAPTER 1
Specific open licences
Article 10

1. Specific open licences may be issued for a specific cultural good which is liable to be temporarily exported from the Community on a regular basis for use and/or exhibition in a third country. The cultural good must be owned by, or be in the legitimate possession of, the particular person or organisation that uses and or exhibits the good.
2. A licence may only be issued provided the authorities are convinced that the person or organisation concerned offers all the guarantees considered necessary for the good to be returned in good condition to the Community and that the good can be so described or marked that there will be no doubt at the moment of temporary export that the good being exported is that described in the specific open licence.
3. A licence may not be valid for a period that exceeds five years.

Article 11

The licence shall be presented in support of a written export declaration or be available in other cases for production with the cultural goods for examination upon request. The competent authorities of the Member State in which the licence is presented may ask for it to be translated into the language, or one of the official languages, of that Member State. In this case, the translation costs shall be met by the licence holder.

Article 12

1. The customs office authorised to accept the export declaration shall ensure that the goods presented are those described on the export licence and that a reference is made to that licence in box 44 of the export declaration if a written declaration is required.
2. If a written declaration is required then the licence must be attached to copy 3 of the single administrative document and accompany the good to the customs office at the point of exit from the customs territory of the Community. Where copy 3 of the single administrative document is made available to the exporter or his representative, the licence shall also be made available to him for use on a subsequent occasion.

CHAPTER 2
General open licences
Article 13

1. General open licences may be issued to museums or other institutions to cover the temporary export of any of the goods that belong to their permanent collection that are liable to be temporarily exported from the Community on a regular basis for exhibition in a third country.
2. A licence may only be issued if the authorities are convinced that the institution offers all the guarantees considered necessary for the good to be returned in good condition to the Community. The licence may be used to cover any combination of goods in the permanent collection at any one occasion of temporary export. It can be used to cover a series of different combinations of goods either consecutively or concurrently.
3. A licence may not be valid for a period that exceeds five years.

Article 14

The licence shall be presented in support of the export declaration. The competent authorities of the Member State in which the licence is presented may ask for it to be translated into the language, or one of the official languages, of that Member State. In this case, the translation costs shall be met by the licence holder.

Article 15

1. The customs office authorised to accept the export declaration shall ensure that the licence is presented together with a list of the goods being exported and which are also described in the export declaration. The list shall be on the headed paper of the institution and each page shall be signed by one of the persons from the institution and named on the licence. Each page shall also be stamped with the stamp of the institution as placed on the licence. A reference to the licence must be made in box 44 of the export declaration.
2. The licence shall be attached to copy 3 of the single administrative document and must accompany the consignment to the customs office at the point of exit from the customs territory of the Community. Where copy 3 of the single administrative document is made available to the exporter or his representative the licence shall also be made available to him for use on a subsequent occasion.

CHAPTER 3

Forms for the licences

Article 16

1. Specific open licences shall be issued on the form, a model of which is in Annex II.
2. General open licences shall be issued on the form a model of which is in Annex III.
3. The licence form shall be produced in printed or electronic form in one or more of the official languages of the Community.
4. The licence shall measure 210 × 297 mm. A tolerance of up to minus 5 mm or plus 8 mm in the length shall be allowed. The paper used shall be white, free of mechanical pulp, dressed for writing purposes and weigh at least 55 g/m^2. It shall have a printed guilloche pattern background in light blue such as to reveal any falsification by mechanical or chemical means.
5. The second sheet of the licence, which shall not have a guilloche pattern background, is for the exporter's own use or records only. The application form to be used shall be prescribed by the Member State concerned.
6. Member States may reserve the right to print the licence forms or may have them printed by approved printers. In the latter case, each must bear a reference to such approval. Each form must bear the name and address of the printer or a mark by which the printer can be identified. It shall also bear a serial number, either printed or stamped, by which it can be identified.
7. Member States shall be responsible for taking any measure necessary in order to avoid the forging of licences. The means of identification adopted by Member States for this purpose shall be notified to the Commission, for communication to the competent authorities of the other Member States.
8. Licences shall be made out by mechanical or electronic means. In exceptional circumstances they may be made out by black ball point pen in block capitals. They shall not contain erasures, overwritten words or other alterations.

SECTION IV

General provisions

Article 1

This Regulation shall enter into force on 1 April 1993.

This Regulation shall be binding in its entirety and directly applicable in all Member States.

Done at Brussels, 30 March 1993.

[Annex not included]

COUNCIL DIRECTIVE 93/7/EEC
of 15 March 1993
on the return of cultural objects unlawfully removed from the territory of a Member State
(OJ L 74/74, 27.3.1993)

THE COUNCIL OF THE EUROPEAN COMMUNITIES,
Having regard to the Treaty establishing the European Economic Community, and in particular Article 100a thereof,
Having regard to the proposal from the Commission[1], In cooperation with the European Parliament[2],
Having regard to the opinion of the Economic and Social Committee[3],
Whereas Article 8a of the Treaty provides for the establishment, not later than 1 January 1993, of the internal market, which is to comprise an area without internal frontiers in which the free movement of goods, persons, services and capital is ensured in accordance with the provisions of the Treaty;
Whereas, under the terms and within the limits of Article 36 of the Treaty, Member States will, after 1992, retain the right to define their national treasures and to take the necessary measures to protect them in this area without internal frontiers;
Whereas arrangements should therefore be introduced enabling Member States to secure the return to their territory of cultural objects which are classified as national treasures within the meaning of the said Article 36 and have been removed from their territory in breach of the abovementioned national measures or of Council Regulation (EEC) No 3911/92 of 9 December 1992 on the export of cultural goods[4];
Whereas the implementation of these arrangements should be as simple and efficient as possible; whereas, to facilitate cooperation with regard to return, the scope of the arrangements should be confined to items belonging to common categories of cultural object; whereas the Annex to this Directive is consequently not intended to define objects which rank as 'national treasures' within the meaning of the said Article 36, but merely categories of object which may be classified as such and may accordingly be covered by the return procedure introduced by this Directive;
Whereas cultural objects classified as national treasures and forming an integral part of public collections or inventories of ecclesiastical institu-

---

1 OJ No C 53, 28.2.1992, p. 11, and OJ No C 172, 8.7.1992, p. 7.
2 OJ No C 176, 13.7.1992, P. 128 and OJ No C 72, 15.3.1993.
3 OJ No C 223, 31.8.1992, p. 10.
4 OJ No L395, 31.12.1992, p. 1.

tions but which do not fall within these common categories should also be covered by this Directive;

Whereas administrative cooperation should be established between Member States as regards their national treasures, in close liaison with their cooperation in the field of stolen works of art and involving in particular the recording, with Interpol and other qualified bodies issuing similar lists, of lost, stolen or illegally removed cultural objects forming part of their national treasures and their public collections;

Whereas the procedure introduced by this Directive is a first step in establishing cooperation between Member States in this field in the context of the internal market; whereas the aim is mutual recognition of the relevant national laws; whereas provision should therefore be made, in particular, for the Commission to be assisted by an advisory committee;

Whereas Regulation (EEC) No 3911/92 introduces, together with this Directive, a Community system to protect Member States' cultural goods; whereas the date by which Member States have to comply with this Directive has to be as close as possible to the date of entry into force of that Regulation; whereas, having regard to the nature of their legal systems and the scope of the changes to their legislation necessary to implement this Directive, some Member States will need a longer period,

HAS ADOPTED THIS DIRECTIVE:

Article 1

For the purposes of this Directive:

1. 'Cultural object' shall mean an object which:

—is classified, before or after its unlawful removal from the territory of a Member State, among the 'national treasures possessing artistic, historic or archaeological value' under national legislation or administrative procedures within the meaning of Article 36 of the Treaty, and

—belongs to one of the categories listed in the Annex or does not belong to one of these categories but forms an integral part of:

—public collections listed in the inventories of museums, archives or libraries' conservation collection.

For the purposes of this Directive, 'public collections' shall mean collections which are the property of a Member State, local or regional authority within a Member States or an institution situated in the territory of a Member State and defined as public in accordance with the legislation of that Member State, such institution being the property of, or significantly financed by, that Member State or a local or regional authority;

—the inventories of ecclesiastical institutions.

2. 'Unlawfully removed from the territory of a Member State' shall mean:

—removed from the territory of a Member State in breach of its rules on the protection of national treasures or in breach of Regulation (EEC) No 3911/92, or

—not returned at the end of a period of lawful temporary removal or any breach of another condition governing such temporary removal.

3. 'Requesting Member State' shall mean the Member State from whose territory the cultural object has been unlawfully removed.

4. 'Requested Member State' shall mean the Member State in whose territory a cultural object unlawfully removed from the territory of another Member State is located.

5. 'Return' shall mean the physical return of the cultural object to the territory of the requesting Member State.

6. 'Possessor' shall mean the person physically holding the cultural object on his own account.

7. 'Holder' shall mean the person physically holding the cultural object for third parties.

Article 2

Cultural objects which have been unlawfully removed from the territory of a Member State shall be returned in accordance with the procedure and in the circumstances provided for in this Directive.

Article 3

Each Member State shall appoint one or more central authorities to carry out the tasks provided for in this Directive.

Member States shall inform the Commission of all the central authorities they appoint pursuant to this Article.

The Commission shall publish a list of these central authorities and any changes concerning them in the C series of the *Official Journal of the European Communities*.

Article 4

Member States' central authorities shall cooperate and promote consultation between the Member States' competent national authorities. The latter shall in particular:

1. upon application by the requesting Member State, seek a specified cultural object which has been unlawfully removed from its territory, identifying the possessor and/or holder. The application must include all information needed to facilitate this search, with particular reference to the actual or presumed location of the object;

2. notify the Member States concerned, where a cultural object is found in their own territory and there are reasonable grounds for believing that it has been unlawfully removed from the territory of another Member State;

3. enable the competent authorities of the requesting Member State to check that the object in question is a cultural object, provided that the check is made within 2 months of the notification provided for in paragraph 2. If it is not made within the stipulated period, paragraphs 4 and 5 shall cease to apply;
4. take any necessary measures, in cooperation with the Member State concerned, for the physical preservation of the cultural object;
5. prevent, by the necessary interim measures, any action to evade the return procedure;
6. act as intermediary between the possessor and/or holder and the requesting Member State with regard to return. To this end, the competent authorities of the requested Member State may, without prejudice to Article 5, first facilitate the implementation of an arbitration procedure, in accordance with the national legislation of the requested State and provided that the requesting State and the possessor or holder give their formal approval.

Article 5

The requesting Member State may initiate, before the competent court in the requested Member State, proceedings against the possessor or, failing him, the holder, with the aim of securing the return of a cultural object which has been unlawfully removed from its territory. Proceedings may be brought only where the document initiating them is accompanied by:

—a document describing the object covered by the request and stating that it is a cultural object,

—a declaration by the competent authorities of the requesting Member State that the cultural object has been unlawfully removed from its territory.

Article 6

The central authority of the requesting Member State shall forthwith inform the central authority of the requested Member State that proceedings have been initiated with the aim of securing the return of the object in question.
The central authority of the requested Member State shall forthwith inform the central authorities of the other Member States.

Article 7

1. Member States shall lay down in their legislation that the return proceedings provided for in this Directive may not be brought more than one year after the requesting Member State became aware of the location

of the cultural object and of the identity of its possessor or holder. Such proceedings may, at all events, not be brought more than 30 years after the object was unlawfully removed from the territory of the requesting Member State. However, in the case of objects forming part of public collections, referred to in Article 1 (1), and ecclesiastical goods in the Member States where they are subject to special protection arrangements under national law, return proceedings shall be subject to a time-limit of 75 years, except in Member States where proceedings are not subject to a time-limit or in the case of bilateral agreements between Member States laying down a period exceeding 75 years.
2. Return proceedings may not be brought if removal from the national territory of the requesting Member State is no longer unlawful at the time when they are to be initiated.

Article 8

Save as otherwise provided in Articles 7 and 13, the competent court shall order the return of the cultural object in question where it is found to be a cultural object within the meaning of Article 1 (1) and to have been removed unlawfully from national territory.

Article 9

Where return of the object is ordered, the competent court in the requested States shall award the possessor such compensation as it deems fair according to the circumstances of the case, provided that it is satisfied that the possessor exercised due care and attention in acquiring the object. The burden of proof shall be governed by the legislation of the requested Member State. In the case of a donation or succession, the possessor shall not be in a more favourable position than the person from whom he acquired the object by that means. The requesting Member State shall pay such compensation upon return of the object.

Article 10

Expenses incurred in implementing a decision ordering the return of a cultural object shall be borne by the requesting Member State. The same applies to the costs of the measures referred to in Article 4 (4).

Article 11

Payment of the fair compensation and of the expenses referred to in Articles 9 and 10 respectively shall be without prejudice to the requesting Member State's right to take action with a view to recovering those amounts from the persons responsible for the unlawful removal of the cultural object from its territory.

Article 12

Ownership of the cultural object after return shall be governed by that law of the requesting Member State.

Article 13

This Directive shall apply only to cultural objects unlawfully removed from the territory of a Member State on or after 1 January 1993.

Article 14

1. Each Member State may extend its obligation to return cultural objects to cover categories of objects other than those listed in the Annex.
2. Each Member State may apply the arrangements provided for by this Directive to requests for the return of cultural objects unlawfully removed from the territory of other Member States prior to 1 January 1993.

Article 15

This Directive shall be without prejudice to any civil or criminal proceedings that may be brought, under the national laws of the Member States, by the requesting Member State and/or the owner of a cultural object that has been stolen.

Article 16

1. Member States shall send the Commission every three years, and for the first time in February 1996, a report on the application of this Directive.
2. The Commission shall send the European Parliament, the Council and the Economic and Social Committee, every three years, a report reviewing the application of this Directive.
3. The Council shall review the effectiveness of this Directive after a period of application of three years and, acting on a proposal from the Commission, make any necessary adaptations.
4. In any event, the Council acting on a proposal from the Commission, shall examine every three years and, where appropriate, update the amounts indicated in the Annex, on the basis of economic and monetary indicators in the Community.

Article 17

The Commission shall be assisted by the Committee set up by Article 8 of Regulation (EEC) No 3911/92. The Committee shall examine any question arising from the application of the Annex to this Directive which may be tabled by the chairman either on his own initiative or at the request of the representative of a Member State.

Article 18

Member States shall bring into force the laws, regulations and administrative provisions necessary to comply with this Directive within nine months of its adoption, except as far as the Kingdom of Belgium, the Federal Republic of Germany and the Kingdom of the Netherlands are concerned, which must conform to this Directive at the latest twelve months from the date of its adoption. They shall forthwith inform the Commission thereof. When Member States adopt these measures, they shall contain a reference to this Directive or shall be accompanied by such reference on the occasion of their official publication. The methods of making such a reference shall be laid down by the Member States.

Article 19

This Directive is addressed to the Member States.

ANNEX

Categories referred to in the second indent of Article 1 (1) to which objects classified as 'national treasures' within the meaning of Article 36 of the Treaty must belong in order to qualify for return under this Directive

A. 1. Archaeological objects more than 100 years old which are the products of:

—land or underwater excavations and finds,
—archaeological sites,
—archaeological collections.

2. Elements forming an integral part of artistic, historical or religious monuments which have been dismembered, more than 100 years old.
3. Pictures and paintings, other than those included in Category 3A or 4, executed entirely by hand on any material and in any medium[1]
3A. Water-colours, gouaches and pastels executed entirely by hand on any material[1]
4. Mosaics in any material executed entirely by hand, other than those falling in Categories 1 or 2, and drawings in any medium executed entirely by hand on any material[1]
5. Original engravings, prints, serigraphs and lithographs with their respective plates and original posters[1].
6. Original sculptures or statuary and copies produced by the same process as the original (1) other than those in category 1.

---

[1] Which are more than fifty years old and do not belong to their orginators.

7. Photographs, films and negatives thereof[1].
8. Incunabula and manuscripts, including maps and musical scores, singly or in collections[1].
9. Books more than 100 years old, singly or in collections.
10. Printed maps more than 200 years old.
11. Archives and any elements thereof, of any kind, on any medium, comprising elements more than 50 years old.
12. (a) Collections[2] and specimens from zoological, botanical, mineralogical or anatomical collections;
(b) Collections[2] of historical, palaeontological, ethnographic or numismatic interest.
13. Means of transport more than 75 years old.
14. Any other antique item not included in categories A 1 to A 13, more than 50 years old.

The cultural objects in categories A 1 to A 14 are covered by this Directive only if their value corresponds to, or exceeds, the financial thresholds under B.

B. **Financial thresholds applicable to certain categories under A (in ecus)**

VALUE:

Whatever the value
—1 (Archaeological objects)
—2 (Dismembered monuments)
—8 (Incunabula and manuscripts)
—11 (Archives)

15 000
—4 (Mosaics and drawings)
—5 (Engravings)
—7 (Photographs)
—10 (Printed maps)

30 000
—3A. (Water colours, gouaches and pastels)

50 000
—6 (Statuary)
—9 (Books)
—12 (Collections)

---

[2] As defined by the Court of Justice in its Judgment in Case 252/84, as follows: 'Collectors' pieces within the meaning of Heading No 99.05 of the Common Customs Tariff are articles which possess the requisite characteristics for inclusion in a collection, that is to say, articles which are relatively rare, are not normally used for their original purpose, are the subject of special transactions outside the normal trade in similar utility articles and are of high value.'

—13 (Means of transport)
—14 (Any other item)
150 000
—3 (Pictures)
The assessment of whether or not the conditions relating to financial value are fulfilled must be made when return is requested. The financial value is that of the object in the requested Member State.

For the Member States which do not have the euro as their currency, the values expressed in euro in the Annex shall be converted and expressed in national currencies at the rate of exchange on 31 December 2001 published in the *Official Journal of the European Communities*. This countervalue in national currencies shall be reviewed every two years with effect from 31 December 2001. Calculation of this countervalue shall be based on the average daily value of those currencies, expressed in euro, during the 24 months ending on the last day of August preceding the revision which takes effect on 31 December. The Advisory Committee on Cultural Goods shall review this method of calculation, on a proposal from the Commission, in principle two years after the first application. For each revision, the values expressed in euro and their countervalues in national currency shall be published periodically in the *Official Journal of the European Communities* in the first days of the month of November preceding the date on which the revision takes effect.

APPENDIX 3

Codes of ethics

UNESCO International Code of Ethics for Dealers in Cultural Property (1999)

Members of the trade in cultural property recognize the key role that trade has traditionally played in the dissemination of culture and in the distribution to museums and private collectors of foreign cultural property for the education and inspiration of all peoples.

They acknowledge the world wide concern over the traffic in stolen, illegally alienated, clandestinely excavated and illegally exported cultural property and accept as binding the following principles of professional practice intended to distinguish cultural property being illicitly traded from that in licit trade and they will seek to eliminate the former from their professional activities.

ARTICLE 1 Professional traders in cultural property will not import, export or transfer the ownership of this property when they have reasonable cause to believe it has been stolen, illegally alienated, clandestinely excavated or illegally exported.

ARTICLE 2 A trader who is acting as agent for the seller is not deemed to guarantee title to the property, provided that he makes known to the buyer the full name and address of the seller. A trader who is himself the seller is deemed to guarantee to the buyer the title to the goods.

ARTICLE 3 A trader who has reasonable cause to believe that an object has been the product of a clandestine excavation, or has been acquired illegally or dishonestly from an official excavation site or monument will not assist in any further transaction with that object, except with the agreement of the country where the site or monument exists. A trader who is in possession of the object, where that country seeks its return within a reasonable period of time, will take all legally permissible steps to co-operate in the return of that object to the country of origin.

ARTICLE 4 A trader who has reasonable cause to believe that an item of cultural property has been illegally exported will not assist in any further transaction with that item, except with the agreement of the country of export. A trader who is in possession of the item, where the country of export seeks its return within a reasonable period of time, will take all legally permissible steps to co-operate in the return of that object to the country of export.

ARTICLE 5 Traders in cultural property will not exhibit, describe, attribute, appraise or retain any item of cultural property with the intention of promoting or failing to prevent its illicit transfer or export. Traders will not refer the seller or other person offering the item to those who may perform such services.

ARTICLE 6 Traders in cultural property will not dismember or sell separately parts of one complete item of cultural property.
ARTICLE 7 Traders in cultural property undertake to the best of their ability to keep together items of cultural heritage that were originally meant to be kept together.
ARTICLE 8 Violations of this Code of Ethics will be rigorously investigated by (a body to be nominated by participating dealers). A person aggrieved by the failure of a trader to adhere to the principles of this Code of Ethics may lay a complaint before that body, which shall investigate that complaint before that body, which shall investigate that complaint.

Results of the complaint and the principles applied will be made public.
Adopted by the UNESCO intergovernmental Committee for Promoting the Return of Cultural Property to its Countries of Origin or its Restitution in Case of Illicit Appropriation at its Tenth Session, January 1999 and endorsed by the 30th General Conference of UNESCO, November 1999.

International Council of Museums' (ICOM) Code of Professional Ethics (adopted in 1986, revised in 2004)

1. Museums preserve, interpret and promote the natural and cultural inheritance of humanity.

Principle: *Museums are responsible for the tangible and intangible natural and cultural heritage. Governing bodies and those concerned with the strategic direction and oversight of museums have a primary responsibility to protect and promote this heritage as well as the human, physical and financial resources made available for that purpose.*

[. . .]

2. Museums that maintain collections hold them in trust for the benefit of society and its development.

Principle: *Museums have the duty to acquire, preserve and promote their collections as a contribution to safeguarding the natural, cultural and scientific heritage. Their collections are a significant public inheritance, have a special position in law and are protected by international legislation. Inherent in this public trust is the notion of stewardship that includes rightful ownership, permanence, documentation, accessibility and responsible disposal.*

ACQUIRING COLLECTIONS

2.1 Collections Policy
The governing body for each museum should adopt and publish a written collections policy that addresses the acquisition, care and use of collections. The policy should clarify the position of any material that will not be catalogued, conserved, or exhibited (*See 2.7; 2.8*).

2.2 Valid Title
No object or specimen should be acquired by purchase, gift, loan, bequest, or exchange unless the acquiring museum is satisfied that a valid title is held. Evidence of lawful ownership in a country is not necessarily valid title.

2.3 Provenance and Due Diligence
Every effort must be made before acquisition to ensure that any object or specimen offered for purchase, gift, loan, bequest, or exchange has not been illegally obtained in or exported from, its country of origin or any intermediate country in which it might have been owned legally (including

the museum's own country). Due diligence in this regard should establish the full history of the item from discovery or production.

2.4 Objects and Specimens from Unauthorised or Unscientific Fieldwork
Museums should not acquire objects where there is reasonable cause to believe their recovery involved the unauthorised, unscientific, or intentional destruction or damage of monuments, archaeological or geological sites, or species and natural habitats. In the same way, acquisition should not occur if there has been a failure to disclose the finds to the owner or occupier of the land, or to the proper legal or governmental authorities.

2.5 Culturally Sensitive Material
Collections of human remains and material of sacred significance should be acquired only if they can be housed securely and cared for respectfully. This must be accomplished in a manner consistent with professional standards and the interests and beliefs of members of the community, ethnic or religious groups from which the objects originated, where these are known (*See also 3.7; 4.3*).

2.6 Protected Biological or Geological Specimens
Museums should not acquire biological or geological specimens that have been collected, sold, or otherwise transferred in contravention of local, national, regional or international law or treaty relating to wildlife protection or natural history conservation.

2.7 Living Collections
When the collections include live botanical and zoological specimens, special considerations should be made for the natural and social environment from which they are derived as well as any local, national, regional or international law, or treaty relating to wildlife protection or natural history conservation.

2.8 Working Collections
The collections policy may include special considerations for certain types of working collection where the emphasis is on preserving cultural, scientific or technical process rather than the object, or where objects or specimens are assembled for regular handling and teaching purposes (*See also 2.1*).

2.9 Acquisition Outside Collections Policy
The acquisition of objects or specimens outside the museum's stated policy should only be made in exceptional circumstances. The governing body

should consider the professional opinions available to them, and the views of all interested parties. Consideration will include the significance of the object or specimen including its context in the cultural or natural heritage, and the special interests of other museums collecting such material. However, even in these circumstances, objects without a valid title should not be acquired (*See also 3.4*).

2.10 Acquisition by Members of the Governing Body and Museum Personnel
Special care is required in considering any item, either for sale, as a donation or as a tax-benefit gift, from members of governing bodies, museum personnel, or the families and close associates of these persons.

2.11 Repositories of Last Resort
Nothing in this *Code of Ethics* should prevent a museum from acting as an authorised repository for unprovenanced, illicitly collected or recovered specimens and objects from the territory over which it has lawful responsibility.

REMOVING COLLECTIONS

2.12 Legal or Other Powers of Disposal
Where the museum has legal powers permitting disposals, or has acquired objects subject to conditions of disposal, the legal or other requirements and procedures must be complied with fully. Where the original acquisition was subject to mandatory or other restrictions these conditions must be observed, unless it can be shown clearly that adherence to such restrictions is impossible or substantially detrimental to the institution and, if appropriate, relief may be sought through legal procedures.

2.13 Deaccessioning from Museum Collections
The removal of an object or specimen from a museum collection must only be undertaken with a full understanding of the significance of the item, its character (whether renewable or non-renewable), legal standing, and any loss of public trust that might result from such action.

2.14 Responsibility for Deaccessioning
The decision to deaccession should be the responsibility of the governing body acting in conjunction with the director of the museum and the curator of the collection concerned. Special arrangements may apply to working collections (*See 2.7; 2.8*).

2.15 Disposal of Objects Removed from the Collections
Each museum should have a policy defining authorised methods for permanently removing an object from the collections through donation, transfer, exchange, sale, repatriation, or destruction, and that allows the transfer of unrestricted title to the receiving agency. Complete records must be kept of all deaccessioning decisions, the objects involved, and the disposition of the object. There will be a strong presumption that a deaccessioned item should first be offered to another museum.

2.16 Income from Disposal of Collections
Museum collections are held in public trust and may not be treated as a realisable asset. Money or compensation received from the deaccessioning and disposal of objects and specimens from a museum collection should be used solely for the benefit of the collection and usually for acquisitions to that same collection.

2.17 Purchase of Deaccessioned Collections
Museum personnel, the governing body, or their families or close associates, should not be permitted to purchase objects that have been deaccessioned from a collection for which they are responsible.

[. . .]

6. Museums work in close collaboration with the communities from which their collections originate as well as those they serve.

Principle: *Museum collections reflect the cultural and natural heritage of the communities from which they have been derived. As such they have a character beyond that of ordinary property which may include strong affinities with national, regional, local, ethnic, religious or political identity. It is important therefore that museum policy is responsive to this possibility.*

ORIGIN OF COLLECTIONS

6.1 Co-operation
Museums should promote the sharing of knowledge, documentation and collections with museums and cultural organisations in the countries and communities of origin. The possibility of developing partnerships with museums in countries or areas that have lost a significant part of their heritage should be explored.

6.2 Return of Cultural Property
Museums should be prepared to initiate dialogues for the return of cultural property to a country or people of origin. This should be undertaken in an impartial manner, based on scientific, professional and humanitarian principles as well as applicable local, national and international legislation, in preference to action at a governmental or political level.

6.3 Restitution of Cultural Property
When a country or people of origin seeks the restitution of an object or specimen that can be demonstrated to have been exported or otherwise transferred in violation of the principles of international and national conventions, and shown to be part of that country's or people's cultural or natural heritage, the museum concerned should, if legally free to do so, take prompt and responsible steps to co-operate in its return.

6.4 Cultural Objects From an Occupied Country
Museums should abstain from purchasing or acquiring cultural objects from an occupied territory and respect fully all laws and conventions that regulate the import, export and transfer of cultural or natural materials.

RESPECT FOR COMMUNITIES SERVED

6.5 Contemporary Communities
Where museum activities involve a contemporary community or its heritage, acquisitions should only be made based on informed and mutual consent without exploitation of the owner or informants. Respect for the wishes of the community involved should be paramount.

6.6 Funding of Community Facilities
When seeking funds for activities involving contemporary communities, their interests should not be compromised. (*See 1.10*).

6.7 Use of Collections from Contemporary Communities
Museum usage of collections from contemporary communities requires respect for human dignity and the traditions and cultures that use such material. Such collections should be used to promote human well-being, social development, tolerance, and respect by advocating multisocial, multicultural and multilingual expression. (*See 4.3*).

6.8 Supporting Organisations in the Community
Museums should create a favourable environment for community support (e.g., Friends of Museums and other supporting organisations), recognise

their contribution and promote a harmonious relationship between the community and museum personnel.

7. Museums operate in a legal manner

Principle: *Museums must conform fully to international, regional, national, or local legislation and treaty obligations. In addition, the governing body should comply with any legally binding trusts or conditions relating to any aspect of the museum, its collections and operations.*

LEGAL FRAMEWORK

7.1 National and Local Legislation
Museums should conform to all national and local laws and respect the legislation of other states as they affect their operation.

7.2 International Legislation
Museum policy should acknowledge the following international legislation which is taken as a standard in interpreting the *ICOM Code of Ethics*:

- *UNESCO Convention for the Protection of Cultural Property in the Event of Armed Conflict* (The Hague Convention, First Protocol, 1954 and Second Protocol, 1999);
- *UNESCO Convention on the Means of Prohibiting and Preventing the Illicit Import, Export and Transfer of Ownership of Cultural Property* (1970);
- *Convention on International Trade in Endangered Species of Wild Fauna and Flora* (1973);
- UN Convention on Biological Diversity (1992);
- *Unidroit Convention on Stolen and Illegally Exported Cultural Objects* (1995);
- *UNESCO Convention on the protection of the Underwater Cultural Heritage* (2001);
- *UNESCO Convention for the Safeguarding of the Intangible Cultural Heritage* (2003).

8. Museums operate in a professional manner

Principle: *Members of the museum profession should observe accepted standards and laws and uphold the dignity and honour of their profession. They should safeguard the public against illegal or unethical professional conduct. Every opportunity should be used to inform and educate the public about the* *aims, purposes, and aspirations of the profession to develop a better public understanding of the contributions of museums to society.*

PROFESSIONAL CONDUCT

8.1 Familiarity with Relevant Legislation
Every member of the museum profession should be conversant with relevant international, national and local legislation and the conditions of their employment. They should avoid situations that could be construed as improper conduct.

8.2 Professional Responsibility
Members of the museum profession have an obligation to follow the policies and procedures of their employing institution. However, they may properly object to practices that are perceived to be damaging to a museum or the profession and matters of professional ethics.

8.3 Professional Conduct
Loyalty to colleagues and to the employing museum is an important professional responsibility and must be based on allegiance to fundamental ethical principles applicable to the profession as a whole. They should comply with the terms of the *ICOM Code of Ethics* and be aware of any other codes or policies relevant to museum work.

8.4 Academic and Scientific Responsibilities
Members of the museum profession should promote the investigation, preservation, and use of information inherent in the collections. They should, therefore, refrain from any activity or circumstance that might result in the loss of such academic and scientific data.

8.5 The Illicit Market
Members of the museum profession should not support the illicit traffic or market in natural and cultural property, directly or indirectly.

8.6 Confidentiality
Members of the museum profession must protect confidential information obtained during their work. In addition, information about items brought to the museum for identification is confidential and should not be published or passed to any other institution or person without specific authorisation from the owner.

8.7 Museum and Collection Security
Information about the security of the museum or of private collections and locations visited during official duties must be held in strict confidence by museum personnel.

8.8 Exception to the Obligation for Confidentiality
Confidentiality is subject to a legal obligation to assist the police or other proper authorities in investigating possible stolen, illicitly acquired, or illegally transferred property.

8.9 Personal Independence
While members of a profession are entitled to a measure of personal independence, they must realise that no private business or professional interest can be wholly separated from their employing institution.

8.10 Professional Relationships
Members of the museums profession form working relationships with numerous other persons within and outside the museum in which they are employed. They are expected to render their professional services to others efficiently and to a high standard.

8.11 Professional Consultation
It is a professional responsibility to consult other colleagues within or outside the museum when the expertise available is insufficient in the museum to ensure good decision-making.

CONFLICTS OF INTEREST

8.12 Gifts, Favours, Loans, or Other Personal Benefits
Museum employees must not accept gifts, favours, loans, or other personal benefits that may be offered to them in connection with their duties for the museum. Occasionally professional courtesy may include the giving and receiving of gifts but this should always take place in the name of the institution concerned.

8.13 Outside Employment or Business Interests
Members of the museum profession, although entitled to a measure of personal independence, must realise that no private business or professional interest can be wholly separated from their employing institution. They should not undertake other paid employment or accept outside commissions that are in conflict with, or may be viewed as being in conflict with the interests of the museum.

8.14 Dealing in Natural or Cultural Heritage
Members of the museum profession should not participate directly or indirectly in dealing (buying or selling for profit), in the natural or cultural heritage.

8.15 Interaction with Dealers
Museum professionals should not accept any gift, hospitality, or any form of reward from a dealer, auctioneer, or other person as an inducement to purchase or dispose of museum items, or to take or refrain from taking official action. Furthermore, a museum professional should not recommend a particular dealer, auctioneer, or appraiser to a member of the public.

8.16 Private Collecting
Members of the museum profession should not compete with their institution either in the acquisition of objects or in any personal collecting activity. An agreement between the museum professional and the governing body concerning any private collecting must be formulated and scrupulously followed.

8.17 Use of the Name and Logo of ICOM
The name of the organisation, its acronym or its logo may not be used to promote or endorse any for-profit operation or product.

8.18 Other Conflicts of Interest
Should any other conflict of interest develop between an individual and the museum, the interests of the museum should prevail.

APPENDIX 4

The 2002 Declaration on the Importance and Value of Universal Museums

The international museum community shares the conviction that illegal traffic in archaeological, artistic, and ethnic objects must be firmly discouraged. We should, however, recognize that objects acquired in earlier times must be viewed in the light of different sensitivities and values, reflective of that earlier era. The objects and monumental works that were installed decades and even centuries ago in museums throughout Europe and America were acquired under conditions that are not comparable with current ones. Over time, objects so acquired – whether by purchase, gift, or partage – have become part of the museums that have cared for them, and by extension part of the heritage of the nations which house them. Today we are especially sensitive to the subject of a work's original context, but we should not lose sight of the fact that museums too provide a valid and valuable context for objects that were long ago displaced from their original source. The universal admiration for ancient civilizations would not be so deeply established today were it not for the influence exercised by the artifacts of these cultures, widely available to an international public in major museums. Indeed, the sculpture of classical Greece, to take but one example, is an excellent illustration of this point and of the importance of public collecting. The centuries-long history of appreciation of Greek art began in antiquity, was renewed in Renaissance Italy, and subsequently spread through the rest of Europe and to the Americas. Its accession into the collections of public museums throughout the world marked the significance of Greek sculpture for mankind as a whole and its enduring value for the contemporary world. Moreover, the distinctly Greek aesthetic of these works appears all the more strongly as the result of their being seen and studied in direct proximity to products of other great civilizations. Calls to repatriate objects that have belonged to museum collections for many years have become an important issue for museums. Although each case has to be judged individually, we should acknowledge that museums serve not just the citizens of one nation but the people of every nation. Museums are agents in the development of culture, whose mission is to foster knowledge by a continuous process of reinterpretation. Each object contributes to that process. To narrow the focus of museums whose collections are diverse and multifaceted would therefore be a disservice to all visitors.

Signed by the Directors of:
The Art Institute of Chicago; Bavarian State Museum, Munich (Alte Pinakothek, Neue Pinakothek); State Museums, Berlin; Cleveland Museum of Art; J. Paul Getty Museum, Los Angeles; Solomon R.

Guggenheim Museum, New York; Los Angeles County Museum of Art; Louvre Museum, Paris; The Metropolitan Museum of Art, New York; The Museum of Fine Arts, Boston; The Museum of Modern Art, New York; Opificio delle Pietre Dure, Florence; Philadelphia Museum of Art; Prado Museum, Madrid; Rijksmuseum, Amsterdam; State Hermitage Museum, St. Petersburg; Thyssen-Bornemisza Museum, Madrid; Whitney Museum of American Art, New York; The British Museum, London

RULES OF PROCEDURE FOR MEDIATION AND CONCILIATION IN ACCORDANCE WITH ARTICLE 4, PARAGRAPH 1, OF THE STATUTES OF THE INTERGOVERNMENTAL COMMITTEE FOR PROMOTING THE RETURN OF CULTURAL PROPERTY TO ITS COUNTRIES OF ORIGIN OR ITS RESTITUTION IN CASE OF ILLICIT APPROPRIATION

Article 1. Scope of the Rules of Procedures for Mediation and Conciliation

1. In accordance with Article 4.1 of the Statutes of the Intergovernmental Committee for Promoting the Return of Cultural Property to its Countries of Origin or its Restitution in case of Illicit Appropriation (hereinafter the 'Statutes'), any request for the return or restitution of cultural property, as defined under Article 3 of the Statutes, which are submitted to the Intergovernmental Committee (hereinafter 'the Committee'), may also be dealt with under a mediation or a conciliation procedure if the parties to the dispute (hereinafter 'the parties') so agree.
2. The rules contained herein apply both to the mediation and conciliation procedures before the Committee unless the Parties agree to amend them before the procedure.

Article 2. Nature of the Procedures and Roles of the Mediator and of the Conciliator

1. For purposes of these Rules, 'Mediation' means a process whereby, with the prior consent of the parties concerned, an outside party intervenes to bring them together and to assist them in reaching an amicable solution of their dispute with respect to the restitution or return of cultural property.
2. A mediation procedure shall require the involvement of one or more individuals who shall act as mediators, chosen by the Parties preferably among independent experts on the return and restitution of cultural property.
3. For purposes of these Rules, 'Conciliation' means a process whereby, subject to their prior consent, the parties concerned submit their dispute with respect to restitution or return of cultural property to a constituted organ for investigation and for efforts to effect an amicable settlement of their dispute.
4. A conciliation commission shall be composed of conciliators who are preferably independent experts on restitution and return of cultural properties whose number shall be mutually agreed upon by the parties concerned.
5. Each party to the dispute shall appoint one or two conciliators. An additional conciliator, which shall be of a nationality different from that of the parties involved, shall be chosen jointly by the parties and will be

the President of the conciliation commission. If the parties cannot agree on that person within 60 days the procedure provided under Article 7.2 below will be followed.

6. A list of potential mediators and conciliators shall be drawn up and maintained by the Secretariat for the information of, and possible use by, the Parties in appointing mediators or conciliators. To that end, each Member State of UNESCO shall be invited to nominate two individuals who could fulfil the role of mediator or conciliator in international cultural property disputes. The list shall be reviewed at two-year intervals when Member States may confirm existing nominations or submit new nominations. The Parties to a mediation or conciliation procedure shall remain free to appoint mediators or conciliators not included in this list.

Article 3. Basic Principles

1. Mediation and conciliation procedures require the consent in writing of the Parties before they may be initiated.
2. Mediation and conciliation procedures shall be conducted in conditions of confidentiality and in accordance with the general principles of fairness, impartiality and good faith.
3. The Parties shall participate in a responsible manner and cooperate in order to proceed as expeditiously as possible.
4. The Parties, the Mediator(s) or the Conciliator(s) shall participate with a view to facilitate an amicable and just solution or settlement of the dispute having due regard to international law and recognized principles.

Article 4. Parties

1. Only UNESCO Member States and Associate Members of UNESCO may have recourse to a mediation or conciliation procedure pursuant to these rules of procedure.
2. States may represent the interests of public or private institutions located in their territory or the interests of their nationals.
3. A request to initiate a mediation or conciliation procedure may be submitted by a member state or associate member of UNESCO with regard to a public or private institution, if the latter are in possession of the cultural property concerned, and if the state mentioned in paragraph 2 has been immediately informed of the request by the initiating member state or associated member of UNESCO and does not object.
4. A representative of each Party shall be present at mediation meetings. Subject to Article 10, paragraph 4, each Party's representative shall have the requisite authority to prepare, with the assistance of the Mediator(s), the terms and conditions of a settlement.

Article 5. Rules of conduct for Mediator(s) and Conciliators
The Mediator(s) and Conciliators shall:
(a) act according to the principles listed in Article 3 paragraph 2.
(b) not act as a representative or counsel of either Party in any proceedings concerning the dispute at issue.

Article 6. Commencement of a Mediation or Conciliation Procedure
1. A mediation or conciliation procedure may be commenced only upon mutual consent of the parties concerned to resort to such procedure. Upon such mutual consent, either party shall submit in writing a request to initiate a mediation or conciliation procedure to the Director-General who shall acknowledge receipt and inform the Chairman of the Committee.
2. The Committee, pursuant to article 4.1 of its Statutes, may also recommend to parties which have a case pending before it to make use of mediation or conciliation procedure.
3. The request shall contain the names and contact information of the parties, including the State mentioned in art. 4 paragraph 2, if any, an indication of the subject of the dispute and the relevant supporting documents.
4. If a mediation or conciliation procedure is initiated, it shall not prejudice the application and the effects of any other procedure or other means of dispute settlement that the parties have undertaken or wish to undertake concurrently or at a later stage.
5. No procedure of mediation or conciliation may prevent or delay any legal proceedings in pursuance of applicable national legislation.

Article 7. Appointment and Replacement of the Mediator(s) or Conciliators
1. The Parties shall appoint (a) Mediator(s) or Conciliators within 60 days of the written request to initiate a procedure of mediation or conciliation and shall inform the Chairman of the Committee accordingly.
2. Failing such appointment, the Director-General of UNESCO shall, after consultation with the Parties concerned, appoint (a) Mediator(s) or Conciliator(s). Such an appointment shall be made as soon as possible.
3. Mediator(s) or Conciliators shall be selected taking into consideration their expertise in the field of restitution and/or their knowledge with regard to the nature of the dispute or the specificity of the cultural property at stake.
4. Any Party, after consultation with the other party, may, in case of breach of any of the obligations set forth under Article 3 (2), request at any stage of the procedure the replacement of the Mediator(s) or Conciliators. The grounds for the requested replacement must be set out clearly. In such a case, the new Mediator(s) or Conciliators must be appointed according to the same procedure originally used.

5. Any vacancies which may occur during a procedure as a result of death, resignation or any other cause shall be filled as soon as possible according to the procedure originally used for appointing these individuals.

Article 8. Conduct of the mediation or conciliation

1. The Parties shall submit to the Mediator(s) or Conciliators the issue which is the subject of the dispute, their position thereon and all relevant documentation. All documentation will be transmitted to the other Party.
2. In consultation with the Parties, the Mediator(s) or Conciliators shall then set the times, places and dates of their meetings and specify in which language(s) documentation and evidence shall be submitted.
3. The Mediator(s) or Conciliators may conduct their own inquiries and research to determine the facts of the dispute.
4. Following the request of a Party, the Mediator(s) or Conciliators may allow witnesses, experts or third parties to provide documentation or evidence.
5. Each Party shall have the right to submit new arguments and documents in writing before the procedure is concluded.
6. Consultations are confidential, no recording shall be made, and information or documents obtained during the procedure shall not be disclosed, unless the Parties agree otherwise.
7. While complying fully with the principles listed in Article 3, paragraph 2, the Mediator(s) or Conciliators may meet and communicate separately with each Party. The information given in this way shall not be disclosed without the express authorization of the Party providing the information.
8. Within a conciliation procedure, unless the parties to the dispute otherwise agree, the Conciliators may decide whether to adopt specific rules of procedure, including with respect to the submission of written pleadings by the Parties.
9. The Mediator(s) or Conciliators shall endeavour to bring the Parties to reach an amicable settlement of the dispute within one year from the date of his/her appointment unless otherwise agreed by the Parties. At the end of the procedure, the Conciliators submit to the Parties a report which includes their recommendations.
10. The Parties may set a time limit for the conclusion of the procedure, beyond which, if no settlement has been reached, the procedure shall be deemed to have been concluded. The Parties may extend the time limit.

Article 9. Information

The Parties shall jointly inform the Committee on the state of progress of the procedure at its following session and its subsequent sessions.

Article 10. Conclusion of the Procedure(s)

1. A mediation or conciliation procedure shall be deemed to have been concluded in one of the following cases:

(a) when all Parties deem that an amicable settlement to that dispute has been reached;

(b) when all of the Parties concerned consent in writing to deem the procedure concluded;

(c) when all Parties to the dispute have set a time limit, and the time limit has expired without a settlement having been reached;

(d) when one of the Parties has notified in writing its withdrawal from the procedure.

2. The Parties shall promptly inform the Chairman of the Committee, who shall inform the Director-General of UNESCO and the Members of the Committee at the next session, of the result of the mediation or conciliation procedure. Any communication of a settlement reached should be done in a coordinated manner.

3. When a procedure has been concluded without a settlement, the issue which is the subject of the dispute shall remain before the Committee as any other unsolved question which has been submitted to it.

4. The outcome of the procedure shall be binding on the Parties only when they reach a binding agreement on it.

Article 11. Costs

1. The Parties shall bear in equal share the costs of the mediation or conciliation procedure unless another arrangement has been agreed. In the event of a withdrawal by a Party, this will not have an affect on the obligation of the Party in question to pay the expenses incurred up to the date of notification of withdrawal.

2. Expenses incurred for witnesses, experts, or legal assistance when requested by only one Party, shall be borne by that Party, unless another arrangement has been agreed.

Bibliography

Abd El Wahed, Maher (2003), 'The 1995 UNIDROIT Convention on Stolen or Illegally Exported Cultural Objects: A View from Egypt', *Worldwide Harmonisation of Private Law and Regional Economic Integration*, 529.

Abramson, Ronald D. and Stephen B. Huttler (1973), 'The Legal Response to the Illicit Movement of Cultural Property', *Law and Policy in International Business*, 932.

Abungu, G. (2009), 'The Declaration: A Contested Issue', in L.V. Prott (ed.), *Witnesses to History*, Paris: UNESCO, p.121.

ACCP Editorial Board (2005), 'Conclusion: Museums at the Center of Public Policy', in K. Fitz Gibbon (ed.), *Who Owns the Past? Cultural Policy, Cultural Property and the Law*, New Brunswick, New Jersey and London: Rutgers University Press in association with American Council for Cultural Policy, p.319.

Adams, John (1998), 'Insurance of Works of Art: Principles, Practice and Problems', in Norman Palmer (ed.), *The Recovery of Stolen Art: A Collection of Essays,* London: Kluwer Law International, p.163.

Adams, R. (ed.) (2001), *Implementing the Native American Graves Protection and Repatriation Act*, Washington: American Association of Museums Technical Information Service.

Akinsha, Konstantin and Grigorii Koslov (1995), *Stolen Treasure: The Hunt for the World's Lost Masterpieces*, London: Weidenfeld & Nicholson.

Akinsha, Konstantin, et al. (1995), *Beautiful Loot: The Soviet Plunder of Europe's Art Treasures*, New York: Random House.

Alder, Christine (2001), *The Illicit Traffic in Asian Antiquities,* paper presented at the Australian Registrars Committee Conference, Melbourne, 9 October 2001, 14, www.savingantiquities.org/pdf/Asian.pdf.

Alder, Christine and Kenneth Polk (2002), 'Stopping this Awful Business: The Illicit Traffic in Antiquities Examined as a Criminal Market', *Art Antiquity and Law*, **7**(1).

Alderman, Kimberly (2007–2008), 'The Ethical Trade in Cultural Property: Ethics and Law in the Antiquity Auction Industry', *ILSA (International Law Students Association) Journal on International & Comparative Law*, 549.

Alford, Kenneth D. (1994), *The Spoils of World War II: The American*

Military's Role in the Stealing of Europe's Treasures, New York: Birch Lane Press.
Allegro, John (1960), *The Dead Sea Scrolls*, London: Penguin Books.
Allegro, John (1990), *The Dead Sea Scrolls: A Reappraisal*, London: Penguin Books.
Amadou-Mahtar M'Bow (1979), 'A Plea for the Return of Irreplaceable Cultural Heritage to Those Who Created It', *Museum*, 31.
Amat, Frédéric (2001), 'Les musées traînent les pieds: le retour des biens culturels dans leur pays d'origine est une cause qui progresse à très petits pas', *Sources UNESCO*, Paris (133) 21.
Ames, M.M. (1987), 'Free Indians from their Ethnological Fate', *Muse*, **5**(2), 14.
Andrews, Carol (1982), *The Rosetta Stone*, London: British Museum Publications.
Anton, Ferdinand, Frederick J. Dockstander, Margaret Trowell and Hans Neuermann (1979), *Primitive Art: Pre-Columbian, North American, Indian, African/Oceanic*, New York: Abrams.
Antoniou, Th. (2004), 'The Evolution of National Cultural Identity in the Light of the Greek Constitution and Community Law', in E. Trova (ed.), *Cultural Heritage and the Law*, Athens-Thessaloniki: Ed. Sakkoulas, 561.
Appiah, A.K. (2006), *Cosmopolitanism: Ethics in a World of Strangers*, New York: W.W. Norton.
Appiah, A.K. (2009), 'Cosmopolitanism: Ethics in a World of Strangers', in L.V. Prott (ed.), *Witnesses to History*, Paris: UNESCO, p.95.
Ardouni, C.D. (1995), 'Vers un trafic licite des biens culturels', *International Journal of Cultural Property*, 4.
Armbrüster, C. (2004), 'La revendication de biens culturels du point de vue du droit international privé', *Revue critique de droit international privé*, p.723.
Aruz, Joan (2009), 'The Impact and Significance of the Statue of Ur-Ningirsen', *Museum International*, **61**(1–2).
Askerud, P. and E. Clément (1997), *Preventing the Illicit Traffic in Cultural Property: A Resource Handbook for the Implementation of the 1970 UNESCO Convention*, Paris: UNESCO.
Association francophone des musées de Belgique (ed.) (2003), 'Les musées et le trafic illicite des oeuvres d'art', *La Vie des musées*, Brussels, AFMB/ICOM Wallonie-Bruxelles, 17.
Association Henri Capitant (ed.) (1991), *La protection des biens culturels*, Paris: Economica.
Association of Art Museum Directors (1971), *Professional Practices in Art Museums*, New York: Association of Art Museum Directors, 2001.

Atwood, Roger (2004), *Stealing History: Tomb Raiders, Smugglers and the Looting of the Ancient World*, New York, NY: St Martin's Press, p.352.

Augustinos, Nicholas (1998), 'The Protection of Cultural Heritage in the Event of Armed Conflict', in Norman Palmer (ed.), *The Recovery of Stolen Art: A Collection of Essays,* London: Kluwer Law International, p.217.

Azoy, Mary Livingston (ed.) (1985), *Peruvian Antiquities: A Manual for United States Customs*, Washington, DC: Organizations of American States, Department of Cultural Affairs.

Bacon, Edward (ed.) (1976), *The Great Archaeologists*, London: Secker and Warburg.

Bacon, Reginald Hugh Spenser (1897), *Benin: The City of Blood*, London, New York: Edward Arnold.

Bai, Liu (1983), *Cultural Policy in the People's Republic of China: Letting a Hundred Flowers Bloom*, Paris: UNESCO.

Baigent, Michael and Richard Leigh (1991), *The Dead Sea Scrolls Deception*, London: Corgi Books.

Baker H.D., R.J. Matthews and J.N. Postgate (1993), *Lost Heritage: Antiquities Stolen from Iraq's Regional Museums*, Fascicle 2, London: British School of Archaeology in Iraq, p.153.

Ballestrazzi, Mireille (1993), 'La Lutte contre le trafic des œuvres d'art', *Museum International*, Paris: UNESCO, **45**(3).

Banks, George (1980), *Moche Pottery from Peru*, London: British Museum Publications.

Baqué, Philippe (1993), 'Le pillage ôte le masque', *Faim Développement Magazine*, Paris: CCFD, (100), December.

Baqué, Philippe (1999), *Un nouvel or noir: Pillage des œuvres d'art en Afrique*, Paris: Éd. Paris Méditerranée, p.192.

Baqué, Philippe (2005), 'Un trafic particulièrement lucratif: enquête sur le pillage des objets d'art', *Le Monde diplomatique*, Paris, January.

Baquedana, Elizabeth (1984), *Aztec Sculpture*, London: British Museum Publications.

Barkan, E. (2001), *The Guilt of Nations: Restitution and Negotiating Historical Injustices*, Baltimore: The Johns Hopkins University Press.

Barkan, E. (2009), 'The Guilt of Nations: Restitution and Negotiating Historical Injustices', in L.V. Prott (ed.), *Witnesses to History*, Paris: UNESCO, p.78.

Barker, L. (2000–3), 'Indeterminacy in International Legal Discourse', *Auckland University Law Review*, 9.

Barker, I. (2006), 'The Protection of Cultural Heritage Items in New Zealand', in B.T. Hoffman (ed), *Art and Cultural Heritage. Law, Policy and Practice*, Cambridge University Press.

Barker, I. (2006), 'Thoughts of an Alternative Dispute Resolution Practitioner on an International ADR Regime for Repatriation of Cultural Property and Works of Art', in Hoffman, B.T. (ed), *Art and Cultural Heritage: Law, Policy and Practice*, Cambridge University Press, p.483.

Barr, Evan (2006), 'From Open-air Bazaar to Buyer Beware: Evolution of the Antiquities Trade', *Museum News*, Washington D.C., AAM, 85 (6), Nov./Dec. 2006, 48.

Bassiouni, Cherif J.M. (1980), *International Criminal Law – A Draft International Criminal Code*, The Netherlands: Sijthoff and Noordhoff, p.98.

Bateman, J.A. et al. (1981), 'Towards a Code of Ethics in Museums', London; *Museum Professionals Group Transactions*, 16.

Batievsky, J. (1995), 'The Protection of Pre-Hispanic Cultural Property in Peru', paper presented at *12th Section on Business Law Biennial Conference*, Paris: International Bar Association.

Bator, P.M. (1982), 'An Essay on the International Trade in Art', *Stanford Law Review*, 275.

Bator, P.M. (1996), *The International Trade in Art*, 2nd edition, Chicago, London: University of Chicago Press.

Battersby, J. (1989), 'Legislative Developments in Australia', in Prott, L.V. and J. Specht (eds), *Protection or Plunder: Safeguarding the Future of Our Cultural Heritage*, Canberra: Australian Government Publishing Service, 92.

Bayraktaroglu, Gulum (2003), 'Harmonization of Private International Law at Different Levels: Communitarization v. International Harmonisation', *European Journal of Law Reform*, 127.

Bedaux, Rogier (1996), 'La destruction du passé au Mali', *Le trafic illicite des biens culturels en Afrique*, Paris: ICOM, p.215.

Bekemans, L. (1993), 'Le Traité de Maastricht et l'Education, la Formation Professionnelle et la Culture', *Revue du Marché Unique Européen*, 2.

Belk, R.W. (1995), *Collecting in a Consumer Society*, London: Routledge.

Bengs, Brian (1996), 'Dead on Arrival? A Comparison of the UNIDROIT Convention on Stolen or Illegally Exported Cultural Objects and U.S. Property Law', *Cultural Property Law*, 503.

Bennett, T. (1988), *Out of Which Past? Critical Reflections on Australian Museum and Heritage Policy*, Brisbane: Institute for Cultural Policy Studies.

Bennett, T. (1995), *The Birth of the Museum: History, Theory, Politics*, London: Routledge.

Bergé, J.S. (2000), 'La Convention d'Unidroit sur les biens culturels:

remarques sur la dynamique des sources en droit international', *Journal du droit international*, 127.

Berrin, K. (2007), 'San Francisco, Mexico, and the Teotihuacan Murals', *Museum International*, 235.

Besternam, Tristram (2009), 'Returning a Stolen Generation', *Museum International*, **61**(1–2).

Beurden, Jos van (2001), *Goden, graven en grenzen. Over kunstroof uit Afrika, Azië en Latijns-Amerika*, Amsterdam: KIT Publishers, 120.

Bibas, St. (1996), 'The Case against Statutes of Limitations for Stolen Art', *International Journal of Cultural Property*, **5**, 73.

Bienkowska, Barbara (1994), *Losses of Polish Libraries during World War II*, Warsaw, Poland: Ministry of Culture and Art, Bureau of the Government Plenipotentiary for the Polish Cultural Heritage abroad, 141.

Bindenagel, J.D. (ed.) (1999), *Washington Conference on Holocaust Era Assets: November 30–December 3, 1998: Proceedings*, Washington: U.S. Government Printing Office.

Biondi, A. (1997), 'The Merchant, the Thief and the Citizen: The Circulation of Works of Art within the European Union', *Common Market Law Review*, 1173.

Blake, J. (2000), 'On Defining the Cultural Heritage', *International & Comparative Law Quarterly*, 49.

Blom, J. (2000), 'Laying Claim to Long-Lost Art: The Hoge Raad of the Netherlands and the Question of Limitation Periods', *International Journal of Cultural Property*, 9.

Boardman, John (1985), *Greek Sculpture, the Classical Period*, London: Thames and Hudson.

Boardman, John and David Finn (1985), *The Parthenon and its Sculptures*, London: Thames and Hudson.

Bodkin, T. (1945), *Dismembered Masterpieces: A Plea for their Reconstruction by International Action*, London: Collins.

Boer, B. (1987), 'Cultural and Natural Heritage: Protection of Movable Cultural Heritage', *Environmental and Planning Law Journal*, 6.

Bogdanos, Matthew (2005), 'The Casualties of War: The Truth about the Iraq Museum', *American Journal of Archaeology*, Boston, Mass.: Archaeological Institute of America, **109**(3), July 2005, 477.

Bogdanos, Matthew (2009), 'The Thieves of Bagdad: A New Way of Looking at the Unification of the Parthenon Sculptures', *Museum International*, **61**(1–2).

Bogdanos, M. and P. William (2005), *Thieves of Baghdad: One Marine's Passion for Ancient Civilizations and the Journey to Recover the World's Greatest Stolen Treasures*, New York: Bloomsbury.

Boguslavskij, M.M. (1994), 'Contemporary Legal Problems of Return of Cultural Property to its Country of Origin in Russia and the Confederation of Independent States', *International Journal of Cultural Property*, **3**(2).

Boguslavskij, Mark (1997), 'Legal Aspects of the Russian Position in regard to the Return of Cultural Property', in E. Simpson (ed.), *The Spoils of War: World War II and Its Aftermath: The Loss, Reappearance and Recovery of Cultural Property*, New York: Harry N. Abrams, p.186.

Bolla, G. (1983), 'Keynote Address: The UNESCO Convention on Illicit Traffic of Art', *New York University Journal of International Law and Politics*, 15.

Bolton, L. (1984), 'Recording Oceanic Collections in Australia: Problems and Questions', *Museum*, 36.

Bolton, L. (1985), *Collection of Inventories and the Return of Information to Oceania: The Australian Experience, 18 March 1985*, Paris: UNESCO, Doc. CLT-85/CONF.202/5.

Borchard, Edwin (1946), 'The Treatment of Enemy Property', *Georgetown Law Journal*, **34**(1), 389.

Borodkin, Lisa (1995), 'The Economics of Antiquities Looting and a Proposed Legal Alternative', *Columbia Law Review*, 377.

Botha, Sarah (2002–3), 'Art Conservation: Problems Encountered in an Unregulated Industry', *Columbia Journal of Law & the Arts*, 251.

Bouchenaki, Mounir (2009), 'Return and Restitution of Cultural Property in the Wake of the 1970 Convention', *Museum International*, **61**(1–2), 139.

Bourguignon, Agnès and Jean-Edouard Choppin (1994), *L'art volé: enquête sur le vol et le trafic d'objets d'art*, Paris: Éditions La Découverte, p.333.

Boyd, W. (2006), 'Museums as Centers of Cultural Understanding', in J.H. Merryman (ed), *Imperialism, Art and Restitution*, Cambridge University Press.

Boylan, P. (1976), 'The Ethics of Acquisition: The Leicestershire Code', *Museums Journal* **75**(4), 165.

Boylan, P. (ed.) (1992), *Museums 2000*, London: Routledge.

Boylan, P.J. (1996), 'ICOM at Fifty', *Museum International*, Paris: UNESCO (191), July–September 1996, 47.

Brabenec, Susan (2000–1), 'The Art of Determining "Stolen Property": United States v. Portrait of Wally, a Painting by Egon Schiele, 105 F. Supp.2d 288, S.D.N.Y. 2000', *University Of Cincinnati Law Review*, 1369.

Bray, T. and T.W. Killion (1994), *Reckoning with the Dead: The Larson Bay Repatriation and the Smithsonian Institution*, Washington: Smithsonian.

Breitkopf, Susan (2007), 'Lost: The Looting of Iraq's Antiquities', *Museum News*, Washington D.C., AAM, **86**(1), Jan/Feb, 44.

Brent, Michel (1993), 'Afrique: le pillage continue . . .', *Le Vif/L'Express*, Paris, (2167), 15–21 January, 34.

Brent, Michel (1994), 'Le grand pillage du Mali', *Le Vif/L'Express*, Paris, (2218), 7 January, 48.

Brent, Michel (1994), 'The Rape of Mali', *Archaeology*, **47**(3), May/June, 26.

Briat, Martine and Judith A. Freedberg (eds) (1996), *Legal Aspects of International Trade in Art – Les aspects juridiques du commerce international de l'art*, Paris; New York: ICC Publishing; The Hague, Boston: Kluwer Law International, p.392.

Brilliant, Richard, Hector Feliciano, Michael Janeway, and András Szántó, (eds) (2001), *Who Owns Culture? Cultural Property and Patrimony Disputes in an Age without Borders*, New York: National Arts Journalism Program.

Broadman, J. (1995), 'Don't Just Berate the Thieves: Look at the Museums and Excavators Too', *The Art Newspaper* (54), December.

Brodie, N. (2001), 'Britannia Waives the Rules? The Licensing of Archaeological Material for Export from the UK', in N. Brodie and K. Walker Tubb (eds), *Illicit Antiquities: The Theft of Culture and the Extinction of Archaeology*, London: Routledge.

Brodie, N. (2003), 'Histoire volée: le pillage et le trafic illicite', *Museum International*, Paris, UNESCO (219–20), 10.

Brodie, N. (2004), 'Export deregulation and the illicit trade in archaeological material', in J.R. Richman & M.P. Forsyth (eds), *Legal Perspectives on Cultural Resources*, Walnut Creek: AltaMira.

Brodie, N. (2006), 'An Archaeologist's View of the Trade in Unprovenanced Antiquities', in B.T. Hoffman (ed.), *Art and Cultural Heritage. Law, Policy and Practice*, Cambridge University Press.

Brodie, Neil (2009), 'Unwanted Antiquities', *Museum International*, **61**(1–2).

Brodie, N. and J. Doole (eds) (1999), *Culture Without Context*, The Newsletter of the Illicit Antiquities Research Centre, Cambridge: McDonald Institute for Archaeological Research, http://www.mcdonald.cam.ac.uk/IARC/cwoc/contents.htm.

Brodie, N. and K.W. Tubb (eds) (2002), *Illicit Antiquities: The Theft of Culture and the Extinction of Archaeology*, (One World Archaeology Series, 42), London: Routledge.

Brodie, N., J. Doole and C. Renfrew (eds) (2001), *Trade in Illicit Antiquities: The Destruction of the World's Archaeological Heritage*, Cambridge: MacDonald Institute for Archaeological Research.

Brodie, N., Doole, J. and Watson, P. (2000), 'Stealing History: The Illicit Trade in Cultural Material', Cambridge: ICOM UK and Museums Association, The McDonald Institute for Archaeological Research.

Brodie, N., J. Doole and P. Watson (2000), *Stealing History: The Illicit Trade in Cultural Material*, Cambridge: MacDonald Institute for Archaeological Research.

Brodie, Neil, M. Kersel, C. Luke and K.W. Tubb (eds) (2006), *Archaeology, Cultural Heritage and the Antiquities Trade*, Gainesville: University of Florida Press.

Brøndum-Nielsen, Johs (1964) *Om der Islandske Handskrifter. vdg. af 'Handskrifikomitean af 1964' Kritiske Bemoerkninger*, Copenhagen: A Critique of the Danish Pamphlet, Facts about the Manuscripts (monograph in Danish).

Browne, Anthony and Pierre Valentin (2005), 'The Art Market in the United Kingdom and Recent Developments in British Cultural Policy', in K. Fitz Gibbon (ed.), *Who Owns the Past? Cultural Policy, Cultural Property and the Law*, New Brunswick, New Jersey and London: Rutgers University Press in association with American Council for Cultural Policy, p.97.

Brown, M.F. (2004), *Who Owns Native Culture?*, Cambridge Mass.: Harvard University Press.

Brown, M.F. and Bruchac, M.M. (2006), 'NAGPRA from the Middle Distance: Legal Puzzles and Unintended Consequences' in J.H. Merryman (ed), *Imperialism, Art and Restitution*, Cambridge University Press.

Brownlie, I. (2003), *Principles of Public International Law*, 6th edition, Oxford University Press.

Bunker, Emma C. (2005), 'The Acquisition and Ownership of Antiquities in Today's Age of Transition', in K. Fitz Gibbon (ed.), *Who Owns the Past? Cultural Policy, Cultural Property and the Law*, New Brunswick, New Jersey and London: Rutgers University Press in association with American Council for Cultural Policy, 311.

Burke, Robert B. and Sam Adeloye (eds) (1986), *A Manual of Basic Museum Security*, Leicester: ICMS, Leicester Museums.

Burnham, Bonnie (1978), *Art Theft, Its Scope, Its Impact, Its Control*, New York: The International Foundation for Art Research, p.205.

Byrne-Sutton, Q. (1988), *Le trafic international des biens culturels sous l'angle de leur revendication par l'Etat d'origine,* Zurich: Schulthess Polygraphischer Verlag.

Byrne-Sutton, Q. (1992), 'The Goldberg Case: A Confirmation of the Difficulty in Acquiring Good Title to Valuable Stolen Cultural Objects', *International Journal of Cultural Property*, **1**, 151.

Byrne-Sutton, Quentin and Fabienne Geisinger-Mariéthoz (eds) (1999),

'Resolution Methods for Art-Related Disputes', *Studies in Art Law*, Vol. 11, Geneva: Schulthess

Byrne-Sutton, Q. and M-A. Renold (eds) (1994), *La libre circulation des Collections d'objets d'art*, Zurich: Schulthess Polygraphischer Verlag.

Byrne-Sutton, Q. and M-A. Renold (eds) (1994), *Les objets d'art dans l'Union Européenne*, Zurich: Schulthess Polygraphischer Verlag.

Byrne-Sutton, Q. and M-A. Renold (eds) (1994), *La réglementation Suisse de l'importation et de l'exportation des biens culturels: Etudes en Droit de l'Art No.5*, Zurich: Schulthess Polygraphischer Verlag.

Cabanne, Pierre (1963), *The Great Collectors*, New York: Farrar, Strauss.

Camarda, G. and T. Scovazzi (eds) (2001), *The Protection of the Underwater Cultural Heritage – Legal Aspects*, Milano.

Cameron, D.F. (1980), *An Introduction to the Cultural Property Export and Import Act*, 2nd edition, Ottawa: Department of the Secretary of State.

Campos, J.D. Gonzales and Virgos Soriano, M. (1988), 'Le commerce international d'art en droit espagnol', in P. Lalive (ed), *International Sales in Works of Art*, Paris: Institute of International Business Law and Practice, and Faculté de Droit de Genève.

Cannon-Brookes, P. (1994), 'Antiquities in the Market-place: Placing a Price on Documentation', *Antiquity*, 68.

Canouts, V. and F.P. McManamon (2001), 'Protecting the Past for the Future: Federal Archaeology in the United States', in N. Brodie, J. Doole, and C. Renfrew (eds), *Trade in Illicit Antiquities: The Destruction of the World's Archaeological Heritage*, Cambridge: McDonald Institute, 97.

Carducci, G. (1997), *La Restitution Internationale Des Biens Culturels Et Des Objets D'Art Volés ou Illicitement Exportés*, Paris: Librairie Générale de Droit et de Jurisprudence.

Carducci, G (2002), 'New Developments in the Law of the Sea: The UNESCO Convention on the Protection of the Underwater Cultural Heritage', *American Journal of International Law*, 419.

Carducci, G. (2006), 'The Growing Complexity of International Art Law: Conflict Of Laws, Uniform Law, Mandatory Rules, UNSC Resolutions and EU Regulations', in B.T. Hoffman (ed), *Art and Cultural Heritage. Law, Policy and Practice*, Cambridge University Press.

Carman, J. (2005), *Against Cultural Property: Archaeology, Heritage and Ownership*, London: Duckworth.

Casanova, Eugenio (1918), 'Gli archivi nei trattati internazionali (Archives in International Treaties)', *Archivi Italiani*, 5.

Casey, Michelle (2006), 'Buried Truth: A Criminological Analysis of the Illicit Antiquities Trade', *Trinity College Law Review*, 119.

Cater, R.R. (1982), 'The Taranaki Panels – A Case-Study in the Recovery of Cultural Heritage', *Museum*, 34.

Caubet, Annie (2009), 'The Historical Context of the Sumerian Discoveries', *Museum International*, **61**(1–2).

Ceram, C.W. (ed.) (1966), *The World of Archaeology (An Anthology)*, London: Thames and Hudson.

Ceram, C.W. (1984), *Gods, Graves and Scholars: The Story of Archaeology*, Harmondsworth: Penguin.

Chamberlain, K. (2002), 'UK Accession to the 1970 UNESCO Convention', *Art Antiquity and Law*, **7**.

Chamberlain, K. (2003), 'The Iraq (United Nations Sanctions) Order 2003 – Is it Human Rights Act-Compatible?', *Art Antiquity and Law*, **8**.

Chamberlain, Russell. (1985), *Loot! The Heritage of Plunder*, New York, N.Y.: Smithmark Pub.

Chaniotis, Angelos (2009), 'Cultural Objects in Cultural Contexts: The Contribution of Academic Institutions', *Museum International*, **61**(1–2).

Chatelain, J. (1976), *Means of Combating the Theft of and Illegal Traffic in Works of Art in the Nine Countries of the EEC*, Commission of the European Communities: Doc, XII 1757/76-E.

Chatelain, J., Rodotà, St. and J. Kohler (1904), 'Das Recht an Denkmälern und Alertumsfunden', *Deutsche Juristenzeitung*, 771

Chenhall, R.G. and P. Homulos (1978), 'Propositions for the Future: Museum Data Standards', *Museum*, **30**(3/4).

Chia, Lan-Po (1975), *The Cave Home of Peking Man*, Peking: Foreign Languages Press.

Chippindale, C. (1993), 'Commercialization: The Role of Archaeological Laboratories and Collectors', *Antiquity*, 67.

Chippindale C. & D.W. Gill, (2000), 'Material Consequences of Contemporary Classical Collecting', *American Journal of Arcaheology*, 104

Clark, Stephen W. (2005), 'The Schiele Matter', in K. Fitz Gibbon (ed.), *Who Owns the Past? Cultural Policy, Cultural Property and the Law*, New Brunswick, New Jersey and London: Rutgers University Press in association with American Council for Cultural Policy, 71.

Cleere, H. (1984), *Approaches to the Archaeological Heritage*, Cambridge University Press.

Clément, Étienne (1994), 'The 1970 UNESCO Convention', *International Criminal Police Review*, 448/449, Special Issue, 71.

Clément, Étienne (1995), 'The 1970 UNESCO Convention on the Means of Prohibiting and Preventing the Illicit Import, Export and Transfer of Ownership of Cultural Property (Paris, 1970)', in Leyten Harrie (ed.), *Illicit Traffic in Cultural Property – Museums against Pillage*, Amsterdam: Royal Tropical Institute.

Clément, Étienne (1995), 'UNESCO Action against Illicit Traffic in

Cultural Property', in ICOM, *Illicit Traffic in Cultural Property*, Paris: ICOM.

Clément, Étienne (2002), 'Le pillage à Angkor: maintenir la pression', *Museum International*, Paris: UNESCO, **54**(1–2), 138.

Cockburn, A.C. (1996), 'Peruvian Antiquities Seized as Sipan artifacts', *The International Foundation for Art Research Reports*, **7&8**.

Cocks, A.G.S. (1995), 'A Dangerously Politicised Issue, Is Laws Obsessed with the Objects rather than the Sites?', *The Art Newspaper*, **52**, October, 27.

Coe, M.C. (1983), 'From Huaquero to Connoisseur: the Early Market in Pre-Columbian Art', in E.H. Boone (ed.), *Collecting the Pre-Columbian Past*, Harvard: Harvard University Press, p.271.

Coggins, C. (1969), 'Illicit Traffic of Pre-Columbian Antiquities', *Art Journal*, New York, 29, Fall, 94.

Coggins, C. (1995), 'A Licit International Traffic in Ancient Art: Let There Be Light!', *International Journal of Cultural Property*, 4.

Coggins, C. (2005), 'Archaeology and the Art Market', in K. Fitz Gibbon (ed.), *Who Owns the Past? Cultural Policy, Cultural Property and the Law*, New Brunswick, New Jersey and London: Rutgers University Press in association with American Council for Cultural Policy, p.221.

Coggins, C. (2005), 'Observations of a Combatant', in K. Fitz Gibbon (ed.), *Who Owns the Past? Cultural Policy, Cultural Property and the Law*, New Brunswick, New Jersey and London: Rutgers University Press in association with American Council for Cultural Policy, p.231.

Collier, J. and V. Lowe (1999), *The Settlement of Disputes in International Law: Institutions and Procedures*, Oxford University Press.

Comando Carabinieri Tutela Patrimonio Artistico (2001), 'La circolazione illecita delle opere d'arte : principio della bona fede – Atti del del 6° Convegno internazionale, Roma, 12–16 giugno 2000', *Bollettino di numismatica*, Roma: Istituto poligrafico e zecca dello Stato, Supplemento al n 36, p.420.

Comando Carabinieri Tutela Patrimonio Culturale (2002), 'Traffico illecito del patrimonio archeologico: internalizzazione del fenomeno e problematiche di contrasto – Atti del del 7° Convegno internazionale, Roma, 25–28 giugno 2001', *Bollettino di numismatica*, Roma: Istituto poligrafico e zecca dello Stato, Supplemento al No. 38, 499.

Comité national marocain de l'ICOM (1997), 'Dossier consacré au trafic illicite des biens culturels', *ICOM Maroc*, Rabat **3**, 3.

Commission des Communautés Européennes (2000), *Rapport de la Commission au Conseil, au Parlement européen et au Comité économique et social sur l'application du règlement (CEE) n° 3911/92 du Conseil concernant l'exportation de biens culturels et de la directive 93/7/CEE du Conseil relative à la restitution de biens culturels ayant quitté illicitement le territoire d'un État membre*, Brussels: Commission des Communautés Européennes, p.23.

Conklin, John E. (1994), *Art Crime*, Westport, Connecticut: Praeger, pp.iii, 326.

Cook, B.F. (1984), *The Elgin Marbles*, London: British Museum Publications.

Cook, B.F. (1992), 'The Transfer of Cultural Property: British Perspectives' in Atti del Convegno internazionale, *Eredita Contestata? Nuove Prospettive per la tutela del patrimonio archeaologico e del territorio*, Rome: Accademia nazionale dei lincei, p.15.

Cooper, Carol (1989), *Hunters and Collectors: Aboriginal and Torres Straits Islands Collections in Overseas Museums*, Canberra: Australian Institute of Aboriginal Studies.

Corbett, P.E. (1959), *The Sculpture of the Parthenon*, Harmondsworth: Penguin.

Cordero, Jorge Sanchez (2003), 'The Protection of Cultural Heritage: A Mexican Perspective', *Worldwide Harmonisation of Private Law and Regional Economic Integration*, 565.

Cornu, M. (2009), 'The Concepts of Original Heritage and Adoptive Heritage in French Legislation', in L.V. Prott (ed.), *Witnesses to History*, Paris: UNESCO, p.326.

Cornu, M. and M.-A. Renold (2010), 'New Developments in the Restitution of Cultural Property: Alternative Means of Dispute Resolution', *International Journal of Cultural Property*, **17**(1).

Cot, J.P. (1972), *International Conciliation*, London: Europa.

Cottrell, Leonard (1959), *Wonders of Antiquity*, London: Longmans, Green and Co.

Cottrell, Leonard (1966), *Digs and Diggers*, London: Lutterworth Press.

Council of Europe (1988), *The Art Trade – Report of the Committee on Culture and Education*, Parliamentary Assembly Doc.5834, Strasbourg: Council of Europe.

Council of Europe (2000), *Directives sur la protection du patrimoine mobilier*, Strasbourg: Council of Europe, p.69.

Council of Europe (2000), *Guidance on the Development of Legislation and Administration Systems in the Field of Cultural Heritage*, Strasbourg: Council of Europe.

Council of Europe (2000), *Guidelines for the Protection of the Movable Heritage*, Strasbourg: Council of Europe, p.69.

Council of Europe (2002), *European Cultural Heritage, Vol.1, Intergovernmental Co-operation: Collected Texts*, Strasbourg: Council of Europe.

Coutau-Bégarie, H. and J-M Schmitt (eds) (1990), *Le patrimoine mobilier: Quelle politique européenne?*, Paris: Economica.

Craven, C. Roy (1976), *Indian Art*, London: Thames and Hudson.

Crewdson, R. (1984), 'Cultural Property – a Fourth Estate?', *Law Society Gazette*.

Crewdson, R. (1996), 'On the Making of Conventions', *International Legal Practitioner*, 21.

Crewdson, R. (2009), 'Getting it Back', in L.V. Prott (ed.), *Witnesses to History*, Paris: UNESCO, p.305.

Croci, G. (2009), 'From Italy to Ethiopia: the Dismantling, Transportation and Re-erection of the Axum Obelisk', *Museum International*, **61**(1–2).

Cunning, A. (2003–2004), 'U.S. Policy on the Enforcement of Foreign Export Restrictions on Cultural Property and Destructive Aspects of Retention Schemes', *Houston Journal of International Law*, 449.

Cuno, J. (2008), *Who Owns Antiquity? Museums and the Battle over Our Ancient Heritage*, Princeton University Press.

Cuno, J. (2005), 'Museums, Antiquities, Cultural Property, and the US Legal Framework for Making Acquisitions', in K. Fitz Gibbon (ed.), *Who Owns the Past? Cultural Policy, Cultural Property and the Law*, New Brunswick, New Jersey and London: Rutgers University Press in association with American Council for Cultural Policy, p.143.

Cuno, J. (2006), 'Beyond Bamiyan: Will the World be Ready Next Time?' in Hoffman, B.T. (ed), *Art and Cultural Heritage. Law, Policy and Practice,* Cambridge University Press, p.41

D'Alton, Martina (1993), *The New York Obelisk*, New York: The Metropolitan Museum of Art.

Dally, B.W. (2006), 'Arbitration of International Cultural Property Disputes: the Experience and Initiatives of the Permanent Court of Arbitration', in B.T. Hoffman (ed.), *Art and Cultural Heritage: Law, Policy and Practice*, Cambridge: Cambridge University Press, p.465.

Daly, Brooks (2005), 'The Potential for Arbitration of Cultural Property Disputes: Recent Developments at the Permanent Court of Arbitration', *Law And Practice International Courts and Tribunals*, 261.

Daniel, Glyn (1968), *The First Civilizations: the Archaeology of their Origins*, London: Thames and Hudson.

Daniel, Glyn (1978), *150 Years of Archaeology*, London: Duckworth.

Daniel, Glyn (1981), *A Short History of Archaeology*, London: Thames and Hudson.

Danish Supreme Court (2009), 'The Icelandic Sagas', in L.V. Prott (ed.), *Witnesses to History*, Paris: UNESCO, p.343.

Dark, Philip J.C. (1973), *An Introduction to Benin Art and Ethnology*, Oxford: Clarendon Press.

Davidson, Marshall B. (ed.) (1962), *The Horizon Book of Lost Worlds*, New York: American Heritage Publishing Company.

Davis, Maurice (2009), 'A First Small Step in a Long Journey', *Museum International*, **61**(1–2).

DeAngelis, I.P. (2006), 'How Much Provenance is Enough? Post-Schultz Guidelines for Art Museum Acquisition of Archaeological Materials and Ancient Art' in Hoffman, B.T. (ed), *Art and Cultural Heritage. Law, Policy and Practice*, Cambridge University Press, p.398

De Ceuster, J. (1993), 'Les Règles Communautaires En Matière De Restitution De Biens Culturels Ayant Quitté Illicitement Le Territoire D'un Etat Membre', *Revue du Marché Unique Européen*, 2.

De Visscher, C. (1935), 'La protection internationale des objets d'art et des monuments historiques', *Revue de Droit International et de Législation Comparée*, 32.

De Visscher, C. (1938), 'La protection des patrimoines artistiques et historiques nationaux: nécessité d'une réglementation nationale', *Mouseïon*, p.43.

De Visscher, F. C. (1949), 'Essays on International Protection of Works of Art', *US Department of State Documents and State Papers,* **I**(15).

Deb, Gitanjali (2005), 'Stealing Gods: Illegal Trade in Indian Antiquities', *Art Antiquity and Law*, **10**(1), March.

Debaux, Geneviève (1993), 'Cher patrimoine', *Faim Développement Magazine*, Paris: CCFD, (100).

Decker, A. (1990), 'Lost Heritage: The Destruction of African Art', *ART News*, p.89.

Delmotte, Hubert (1997), 'Les services de police', *La Vie des musées,* Brussels: AFMB/ICOM Wallonie-Bruxelles, 12.

Delouis, Dominique (1996), *A Study on Access to Databases on Stolen Cultural Property Items Databases – Minutes of Interviews and Documents*, Paris: UNESCO Division of Cultural Heritage.

Demakopoulu, K. and N. Divan-Valakou (1997) *The Aidonia Treasure*, Athens: Greek Ministry of Culture, Archeological Receipts Fund.

Dembélé, M. and J. van der Waals (1991), 'Looting the Antiquities of Mali', *Antiquity*, **65**, 904.

Department of Culture, Media and Sport (2004), *The 1970 UNESCO Convention – Guidance for Dealers and Auctioneers in Cultural Property*, London: Department of Culture, Media and Sport.

Department of Culture Media and Sport (UK) (2005), *Guidance for the Care of Human Remains in Museums*, London: Department of Culture, Media and Sport.

Derout, Anne (1993), *La protection des biens culturels en droit communautaire*, Rennes: Editions Apogée.

Des Portes, Elisabeth (1996), 'ICOM et la lutte contre le trafic illicite des biens culturels', *Museum International*, Paris: UNESCO, (191), July–September 1996, 51.

Des Portes, Elisabeth (1997), 'Patrimoine artistique, morale et politique', *Le Monde*, Paris, Tuesday 14 January 1997, 15.

Deuel, Leo (1962), *The Treasures of Time*, London: Souvenir Press.

Dietrich, Reinhard (2002), 'Cultural Property on the Move – Legally, Illegally', *International Journal of Cultural Property*, **11**(2).

Dobinson, C. and S. Denison (1995), *Metal Detecting and Archaeology in England*, London: English Heritage.

Dodwell, C.R. (1980), *Jewish Art Treasures from Prague*, London: Lund Humphries with the Whitworth Art Gallery, University of Manchester.

Douglas, David C. (ed.) (1969), *English Historical Documents, vol. IV, 1327–1485*, Oxford University Press.

Douglas, Frederick Silvester North (1813), *Essay on Certain Points of Resemblance between the Ancient and Modern Greeks*, London: John Murray.

Drimmer, Jonathan (1997–8), 'Hate Property: A Substantive Limitation for America's Cultural Property Laws', *Tennessee Law Review*, 691.

Dromgoole, Sarah (2003), *The Protection of the Underwater Cultural Heritage: Legal Aspects*, Guido Camarda and Tullio Scovazzi (eds), Milan: Giuffre, p.453.

Dromgoole, Sarah (ed.) (2006), *The Protection of the Underwater Cultural Heritage – National Perspectives in Light of the UNESCO Convention 2001*, Leiden

Droz, G. (1997), 'Convention d'UNIDROIT sur les biens volés ou illicitement exportés', *Revue Critique de Droit International Privé*, 1.

Duboff, Leonard D. (ed.) (1975), *Art Law – Domestic and International (Collection of Papers)*, New Jersey: Fred B. Rothman.

DuBoff, L. et al. (1976), 'Proceedings of the Panel on the US Enabling Legislation of the UNESCO Convention on the Means of Prohibiting and Preventing the Illicit Import, Export and Transfer of Ownership of Cultural Property', *Syracuse Journal of International Law and Commerce*, 4.

Duboff, Leonard D. (1977), *The Deskbook of Art Law*, Washington: Federal Publishers, p.71.

Duquesne, J. (1982), 'Le libre échange des œuvres d'art', in Van der Abeele (ed.) *Le Marché Commun et le marché de l'art*, 35 (37), Brussels: Editions de l'Université Libre de Bruxelles.

Dworkin, R. (1986), 'Can a Liberal State Support Art?', in *A Matter of Principle*, Oxford: Clarendon Press, p.221.

Ede, James (1998), 'Ethics, the Antiquities Trade, and Archaeology', *International Journal of Cultural Property*, **7**, 128.
Edson, Gary (ed.) (1997), *Museum Ethics*, Routledge, London.
Edwards, I.E.S. (1961), *The Pyramids of Egypt*, Harmondsworth: Penguin.
Eichwede, W. (1997), 'Models of Restitution (Germany, Russia, Ukraine)', in E. Simpson (ed.), *The Spoils of War: World War II and Its Aftermath: The Loss, Reappearance and Recovery of Cultural Property*, New York: Harry N. Abrams, 216.
Elen, J. Albert (1989), *Missing Old Master Drawings from the Koenigs Collection*, The Hague: Netherlands Office for Fine Arts.
Elia, R. (1994), 'The World Cannot Afford Many More Collectors with a Passion for Antiquities', *The Art Newspaper* **41**, October, 19.
Elia, R.J. (1997), 'Looting, Collecting, and the Destruction of Archaeological Resources', *Nonrenewable Resources*, **6**(2).
Elia, R.J. (2001), 'Analysis of the Looting, Selling, and Collecting of Apulian Red-figure Vases: A Quantitative Approach', in N. Brodie, J. Doole & C. Renfrew (eds), *Trade in Illicit Antiquities: the Destruction of the World's Archaeological Heritage*, Cambridge: McDonald Institute for Archaeological Research.
Elia, R.J. (2009), 'Preventing Looting through the Return of Looted Archaeological Objects', *Museum International*, **61**(1–2).
Ellis, R. (2002), 'The Fred Schultz Case – An Example of International Cooperation between Police, Archaeologists and Legal Experts', in UNESCO, Korean National Commission (ed.), *International Expert Meeting on the Return of Cultural Property and the Fight against its Illicit Trafficking, 30 September–3 October 2002, Seoul, Republic of Korea*, Seoul: Korean National Commission for UNESCO, 106.
Emetz, I. and A. Golentzov (1993), 'The Pillage of the Ancient Tombs in the Crimea', *International Journal of Cultural Property*, **2**(2).
Emmerich, André (2005), 'Improving the Odds: Preservation through Distribution', in K. Fitz Gibbon (ed.), *Who Owns the Past? Cultural Policy, Cultural Property and the Law*, New Brunswick, New Jersey and London: Rutgers University Press in association with American Council for Cultural Policy, p.247.
Endere, M.L. (2009), 'The Return of Inakayal to Patagonia', in L.V. Prott (ed.), *Witnesses to History*, Paris: UNESCO, 283.
Epstein, Jeremy G. (2005), 'The Hazards of Common Law Adjudication', in K. Fitz Gibbon (ed.), *Who Owns the Past? Cultural Policy, Cultural Property and the Law*, New Brunswick, New Jersey and London: Rutgers University Press in association with American Council for Cultural Policy, 123.

Esterow, Milton (1967), *The Art Stealers*, London: Weidenfeld and Nicolson.

Eyo, Ekpo O. (1986), *The Threat to National Art Treasures: The Illicit Traffic in Stolen Art, the Challenge to our Cultural Heritage*, Paris: UNESCO.

Fagan, Brian (1977), *Elusive Treasure*, London: Macdonald and Jones Publishers Ltd.

Fagan, Brian M. (1978), *Quest for the Past – Great Adventures in Archaeology*, Reading, London: Addison-Wesley.

Fagg, William (1978), *Divine Kingship in Africa*, London: British Museum Publications.

Failing, P. (1990), 'Judd and Panza Square off', *ART News*, **89**(9).

Faith, Nicholas (1985), *Sold – The Revolution in the Art Market*, London: Hamish Hamilton.

Feather, J. (1997), 'Disputed Titles in Antiquarian Books', *Art, Antiquity & Law*, 373.

Fechner, Frank (1991), *Rechtlicher Schutz archäologischen Kulturguts. Regelungen im innerstaatlichen Recht, im Europa- und Völkerrecht sowie Möglichkeiten zu ihrer Verbesserung*, Berlin: Duncker und Humblot, p.131.

Fechner, Frank (1997), 'Strategies for the Preservation of Cultural Heritage in a Single European Market', *Tel Aviv University Studies in Law*, 169.

Fechner, F. (1998), 'The Fundamental Aims of Cultural Property Law', *International Journal of Cultural Property*, 7.

Fechner, F., T. Oppermann, and L.V. Prott (eds) (1996), *Prinzipien des Kulturgüterschutzes. Ansätze im deutschen, europäischen und internationalen Recht*, Berlin: Duncker and Humblot.

Federal Office of Culture, Switzerland (1999), *International Transfer of Cultural Objects: UNESCO Convention of 1970 and UNIDROIT Convention*, Report of the Working Group, Berne: Federal Office of Culture, X, 42.

Federal Office of Culture, Switzerland (2002), 'Commerce des biens culturels: redéfinir les règles du jeu', *OFC (Office Fédéral de la Culture) Journal*, Berne, 5.

Feldman, M.B. (1976), 'Proceedings of the Panel on the U. S. Enabling Legislation of Import, Export and Transfer of Ownership of Cultural Property', *Syracuse Journal of International Law and Commerce*, **4**, 7.

Feliciano, Hector (1997), *The Lost Museum: The Nazi Conspiracy to Steal the World's Greatest Works of Art*, New York: Basic Books.

Ferguson, T.J., R. Anyon and E.J. Ladd (2009), 'The Denver Art Museum', in L.V. Prott (ed.), *Witnesses to History*, Paris: UNESCO, p.255.

Ferrer-Correia, A., 'La vente nationale d'objets d'art sous l'angle de la protection patrimoine culturel', *Annuaire de l'Institute de Droit International* (64-I), 1991, session de Bâle, 90.

Ferri, Paolo Giorgio (2009), 'New Types of Cooperation between Museums and Countries of Origin', *Museum International*, **61**(1–2).

Fforde, C., J. Hubert and P. Turnbull (eds.) (2002), *The Dead and Their Possessions: Repatriation in Principle, Policy and Practice*, (One World Archaeology Series, 43), London: Routledge.

Fforde, Cressida (2009), 'From Edinburgh University to the Ngarrinjeri Nation, South Australia', *Museum International*, **61**(1–2).

Fiddick, J.M. (1983), *Research Note (on Elgin Marbles)*, London: House of Commons.

Fiedler, W. (ed.) (1991), *Internationaler Kulturguterschutz und deutsche Frage*, [International Protection of Cultural Objects and German Issues], Berlin: Gebr. MannVerlag, (in German).

Fincham, D. (2009), 'Iran v. Barakat: Iran Wins Barakat Appeal', in L.V. Prott (ed.), *Witnesses to History*, Paris: UNESCO, p.388.

Finlay, Ian (1977), *Priceless Heritage: The Future of Museums*, London: Faber and Faber.

Finley, G. et al. (1986), 'Being a Curator Is the Most Impossible Profession on Earth', *Muse*, **3**(4), 15.

Fitz Gibbon, K. (ed.) (2005), *Who Owns the Past? Cultural Policy, Cultural Property and the Law*, New Brunswick, New Jersey and London: Rutgers University Press in association with American Council for Cultural Policy.

Fitz Gibbon, K. (2005), 'Alternatives to Embargo', in *Who Owns the Past? Cultural Policy, Cultural Property and the Law*, New Brunswick, New Jersey and London: Rutgers University Press in association with American Council for Cultural Policy, p.291.

Fitz Gibbon, K. (2005), 'Editor's Note: The Illicit Trade – Fact or Fiction', in *Who Owns the Past? Cultural Policy, Cultural Property and the Law*, New Brunswick, New Jersey and London: Rutgers University Press in association with American Council for Cultural Policy, p.179.

Fitz Gibbon, K. (2005), 'The Elgin Marbles: A Summary', in *Who Owns the Past? Cultural Policy, Cultural Property and the Law*, New Brunswick, New Jersey and London: Rutgers University Press in association with American Council for Cultural Policy, p.109.

Flandrin, Philippe (1996), *Le Musée des pillards: récit*, Paris: Éditions du Félin, 285.

Flandrin, Philippe (2004), *Le pillage de l'Irak: main basse sur la Mésopotamie*, Monaco: Éditions du Rocher, p.209.

Forbes, Stephanie O. (1996), 'Current Efforts to Protect Cultural Property', *The Transnational Lawyer*, 235.

Forrest, C. (2003), 'Strengthening the International Regime for the Prevention of the Illicit Trade in Cultural Heritage', *Melbourne Journal of International Law*, 592.

Forrest, C. (2004), 'Australia's Protection of Foreign States' Cultural Heritage', *University of New South Wales Law Journal*, 27.

Forrest, C. (2005), 'The Protection of Cultural Heritage in South Africa and the Implementation of the 1970 UNESCO Convention', *Art Antiquity and Law*, **10**(1).

Fourmile, H. (1989), 'Who Owns the Past? – Aborigines as Captives of the Archives', *Aboriginal History*, 13.

Fox, Claudia (1993–4), 'The UNIDROIT Convention on Stolen or Illegally Exported Cultural Objects: An Answer to the World Problem of Illicit Trade in Cultural Property', *American University Journal of International Law and Policy*, p.225.

Francioni, Fr. (2007), 'A dynamic evolution of concept and scope: from cultural property to cultural heritage', in A. Yusaf (ed.), *Standard setting in UNESCO, Volume 1: Normative action in education, science and culture,* Essays in commemoration of the sixtieth Anniversary of UNESCO, Paris, p.221.

Francioni, Francesco (1998), 'Le commerce illicite d'objets d'art et son contrôle: la Convention d'UNIDROIT de 1995', *Revue du Marché Unique Européen*, (2), 69.

Francioni, Fr. and Lenzerini, F. (2006) 'The Obligation to Prevent and Avoid Destruction of Cultural Heritage: from Bamiyan to Iraq', in B.T. Hoffman (ed), *Art and Cultural Heritage. Law, Policy and Practice*, Cambridge University Press.

Frankena, William K. (1973), *Ethics*, 2nd edition, Englewood Cliffs, N.J.: Prentice-Hall.

Fraoua, R. (1985), *Le trafic illicite des biens culturels et leur restitution: analyse des réglementations nationales et internationales; critiques et propositions*, Fribourg: Editions Universitaires Fribourg Suisse, VIII, p.279.

Fraoua, R. (1986), *Convention concernant les mesures à prendre pour interdire et empêcher l'importation, l'exportation et le transfert de propriété illicites de biens culturels (Paris, 1970) – Commentaire et aperçu de quelques mesures nationales d'exécution*, Paris: UNESCO Doc. CC–86/WS/40.

Fraoua, R. (1995), 'Le projet de convention de l'UNIDROIT sur le retour international des biens culturels volés ou illicitement exportés', *Aktuelle Juristische Praxis*, 317.

Freidel, D. (2009), 'The Mayan Temple Facade', in L.V. Prott (ed.), *Witnesses to History*, Paris: UNESCO, p.217.

Frigo, M. (1986), *La protezione dei beni culturali nel diritto internazionale*, Milan: Dott. A. Giouffrè Editore.
Frigo, M. (1993), 'The Proposed EEC Council Directive on the Return of Unlawfully Exported Cultural Objects', *International Journal of Cultural Property*, 2.
Frigo, M. (2001), 'Il comercio di opere d'arte e la circolazione dei beni culturali tra diritto internazionale, diritto comunitario e diritto interno', in *La circolazione internazionale dei beni culturali*, Milan: Giuffrè, 3.
Frigo, M. (2001), *La circolazione internazionale dei beni culturali: Diritto internazionale, diritto comunitario e diritto interno*, Milan: Giuffrè, p.342.
Frigo, M. (2004), 'Cultural Property v. Cultural Heritage: A "Battle of Concepts" in International Law?', *International Review of the Red Cross*, **86**(854), 367.
Fuchs, Elisa (1992), *Göttinnen, Gräber und Geschäfte von der Plünderung fremder Kulturen*, Zürich: Erklärung von Bern, p.120.
Fuentes Camacho, V. (1993), *El trafico illicito internacional de bienes culturales* [International Illicit Traffic in Cultural Objects], Madrid: Editorial Beramar, 456, (in Spanish).
Gabriel, Mille (2009), 'The Return of Cultural Heritage from Denmark to Greenland', *Museum International*, **61**(1–2).
Ganslmayr, Herbert (1979), 'Return and restitution of cultural property', *Museum*, **31**(1), UNESCO, 12.
Garabello, R. and T. Scovazzi (eds) (2003), *The Protection of the Underwater Cultural Heritage – Before and After the 2001 UNESCO Convention*, Leiden.
Garel, Michael (1991), *D'une main forte: manuscrits hébreux des collections françaises*. Paris: Bibliothèque Nationale.
Garnett, Henry (1964), *Treasures of Yesterday*, London: Library of Modern Knowledge.
Gathercole, Peter and David Lowenthal (eds) (1990), *The Politics of the Past*, London and Boston: Unwin Hyman.
Gaultier-Kurhan, C. (2001), *Le patrimoine culturel africain*, Paris: Maisonneuve & Larose.
Gegas, Evangelos (1997–8), 'International Arbitration and the Resolution of Cultural Property Disputes: Navigating the Stormy Waters Surrounding Cultural Property', *Ohio State Journal on Dispute Resolution*, p.129.
George, Tanya Evelyn (2005), 'Using Customary International Law to Identify "Fetishistic" Claims to Cultural Property', *New York University Law Review*, 1207.
Gerstenblith, P. (1995), 'Identity and Cultural Property: The Protection of Cultural Property in the United States', *Boston University Law Review*, 75.

Gerstenblith, P. (2000–1), 'The Public Interest in the Restitution of Cultural Objects', *Connecticut Journal of International Law*, 197.

Gerstenblith, P. (2003), 'Acquisition and Deacquisition of Museum Collections and the Fiduciary Obligations of Museums to the Public', *Cardozo Journal of International and Comparative Law*, 11.

Gerstenblith, P. (2004), *Art, Cultural Heritage, and the Law*, Durham, N.C: Carolina Academic Press.

Gersternblith, P. (2009), 'The McClain/Schultz Doctrine: Another Step against Trade in Stolen Antiquities', in L.V. Prott (ed.), *Witnesses to History*, Paris: UNESCO, p.346.

Gerstenblith, P. and Lucille Roussin (2007), 'International Cultural Property', *The International Lawyer*, 613.

Ghoshray, Saby (2007–8), 'Repatriation of the Kohinoor Diamond: Expanding the Legal Paradigm for Cultural Heritage', *Fordham International Law Journal*, 741.

Gibson, McGuire and Augusta McMahon (1992), *Lost Heritage: Antiquities Stolen from Iraq's Regional Museums*, Fascicle 1, Chicago: American Association for Research in Baghdad, 54.

Gill, D. and C. Chippindale (1993), 'Material and Intellectual Consequences of Esteem for Cycladic Figures', *American Journal of Archaeology*, 97.

Gill, D. and C. Chippindale (2002), 'The Trade in Looted Antiquities and the Return of Cultural Property: A British Parliamentary Inquiry', *International Journal of Cultural Property*, **11**(1).

Gill, D. and C. Chippindale (2006), 'From Boston to Rome: Reflections on Returning Antiquities', *International Journal of Cultural Property*, 13.

Gillman, D. (2006), *The Idea of Cultural Heritage*, Leicester: Institute of Art and Law.

Gimbrère, Sabine and T. Pronk (1992), 'The Protection of Cultural Property: From UNESCO to European Community with Special Reference to the Case of the Netherlands', *Netherlands Yearbook of International Law*, 23.

Gimpel, Jean (1969), *The Cult of Art*, New York: Stein and Day.

Girsberger, Daniel (1997), 'Das internationale Privatrecht der nachrichtenlosen Vermögen in der Schweiz (Private international law and unclaimed property in Switzerland)', Berne: Helbing & Lichtenhahn with Kluwer Law International, p.80.

Gislason, Gylfi P. (1961), *The Manuscripts Case (Handritamalio)*, Serberg: Ministry of Education, (in Icelandic).

Godart, Louis (2009), 'Artistic Heritage and the Return of Masterpieces', *Museum International*, **61**(1–2).

Gold, Leonard Singer (1988), *A Sign and a Witness – 2000 Years of Hebrew Books and Illuminated Manuscripts*, New York: Oxford University Press.

Goldberg, Adam (2006), 'Reaffirming McClain: The National Stolen Property Act and the Abiding Trade in Looted Cultural Objects', *UCLA (University of California, Los Angeles) Law Review*, 1031.

Gordon, J.B. (1971), 'The UNESCO Convention on the Illicit Movement of Art Treasures', *Harvard International Law Journal*, 12.

Gorman, M. and P.W. Winkler (1988), *Anglo-American Cataloguing Rules*, 2nd edition, 1988 revision, London: Library Association.

Gosden, C. and C. Knowles (2001), *Collecting Colonialism: Material Culture and Colonial Change*, Oxford: Berg.

Gößwald, Udo (2009), 'ICOM Statement on Reclaiming Cultural Property', *Museum International*, **61**(1–2).

Goy, R. (1979), 'Le retour et la restitution des biens culturels à leur pays d'origine en cas d'appropriation illégale', *Revue Générale de Droit International Public*, 83.

Goyder, J. (1992), 'Free Movement of Cultural Goods and European Community Law', *International Journal of Cultural Property*, 1.

Goyder, J. (1993), 'European Community Free Movement of Cultural Goods and European Community Law Part III: Two New Legislative Proposals', *International Journal of Cultural Property*, 2.

Graepler, Daniel and Mazzei, Marina (1993), *Fundort: unbekannt. Raubgrabungen zerstören das archäologische Erbe: eine Dokumentation*, Munich: Druck Biering GmbH, p.96.

Grammatikaki-Alexiou, A. (2002), *International Trade of Cultural Property and Private International Law*, Thessaloniki: Sakkoulas Publications, XV, 410, (in Greek).

Grammatikaki-Alexiou, A. (2004), 'The combat of the Illicit Traffic in Cultural Goods: The UNIDROIT Convention', in E. Trova (ed.), *Cultural Heritage and the Law*, Athens-Thessaloniki: Ed. Sakkoulas, p.253.

Grammatikaki-Alexiou, A., A. Strati, E. Mouameletzi and D. Anagnostopoulou (2001), *Legal and Illegal Movement of Cultural Goods under the Scope of International, Community and Greek law*, Athens: Ant. N. Sakkoulas.

Grant, A. (ed.) (1994), *Spectrum: the U.K. Museum Documentation Standard*, Cambridge: The Museum Documentation Association.

Green, Ernestene L. (ed.) (1984), *Ethics and Values in Archaeology*, New York: Free Press.

Greenfield, J. (2007), *The Return of Cultural Treasures*, 3rd revised edition, Cambridge University Press.

Grifiths, T. (1996), *Hunters and Collectors*, Melbourne: Cambridge University Press.

Grimsted, P.K. (2009), 'From Nazi Plunder to Russian Restitution', in L.V. Prott (ed.), *Witnesses to History*, Paris: UNESCO, p.295.

Grimsted, P.K., F.J. Hoogewould and E. Katelaar (eds) (2007), *Returned from Russia: Nazi Archival Plunder in Western Europe and Recent Restitution Issues*, Builth Wells, Wales: Institute of Art and Law.

Groube, L. (1984), 'The Ownership of Diversity: The Problem of Establishing a National History in a Land of Nine Hundred Ethnic Groups', in I. McBryde (ed.), *Who Owns the Past?*, Papers from the Annual Symposium of the Australian Academy of the Humanities, Melbourne: Oxford University Press, p.49.

Guerrero, Blanca Alva (2009), 'Repatriation of Cultural Properties: the Peruvian Experience', *Museum International*, **61**(1–2).

Guillotreau, Ghislaine (1999), *Art et crime: la criminalité du monde artistique, sa répression*, Paris: Presses Universitaires de France, p.299.

Hall, A.R. (1947), 'Return of Looted Objects of Art to Countries of Origin: Memorandum by the State Department', *Department of State Bulletin*, **16**(399).

Hall, A.R. (1951), 'The Recovery of Cultural Objects Dispersed During World War II', *Department of State Bulletin*, **25**(635).

Hall, A.R. (1954), 'The US Program for the Return of Historic Objects to Countries of Origin, 1944–1954', *Department of State Bulletin*, **31**(797).

Hallman, Robert (2005), 'Museums and Cultural Property: A Retreat from the Internationalist Approach', *International Journal of Cultural Property*, **12**(2).

Hampe Martinez, T. (2008), 'Cómo recuperar el patrimonio documental Uevado a Chile durante la guerra del Pacifico?' *Revista Peruana de Derecho Internacional*, 77.

Handler, R. (1991), 'Who Owns the Past? History, Cultural Property, and the Logic of Possessive Individualism', in B. Williams (ed.), *The Politics of Culture*, Washington: The Smithsonian Institution Press, p.63.

Harding, Sarah (1999), 'Value, Obligation and Cultural Heritage', *Arizona State Law Journal*, 291.

Harding, Sarah (2003), 'Cultural Property and the Limitations of Preservation', *Law and Policy*, 17.

Harvey, K. and P. Young (1994), *Data Content Standards: A Directory*, Unpublished document prepared for limited distribution, Ottawa: Canadian Heritage Information Network.

Harwood, R. (2003), 'Dealing in Cultural Objects (Offenses) Act 2003', *Art Antiquity and Law*, VIII, 347.

Hatti, Vivek (1999–2000), 'India's Right to Reclaim Cultural and Art Treaures from Britain under International Law', *George Washington Journal of International Law and Economics*, 465.

Hawkes, Jacquetta (ed.) (1963), *The World of the Past*, London: Thames and Hudson.

Hawkes, Jacquetta (1974), *Atlas of Ancient Archaeology*, London: Heinemann.
Hawkins, Ashton and Judith Church (2005), 'A Tale of Two Innocents: The Rights of Former Owners and Good-Faith Purchasers of Stolen Art', in K. Fitz Gibbon (ed.), *Who Owns the Past? Cultural Policy, Cultural Property and the Law*, New Brunswick, New Jersey and London: Rutgers University Press in association with American Council for Cultural Policy, p.57.
Hawkins, Ashton, Richard Rothman and David Goldstein (1995–6), 'A Tale of Two Innocents: Creating an Equitable Balance between the Rights of Former Owners and Good Faith Purchasers of Stolen Art', *Fordham Law Review*, 64.
Hawthorne, Nathaniel (1941), *English Notebooks (1856)*, New York: The Modern Language Association of America.
Hay, John (1973), *Ancient China*, London: The Bodley Head.
Haynes, D.E.L. (ed.) (1962), *An Historical Guide to the Sculptures of the Parthenon*, London: British Museum Publications.
Hayton, David J. (1998), 'Selling, Giving and Acquiring Works of Art in Breach of Trust', in Norman Palmer (ed.), *The Recovery of Stolen Art: A Collection of Essays,* London: Kluwer Law International, p.122.
Hemming, John (1993), *The Conquest of the Incas*, London: Macmillan.
Henry, D. (1995), 'Back from the Brink: Canada's First Nations' Right to Preserve Canadian Heritage', *University of British Columbia Law Review*, Special Issue 5.
Herczl, Moseh Y. (1993), 'Anti-Jewish Legislation', in *Christianity and the Holocaust of Hungarian Jewry*, New York: New York University Press, p.81.
Hermannsson, Haldór (1929), 'Icelandic Manuscripts', *Islandica*, Vol. xix, New York: Cornell University Library.
Herscher, Ellen (1983), 'The Antiquities Market: News and Commentary on the Illicit Traffic in Antiquities', *Journal of Field Archaeology*, Association for Field Archaeology, 10.
Hiat, Philip (ed.) (1987), *A Visual Testimony – Judaica from the Vatican Library*, Miami, Florida, New York: Center for Fine Arts Association and the Union of American Hebrew Congregations.
Hideo, Fuji and Kazumi Oguchi (1996), *Lost Heritage: Antiquities Stolen from Iraq's Regional Museums*, Fascicle 3, Tokyo: The Institute for Cultural Studies of Ancient Iraq, p.43.
Hill, Charles (1998), 'Recovering Stolen Art: Practical Recovery Issues and the Role of the Law Enforcement Agencies', in Norman Palmer (ed.), *The Recovery of Stolen Art: A Collection of Essays,* London: Kluwer Law International, p.177.

Hill Jr., Thomas E. (2002), 'Basic Respect and Cultural Diversity', in *Respect Pluralism and Justice – Kantian Perspectives*, New York: Oxford University Press, p.59.

Hiller, Armin (1997), 'The German-Russian Negotiations over the Contents of the Russian Repositories', in E. Simpson (ed.), *The Spoils of War: World War II and Its Aftermath: The Loss, Reappearance and Recovery of Cultural Property*, New York: Harry N. Abrams, p.179.

His Majesty's Stationery Office (1945), *World of Art in Italy – Losses and Survivals in the War*, vols. 1 and 2 compiled by Hugh Braun and issued by the British Committee on the Preservation and Restitution of Works of Art, Archives and other Material in Enemy Hands, London: HMSO.

His Majesty's Stationery Office (1946), *Works of Art in Malta – Losses and Survivals in the War*, vols. 1 and 2 compiled by Hugh Braun and issued by the British Committee on the Preservation and Restitution of Works of Art, Archives and other Material in Enemy Hands, London: HMSO.

Hitchens, C. (ed.) (1997), *The Elgin Marbles: Should they be Returned to Greece?* London: Chatto & Windus.

Hobhouse, John Cam (1813), *A Journey through Albania and other Provinces of Turkey in Europe and Asia to Constantinople during the Years of 1809 and 1810*, London: James Cawthorn, especially letters xxi and xxiii.

Hoffman, B.T. (1993), 'The Spoils of War', *Archaeology*, November–December 1993, 37.

Hoffman, B.T. (ed.) (2006), *Art and Cultural Heritage: Law, Policy and Practice,* Cambridge University Press.

Hoffman, B.T. (2006), 'European Union Legislation Pertaining to Cultural Goods', in B.T. Hoffman (ed), *Art and Cultural Heritage. Law, Policy and Practice*, Cambridge University Press.

Hoffman, B.T. (2006), 'International Art Transactions and the Resolution of Art and Cultural Property Disputes: A United States Perspective', in B.T. Hoffman (ed), *Art and Cultural Heritage. Law, Policy and Practice*, Cambridge University Press.

Hollander, Barnett (1959), *The International Law of Art*, London: Bowes & Bowes, especially Chapter 1.

Holmes, R. (2007), *The Hottentot Venus: The Life and Death of Saartjie Baartman: Born 1789 – Buried 2002*, London: Bloomsbury Publishing.

Home, Robert (1982), *City of Blood Revisited – A New Look at the Benin Expedition of 1897*, London: Rex Collins.

Hopkirk, Peter (1980), *Foreign Devils on the Silk Road*, London: John Murray.

Horne, Donald (1984), *The Great Museum: The Re-Presentation of History*, London, Sydney: Pluto Press.

House of Commons, Culture Media and Sport Committee, (2000), *Cultural Property: Return and Illicit Trade. Volume I: Report and Proceedings of the Committee*, London: The Stationery Office Ltd.

House of Commons, Culture, Media and Sport Committee, (2000), *Seventh Report: Cultural Property: Return and Illicit Trade*, (HC 371–1), London: The Stationery Office Ltd.

Hoving, T. (1975), *The Chase, the Capture: Collecting at the Metropolitan*, New York: Metropolitan Museum of Art.

Howe Jr., Thomas Carr (1946), *Salt Mines and Castles: The Discovery and Restitution of Looted European Art*, New York: Bobbs-Merrill.

Hudson, K. (1989), 'The Flipside of Professionalism', *Museums Journal*, 88 (4), 188.

Hughes, J. (2000), 'The Trend Toward Liberal Enforcement of Repatriation Claims in Cultural Property Disputes' *George Washington International Law Review*, 33.

Hughes, V. (1994), 'International Efforts to Secure the Return of Stolen or Illegally Exported Cultural Objects: Has Unidroit found a Global Solution?' *The Canadian Yearbook of Int'l Law*, 219

Hughes, V. (1996), *The UNIDROIT Convention on Stolen and Illegally Exported Cultural Objects*, Ottawa: Canadian Museums Association Proceedings of Legal Affairs and Management Symposium.

Hughes, V. and Laurie Wright (1994), 'International Efforts to Secure the Return of Stolen or Illegally Exported Cultural Objects: Has UNIDROIT Found a Global Solution?', *The Canadian Yearbook of International Law*, 32.

Hunt S., E.W. Jones and M.E. McAllister (1992), *Archaeological Resource Protection*, Washington: Preservation Press.

ICOM (1979), 'Study on the Principles, Conditions and Means for the Restitution or Return of Cultural Property in View of Reconstituting Dispersed Heritage', *Museum*, 31.

ICOM (1981), *International Committee on Museum Security: Museum Security Survey*, based on a document by G.H.H. Schröder, edited by D. Menkes and translated by M. de Moltke. Paris: ICOM.

ICOM (1993), 'Focus: Cultural Property and Illicit Traffic', *ICOM News*, Paris, **46**(3).

ICOM (1994), *Final Report of the UNESCO–ICOM Regional Workshop on Illicit Traffic in Cultural Property (Arusha, Tanzania, September 1993)*, Paris: ICOM.

ICOM (1994), *Final Report of UNESCO–ICOM Regional Workshop on Illicit Traffic in Cultural Property (Bamako, Mali, 1994)*, Paris: ICOM.

ICOM (1996), *Illicit Traffic of Cultural Property in Africa*, Paris: ICOM, 274.

ICOM (1996), *Illicit Traffic of Cultural Property in Latin America*, Paris: ICOM, 206.

ICOM (1996), *Manuel des normes: Documentation des collections africaines* [*Handbook of Standards: Documenting African Collections*] (also in Arabic), Paris: ICOM, 65.

ICOM (1997), *Atelier sur la protection du patrimoine culturel africain, Amsterdam, 22–24 octobre 1997: documents de travail*, Paris: ICOM.

ICOM (1997), *Pillage à Angkor* [*Looting in Angkor*] réimpression mise à jour, (*Cent objets disparus* [*One Hundred Missing Objects*]) Paris: ICOM-EFEO, p.102.

ICOM (1997), *Pillage en Afrique* [*Looting in Africa*] (*Cent objets disparus* [*One Hundred Missing Objects*]), Paris: ICOM, p.143.

ICOM (1997), *Pillage en Amérique latine* [*Saqueo en América Latina – Looting in Latin America*], (*Cent objets disparus* [*One hundred missing objects*]), Paris: ICOM, p.143.

ICOM (1998), *Actes de l'atelier pour la protection du patrimoine et la lutte contre le trafic illicite des biens culturels dans les pays arabes, Hammamet, Tunisie, 2–4 juin 1998*/ICOM et Institut national du patrimoine de Tunisie, en collaboration avec l'UNESCO, Paris: ICOM, pp.74, 111 (in French and Arabic).

ICOM (2000), *Pillage en Europe* [*Looting in Europe*], (*Cent objets disparus* [*One hundred missing objects*]), Paris: ICOM, p.127.

ICOM (2000), *Red List, Stop the Looting of African Archaeological Objects: Protect Our Common Heritage*, Paris: ICOM, p.8.

ICOM (2003), *Emergency Red List of Iraqi Antiquities at Risk*, (Folder), Paris: ICOM.

ICOM (2003), *Lista roja de bienes culturales latinoamericanos en peligro* [*Red List of Latin-American Cultural Objects at Risk*], Paris: ICOM, p.68.

ICOM (2003), *Liste rouge d'urgence des antiquités irakiennes en péril*, Paris: ICOM.

ICOM (AFRICOM programme) (1996), *Handbook of Standards – Documenting African Collections*, Paris: ICOM.

ICOM/International Committee for Documentation (CIDOC) (1995), *International Directory of Thesauri for Object Names*, edited by T. Petersen and translated by C. Arminjon, (text available in French and English, in print and electronic editions from ICOM or from the *Art and Architecture Thesaurus*), Paris: ICOM.

ICOM/International Committee for Documentation (CIDOC) (1995), *International Guidelines for Museum Object Information: The CIDOC*

Information Categories, (text available in French and English, in print and electronic editions from ICOM or from the *Art and Architecture Thesaurus*), Paris: ICOM.

ICOM ad hoc Committee for the Return of Cultural Property (2009), 'Return of Cultural Property to their Countries of Origin: Bangladesh, Mali, Western Samoa – A Preliminary Survey of Three National Situations', in L.V. Prott (ed.), *Witnesses to History*, Paris: UNESCO, p.182.

ICOM, Comité Peruano (2003), *Encuentro trinacional de lucha contra el tráfico ilícito de bienes culturales*, Lima: Comité Peruano del Consejo Internacional de Museos, 45.

Iglesias Kuntz, Lucía (1999), 'À la recherche de l'art perdu', *Le Courrier de l'UNESCO*, Paris, **52**(3).

Iliadou, E. (2004), 'Common Cultural Heritage and Cultural Pluralism under the EC Treaty', in E. Trova (ed.), *Cultural Heritage and the Law*, Athens-Thessaloniki: Ed. Sakkoulas, p.589.

Impey, Oliver and Arthur McGregor (1985), *The Origins of Museums*, Oxford: Clarendon Press.

Institute of Art and Law (1996), *Export Licensing and the International Market*, papers from a seminar held in London on 19 March 1996, Leicester: Institute of Art and Law.

Institute of Art and Law (1996), *Title and Time in Art and Antiquity Claims*, papers from a Seminar held in London on 19 March 1996, Leicester: Institute of Art and Law.

International Bureau of the Permanent Court of Arbitration (2004), *Resolution of Cultural Property Disputes, Permanent Court of Arbitration/Peace Palace Papers*, The Hague: Kluwer Law International, p.7.

International Bureau of the Permanent Court of Arbitration (ed.) (2004), *Resolution of Cultural Property Disputes: Papers Emanating from the Seventh PCA International Law Seminar, May 23, 2003*, The Hague: Kluwer Law International.

International Bureau of the Permanent Court of Arbitration (ed.) (2004), *Resolution of Cultural Property Disputes*, The Netherlands: Kluwer Law International.

International Committee for Museum Security (ICMS) (2006), *Thefts in Museums: Causes, Effects, Conclusions*, Warsaw, Gdansk: ICMS, 216.

International Institute of Higher Studies in Criminal Sciences (1994), *The Penal Protection of Works of Art*, Syracuse, Italy: IIHSC, Univ. Catania.

International Law Association (ILA) (2004), *Report of the Cultural Heritage Law Committee*, London: ILA.

INTERPOL (1994), *International Criminal Police Review*, Lyon: ICPO-INTERPOL General Secretariat, (448/449), May–June/July–August.

INTERPOL (1997), *Third International Symposium on Works of Art,*

Antiques and Cultural Property, Lyon, France, 1996: Minutes, Lyon: INTERPOL, p.11.

INTERPOL (1998), *Deuxième conférence internationale sur le trafic illicite des œuvres d'art volées dans les pays d'Europe centrale et orientale, Budapest, Hongrie, 9–11 juin 1998: compte rendu*, Lyon: OIPC/INTERPOL, p.27.

INTERPOL (2002), *5th International Symposium on Works of Art, Antiques and Cultural Property, Lyon, 29–31 October 2002: Minutes*, Lyon: INTERPOL, http://www.interpol.int/Public/WorkOfArt/Conferences/Symposium5/Minutes.asp.

INTERPOL (2003), *Conférence internationale sur les biens culturels volés en Iraq, Lyon, 5–6 mai 2003: compte rendu*, Lyon: OIPC/Interpol.

INTERPOL (2004), *Conférence régionale sur le trafic illicite de biens culturels volés en Iraq, Amman, Jordanie, 1er–2 juin 2004: compte rendu et recommandations*, Lyon: INTERPOL, 10 p. & 7 p. d'annexes.

INTERPOL (2004), *Première réunion de la Cellule spéciale d'Interpol chargée de retrouver les biens culturels volés en Irak et de lutter contre le trafic illicite de ces biens, 12 et 13 novembre 2003: recommandations*, Lyon: INTERPOL.

INTERPOL (2004), *Quatrième conférence internationale sur le trafic illicite des biens culturels volés en Europe centrale et orientale, Sinaïa City, Roumanie, 7–9 septembre 2004: recommandations*, Lyon: OIPC/Interpol.

INTERPOL (2004), *Second Meeting of the Interpol Tracking Task Force to Fight the Illicit Trafficking of Cultural Property Stolen in Iraq, Amman, Jordan, 30th and 31st May 2004: Recommendations,* http://www.interpol.int/Public/WorkOfArt/Iraq/meetings/Recommendations200405.asp.

INTERPOL (2005), *6th International Symposium on the Theft of and the Illicit Traffic in Works of Art, Cultural Property and Antiques, Lyon, France, from 21 to 23 June 2005: Recommendations*, Lyon: INTERPOL, http://www.interpol.int/Public/WorkofArt/Conferences/20050621/recommendations.asp.

INTERPOL (2005), *Second Meeting of the Interpol Expert Group (IEG) on Stolen Cultural Property France, Lyon, 22 February 2005: Recommendations,* Lyon: INTERPOL, http://www.interpol.int/Public/WorkOfArt/Conferences/20050222/recommendations.asp.

Ireland, Law Reform Commission (1997), *The Law Reform Commission Report on the UNIDROIT Convention on Stolen and Illegally Exported Cultural Objects*, Dublin: Law Reform Commission.

Isar, Y. Raj (1986), *The Challenge to our Cultural Heritage: Why Preserve the Past? Proceedings of a Conference on Cultural Preservation, Washington, D.C. 8–10 April 1984*, Washington: Smithsonian Institution Press and Paris: UNESCO.

James, T.G.H. (1981), *The British Museum and Ancient Egypt*, London: British Museum Publications.
Jamieson, H.H. (1995), 'The Protection of Australia's Movable Cultural Heritage', *International Journal of Cultural Property*, 4.
Janus, Christopher G. and William Brashler (1975), *The Search for Peking Man*, New York: Macmillan.
Jayme, Eric (2005), 'Globalization in Art Law: Clash of Interests and International Tendencies', *Vanderbilt Journal of Transnational Law*, 928.
Jenkins, P. (1995), *The UNIDROIT Convention on Stolen or Illegally Exported Cultural Objects*, London: UK Department of National Heritage.
Jenkins, P. (1996), 'The UNIDROIT Convention on Stolen and Illegally Exported Cultural Objects', *Art Antiquity and Law*, 1.
Jernigan, Christopher G. (1994), 'Protecting National Treasures in a Single-market EC', *Boston College International and Comparative Law Review*, 17.
Jote, Kifle (1994), *International Legal Protection of Cultural Heritage*, Stockholm: Juristförlaget, 346.
Kaiku, R. (1980), 'Restoration of National Cultural Property: The Case of Papua New Guinea', in R. Edwards and J. Stewart (eds), *Preserving Indigenous Cultures: A New Role for Museums*, Canberra: Australian Government Publishing Service, p.175.
Kaplan, F.E.S. (ed.) (1994), *Museums and the Making of 'Ourselves': The Role of Objects in National Identity*, London: Leicester University Press.
Kaplan, W. (1986), 'Assistance under the 1970 UNESCO Cultural Property Convention: Canada's Request to the United States', *Stanford Journal of International Law*, 22.
Karakostas, I. (1994), 'Archaeological Heritage: The View of the Private Possessor', Institute of Hellenic Constitutional History and Constitutional Law, Archaeological Heritage (International Conference, 1992), *Περιβάλλον & Δίκαιο*, 1.
Karydis, G. (1994), 'Le juge communautaire et la préservation de l'identité culturelle nationale', *Revue Trimestrielle de Droit Européen*, 4.
Kassimatis, G. (ed.) (1995), *Archaeological Heritage: Current Trends in its Legal Protection*, Athens: P. Sakkoulas Bros. Publishers.
Katsirea, I. (2001), *Cultural Diversity and European Integration in Conflict and in Harmony*, Athens-Komotini: Ant. N. Sakkoulas.
Kaye, Lawrence (1996), 'The Future of the Past: Recovering Cultural Property', *Cardozo Journal of International & Comparative Law*, 23.
Kaye, Lawrence M. (1998), 'The Statute of Limitations in Art Recovery Cases: An Overview', *International Foundation for Art Research Journal*, **1**(3).
Kelly, L. and P. Gordon (2002), 'Developing a Community of Practice:

Museums and Reconciliation in Australia', in R. Sandell (ed.), *Museums, Society and Inequality*, London: Routledge, p.153.

Kelly, L., P. Gordon and T. Sullivan (2001), *'We Deal with Relationships: Not just Objects': An Evaluation of Previous Possessions, New Obligations, Green Paper*, Sydney: Australian Museum Audience Research Centre.

Kelly, Michael (1995–6), 'Conflicting Trends in the Flourishing International Trade of Art and Antiquities: Restitutio in Integrum And Possessio Animo', *Dickinson Journal of International Law*, 31.

Kenyon, Andrew and Simon McKenzie (2002), 'Recovering Stolen Art: Legal Understandings in the Australian Art Market', *University of Tasmania Law Review*, 1.

Kiernan, V.G. (1969), *The Lords of Human Kind: European Attitudes to the Outside World in the Imperial Age*, London: Weidenfeld and Nicolson.

Kinderman, Spencer (1993), 'The UNIDROIT Draft Convention on Cultural Objects: An Examination of the Need for a Uniform Legal Framework for Controlling the Illicit Movement of Cultural Property', *Emory International Law Review*, 457.

Kirgis, F.L. (1983), *Prior Consultation in International Law*, Charlottesville: University of Virginia Press.

Kirkpatrick, S.D. (1992), *Lords of Sipan: A True Story of Pre-Inca Tombs, Archaeology, and Crime*, New York: Willima Morrow.

Klausewitz, W. (1985), 'Museumsethik in Deutschland', *Museumskunde*, **50**(1), 2–27.

Knop, K. (2002), *Diversity and Self-Determination in International Law*, Cambridge University Press.

Knox, Christine (2005–6), 'They've Lost their Marbles: 2002 Universal Museums' Declaration, the Elgin Marbles and the Future of the Repatriation Movement', *Suffolk Transnational Law Review*, 315.

König, H. (2007), 'Claims for the Restitution of Holocaust-Era Cultural Assets and their Resolution in Germany', *Art Antiquity and Law*, XII, 59.

Kono, T. (2004), 'UNESCO Convention on the Means of Prohibiting and Preventing the Illicit Import Export and Transfer of Ownership of Cultural Property and its Implementation in Japan', in N. Urtnasan and N. Hellmann (eds), *UNESCO Regional Workshop on the Illicit Traffic of Cultural Property, October 29 – November 2, 2003, Ulaanbaatar*, Bejing: UNESCO Office Bejing, Mongolian National Commission for UNESCO, 62.

Kono, T. (2009), 'Japanese Swords Taken during the Occupation after the Second World War', in L.V. Prott (ed.), *Witnesses to History*, Paris: UNESCO, 173.

Kono, T. and Eriko Kani (2003), 'Japan's Measures for the Implementation of the 1970 Convention', *Art Antiquity and Law* 8, 107.

Korka, Elena (2009), 'Final Synthesis and Conclusions of the Athens Conference', *Museum International*, **61**(1–2).

Koskenniemi, M. (1989), *From Apology to Utopia: The Structure of International Legal Argument*, Cambridge University Press

Kostenevich, Albert (1995), *Hidden Treasures Revealed: Impressionist Masterpieces and Other French Paintings Preserved by the State Hermitage Museum, St. Petersburg*, New York: Harry N. Abrams, Ministry of Culture of the Russian Federation & the State Hermitage Museum.

Koumantos, G. (1995), 'La protection des biens culturels en droit civil', in Institute of Hellenic Constitutional History and Constitutional Law (ed.), *Archaeological Heritage International Conference, Athens 1992*, Athens: Sakkoulas Bros.

Kowalski, W. (1994), *Liquidation of the Effects of World War II in the Area of Culture*, Warsaw: Institute of Culture, p.115.

Kowalski, W. (1996), 'Introduction to International Law of Restitution of Works of Art Looted during Armed Conflicts – Part II', *Spoils of War* (3), December 1996, 10–11, National Archives Library, http://www.dhh-3.de/biblio/bremen/sow3.

Kowalski, W. (1998), *Art Treasures and War: A Study on the Restitution of Looted Cultural Property, Pursuant to Public International Law*, London: Institute of Art and Law.

Kowalski, W. (2001), *Restitution of Works of Art in RCADI*, Vol. 288, p.17

Kowalski, W. (2001), 'Repatriation of Cultural Property following a Cession of Territory or Dissolution of Multinational States', *Art Antiquity and Law*, **VI**, 139.

Kowalski, W. (2002), *Restitution of Works of Art Pursuant to Private and Public International Law in Hague Academy of International Law – Recueil de cours 2002*, The Hague: Martinus Nijhoff.

Kowalski, W. (2005), 'Types of Claims for Recovery of Lost Cultural Property', *MUSEUM International: Protection and restitution*, Volume 57, No. 4, No.228

Kowalski, W. (2009), '"Restitution": Art Treasures and War', in L.V. Prott (ed.), *Witnesses to History*, Paris: UNESCO, p.163.

Kozloff, Arielle (2005), 'The Antiquities Market: When, What, Where, Who, Why . . .', in K. Fitz Gibbon (ed.), *Who Owns the Past? Cultural Policy, Cultural Property and the Law*, New Brunswick, New Jersey and London: Rutgers University Press in association with American Council for Cultural Policy, p.183.

Kreder, Jennifer Anglim (2005), 'The Choice Between Civil and Criminal Remedies in Stolen Art Litigation', *Vanderbilt Journal of Transnational Law*, 1199.

Kroeber, A.L. (1952), *The Nature of Culture*, University of Chicago Press.

Kurtz, Michael J. (1985), *Nazi Contraband: American Policy on the Return of European Cultural Treasures, 1945–1955*, New York: Garland.

Kurzweil, H., L.V. Gagion and L. De Walden (2005), 'The Trial of the Sevso Treasure: What a Nation Will Do in the Name of Its Heritage', in K. Fitz Gibbon (ed.), *Who Owns the Past? Cultural Policy, Cultural Property and the Law*, New Brunswick, New Jersey and London: Rutgers University Press in association with American Council for Cultural Policy, 83.

Lacouture, Jean (1975), *André Malraux*, London: Andre Deutsch, p.49.

Lalive, P. (1975), 'L'application du droit public étranger', Institut de droit International, Annuaire, Session de Wiesbaden, Paris: Karger.

Lalive, P. (1993), 'Le projet de Convention de l'Unidroit sur les biens culturels volés ou illicitement exportés', in M. Briat and J. Freedberg (eds), *Legal Aspects of International Art Trade*, The Hague: Kluwer Law International.

Lalive, P. (1996), 'Réflexions transfrontières sur les biens culturels', *La Comunità Internazionale* 51, 450.

Lalive, P. (1996), 'Une avancée du droit international: la convention de Rome d'UNIDROIT sur les biens culturels volés ou illicitement exportés', *Uniform Law Review*, 1.

Lalive, P. (1997), 'La convention d'UNIDROIT sur les biens culturels volés ou illicitement exportés (du 24 juin 1995)', *Revue Suisse de Droit International et de Droit Européen*, Geneva, **1**, 13.

Lalive, P. (2009), 'A Disturbing International Convention: The UNIDROIT Convention on Cultural Objects', in L.V. Prott (ed.), *Witnesses to History*, Paris: UNESCO, p.322.

Lâm, M.C. (1992), 'Making Room for Peoples at the United Nations: Thoughts Provoked by Indigenous Claims to Self-Determination', *Cornell International Law Journal*, 25.

Lâm, M.C. (2000), 'Indigenous Peoples' Conception of their Self-Determination in International Law', in C. Lynch and M. Loriaux (eds), *Law and Moral Action in World Politics*, Minneapolis: University of Minnesota Press.

Langlois, Walter G. (1966), *André Malraux – the Indo China Adventure*, London: Pall Mall.

Le Coq, Albert von (1928), *Buried Treasures of Chinese Turkestan*, London: Allen and Unwin.

Le Farge, Henry (ed.) (1946), *Lost Treasures of Europe*, London: B. J. Batsford; New York: Pantheon Books.

Leakey, Mary (1984), *Disclosing the Past*, London: Weidenfeld and Nicholson.

Lecrenier, S. (1990), *La libre circulation des œuvres d'art dans la Communauté Européenne*, Paris: ICC Publishing/Kluwer, Law and Taxation Publishers.

Lee, R.F. (2000), 'The Antiquities Act', *Journal of the Southwest*, 42.

Legendre, Jacques (2003), *La protection des biens culturels africains: actes du colloque du 28 mars 2003*, Paris: Sénat, p.63.

Legget, J. (2000), *Restitution and Repatriation: Guidelines for Good Practice*, London: Museums and Galleries Commission.

Lehman, Jennifer (1997), 'The Continued Struggle with Stolen Cultural Property: The Hague Convention, the UNESCO Convention, and the UNIDROIT Draft Convention', *Arizona Journal of International and Comparative Law*, 527.

Lenzner, N. (1994), 'The Illicit International Trade in Cultural Property: Does the UNIDROIT Convention Provide an Effective Remedy for the Shortcomings of the UNESCO Convention?', *University of Pennsylvania Journal of International Business Law*, **15**, 469.

Leonhard, Adam (1949), *Primitive Art*, Harmondsworth: Pelican.

Lerner, Ralph E. and Judith Bresler (2005), *Art Law: The Guide for Collectors, Investors, Dealers and Artists*, 3rd edition, New York: Practising Law Institute.

Levenson, Jay A. (1991), *Circa 1492: Art in the Age of Exploration*, New Haven: Yale University Press.

Lewis, G. (1992), 'Cultural Property in the Community', in S. Pearce (ed.), *Museums and Europe 1992*, London: The Athlone Press, New Jersey: Atlantic Highlands.

Lewis, G. (2004), 'Legal and Ethical Considerations in the Repatriation of Stolen and Illegally Exported Cultural Property: Is There a Means to Settle Disputes?', http://icom.museum.

Lewis, G. (2006), 'The "Universal Museum": a case of special pleading?', in B.T. Hoffman (ed), *Art and Cultural Heritage. Law, Policy and Practice*, Cambridge University Press.

Lewis G. (2009), 'A View in 1981 on the Founding of the Committee', in L.V. Prott (ed.), *Witnesses to History*, Paris: UNESCO, p.29.

Ley, John (1991), *Australia's Protection of Movable Cultural Heritage*, Canberra: Australian Government Publishing Service.

Leyten, Harrie (ed.) (1995), *Illicit Traffic in Cultural Property: Museums against Pillage*, Amsterdam: Royal Tropical Institute in collaboration with Musée National du Mali, Bamako, p.104.

Lipe, William D. (1974), 'A Conservation Model for American Archaeology', *The Kiva*, **39**(1–2).

Lipe, William D. (1984), 'Value and Meaning in Cultural Resources', in Henry Cleere (ed.), *Approaches to the Archaeological Heritage: A*

Comparative Study of World Cultural Resource Management Systems, Cambridge University Press.

Lissnar, Ivar (1957), *The Living Past–The Great Civilization of Mankind*, translated from German by J. Maxwell Brownjohn, London: The Reprint Society & Jonathan Cape.

Liston, David (ed.) (1993), *Museum Security and Protection: A Handbook for Cultural Heritage Institutions,* London, New York: ICOM and Routledge.

Lloyd, Seton (1947), *Foundations in the Dust*, London: Oxford University Press.

Lomans, A., K. Mortelmans, H. Post and J.Watson (1992), *Culture and Community Law–Before and after Maastricht*, Netherlands: Kluwer Law and Taxation Publishers.

Lowenthal, Constance (1991), 'Stolen Art: A Positive Move toward International Harmony', *Museum News*, **70**(5).

Lowenthal, D. (1985), *The Past is a Foreign Country*, Cambridge University Press.

Lowenthal, D. (1990), 'Conclusion: Archaeologists and Others', in P. Gathercole and D. Lowenthal (eds), *The Politics of the Past*, London: Unwin Hyman, p.302.

Lynott, Mark J. and Alison Wylie (eds) (2000), *Ethics in American Archaeology*, 2nd revised edition, Washington, D.C.: Society for American Archaeology.

M'Bow, A.M. (1979), 'Plea for the Return of an Irreplaceable Heritage to "Those Who Created It": An Appeal by the Director-General of UNESCO', *Museum*, 31.

M'Bow, A.M. (2009), 'A Plea for the Return of an Irreplaceable Cultural Heritage to Those Who Created It', in L.V. Prott (ed.), *Witnesses to History*, Paris: UNESCO, p.30.

Macdonald, R.R. (1993), 'A Code of Ethics for United States Museums', *Museum International*, 177.

Maclagan, Eric (1949), *The Bayeux Tapestry*, Harmondsworth: Penguin.

Macpherson, C.P. (1962), *The Political Theory of Possessive Individualism: Hobbes to Locke*, Oxford: Clarendon Press.

Magán Perales, José María (2001), *La circulación ilícita de bienes culturales*, Madrid: Lex Nova, p.526.

Magnusson, Magnus (1980), 'Can we Have our Past back?' in *Magnus on the Move*, Edinburgh: Macdonald, 73.

Magnusson, Magnus (1987), *Iceland Saga*, London: Bodley Head.

Malraux, André (1967), *Museums without Walls*, London: Secker and Warburg.

Malraux, André (1968), *Antimemoirs*, London: Hamish Hamilton.

Malraux, André (1978), *The Voices of Silence*, Princeton University Press.

Maniscalco, Fabio (2006), 'Archaeological Looting and the Protection of Cultural Property in Nigeria', *Webjournal on cultural patrimony*, Università degli Studi di Napoli, 1.

Mann, Vivian B. (1989), *Gardens and Ghettos: The Art of Jewish Life in Italy*, Berkeley: University of California Press.

Margue, T. (1993), 'L'Exportation des Biens Culturels dans le Cadre du Grande Marché', *Revue du Marché Unique Européen*, p.2.

Mariam, Haile (2009), 'The Cultural Benefits of the Return of the Axum Obelisk', *Museum International*, **61**(1–2).

Marin, Jean-Yves (2003), 'Œuvres d'art: halte au pillage', *Le Monde*, Paris, 7 May 15.

Marks, P. (1998), 'The Ethics of Art Dealing', *International Journal of Cultural Property*, **7**, 116.

Marks, P. (ed.) (2005), 'Dealers Speak', in K. Fitz Gibbon (ed.), *Who Owns the Past? Cultural Policy, Cultural Property and the Law*, New Brunswick, New Jersey and London: Rutgers University Press in association with American Council for Cultural Policy, p.191.

Marques dos Santos, A. (1996), 'Projecto de Convenção do. UNIDROIT sobre a Restituição Internacional dos Bens Culturals Roubados ou Ilicitamente Epxortados', in Instituto Nacional de Administracao, *Direito do Património Cultural*, Oeiras: Instituto Nacional de Administracao, p.61.

Mason, Sir Anthony (1998), 'Exploiting the Weaker Party: Unconscionable, Unequal and Disadvantageous Transactions in Art', in Norman Palmer (ed.), *The Recovery of Stolen Art: A Collection of Essays,* London: Kluwer Law International, 109.

Massy, Laurence (1997), 'La protection du patrimoine religieux en Pologne: présentation de la situation', *La Vie des musées*, Brussels: AFMB/ICOM Wallonie-Bruxelles, 12, 87.

Massy, Laurence (2000), *Le vol d'œuvres d'art: une criminalité méconnue*, Brussels: Bruylant, 202.

Mastalir, R.W. (1992–3), 'A Proposal for Protecting the "Cultural" and "Property" Aspects of Cultural Property under International Law', *Fordham International Law Journal*, 16.

Matsuda, David (2005), 'Subsistence Diggers', in K. Fitz Gibbon (ed.), *Who Owns the Past? Cultural Policy, Cultural Property and the Law*, New Brunswick, New Jersey and London: Rutgers University Press in association with American Council for Cultural Policy, p.255.

Mattera, A. (1990), 'La règle dérogatoire de l'article 36 du Traité CEE, la protection du patrimoine artistique, historique ou archéologique national et la libre circulation des objets d'art à l'intérieur de la

Communauté', in *Le Marché Unique Européen, ses règles, son fonctionnement,* Paris: Jupiter, 2nd edition.
Mattera, A. (1993), 'La libre circulation des œuvres d'art à l'intérieur de la Communauté et la protection des trésors nationaux ayant une valeur artistique, historique ou archéologique', *Revue du Marché Unique Européen*, 2.
Matyk, S. (2009), 'The Cypriot Icons in the Netherlands (Lans Case)', in L.V. Prott (ed.), *Witnesses to History*, Paris: UNESCO, p.386.
Maurer, E. (1997), 'The Role of the State Department regarding National and Private Claims for the Restitution of Stolen Cultural Property', in Elizabeth Simpson (ed.), *The Spoils of War: World War II and Its Aftermath: The Loss, Reappearance and Recovery of Cultural Property*, New York: Harry N. Abrams.
Maurice, C. and R. Turnor (1992), 'The Export Licensing Rules in the United Kingdom and the Waverley Criteria', *International Journal of Cultural Property*, 1.
Mayo, Margaret Ellen (2005), 'Collecting Ancient Art: A Historical Perspective', in K. Fitz Gibbon (ed.), *Who Owns the Past? Cultural Policy, Cultural Property and the Law*, New Brunswick, New Jersey and London: Rutgers University Press in association with American Council for Cultural Policy, p.133.
McIntosh, Molly L. (2006–7), 'Exploring Machu Picchu: An Analysis of the Legal and Ethical Issues Surrounding the Repatriation of Cultural Property', *Duke Journal of Comparative & International Law*, 199.
McIntosh, R.J. and S.K. McIntosh (1986), 'Dilettantisme et pillage: trafic illicite d'objets d'art anciens du Mali', *Museum International*, Paris: UNESCO, **38** (1).
McIntosh, R.J. and Peter R. Schmidt, (eds) (1996), *Plundering Africa's Past*, Bloomington: Indiana University Press, p.289.
McIntosh R.J., T. Togola and S.K. McIntosh (1995), 'The Good Collector and the Premise of Mutual Respect among Nations', *African Arts*, Autumn 1995, 60.
McKenzie, Simon (2002), 'Illicit Antiquities, Criminological Theory and the Deterrent Power of Criminal Sanctions for Targeted Populations', *Art Antiquity and Law*, **7**(2).
McKenzie, S.R.M. (2005), *Going, Going, Gone: Regulating the Market in Illicit Antiquities*, London: Institute of Art and Law.
McLeod, M.D. (1981), *The Asante*, London: British Museum Publications.
Mead, H.M. (1990), *The Wanderings of the Carved House, Mataatua*, Whakatane, New Zealand: Te Runanga o Ngati Awa.
Mead, H.M. (2009), 'The Mataatua Declaration and the Case of the

Carved Meeting House, Mataatua', in L.V. Prott (ed.), *Witnesses to History*, Paris: UNESCO, p.208.
Melikian, S. (1995), 'A Degree of Destruction Unprecedented in the History of the World – And Yet I Support Collecting', *The Art Newspaper* (52), October 1995, 27.
Merrill, W.L., E.J. Ladd and T.J. Ferguson (2009), 'The Return of the Ahayu:da to Zuni Pueblo', in L.V. Prott (ed.), *Witnesses to History*, Paris: UNESCO, p.255.
Merrill, W.I., E.J. Ladd and T.J. Ferguson (2009), 'The Smithsonian Institution', in L.V. Prott (ed.), *Witnesses to History*, Paris: UNESCO, p.257.
Merrills, J.G. (1987), 'The Role and Limits of International Adjudication', in Butler, W.E. (ed.), *International Law and the International System*, Dordrecht: M. Nijhoff.
Merryman, J.H. (2000), *Thinking about the Elgin Marbles: Critical Essays on Cultural Property, Art and Law*, The Hague: Kluwer Law International.
Merryman, J.H. (ed.) (2006), *Imperialism, Art and Restitution*, Cambridge University Press.
Merryman, J.H. (1974), 'A Course in Art and the Law', *Journal of Legal Education*, 26.
Merryman, J.H. (1983), 'International Art Law: From Cultural Nationalism to a Common Cultural Heritage', *New York University Journal of International Law and Politics*, 15.
Merryman, J.H. (1985), 'Thinking of the Elgin Marbles', *Michigan Law Review*, 83.
Merryman, J.H. (1986) 'Two ways of thinking about cultural property', *American Journal of International Law*, 80.
Merryman, J.H. (1988), 'The Retention of Cultural Property', *University of California Davis Law Review*, 21.
Merryman, J.H. (1989), 'Cultural Property Export Controls', *UFITA*, 63.
Merryman, J.H. (1989), 'The Public Interest in Cultural Property', *California Law Review*, 77.
Merryman, J.H. (1990), 'Projection of the Cultural Heritage. U.S. Law in an Era of Democratization: Section IV', *American Journal of Comparative Law Supplement*, 38.
Merryman, J.H. (1992), 'Limits on State Recovery of Stolen Artifacts: Peru v. Johnson', *International Journal of Cultural Property*, **1**(1).
Merryman, J.H. (1994), 'The Nation and the Object', *International Journal of Cultural Property*, 3.
Merryman, J.H. (1995), 'A Licit International Trade in Cultural Objects', *International Journal of Cultural Property*, 4.

Merryman, J.H. (1995), 'What do Matisse, Van Gogh and Hitler Have in Common?', *University of British Columbia Law Review*, 273.

Merryman, J.H. (1996), 'Archaeologists Are not Helping', *The Art Newspaper*, London, VII (55), January 1996, 26.

Merryman, J.H. (1996), 'Note on the Marquis de Somerueles', *International Journal of Cultural Property*, 5.

Merryman, J.H. (1996), 'The UNIDROIT Convention: Three Significant Departures from the Urtext', *International Journal of Cultural Property*, **5**, 11.

Merryman, J.H. (1998), 'Cultural Property Ethics', *International Journal of Cultural Property*, **7**, 1.

Merryman, J.H. (1998), 'The Free International Movement of Cultural Property', *New York University Journal of International Law and Politics*, **31**(1), 1–14, available at www.law.nyu.edu/journals/jilp/main/issues/31/pdf/31a.pdf, www.culturalpolicycouncil.org/readings/MerrymanFreeInternationalMovement.pdf.

Merryman, J.H. (2000), 'Cultural Property, International Trade, and Human Rights', *Occasional Papers in Intellectual Property*, New York, NY: Benjamin N. Cardozo School of Law, Yeshiva University, **9**, 21, http://www.cardozo.yu.edu/news_events/papers/9.pdf.

Merryman, J.H. (2001), 'Cultural Property, International Trade and Human Rights', *Cardozo Arts & Entertainment*, 51.

Merryman, J.H. (2002), 'Who Owns the Past?' in J.H. Merryman & A.E. Elsen (eds.), *Law, Ethics and the Visual Arts*, 4th edition, the Netherlands: Kluwer Law International.

Merryman, J.H. (2005), 'A Licit International Trade in Cultural Objects', in K. Fitz Gibbon, *Who Owns the Past? Cultural Policy, Cultural Property and the Law*, New Brunswick, New Jersey and London: Rutgers University Press in association with American Council for Cultural Policy, p.269.

Merryman, J.H. (2005), 'Cultural Property Internationalism', *International Journal of Cultural Property*, **12**(1).

Merryman, J.H. (2006), 'Whither the Elgin Marbles?', in J.H. Merryman (ed), *Imperialism, Art and Restitution*, Cambridge University Press.

Merryman, J.H. and A.E. Elsen (2002), *Law, Ethics, and the Visual Arts*, London, New York: Kluwer Law International, xviii, 1342.

Merryman, J.H. and J.A.R. Nafziger (1994), 'Private International Law of Cultural Property in the United States', *American Journal of Comparative Law Supplement*, 42.

Messenger, Phyllis Mauch (ed.) (1999), *The Ethics of Collecting Cultural Property: Whose culture? Whose property?*, 2nd updated and enlarged edition, Albuquerque: University of New Mexico Press, pp.xxviii, 301.

Meyer, K.E. (1972), *The Maya Crisis: A Report on the Pillaging of Maya Sites in Mexico and Guatemala*, New York: Center for Inter-American Relations.

Meyer, K.E. (1973), *The Plundered Past*, New York: Atheneum.

Michaelis, Adolf (1871), *Der Parthenon*, Leipzig: von Brietkopf und Hartel (in German).

Michaelis, Adolf (1882), *Ancient Marbles in Great Britain*, translated by C.A.M. Fennell, Cambridge University Press.

Mihan, George (1944), *Looted Treasure: Germany's Raid on Art*, London: Alliance.

Mihesuah, D.A. (2000), *Repatriation Reader: Who Owns American Indian Remains?* Lincoln: University of Nebraska Press.

Mille, G. (2009), 'The Return of Cultural Heritage from Denmark to Greenland', *Museum International*, 61(1–2).

Mille, G. and J. Dahl (eds) (2008), *UTIMUT: Past Heritage, Future Partnerships. Discussions on Repatriation in the 21st Century*, Copenhagen: Greenland National Museum and Archives (NKA)/International Work Group for Indigenous Affairs (IWGIA), (Papers from the Conference on Repatriation of Cultural Heritage, Nuuk, Greenland 13–15 February 2007).

Miller, Crane H. (1973), *International Law and Marine Archaeology*, Massachusetts Academy of Applied Science.

Miller, Mary Ellen (1986), *The Art of Mesoamerica*, London: Thames and Hudson.

Miniham, J. (1977), *The Nationalization of Culture: The Development of State Subsidies to the Arts in Great Britain*, London: Hamish Hamilton.

Ministerial Advisory Panel on Illicit Trade (2000), *Report*, London: Department for Culture, Media and Sport.

Ministerio de Cultura, Colombia (2003), *III Taller regional contra el tráfico ilícito de bienes culturales muebles. Taller de preparación de la Lista roja de bienes culturales en peligro en América Latina : Memorias Talleres, 23 al 26 de abril de 2002, Bogotá, Colombia/Jorge Caballero (coord.)*, Bogotá: Imprenta Nacional, 167 (Campaña nacional contra el tráfico ilícito de bienes culturales muebles).

Ministerio de Cultura, Colombia (2003), *Programa de formación: Acercamiento a la valoración y protección del patrimonio cultural mueble. Memorias de los cursos 2000–2002, Bogotá, Cartagena, Medellín, Cali, Bucamaranga, Manizales, Santa Marta*, Bogotá: Imprenta Nacional, 133 (Campaña nacional contra el tráfico ilícito de bienes culturales).

Monreal, Luis (2001), 'Reconstitution de patrimoines culturels dispersés: problèmes et possibilités', *Museum International*, Paris: UNESCO, No. 212 (vol. 53, No.4), Oct.-Dec., 73.

Montagu, A. (1993–1994), 'Recent Cases on the Recovery of Stolen Art – The Tug of War between Owners and Good Faith Purchasers', *Columbia VLA (Volunteer Lawyers for the Arts) Journal of Law and the Arts*, 18.
Montejo, V.D. (1999), 'The Year Bearer's People: Repatriation of Ethnographic and Sacred Knowledge to the Jakaltek Maya of Guatemala', *International Journal of Cultural Property*, 8.
Morin, E. και S. Nair (1998), Μια πολιτική πολιτισμού, Μετάφραση από τα Γαλλικά, Αθήνα: Νέα Σύνορα Λιβάνης.
Morin, Edgar (1987), *L'Imperialismo Culturale*, Athens: Herodotos.
Morris, Ramona (2005), 'ATADA: Building Ethical Consensus through Trade Organization', in K. Fitz Gibbon (ed.), *Who Owns the Past? Cultural Policy, Cultural Property and the Law*, New Brunswick, New Jersey and London: Rutgers University Press in association with American Council for Cultural Policy, p.201.
Mosuwadoga, G. (1980), 'Restitution of Collections', *Council of Museum Anthropologists Bulletin*, 5.
Moulin, Annie (1997), 'Œuvres d'art et antiquités (S.A.G.P.)', *La Vie des musées*, Brussels: AFMB/ICOM Wallonie-Bruxelles, 12.
Moustakas, J. (1984), 'Group Rights in Cultural Property: Justifying Strict Inalienability', *Cornell Law Review*, 74.
Muensterberger, W. (1994), *Collecting: An Unruly Passion: Psychological Perspectives*, Princeton University Press.
Mulongo, A.H. (1992) *Retour et restitution des biens culturels, L'affaire du crâne de Broken Hill, Museum*, Paris: UNESCO, No. 174, Vol. XLIV, No. 2.
Müller-Katzenburg, A. (1996), *Internationale Standards im Kulturgüterverkehr und ihre Bedeutung für das Sach- und Kollisionsrecht*, Berlin: Duncker & Humblot.
Müller-Katzenburg, A (2009), 'Possession and Ownership of Stolen or Otherwise Lost Works of Art', in L.V. Prott (ed.), *Witnesses to History*, Paris: UNESCO, 314.
Mulvaney, John (1985), 'A Question of Values: Museums and Cultural Property', in *Who owns the past?*, Oxford University Press.
Munjeri, Dawson (2009), 'The Reunification of a National Symbol', *Museum International*, **61**(1–2).
Murphy, B. (2009), 'Sharing Knowledge: Digital Heritage', in L.V. Prott (ed.), *Witnesses to History*, Paris: UNESCO, p.254.
Murphy, J.D. (1994), 'The People's Republic of China and the Illicit Trade in Cultural Property', *International Journal of Cultural Property*, **3**(2).
Murphy, J.D. (1995), 'The Imperilment of Cultural Property in the People's Republic of China', *University of British Columbia Law Review*, Special Issue, 91.

Murphy, J.D. (1995), *Plunder and Preservation: Cultural Property Law and Practice in the People's Republic of China*, Oxford University Press, pp.xvi, 205.

Museums and Galleries Commission (United Kingdom) (2000), *Restitution and Repatriation: Guidelines for Good Practice*, London: Museums and Galleries Commission.

Museums and Galleries Commission (United Kingdom) (2009), 'Excerpts from "Restitution and Repatriation: Guidelines for Good Practice" 2000', in L.V. Prott (ed.), *Witnesses to History*, Paris: UNESCO, p.130.

Myles, K. (1982), *Should Finding Mean Keeping? UNESCO Radio*, Doc. PI/R/1825, Paris: UNESCO.

Nafziger, J.A.R. (1972), 'Regulation by the International Council of Museums: An Example of the Role of Non-Governmental Organizations in the Transnational Legal Process', *Denver Journal of International Law and Policy*, 2.

Nafziger, J.A.R. (1975), 'Article 7 (a) of the UNESCO Convention' in L.D. DuBoff (ed.) *Art Law: Domestic and International*, South Hackensack: Fred B. Rothman & Co., 387.

Nafziger, J.A.R. (1983), 'Comments on the Relevance of Law and Culture to Cultural Property Law', *Syracuse Journal of International Law & Commerce*, 10.

Nafziger, J.A.R. (1985), 'International Penal Aspects of Protecting Cultural Property', *International Lawyer*, 19.

Nafziger, J.A.R. (1987), 'Repose Legislation: A Threat to the Protection of the World's Cultural Heritage', *California Western International Law Journal* 250.

Nafziger, J.A.R. (1995), 'The New Fiduciary Duty of United States Museums to Repatriate Cultural Heritage: The Oregon Experience', *University of British Columbia Law Review*, 29.

Nafziger, J.A.R. (1998), 'Seizure and Forfeiture of Cultural Property by the United States', *Villanova Sports & Entertainment Law Journal*, 5.

Nafziger, J.A.R. (1999), 'The Native Americans Graves Protection and Repatriation Act in its First Decade', *International Journal of Cultural Property*, 8.

Nagashima, M. (2002), *The Lost Heritage: The Reality of Artifact Smuggling in Southeast Asia*, Bangkok: Post Books.

Nahlik, S.E. (1967), 'La protection internationale des biens culturels en cas de conflit armé', *Recueil des Cours de l'Académie de Droit International de La Haye*, 120.

Nahlik, S.E. (1980), 'The Case of the Displaced Art Treasures', *German Yearbook of International Law*, 23.

Nahlik, S.E. (1981–3), 'International Co-operation to Prevent Illicit Traffic of Cultural Property', *Annuaire de l'Association des Anciens Auditeurs de l'Académie de la Haye*, 51.

Nahlik, S.E. (ed.) (1988), *International Dimensions of Humanitarian Law*, Paris: UNESCO.

Narajno, T. (1996), 'Musing on Two World Views', in B. Meister (ed.), *Mending the Circle: A Native Smithsonian and other Repatriation Policies*, New York: American Indian Ritual Object Repatriation Foundation, 27.

Nason, J.A. (1997), 'Beyond Repatriation: Cultural Policy and Practice for the Twenty-First Century', in B. Ziff and P.V. Pao (eds), *Borrowed Power: Essays on Cultural Appropriation*, New Brunswick: Rutgers University Press, p.291.

Neeru, Misra (2003), *Prevention of Illicit Traffic in Cultural Property, New Delhi, 25 July 2003: Workshop Proceedings*, New Delhi: UNESCO New Delhi Office, 60.

Négri, Vincent (1997), 'Genèse et principes de la convention UNIDROIT du 24 juin 1995 sur les biens culturels volés ou illicitement exportés', *ICOM France*, lettre du Comité national français, Paris, (22), octobre 1997.

Nicholas, H. Lynn (1994), *The Rape of Europa: The Fate of Europe's Treasures in the Third Reich and the Second World War*, New York: Alfred A. Knopf.

Nicholas, T. (1993) 'EEC Measures on the Treatment of National Treasures', *Loyola of Los Angeles International and Comparative Law Review*, 16.

Nicklin, Keith (1981), 'Pillage et restitution: à propos de la région de Cross River, Nigéria', *Museum international*, Paris: UNESCO, **33**(4), 259.

Niec, H. (1971), 'Sovereign Rights to Cultural Property', *Polish Yearbook of International Law*, 4.

Niec, H. (1980), *Ojezyzna Dzieta Sztuki*, Warsaw-Krakow: Panstwowe Wydawnictwo Naukowe.

Niec, H. (ed.) (1998), *Cultural Rights and Wrongs*, Paris: UNESCO.

Niedobitek, M. (1995), 'Die Kulturelle Dimension im Vertrag über die Europäische Union', *Europarecht*, 349.

Nielsen-Becker, Hans and Ole Widding (1972), *Arne Magnusson, the Great Manuscript Collector (Arne Magnusson. Der Store handskriftsamler)*, translated by Robert W. Mattil, Odense: Odense University Press.

Niezen, R. (2000), *Spirit Wars: Native North American Religions in the Age of Nation Building*, Berkeley: University of California Press.

Niezen, R. (2003), *The Origins of Indigenism: Human Rights and the Politics of Identity*, Berkeley: University of California Press.

Noonan, Rebecca (2005), 'Immunity from Seizure?', in K. Fitz Gibbon (ed.), *Who Owns the Past? Cultural Policy, Cultural Property and the*

Law, New Brunswick, New Jersey and London: Rutgers University Press in association with American Council for Cultural Policy, p.45.

Noorbergen, Rene (1983), *Treasures of Lost Races – Discovering the Riches of Ancient Civilizations*, London: W. H. Allen.

Nott, S. (1984), 'Title to Illegally Exported Items of Historic or Artistic Worth', *International Comparative Law Quarterly*, 206.

O'Connell, Mary Ellen (2004), 'Occupation Failures and the Legality of Armed Conflict: The Case of Iraqi Property', *Art Antiquity and Law*, **9**(4), December.

O'Keefe, P.J. (1994), *Feasibility of an International Code of Ethics for Dealers in Cultural Property for the Purpose of More Effective Control of Illicit Traffic in Cultural Property*, UNESCO Document CLT-94/ WS/11, Paris: UNESCO, 99, http://unesdoc.UNESCO.org/images/0009/000985/098554Eo.pdf.

O'Keefe, P.J. (1997), *Le Commerce des antiquités: combattre les destructions et le vol*, Paris: Editions UNESCO, p.158.

O'Keefe, P.J. (1997), *Trade in Antiquities: Reducing Destruction and Theft*, Paris: UNESCO and London: Archetype.

O'Keefe, P.J. (2000), *Commentary on the UNESCO 1970 Convention on Illicit Traffic*, Leicester: Institute of Art and Law.

O'Keefe, P.J. (2002), *Shipwrecked Heritage: A Commentary on the UNESCO Convention on Underwater Cultural Heritage*, Leicester: Institute of Art and Law.

O'Keefe, P.J. (1994), 'Mauritius Scheme for the Protection of Material Cultural Heritage', *International Journal of Cultural Property*, **3**(2).

O'Keefe, P.J. (1995), 'Protection of the Material Cultural Heritage: The Commonwealth Scheme', *International and Comparative Law Quarterly*, 44.

O'Keefe, P.J. (1995), 'Provenance and Trade in Cultural Heritage', *University of British Columbia Law Review*, Special Issue, 259.

O'Keefe, P.J. (1996), 'Activities of International Organisations in the Protection of Cultural Objects', *International Legal Consultant, Cultural and Natural Heritage Law*, 88.

O'Keefe, P.J. (1998), 'Dealers Ethics and Theft', in Norman Palmer (ed.), *The Recovery of Stolen Art: A Collection of Essays,* London: Kluwer Law International, p.201.

O'Keefe, P.J. (2001), 'Unlawful Traffic In Cultural Heritage and UNESCO', *Media & Arts Law Review*, 139–141.

O'Keefe, P.J. (2006), 'Using UNIDROIT to Avoid Cultural Heritage Disputes: Limitation Periods', *Willamette Journal of International Law & Dispute Resolution*, 227.

O'Keefe, P.J. (2007), *Commentary on the UNESCO 1970 Convention on Illicit Traffic*, 2nd edition, Crickadarn: Institute of Art and Law.
O'Keefe, P.J. (2009), 'A Comparison of the Washington and Vilnius Principles and Resolution 1205', in L.V. Prott (ed.), *Witnesses to History*, Paris: UNESCO, p.158.
O'Keefe, P.J. (2009), 'Repatriation of Sacred Objects', in L.V. Prott (ed.), *Witnesses to History*, Paris: UNESCO, p.225.
O'Keefe, P.J. (2009), 'The Tattooed Maori Head (toi moko) in the City of Rouen Museum', in L.V. Prott (ed.), *Witnesses to History*, Paris: UNESCO, p.290.
O'Keefe, P.J. and L.V. Prott (1989), *Law and the Cultural Heritage: Volume I: Discovery and Excavation* and *Volume III: Movement*, London: Butterworths.
O'Keefe, R. (1999), 'The meaning of 'cultural property' under the 1954 Hague Convention', *Netherlands International Law Review*, 26.
Olivier M. (1996), 'The UNIDROIT Convention: Attempting to Regulate the International Trade and Traffic of Cultural Property', *Golden Gate University Law Review*, 26.
Ortiz, G. (1994), *The George Ortiz Collection: In Pursuit of the Absolute: Art of the Ancient World*, London: Royal Academy of Arts.
OSS Art Looting Investigation Unit (2000), *Reports, 1945–46*, Washington, D.C.: National Archives and Records Administration, (microfilm), http://www.archives.gov/research_room/holocaust_era_assets/art_provenance_and_claims/oss_art_looting_investigation_unit_reports.html
Palmer, N. (ed.) (1998), *The Recovery of Stolen Art: A Collection of Essays*, London: Kluwer Law International.
Palmer, N. (1993), 'Treasure Trove and Title to Discovered Antiquities', *International Journal of Cultural Property*, 2.
Palmer, N. (1995), Editorial, *International Journal of Cultural Property*, 4.
Palmer, N. (1998), 'Conversion, Trespass and Title to Art Works', in *The Recovery of Stolen Art: A Collection of Essays,* London: Kluwer Law International, p.33.
Palmer, N. (1998), 'Statutory, Forensic and Ethical Initiatives in the Recovery of Stolen Art and Antiquities', in *The Recovery of Stolen Art: A Collection of Essays,* London: Kluwer Law International, p.1.
Palmer, N. (2000), *Museums and the Holocaust: Law, Principle and Practice*, Leicester: Institute of Art and Law.
Palmer, N. (2003), 'Arbitration and the Applicable Law', in The Permanent Court of Arbitration/Peace Palace Papers (ed.), *Resolution of Cultural Property Disputes*, Kluwer Law International, p.291.
Palmer, N. (2003), 'Litigation, the Best Remedy?', in The Permanent Court

of Arbitration/Peace Palace Papers (ed.), *Resolution of Cultural Property Disputes*, Kluwer Law International, p.265.

Palmer, N. (2007), 'Spoliation and Holocaust-Related Cultural Objects: Legal and Ethical Models for the Resolution of Claims', *Art Antiquity and Law*, **XII**, 1.

Palmer, N. (2009), 'Litigation: The Best Remedy?', in L.V. Prott (ed.), *Witnesses to History*, Paris: UNESCO, p.358.

Palmer, N. and Anthony Hudson (1998), 'Improving Stolen Art', in Norman Palmer (ed.), *The Recovery of Stolen Art: A Collection of Essays,* London: Kluwer Law International, p.127.

Palmer, N. and J. Goyder (1992), 'Free Movement of Cultural Goods and the European Community', in S. Pearce (ed.), *Museums and Europe 1992*, London: The Athlone Press, New Jersey: Atlantic Highlands.

Pantos, P. (2005), *Codification of the Legislation on Cultural Heritage*, t. I and t. II, Athens: Greek Ministry of Culture.

Papademetriou, Theresa (1996), 'International Aspects of Cultural Property: An Overview of Basic Instruments and Issues', *International Journal of Legal Information*, 270.

Papageorge Kouroupas, M. (1998), 'Illicit Trade in Cultural Objects', *The Getty Conservation Institute Newsletter*, 13.

Papagiannis, D. (2004), 'The Notion of Cultural Goods under Community Law', in E. Trova (ed.), *Cultural Heritage and the Law*, Athens-Thessaloniki: Ed. Sakkoulas, 607.

Park, Sue (2002), 'The Cultural Property Regime in Italy: An Industrialized Source Nation's Difficulties in Retaining and Recovering its Antiquities', *University of Pennsylvania Journal of International Business Law*, 931.

Parkhouse A. (2006), 'The Illicit Trade in Cultural Objects: Recent Developments in the United Kingdom', in B.T. Hoffman (ed), *Art and Cultural Heritage. Law, Policy and Practice*, Cambridge University Press.

Parsons, N. and A.K. Segobye (2009), 'From Banyoles to Botsawa: The Return of a Bushman to Africa', in L.V. Prott (ed.), *Witnesses to History*, Paris: UNESCO, 391.

Paterson, R. (1993), 'Bolivian Textiles in Canada', *International Journal of Cultural Property*, 2.

Paterson, R.K. (1996), 'The "Curse of the London Nataraja"', in Canadian Museums Association, *Legal Affairs and Management Symposium, Ottawa, 1–2 March 1996*, Ottawa: Canada Museums Association, p.251.

Paterson, R.K. (2006), 'Resolving Material Culture Disputes: Human Rights, Property Rights and Crimes against Humanity', *Willamette Journal of International Law and Dispute Resolution*, 14.

Patt, Jodi (2001–2), 'The Need to Revamp Current Domestic Protection for Cultural Property', *Northwestern University Law Review*, 1207.

Pearce, S.M. (1995), *On Collecting: An Investigation into Collecting in the European Tradition*, London: Routledge.

Pearlstein, William G. (2005), 'Cultural Property, Congress, the Courts and Customs: The Decline and Fall of the Antiquities Market?', in K. Fitz Gibbon (ed.), *Who Owns the Past? Cultural Policy, Cultural Property and the Law*, New Brunswick, New Jersey and London: Rutgers University Press in association with American Council for Cultural Policy, p.9.

Pearson, Kenneth and Patricia Connor (1968), *The Dorak Affair*, New York: Atheneum.

Peers, L.L. and Brown, A.K. (eds) (2003), *Museums and Source Communities: A Routledge Reader*, London: Routledge.

Pendergast, D.M. (1991), 'And the Loot Goes on: Winning Some Battles, but not the War', *Journal of Field Archaeology*, **18**(1).

Pendergast, D.M. (1994), 'Looting the Maya World: The Other Losers', *Public Archaeology Review*, 2, September, 2.

Penslar, Robin Levin (ed.) (1995), *Research Ethics: Cases and Materials*, Bloomington: Indiana University Press.

Pentz, P. (ed.) (2004), *Utimut – Return*, Copenhagen: National Museum of Denmark.

Pérez, Capella (1991), *Jornades sobre protecció legal de Patrimonio Arqueològic: Dossier de Patrimoni Cultural*, Barcelona: Diputació de Barcelona.

Perkins, J. (1995), 'CIMI and CHIO: Cultural Heritage Information – the Short and the Long of it', *Spectra*, **22**(3).

Pescatore, P. (1985), 'Le commerce de l'art et le Marché Commun', *Revue Trimestrielle de Droit Européen*, a.XXI(1).

Peters, K.M. (1983), 'The Conservation of a Maori Meeting House – a "Living" Artefact', *AGMANZ News*, **14**(2).

Petersen, T. (1994), *Art and Architecture Thesaurus (AAT)*, 2nd edition, New York: Oxford University Press.

Petropoulos, Jonathan (1996), *Art as Politics in the Third Reich*, Chapel Hill: University of North Carolina Press.

Petropoulos, Jonathan (2000), *The Faustian Bargain: The Art World in Nazi Germany*, New York: Oxford University Press.

Phelan, Marilyn (1998), 'Cultural Property, International Trade and Human Rights', *Public International Law*, 447.

Phelan, Marilyn (1998), 'The UNIDROIT Convention on Stolen or Illegally Exported Cultural Objects Confirms a Separate Property Status for Cultural Treasures', *Villanova Sports & Entertainment Law Journal*, 31.

Pickard, R. (2003), *European Cultural Heritage: A Review of Policies and Practice*, Strasbourg: Council of Europe Publishing, Vol. II, 53.

Pierron, Véronique (1992), 'L'UNESCO et le trafic illicite des biens culturels', *Archéologia*, Dijon, **284**, November, 4.

Platzman, S. (1992), 'Objects of Controversy', *American University Law Review*, 41.

Poli, J. Fr. (1996), *La Protection des Biens culturels meubles*, Paris: Librairie générale de Droit et de Jurisprudence.

Poli, J. Fr. (1998), 'Droit Communautaire, compétences culturelles des états membres', *Revue du Marché Commun et de l' Union Européenne*, 89.

Polk, Milbry and Angela M.H. Schuster (2005), *The Looting of the Iraq Museum, Baghdad: The Lost Legacy of Ancient Mesopotamia*, New York: Harry N. Abrams, 256.

Pomerance, M. (1976), 'The United States and Self-Determination: Perspectives on the Wilsonian Conception', *American Journal of International Law*, 70.

Popper, William A.M. (1899), *The Censorship of Hebrew Books*, New York: Burt Franklin.

Post, H. (1995), 'The Protection of Archaeological Property and the Internal Market', in G. Kassimatis, (ed.), *Archaeological Heritage: Current Trends in its Legal Protection*, Athens: P. Sakkoulas Bros. Publishers.

Prescott, William H. (1974), *The World of Aztecs*, New York: Tudor Publishing Co.

Prott, L.V. (1996), *Report of the UK Department of National Heritage on the 1970 UNESCO Convention concerning the Illicit Import, Export and Transfer of Cultural Property, 21 March*, London: UK Department of National Heritage.

Prott, L.V. (1997), *Commentary on the UNIDROIT Convention on Stolen and Illegally Exported Cultural Objects 1995*, Leicester: Institute of Art and Law.

Prott, L.V. (2000), *Biens culturels volés ou illicitement exportés: commentaire relatif à la Convention d'UNIDROIT 1995*, Paris: UNESCO, p.219.

Prott, L.V. (1988), 'Cultural Rights as Peoples' Rights in International Law', in J. Crawford (ed.), *The Rights of Peoples*, Oxford: Clarendon Press.

Prott, L.V. (1989), 'Problems of Private International Law for the Protection of Cultural Heritage', *Recueil des Cours de l'Académie de Droit International*, 215.

Prott, L.V. (1992), 'The Preliminary Draft UNIDROIT Convention on Stolen or Illegally Exported Cultural Objects', *International and Comparative Law Quarterly*, 41.

Prott, L.V. (1993), 'The Protocol to the Convention for the Protection of Cultural Property in the Event of Armed Conflict (The Hague Convention of 1954)', *Humanitäres Völkerrecht – Informationsschriften, German Red Cross*, Year 6, 4, pp.191.

Prott, L.V. (1996), 'Kulturgüterschutz nach der UNIDROIT Konvention und nach der UNESCO Konvention'[Protection of Cultural Property according to the UNIDROIT and UNESCO Conventions], *Zeitschrift für Vergleichende Rechtswissenschaft*, 95, 188 (in English).

Prott, L.V. (1996), 'The Protocol to the Convention for the Protection of Cultural Property in the Event of Armed Conflict (The Hague Convention of 1954)', in Martine Briat and Judith A. Freedberg (eds), *Legal Aspects of International Trade in Art – Les aspects juridiques du commerce international de l'art*, Paris; New York: ICC Publishing; The Hague; Boston: Kluwer Law International, p.163.

Prott, L.V. (1996), 'UNESCO and UNIDROIT: A Partnership against Illicit Trafficking', *Uniform Law Review*, 1.

Prott, L.V. (1997), 'Principles for the Resolution of Disputes concerning Cultural Heritage Displaced during the Second World War', in E. Simpson (ed.), *The Spoils of War: World War II and Its Aftermath: The Loss, Reappearance and Recovery of Cultural Property*, New York: Harry N. Abrams, 221–224. New York: Harry N. Abrams.

Prott, L.V. (1997), 'Why UNIDROIT is Good for Museums! [L'effet positif de la Convention UNIDROIT sur les musées]', *INTERCOM newsletter* [*Bulletin de l'INTERCOM*], Ottawa, Ont., 1.

Prott, L.V. (1998), 'Understanding One Another on Cultural Rights', in H. Niec (ed.), *Cultural Rights and Wrongs*, Paris: UNESCO, p.161.

Prott, L.V. (1998), 'UNESCO and UNIDROIT: A Partnership against Trafficking in Cultural Objects', in Norman Palmer (ed.), *The Recovery of Stolen Art: A Collection of Essays,* London: Kluwer Law International, p.205.

Prott, L.V. (2005), 'The International Movement of Cultural Objects', *International Journal of Cultural Property*, **12**(2).

Prott, L.V. (2009), 'Note on Terminology', in L.V. Prott (ed.), *Witnesses to History*, Paris: UNESCO.

Prott, L.V. (2009), 'The Ethics and Law of Returns', *Museum International,* **61**(1–2).

Prott, L.V. (2009), 'The History and Development of Processes for the Recovery of Cultural Heritage', in L.V. Prott (ed.), *Witnesses to History*, Paris: UNESCO, p.2.

L.V. Prott (ed.) (2009), *Witnesses to History*, Paris: UNESCO.

Prott, L.V. (2009), 'The Parthenon Marbles', in L.V. Prott (ed.), *Witnesses to History*, Paris: UNESCO, p.214.

Prott, L.V. and P.J. O'Keefe (1983), *Implementation of the 1970 Convention on the Means of Prohibiting and Preventing the Illicit Import, Export and Transfer of Ownership of Cultural Property*, UNESCO Doc. CLT-83/WS/16, Paris: UNESCO.

Prott, L.V. and P.J. O'Keefe (1983), *Mesures législatives et réglementaires nationales visant à lutter contre le trafic illicite de biens culturels*, Paris: UNESCO, p.144.

Prott, L.V. and P.J. O'Keefe (1983), *National Legal Control of Illicit Traffic in Cultural Property* UNESCO doc. CLT/83/WS/16, Paris: UNESCO.

Prott, L.V. and P.J. O'Keefe (1988), *Handbook of National Regulations Concerning the Export of Cultural Property*, UNESCO doc. CC.88/WS/27, Paris: UNESCO.

Prott, L.V. and P.J. O'Keefe (1992), '"Cultural Heritage" or "Cultural Property"?', *International Journal of Cultural Property*, 1.

Prott, L.V. and J. Specht (eds) (1989), *Protection or Plunder: Safeguarding the Future of Our Cultural Heritage*, Canberra: Australian Government Publishing Service.

Przyborowska-Klimczak, A. (1989–90), 'Les notions de "biens culturels" et de "patrimoine culturel mondial" dans le droit international', *Polish Yearbook of International Law*, **XVIII**, 51.

Putman, J. (1992), 'Common Markets and Cultural Identity: Cultural Property Export Restrictions in the European Economic Community', *University of Chicago Legal Forum*, 457.

Quatremère de Quincy, A-C. (1796), 'Extracts from Letters to General Miranda 1796', in L.V. Prott (ed.) (2009), *Witnesses to History*, Paris: UNESCO, p.19.

Quatremère de Quincy, A-C. (1796), *Lettres* à *Miranda sur le déplacement des monuments de l' art de l'Italie*, [Letters to Miranda on the Displacement of the Artistic Works of Italy], in E. Pommier, (ed.) (1989), Librairie du bicentenaire de La Révolution Française, Paris: Macula.

Radcliffe, Julian (1998), 'The Work of the International Art and Antiquities Loss Register', in Norman Palmer (ed.), *The Recovery of Stolen Art: A Collection of Essays,* London: Kluwer Law International, p.189.

Raschèr, Andrea F.G. (2000), *Kulturgütertransfer und globalisierung: UNESCO-Konvention 1970, Unidroit-Konvention 1995, EG-Verordnung 3911/92, EG-Richtlinie 93/7, Schweizerisches Recht*, Zurich: Schulthess Juristische Medien AG.

Raschèr, Andrea F.G., Marc Bauen, Yves Fischer and Marie-Noëlle Zen-Ruffinen (2005), *Cultural Property Transfer*, Zürich: Schulthess.

Redmond-Cooper, R. (1998), 'Time Limits in Actions to Recover Stolen Art', in Norman Palmer (ed.), *The Recovery of Stolen Art: A Collection of Essays,* London: Kluwer Law International, p.145.

Redmond-Cooper, R. (2009), 'Limitation of Actions in Art and Antiquity Claims', in L.V. Prott (ed.), *Witnesses to History*, Paris: UNESCO, p.318.

Reich, N. (1994), 'The "November revolution" of the European Court of Justice: Keck, Meng and Audi revisited', *Common Market Law Review*, 31.

Reichelt, G. (1993), 'Die Rolle von UNIDROIT für den Internationalen Kulturgüterschutz', *Europa im Aufbruch: Festschrift Fritz Schwind zum 80. Geburtsag*, 205.

Renfrew, Colin (1995), 'Art Fraud: Raiders of the Lost Past', *Journal of Financial Crime*, **3**(1).

Renfrew, Colin (2000), *Loot, Legitimacy and Ownership*, London: Duckworth.

Renold, M. (2004), 'Stolen Art: The Ubiquitous Question of Good Faith', in The Permanent Court of Arbitration/Peace Palace Papers (ed.), *Resolution of Cultural Property Disputes*, The Hague: Kluwer Law International.

Renold, M-A. (2009), 'Stolen Art: The Ubiquitous Question of Good Faith', in L.V. Prott (ed.), *Witnesses to History*, Paris: UNESCO, p.309.

Renold, M-A. and P. Gabus (eds) (2004), *Claims for the Restitution of Looted Art*, Geneva: Schulthess, (in English, French and German).

Reppas, Michael (1998–9), 'The Deflowering of the Parthenon: A Legal and Moral Analysis on Why the "Elgin Marbles" Must Be Returned to Greece', *Fordham Intellectual Property, Media & Entertainment Law Journal*, 911.

Rheims, Maurice (1961), *The Strange Life of Objects*, New York: Atheneum.

Rigaux, F. (1995), 'Libre circulation des biens culturels et protection des trésors nationaux', *European Review of Private Law*, 2.

Rijn, M. van (1993), *Hot Art, Cold Cash*, London: Little Brown and Co.

Riou, A. (1996), *Le droit de la culture et le droit à la culture*, Paris: Editions ESF, 35.

Ripley, Dillon (1970), *The Sacred Grove – Essays on Museums*, London: Victor Gollancz.

Rivet, Paul (1973), *Maya Cities*, London: Elek Books.

Rivière, F. (2008), *Proceedings of the Athens International Conference: 17–18 March* (UNESCO, Blackwells), (2009), Editorial in *Museum International*, **61**(1–2), (in English and French).

Roberts, D.A. (ed.) (1990), *Terminology for Museums – Proceedings of an International Conference, held in Cambridge England, 1988*, Cambridge: The Museum Documentation Association.

Robinson, N. (1949), 'Repatriations and Restitution in International Law', *Jewish Yearbook of International Law*, 1.

Rodotà, St. (1984), 'Les aspects de droit civil de la protection internationale

des biens culturels', in Conseil de l'Europe, *La protection juridique internationale des biens culturels, Actes du treizième Colloque de Droit Europeen (Delphes, 20–22 septembre 1983)*, Strasbourg: Conseil de l'Europe, 108.
Rogers, W.D. (1973), 'The Legal Response to the Illicit Movement of Cultural Property', *Law and Policy in International Business*, 5.
Rolf, D.C. (1996), 'The Union of India Vs. Bumper Development Corporation: A Canadian's International Art Litigation Experience', in Canadian Museums Association, *Legal Affairs and Management Symposium, Ottawa, 1–2 March 1996*, Ottawa: Canadian Museums Association, 265.
Rosenbaum, Lee (2009), 'Art History Meets Archaeology: Considering Cultural Context in American Museums', *Museum International*, **61**(1–2).
Ross, M. (1995), 'Cultural Protection: A Matter of Union Citizenship or Human Rights?', in N. Neuwahl and A. Rosas (eds), *The European Union and Human Rights*, The Hague/Boston/London: Martinus Nijhoff Publishers, p.235.
Rostomian, Predita (2002–3), 'Looted Art in the U.S. Market', *Rutgers Law Review*, 271.
Roth, Ling H. (1903), *Great Benin: Its Customs, Art and Horrors*, Halifax: F. King and Sons.
Rothenberg, Jacob (1977), *'Decensus ad Terram': The Acquisition and Reception of the Elgin Marbles*, New York and London: Garland.
Roux, Emmanuel (de) and Roland-Pierre Paringaux (1999), *Razzia sur l'art*, Paris: Fayard, p.349.
Rowan, J. (2009), '7 million to Renovate Meeting House', in L.V. Prott (ed.), *Witnesses to History*, Paris: UNESCO, p.212.
Roxan, David and Ken Davie (1965), *The Rape of Art: The Story of Hitler's Plunder of the Great Masterpieces of Europe*, New York: Couard-McCann.
Royal Canadian Mounted Police (1994), *Theft of Cultural Property in Canada*, Ottawa, Ontario: Interpol Ottawa.
Russell, John Malcolm (2003), 'Art loss in Iraq', *International Foundation for Art Research Journal*, **6**(1 & 2).
Ryan, Lyndall (1981), *The Aboriginal Tasmanians*, St. Lucia, Queensland: University of Queensland Press.
Salem, Aisha (2005), 'Finders Keepers? The Repatriation of Egyptian Art', *Journal of Technology Law & Policy*, 173.
Sanborn, A. (2009), 'The Reunification of the Kwakwaka'wakw Mask with its Cultural Soul', *Museum International*, **61**(1–2).
Sandrock, O. (1988), 'Foreign Laws Regulating the Export of Cultural Property: The Respect Due to them by the Judge of the Lex Fori', in

P. Lalive (ed.), *International Sales of Works of Art*, Paris: Institute of International Business Law & Practice and Geneva: Faculté de Droit de Genève.

Schick, Jürgen (1998), *The Gods Are Leaving the Country: Art Theft from Nepal*, translated from German by Philip H. Pierce. Rev. English edition (Original Title: *Die Götter verlassen das Land*), Bangkok: Orchid Press, p.209.

Schmidt, F. (1992), 'Codes of Museum Ethics and the Financial Pressure on Museums', *Museum Management and Curatorship*, **11**(2).

Schneider, M. (1995), 'The UNIDROIT Convention on Stolen or Illegally Exported Cultural Objects', www.city.ac.uk/artspol/schneider.html.

Schneider, M. (1997), 'The UNIDROIT Convention on Cultural Property: State of Play and Prospects for the Future', *UNIDROIT Research Officer*, 494.

Schultsz, J.C. 'Dutch Antecedents and Parallels to Article 7 of the EEC Contracts Convention of 1980', *Rabels Zeitschrift für ausländisches und internationales Privatrecht*, 47.

Scovazzi, T. (2009), 'Diviser c'est détruire: Ethical Principles and Legal Rules In The Field of Return of Cultural Properties', paper presented in the 15th Session of the Intergovernmental Committee for Promoting the Return of Cultural Property to Its Countries of Origin or Its Restitution in Case of Illicit Appropriation (11–13 May 2009), Paris: UNESCO.

Scovazzi, T. (2009), 'Legal Aspects of the Axum Obelisk Case', *Museum International*, 61(1–2).

Scovazzi, T. (2010), *A Second Italian Case on Cultural Properties Enmeshed in Fishing Nets*, available at http//www.mepielanebulletin.gr/default.aspx?pid=18&CategoryId=4&ArticleId=17&Article=A-Second-Italian-Case-on-Cultural-Properties-Enmeshed-in-Fishing-Nets

Seabrook, J.B. (1974), 'Legal Approaches to the Trade in Stolen Antiquities', *Syracuse Journal of International Law and Commerce*, 2.

Sease, Catherine (1997), 'Conservation and the Antiquities Trade', *Journal of the American Institute for Conservation*, Washington, D.C., AIC, 36 (1), 49–58, http://aic.stanford.edu/jaic/articles/jaic36-01-004.html.

Seferiades, S. (1932), 'La question du repatriement des "Marbres d'Elgin" considérée plus spécialement au point de vue de droit des gens', *Revue de Droit International*, 3.

Seibert, Sam, Tony Clifton, George Wehrfritz, Matt Forney, Gretchen Luchsinger, and Kay Itoi (1994), 'Art Pirates – The Booming Trade in Smuggled Chinese Treasures', *Newsweek*, August 22, 36.

Shapiro, Harry Lionel (1974), *Peking Man*, New York: Simon and Schuster.

Shelley, Henry C. (1911), *The British Museum, its History and Treasures*, Boston: L. C. Page and Company.

Shulevitz, J. (1990), 'Pillaged and Plundered', *ART News*, New York, December 1990, 85.

Shyllon, F. (1998), 'One Hundred Years of Looting Nigerian Art Treasures: 1897–1996', *Art Antiquity and Law*, **3**(3).

Shyllon, F. (2002), 'The Recovery of Cultural Objects by African States through the UNESCO and UNIDROIT Conventions and the Role of Arbitration', *Uniform Law Review*, 2.

Shyllon, F. (2003), 'Negotiations for the Return of Nok Sculptures from France to Nigeria – An Unrighteous Conclusion', *Art Antiquity and Law*, **VIII**, 133.

Shyllon, F. (2003), 'Private Law beyond Markets for Goods and Services: The Example of Cultural Objects', *Worldwide Harmonisation of Private Law and Regional Economic Integration*, 511.

Shyllon F. (2009), 'The Recovery of Cultural Objects by African States through the UNESCO and UNIDROIT Conventions and the Role of Arbitration', in L.V. Prott (ed.), *Witnesses to History*, Paris: UNESCO, 369.

Sidorsky, E. (1996), 'The 1995 UNIDROIT Convention on Stolen or Illegally Exported Cultural Objects: The Role of International Arbitration', *International Journal of Cultural Property*, 5.

Siehr, K. (1992), 'Preliminary Draft UNIDROIT Convention on Stolen or Illegally Exported Cultural Objects (Approved by the UNIDROIT Study Group on the International Protection of Cultural Property at Its Third Session on 26 January 1990)', *International Journal of Cultural Property*, Berlin, New York: Walter de Gruyter, **1**(1).

Siehr, K. (1992), 'The UNIDROIT Draft Convention on the International Protection of Cultural Property', *International Journal of Cultural Property*, **1**(2).

Siehr, K. (1993), 'International Art Trade and the Law', *Recueil des Cours de l'Académie de Droit International*, 243.

Siehr, K. (1995), 'Vereinheithcliung des Mobilaraschenrechts in Europa, insbesondere im Hinblick auf Kulturgüter', *RABELSZ*, 454.

Siehr, K. (1996), 'Kultursgüterschutz innerhalb der Europäischen Union', *ZvglRWiss*, 170.

Siehr, K. (1997), 'The Protection of Cultural Heritage and International Commerce', *International Journal of Cultural Property*, 304.

Siehr, K. (1998), 'The Protection of Cultural Property: The 1995 UNIDROIT Convention and the EEC Instruments of 1992/93 Compared', *Uniform Law Studies*, 671.

Siehr, K. (2001), 'Resolution of Disputes in International Art Trade – Third Annual Conference of the Foundation "The Venice Court of National and International Arbitration"', *Conference Scene*, 64.

Silverberg, Robert (1962), *Lost Cities and Vanished Civilizations*, Philadelphia and New York: Chilton.
Silverberg, Robert (ed.) (1985), *Great Adventures in Archaeology: An Anthology*, Harmondsworth: Penguin.
Silverman, H. (1993), 'Who Owns the Past? – The Potential Privatization of Archaeology in Peru', *Public Archaeology Review*, 1.
Simpson, Elizabeth (ed.) (1997), *The Spoils of War: World War II and Its Aftermath: The Loss, Reappearance and Recovery of Cultural Property*, New York: Harry N. Abrams.
Simpson, M. (1997), *Museums and Repatriation: An Account of Contested Items in Museum Collections in the UK, with Comparative Material from Other Countries*, London: Museums Association.
Simpson, M. (2001), *Making Representations: Museums in the Post-Colonial Era*, revised edition, London: Routledge.
Simpson, M. (2009), 'Museums and Restorative Justice: Heritage, Repatriation and Cultural Education', *Museum International*, **61**(1–2).
Simpson, M. (2009), 'Posing a Challenge for the Future', in L.V. Prott (ed.), *Witnesses to History*, Paris: UNESCO, p.240.
Simpson, M. (2009), 'The Repatriation of Haida Ancestors', in L.V. Prott (ed.), *Witnesses to History*, Paris: UNESCO, p.260.
Singer, Peter (ed.) (1993), *A Companion to Ethics*, Blackwell Companions to Philosophy, Oxford: Blackwell.
Singh K. (2009), 'Universal Museums: The View from Below', in L.V. Prott (ed.), *Witnesses to History*, Paris: UNESCO, p.123.
Sljivic, A. (1997–8), 'Why Do You Think it's You? An Exposition of the Jurisprudence Underlying the Debate between Cultural Nationalism and Cultural Internationalism', *George Washington Journal of International Law & Economics*, 31.
Smith, A. (1916), 'Lord Elgin and his Collection', *Journal of Hellenistic Studies*, 36.
Smith, G.S. and J.E. Ehrenhard (eds) (1991), *Protecting the Past*, Florida: CRC Press.
Smith, Joseph Lindon (1956), *Tombs, Temples, and Ancient Art*, Norman: University of Oklahoma Press.
Smith, Sir John (1998), 'Rewards for the Return of Lost or Stolen Property: The Civil and Criminal Law', in Norman Palmer (ed.), *The Recovery of Stolen Art: A Collection of Essays,* London: Kluwer Law International, p.171.
Smyth, Craig Hugh (1988), *Repatriation of Art from the Collection Point in Munich after World War II: Background and Beginnings with Reference Especially to the Netherlands*, Maarssen, Netherlands: G. Schwartz.
Snyder, Fr. (1994), 'Soft Law and Institutional Practicc in the European

Community', in S. Martin (ed.), *The Construction of Europe: Essays in Honour of Émile Noël*, Dordrecht: Kluwer.
Solomon, Andrew (2005), 'Art in Jeopardy', in K. Fitz Gibbon (ed.), *Who Owns the Past? Cultural Policy, Cultural Property and the Law*, New Brunswick, New Jersey and London: Rutgers University Press in association with American Council for Cultural Policy, p.239.
Soudijin, Melvin and Edgar Tijhuis (2003), 'Some Perspectives on the Illicit Antiquities Trade in China', *Art Antiquity and Law*, **8**(2).
Spagna Musso, E. (1961), *Lo Stato di cultura nella Constituzione italiana*, Naples: Morano.
Specth, J. (2009), 'Comments on the Establishment of the Committee', in L.V. Prott (ed.), *Witnesses to History*, Paris: UNESCO, p.28.
Spencer, Ronald D. (2005), 'The Expert and the Object', in K. Fitz Gibbon (ed.), *Who Owns the Past? Cultural Policy, Cultural Property and the Law*, New Brunswick, New Jersey and London: Rutgers University Press in association with American Council for Cultural Policy, p.159.
Squires, D.F. (1969), 'Schizophrenia: The Plight of the Natural History Curator', *Museum News*, **47**(7), 18.
St. Clair, W. (1998), *Lord Elgin and the Marbles*, Oxford, New York: Oxford University Press.
St. Clair W. (2006), 'Imperial Appropriations of the Parthenon', in J.H. Merryman (ed), *Imperialism, Art and Restitution* Cambridge University Press.
St. Clair Harvey, Archer and P.J. O'Keefe (2001), *Art, Antiquity and the Law: Preserving our Global Cultural Heritage*, Piscataway, N.J.: Rutgers University Press.
Stagos, P. (1986), 'The Free Movement of Artistic Goods in the Community and the Cultural Dimension of European Integration', *Greek European Law Review*, 683.
Stagos, P. (2004), 'European Union Activities in the Area of Culture: Between the Coercions of National Cultural Policies and Organized Professional Interests', in E. Trova (ed.), *Cultural Heritage and the Law*, Athens-Thessaloniki: Ed. Sakkoulas, p.573.
Staley, D.P. (1993), 'St. Lawrence Island's Subsistence Diggers: A New Perspective on Human Effects on Archaeological Sites', *Journal of Field Archaeology*, 20.
Stamatoudi, I. (1997), 'The Law and the Ethics Deriving from the Parthenon Marbles Case', *Web Journal of Current Legal Issues*, 3, 12 (www.ncl.ac.uk/~nlawwww/) and (1998) *Yearbook of Current Legal Issues*, Blackstone Press.
Stamatoudi, I. (1997), 'Specific performance in non-contractual obligation. A comparative study in French and Greek law', *Nomiki Epitheorissi*, 50.

Stamatoudi, I. (1998), 'Subsidiarity in the Maastricht Treaty', *Annales de la Faculté de Droit d'Istanbul*, 239.

Stamatoudi, I. (1998), 'The National Treasures Exception in Article 36 EC: How Many of them Fit the Bill?', *Art Antiquity and Law*, 3.

Stamatoudi, I. (2000), 'Restitution of Stolen and Illegally Exported Cultural Objects', in P. Torremans (ed.), *Legal Convergence in the Enlarged Europe of the New Millennium,* the Netherlands: Kluwer Law International, p.109.

Stamatoudi, I. (2002), 'Legal Grounds for the Return of the Parthenon Marbles', *Revue Hellénique de Droit International*, 2.

Stamatoudi, I. (2004), 'Legal Issues Associated with the Return of the Parthenon Marbles', in M. Μαρούλη-Ζηλεμένου (ed.), *Ο Παρθενώνας. Η Επιστροφή των Γλυπτών*, Athens: Ι. Σιδέρης, p.214.

Stamatoudi, I. (2004), 'National Cultural Treasures and Free Movement of Goods in the Single Market', in E. Trova (ed.), *Cultural Heritage and the Law*, Athens-Thessaloniki: ed. Sakkoulas, p.261.

Stamatoudi, I. (2004), 'The Protection of Intangible Property by Means of the UNESCO Convention on the Safeguarding of Intangible Heritage and Intellectual Property Law', *Revue Hellénique de Droit International*, 57.

Stamatoudi, I. (2009), 'Mediation and Cultural Diplomacy', *Museum International*, **61**(1–2).

Stanton, J.E. (2009), 'Snapshots on the Dreaming: Photographs of the Past and Present (2009)', in L.V. Prott (ed.), *Witnesses to History*, Paris: UNESCO, p.242.

Staunton, I. and M. McCarthy (eds) (1981), *Lost Heritage: A Report of the Symposium on the Return of Cultural Property held at the Africa Centre, 21 May 1981*, London: Commonwealth Arts Association and the Africa Centre.

Stein, Aurel M. (1912), *Ruins of Desert Cathay (Personal Narrative of Explorations in Central Asia and Westernmost China)*, 2 vols, London: Macmillan, especially Chapter 66.

Steiner, J. (1994), 'Subsidiarity under the Maastricht Treaty', in D. O'Keefe and P. Twomey (eds), *Legal Issues of the Maastricht Treaty*, Chichester: Wiley Chancery Law.

Stetie, S. (1981), 'The View of UNESCO's Inter-governmental Committee', in I. Staunton and M. McCarthy (eds), *Lost Heritage: A Report of the Symposium on the Return of Cultural Property held at the Africa Centre, 21 May 1981*, London: Commonwealth Arts Association and the Africa Centre.

Stewart, W.G. (2001), 'The Marbles: Elgin or Parthenon?', *Art Antiquity and Law*, **6**, 37.

Struell, Fabienne (1997), 'Cultural Property: Recent Cases under the Convention on Cultural Property Implementation Act', *The International Lawyer*, 31.

Sullivan, T.J. (2002), 'M. Abraham and D.J.G. Griffin, NAGPRA: Effective Repatriation Programs and Cultural Change in Museums', *Curator*, 43.

Sutcliffe, Ray (1978), *Chronicle*, London: BBC.

Sveinsson, Einar Ol. (1959), *Handritamdlio – The Manuscripts Case*, Reykjavik: Icelandic Literary Society, (monograph in Icelandic).

Symeonides, Symeon (2005), 'A Choice-of-law Rule for Conflicts Involving Stolen Cultural Property', *Vanderbilt Journal of Transnational Law*, 1177.

Talley, M.K. (1993), 'Ethics and the Morality of Conservation/Restoration Practices', in P. Berghuis and P.A. Terwen (eds), *How Safe is your Object? A Concise Manual of Preventive Conservation*, Amsterdam: Reinwardt Academie, p.1.

Taschner, C. (1992), 'Kulturgüterschutz aus der Sicht des EG-Rechts', in Gerte Reichelt (ed.), *Internationaler Kulturgüterschutz, Wiener Symposium 18/19 Oktober 1990*, Wien: Manzsche Verlag, 97.

Taylor, Ch. (1994), 'The Politics of Recognition', in Amy Gutmann (ed.), *Multiculturalism: Examining the Politics of Recognition*, Princeton University Press, p.25.

Taylor, Francis Henry (1945), *Babel's Tower – The Dilemma of the Modern Museum*, New York: Columbia University Press.

Taylor, Francis Henry (1948), *The Taste of Angels – A History of Art Collecting from Rameses to Napoleon*, London: Hamish Hamilton.

Taylor, Jason (2005–6), 'The Rape and Return of China's Cultural Property: How Can Bilateral Agreements Stem the Bleeding of China's Cultural Heritage in a Flawed System?', *Loyola University Chicago International Law Review*, 233.

Taylor, P.M. (ed.) (1994), *Fragile Traditions: Indonesian Art in Jeopardy*, Honolulu: University of Hawaii.

Theophile, Erich and Cynthia Rosenfield (2005), 'The Kathmandu Valley Preservation Trust', in K. Fitz Gibbon (ed.), *Who Owns the Past? Cultural Policy, Cultural Property and the Law*, New Brunswick, New Jersey and London: Rutgers University Press in association with American Council for Cultural Policy, p.305.

Thomas, D.H. (2006) 'Finders Keepers and Deep American History: Some Lessons in Dispute Resolution' in J.H. Merryman (ed) (2006), *Imperialism, Art and Restitution*, Cambridge University Press.

Thorleifsen, Daniel (2009), 'The Repatriation of Greenland's Cultural Heritage', *Museum International*, **61**(1–2).

Thorndike, Joseph J. (ed.) (1979), *Discovery of Lost Words*, New York: American Heritage Publishing Co.

Thornes, R. (1995), *Protecting Cultural Objects through International Documentation Standards – A Preliminary Survey*, Santa Monica: The Getty Art History Information Program, J. Paul Getty Trust.

Thornes, R. (1997), *Protecting Cultural Objects in the Global Information Society*, Los Angeles: The Getty Information Institute, p.81.

Thornton, R. (2009), 'Repatriation as Healing the Trauma of History', in L.V. Prott (ed.), *Witnesses to History*, Paris: UNESCO, p.239.

Tijhuis, Edgar A.J.G. (2006), 'The Illicit Art and Antiquities Trade: An Emerging Criminal Market', *Standing Group Organised Crime eNewsletter,* Colchester, European Consortium for Political Research, **5**(3), Sept. 2–3, http://www.essex.ac.uk/ECPR/standinggroups/crime/documents/SGOC_Vol5_3.pdf.

Tijhuis, Edgar A.J.G. (2006), *Transnational Crime and the Interface between Legal and Illegal Actors: The Case of the Illicit Art and Antiquities Trade*, Nijmegen: Wolf Legal Publishers, p.250.

Timmins, J. (2002) 'The Macchiaioli Affair: Lost and Found in Italy', *Art Antiquity and Law*, **VII**, 109.

Toman, Jiri (1996), *The Protection of Cultural Property in the Event of Armed Conflict: Commentary on the Convention for the Protection of Cultural Property in the Event of Armed Conflict and its Protocol, signed on 14 May, 1954 in the Hague, and on Other Instruments of International Law Concerning Such Protection*, Aldershot, England; Brookfield, Vt, USA: Dartmouth Publishers.

Tompa, Peter K. and Ann M. Brose (2005), 'A Modern Challenge to an Age-Old Pursuit: Can Cultural Patrimony Claims and Coin Collecting Coexist', in K. Fitz Gibbon (ed.), *Who Owns the Past? Cultural Policy, Cultural Property and the Law*, New Brunswick, New Jersey and London: Rutgers University Press in association with American Council for Cultural Policy, p.205.

Tomuschat, Ch. (1988), 'Rechtliche Aspekte des Gemeinschaftshandels im Bereich Kultur', in *Fédération Internationale pour le Droit Européen (Hrsg), Legal Aspects of Community Action in the Field of Culture*, 1.

Torres de Aráuz, Reina (1982), 'Museums and the Containment of Illicit Traffic', *Museum*, Paris: UNESCO, **34**(2).

Trova, E. (ed.) (2004), *Cultural Heritage and the Law*, Athens-Thessaloniki: Ed. Sakkoulas.

True, M. and A. Kozloff (1994), 'Barbara and Lawrence Fleischman: Guardians of the Past', in J. Harris (ed.), *A Passion for Antiquities: Ancient Art from the Collection of Barbara and Lawrence Fleischman*, Malibu: The J. Paul Getty Museum.

Tubb, K.W. (ed.) (1995), *Antiquities Trade or Betrayed: Legal, Ethical and Conservation Issues*, London: Archetype Publications.
Tubb, K.W. and C. Sease (1996), 'Sacrificing the Wood for Trees – Should Conservation Have a Role in the Antiquities Trade?', in A. Roy and P. Smith (eds), *Archaeological Conservation and Its Consequences*, London: International Institute for Conservation of Historic and Artistic Works.
Tung-Lai, Margue (1993), 'L'exportation des biens culturels dans le cadre du Grand Marché', *Revue du Marché Commun et de l'Union Européenne*, 2.
Turner, S. (2009), 'Cultural Property as National Heritage and Common Human Heritage: The Problem of Reconciling Common and Individual Interests', in L.V. Prott (ed.), *Witnesses to History*, Paris: UNESCO, p.110.
Tymchuk, M. (1985), 'Museums, Anthropology and Skeletal Remains', *The International Journal of Museum Management and Curatorship*, **4**(4).
Tytgat, Christiane (2009), 'The 1997 Exhibition and the Reunification Process', *Museum International*, **61**(1–2).
Ullberg, A.D. and P. Ullberg (1974), 'A Proposed Curatorial Code of Ethics', *Museum News*, **52**(8).
Ulph, Janet (1998), 'Tracing and Recovering Stolen Art on the Proceeds of Sale', in Norman Palmer (ed.), *The Recovery of Stolen Art: A Collection of Essays,* London: Kluwer Law International.
UNESCO (1961), *Intergovernmental Conference on the Protection of Cultural Property in the Event of Armed Conflict – The Hague, 1954: Records of the Conference*, The Hague: UNESCO.
UNESCO (1970), *Cultural Rights as Human Rights*, Paris: UNESCO.
UNESCO (1974), *An Illustrated Inventor of Famous Dismembered Works of Art – European Painting*, Paris: UNESCO.
UNESCO (1976), *Moving towards Change: Some Thoughts on the New International Economic Order*, Paris: UNESCO.
UNESCO (1982), *The Cultural Heritage of Mankind: A Shared Responsibility*, Paris: UNESCO, Doc.CLT-82/WS/27.
UNESCO (1984), *Protection of Movable Cultural Property, vols. I and II, Compendium of Legislative Texts*, Paris: UNESCO.
UNESCO (1985), *Conventions and Recommendations Concerning the Protection of the Cultural Heritage*, Paris: UNESCO.
UNESCO (1992), *Final Report of the National Workshop on the Means of Preventing the Illicit Traffic in Cultural Property in Cambodia organized by UNESCO in Phnom Penh, Cambodia, 20–24 July 1992*, Phnom Penh: UNESCO.
UNESCO (1993), *Report by the Intergovernmental Committee for Promoting the Return of Cultural Property to its Countries of Origin or its Restitution*

in Case of Illicit Appropriation on its Activities (1991–1993), Paris: UNESCO, Doc. 27C/102, 21, September.

UNESCO (1995), *Reports from Member States on measures they have adopted to implement the Convention on Preventing and Prohibiting the Illicit Import, Export and Transfer of Ownership of Cultural Property (1970)*, Paris: UNESCO, Doc. 28 C/35, 28 C/35Add and 28 C/35 Add.2 UNESCO programme documents (in English, French, Arabic, Russian, Spanish, and Chinese).

UNESCO (1996), *Guidelines of the Use of the Standard Form Concerning Requests for Return or Restitution*, Paris: UNESCO Doc. 66-86/W5/3.

UNESCO (1997), *La lutte contre le trafic illicite des biens culturels – Guide pour la mise en œuvre de la Convention de 1970,* Paris: UNESCO, 1997 (English), 2000 (French), 312.

UNESCO (2000), *No to Illicit Traffic in Cultural Property*, Paris: UNESCO.

UNESCO (2006), *Mesures juridiques et pratiques contre le trafic illicite des biens culturels – Manuel de l'UNESCO*, Paris: UNESCO, p.44.

UNESCO (2009), 'Principles & Guidelines for the Protection of the Heritage of Indigenous People: Extracts', in L.V. Prott (ed.), *Witnesses to History*, Paris: UNESCO, p.353.

UNESCO and Instituto Nacional de Patrimonio Cultural del Ecuador (1999), *Primer curso de formación para el control de tráfico ilícito de bienes culturales patrimoniales*, (Serie Conservación, restauración, promoción y difusión del patrimonio cultural de la Nación), Quito: UNESCO-Quito, Instituto Nacional de Patrimonio Cultural, 97.

UNESCO and UNIDROIT (2005), *The Fight Against Illicit Traffic in Cultural Property: International Developments*, Paris: UNESCO and UNIDROIT Cooperation, 536.

UNESCO, Bangkok (1992), *Final Report of the Regional Workshop on the Convention on the Means of Prohibiting and Preventing the Illicit Import, Export and Transfer of Ownership of Cultural Property organized by UNESCO in co-operation with SEAMEO/ SPAFA in Jomtie, Thailand, February 24–28, 1992*, Bangkok, Thailand: SPAFA.

UNESCO, Korean National Commission (2002), *International Expert Meeting on the Return of Cultural Property and the Fight against its Illicit Trafficking, 30 September–3 October 2002, Seoul, Republic of Korea,* Seoul: Korean National Commission for UNESCO, p.259.

UNESCO, Korean National Commission (2007), *Forum on the Return of Korean Cultural Property Displaced to Japan during Occupation or War*, Seoul: Korean National Commission for UNESCO, (in Korean and English).

UNESCO, Oficina Regional de Cultura Para América Latina y el Caribe

(2003), *Tráfico ilícito de bienes culturales en América Latina y el Caribe,* La Habana: ORCALC, p.83.
UNESCO, *Statutes of the Intergovernmental Committee for Promoting the Return of Cultural Property to its Countries of Origin or its Restitution in Case of Illicit Appropriation*, http://www.unesco.org/culture/laws/committee/html_eng/statuts.shtml.
UNSDRI (1976), *The Protection of the Artistic and Archaeological Heritage: A View from Italy and India*, Rome: UNSDRI, Publication No. 13.
Van Heese, M. (2006), 'The Fight against Illicit Traffic in Cultural Goods – The Dutch Approach', *Art Antiquity and Law*, 11.
Varine-Bohan, Hugues de (2001), 'Viol et vol des cultures: un aspect de la dégradation des termes de l'échange culturel entre les nations', *Museum International*, Paris: UNESCO, No. 212, (Vol. 53, No. 4), Oct.–Dec., 83.
Verheul, J.P. (1984), 'Foreign Export Prohibition: Cultural Treasures and Minerals', *Netherlands International Law Review*, 31.
Villanueva, Robin Hardy (1995–6), 'Free Trade and the Protection of Cultural Property: The Need for an Economic Incentive to Report Newly Discovered Antiquities', *George Washington Journal of International Law and Economics*, 547.
Vincent, Steven (2005), 'Indian Givers', in K. Fitz Gibbon (ed.), *Who Owns the Past? Cultural Policy, Cultural Property and the Law*, New Brunswick, New Jersey and London: Rutgers University Press in association with American Council for Cultural Policy, 33.
Virgos Soriano, M. (1998), 'Le commerce international d'art en droit espagnol', in P. Lalive (ed), *International Sales in Works of Art*, Paris: Institute of International Buisness Law and Practice, and Faculté de Droit de Genève, 341, at 356.
Vitelli, Karen D. (1996), 'A Case Study in Archaeological Context: Paleolithic Obsidian from Franchthi Cave', in *Archaeological Ethics*, California: AltaMira Press.
Vitrano, V. (1994), 'Protecting Cultural Objects in an Internal Border-free EC: the EC Directive and Regulation for the Protection and Return of Cultural Objects', *Fordham International Law Journal*, 17.
von Hagen, Victor W. (1964), *The Desert Kingdom of Peru*, London: Weidenfeld and Nicolson.
von Plehwe, T. (1995), 'European Union and the Free Movement of Cultural Goods', *European Law Review*, 431.
von Segesser, G. and A. Jolles (2005), 'Switzerland's New Federal Act on the International Transfer of Cultural Property: An Update and a Perspective from the Art Trade', *Art Antiquity and Law*, X, 175.
Voudouri, D. (1994), 'Circulation et protection des biens culturels dans l'Europe sans frontières', *Revue du Droit Public*, 483.

Voudouri, D. (1995), 'The Idea of a Common European Cultural Heritage, in the Perspective of the Abolition of Internal Frontiers', in G. Kassimatis (ed.), *Archaeological Heritage: Current Trends in its Legal Protection*, Athens: P. Sakkoulas Bros. Publishers.

Voutsakis, V. 'The Protection of Cultural Heritage in Greece: Political Principles and Legislative Choices', in S. Voutsaki and P. Cartledge, *Ancient Monuments and Modern Identities: The History of Archaeology in 19th and 20th Century Greece*, London: Ashgate, forthcoming.

Vrdoljak, A.F. (2008), *International Law, Museums and the Return of Cultural Objects*, Cambridge University Press.

Vrdoljak, A.F. (2009), 'International Law, Museums and the Return of Cultural Objects', in L.V. Prott (ed.), *Witnesses to History*, Paris: UNESCO, p.193.

Vrettos, Theodore (1974), *A Shadow of Magnitude – The Acquisition of the Elgin Marbles*, New York: Putnam.

Walden, D.A. (1995), 'Canada's Cultural Property Export and Import Act: The Experience of Protecting Cultural Property', *University of British Columbia Law Review,* Special Issue, 203.

Waldem, D.A. (2009), 'The Return of Ancient Textiles to Bolivia from Canada', in L.V. Prott (ed.), *Witnesses to History*, Paris: UNESCO, p.410.

Waldron, J. (1993), 'Can Communal Goods Be Human Rights?', in *Liberal Rights*, Cambridge University Press, p.339.

Walsh, James (1991), 'Your Masterpiece Is Missing', *Time*, November 25 1991.

Walzer, M. (1994), 'Comment', in Amy Gutmann (ed.), *Multiculturalism: Examining the Politics of Recognition*, Princeton University Press, p.99.

Warren, J. (1992), '1992 and the Movement of Works of Art', in S. Pearce (ed.), *Museums and Europe 1992*, London: The Athlone Press, New Jersey: Atlantic Highlands.

Warring, Jane (2005), 'Underground Debates: the Fundamental Differences of Opinion that Thwart UNESCO's Progress in Fighting the Illicit Trade in Cultural Property', *Emory International Law Review*, 227.

Watson, P. (1997), *Sotheby's: Inside Story*, London: Bloomsbury.

Watson, P. and Cecilia Todeschini (2006), *The Medici Conspiracy: The Illicit Journey of Looted Antiquities from Italy's Tomb Raiders to the World's Greatest Museums*, New York: BBS Public Affairs, p.379.

Watt, Horatia Muir (1992), 'La revendication internationale des biens culturels: à propos de la décision américaine Eglise Autocéphale', *Revue Critique de Droit international privé*, **81**(1) January–March, 20

Weatherill, St. and P. Beaumont (1995), *EC Law*, 2nd edition, London, New York: Penguin Books.

Webster, G.C. (1995), 'The Potlatch Collection Repatriation', *University of British Columbia Law Review*, Special Issue, 137.
Wechsler, Helen (2001), *Museum Policy and Procedure for Nazi-Era Issues – Resource Report,* Washington, D.C.: American Association of Museums.
Weihe, H.K. (1995) 'Licit International Traffic in Cultural Objects', *International Journal of Cultural Property*, 4.
Weihe, H.K. (1996), 'Licit International Trade in Cultural Objects for Art's Sake', in Martine Briat and Judith A. Freedberg (eds), *Legal Aspects of International Trade in Art – Les aspects juridiques du commerce international de l'art*, Paris, New York: ICC Publishing; The Hague, Boston: Kluwer Law International.
Weil, S. (1988), 'The Ongoing Pursuit of Professional Status: The Progress of Museum Work in America', *Museum News*, **67**(2).
Weisberg, Richard H. (1996), *Vichy Law and the Holocaust in France*, New York: New York University Press for the Vidal Sassoon International Center for the Study of Antisemitism, p.447.
Weisz, Jackie (compiler) (2000), *Codes of Ethics and Practice of Interest to Museums*, Washington, D.C.: American Association of Museums.
Welsh, P.H. (1992), 'Repatriation and Cultural Preservation: Potent Objects, Potent Pasts', *University of Michigan Journal of Law Reform*, 25.
Wendt, A. (1980), 'Reborn to Belong: Culture and Colonialism in the Pacific', in R. Edwards and J. Stewart (eds), *Preserving Indigenous Cultures: A New Role for Museums*, Canberra: Australian Government Publishing Service, p.25.
Wengler, W. (1962), 'Conflicts of Laws, Problems relating to Restitution of Property in Germany', *International and Comparative Law Quarterly*, 11.
Werth, Alexander (1964), *Russia at War*, New York: Caroll and Graf.
White, Shelby (2005), 'Building American Museums: The Role of the Private Collector', in K. Fitz Gibbon (ed.), *Who Owns the Past? Cultural Policy, Cultural Property and the Law*, New Brunswick, New Jersey and London: Rutgers University Press in association with American Council for Cultural Policy, 165.
Whitehouse, David and Ruth Whitehouse (1975), *Archaeological Atlas of the World*, London: Thames and Hudson.
Whitfield, Roderick and Anne Farrer (1990), *Caves of the Thousand Buddhas: Chinese Art from the Silk Route*, London: British Museum Publications.
Wilkes, Nicole (2000–1), 'Public Responsibilities of Private Owners of Cultural Property: Toward a National Art Preservation Statute', *Columbia VLA (Volunteer Lawyers for the Arts) Journal of Law & the Arts*, 177.
Willaumez, Marie-France (1995), 'Patrimoine africain: Quels succès, quels périls?', *La Vie des musées*, Brussels: AFMB/ICOM Wallonie-Bruxelles, 10.

Willett, Frank and Ekpo O. Eyo (1980), *Treasures of Ancient Nigeria*, New York: Alfred A. Knopf in association with the Detroit Institute of Arts.

Williams, Sharon A. (1978), *The International and National Protection of Movable Cultural Property: A Comparative Study*, Dobbs Ferry, NY: Oceana Publications.

Williams, Sue (2000), 'Lutter contre le Comité des sanctions et le marché international des antiquités irakiennes', *Sources UNESCO*, 123.

Williams, Sue (2000), 'The Sanctions Committee and the International Market', *UNESCO Sources*, 123.

Williams, Sue and A.L. Martin (1999), 'Moraliser le marché de l'art: responsabiliser les marchands d'art est nécessaire, mais non suffisant, pour lutter contre le trafic d'objets volés', *Sources UNESCO*, 110.

Williams, Sue and A.L. Martin (1999), 'The Importance of Being Honest: UNESCO's Return and Restitution Committee Proposes a Good Behavior Code for Dealers in Cultural Property', *UNESCO Sources*, 110.

Wilson, Christopher (2009), 'Implications and Challenges of Repatriating and Reburying Ngarrindjeri Old People from the Edinburgh Collection', *Museum International*, **61**(1–2).

Wilson, Derek (1981), *The World Atlas of Treasure*, London: Williams Collins.

Wippman, D. (ed.) (1998), *International Law and Ethnic Conflict*, Ithaca, NY: Cornell University Press.

Wittlin, Alma Stephanie (1949), *The Museum, its History and its Tasks in Education*, London: Routledge and Kegan Paul.

Wittlin, Alma (1970), *Museums in Search of a Usable Future,* MIT Press.

Wondrausch, Heather Dean (ed.) (1990), *Egyptian Museum: Berlin (White Catalogue)*, Berlin: Ägyptisches Museum.

Woodall, J. Ned (ed.) (1990), 'Predicaments, Pragmatics, and Professionalism: Ethical Conduct in Archaeology', *Society of Professional Archaeologists, N.p., SOPA Special Publication*, 1.

Woolley, Sir Charles Leonard (1947), *A Record of the Work Done by the Military Authorities for the Protection of the Treasures of Art and History of War Areas*, London: His Majesty's Stationery Office.

Woolley, Sir Charles Leonard (1958), *History Unearthed*, London: Ernest Benn.

World Archaeological Congress (WAC) (1990), 'First Code of Ethics', *Anthropology Today*, 6.

Wyatt, D. and A. Dashwood (1993), *European Community Law*, London: Sweet & Maxwell, 3rd edition.

Wyliw, A. (1995), 'Archaeology and the Antiquities Market: the use of "looted" data', in M.J. Lynott and A. Wylie (eds.), *Ethics in American*

Archaeology: Challenges for the 1990s, Washington D.C.: Society for American Archaeology.
Wyss, M. (1992), 'The Protection of the Cultural Heritage and its Legal Dimensions: The Heidelberg Symposium 22–23 June 1990', *International Journal of Cultural Property*, 232.
Wyss, M. Ph. (1992), *Kultur als eine Dimension der Völkerrechtsordnung: Von Kulturgüterschutz zur internationalen kulturellen Kooperation*, Zurich: Schultthess Polygraphischer Verlag.

['X' stands for unknown author]

X (1945), 'Removal of German Art Objects to the United States', *Department of State Bulletin*, **13**(327), 499.
X (1975), 'The Acquisition of Cultural Property: New Australian Museum Policy', *Mankind*, **10**, 279.
X (1976), 'Legal Aspects of the International Traffic in Stolen Art: Symposium', *Syracuse Journal of International Law and Commerce*, 4.
X (1979), 'A Brief History of the Creation by UNESCO of an Intergovernmental Committee for Promoting the Return of Cultural Property to its Countries of Origin or its Restitution in Case of Illicit Appropriation', *Museum*, 31.
X (1992), *Curbing Illicit Traffic in Cultural Property: U.S. Assistance under the Convention of Cultural Property Implementation Act*, Washington, D.C.: U.S. Information Agency.
X (1995), 'Protecting Mali's Cultural Heritage', *African Arts Magazine*, Los Angeles: University of California, **28** (4), 112.
X (1996), 'Illicit Traffic: New International Convention Combats Illegal Art Sales in the Private Sector', *Museum International*, Paris: UNESCO (190), April–June, 60.
X (1997), 'Des solutions contre le trafic illicite: restitution, accord', *Les Nouvelles de l'ICOM*, Paris, **50**(4).
X (1997), 'Illicit Traffic: France Joins 1970 UNESCO Convention on Illicit Traffic', *Museum International*, Paris: UNESCO, p.195.
X (1997), 'Illicit Traffic: Recent Publications Highlight Growing International Concern', *Museum International*, 194.
X (1997), 'Non au pillage des cultures!', in *Vers un développement solidaire*, Lausanne, Déclaration de Berne (176), June 2004, 31 (Numéro spécial, existe aussi en allemand).
X (1997), 'Trafic illicite: de nouvelles publications soulignent la préoccupation croissante de la communauté internationale', *Museum International*, Paris: UNESCO, 194.
X (1997), 'Trafic illicite: une nouvelle convention internationale pour lutter

contre le trafic illicite d'objets d'art sur le marché privé', *Museum international*, Paris: UNESCO, p.190.

X (1999) *The Oe-Kyujanggak Books: What Are the Problems?*, Kyujanggak: Seoul National University.

X (2000), 'Provenance and Due Diligence', *The International Foundation for Art Research Journal*, New York, **3**(3 & 4).

X (2001), 'Cultural Heritage: An Ongoing Crusade', *UNESCO Sources*, Paris: UNESCO (128), November 2000, April, 10–15.

X (2001), 'Dossier: Contre les pilleurs et les vandales, sauvons nos trésors', *Le Courrier de l'UNESCO*, **54**(4).

X (2001), 'Patrimoine sous-marin: sus aux pirates!', *Sources UNESCO*, Paris, (140), December, 4.

X (2001), 'Trade not traffic: A Special Report on Invaluable and Trace's Recent "Due Diligence Seminar"', *Invaluable and Trace*, 150.

X (2001), *UNIDROIT Convention on Stolen or Illegally Exported Cultural Objects: Explanatory Report*, Paris: UNIDROIT Secretariat, p.476.

X (2002), 'Rechtsschutz für Kulturgut', *Museumskunde*, Berlin: Deutscher Museumsbund, **65**(1).

X (2003), 'The UK Makes it a Criminal Offence to Hold Iraqi Cultural Property', in *Keeping up with Art and Cultural Assets*, London: Withers LLP, p.8.

X (2003), 'UK Ratifies UNESCO Convention on Stolen and Illegally Exported Art and Introduces New Criminal Offence of Dealing in Stolen Cultural Property', in *Keeping up with Art and Cultural Assets,* London: Withers LLP.

X (2004), 'Stoppt den Ausverkauf der Kulturen!', *EvB Magazin*, Zürich, Erklärung von Bern, Special issue 4 (also in French).

X (2006), 'Les biens culturels', *LEGICOM*, (36), 2006/2, Editions Victoires, 164.

X (2009) Conclusions of the Athens International Conference on the Return of Cultural Objects to their Countries of Origin, *Museum International*, **61**(1–2).

Xiaoxue, Zhou (1998), 'Sus au trafic! La Chine intensifie son action contre le trafic illicite de ses oeuvres d'art', *Sources UNESCO*, 105.

Yeide, Nancy H., Konstantin Akinsha and Amy L. Walsh (2001), *The AAM Guide to Provenance Research*, Washington, D.C.: American Association of Museums.

Yi, Tae-jin and Choong-Hyun Paik (2009), 'The Korean Archives (The Oe-kyujanggak Books)', in L.V. Prott (ed.), *Witnesses to History*, Paris: UNESCO, p.300.

Youngbird, M. (2009), 'The Web that Connects the Heart and the Mind', in L.V. Prott (ed.), *Witnesses to History*, Paris: UNESCO, p.256.

Zainab Bahrani, (2004),'British and Swiss Get Tough About Smuggling in the Fray', *Wall Street Journal*, 18 February.

Βουδούρη Δ. (1992), *Η προστασία της πολιτιστικής κληρονομιάς στην προοπτική της ενιαίας ευρωπαϊκής αγοράς*, Αθήνα – Θεσσαλονίκη: Εκδόσεις Σάκκουλα.

Βουδούρη Δ. και Α. Στρατή (επιμ.) (1999), 'Η προστασία της πολιτιστικής κληρονομιάς σε διεθνές και ευρωπαϊκό επίπεδο - Κείμενα, Ινστιτούτο Συνταγματικών Ερευνών', *Κείμενα Δημοσίου Δικαίου*, αριθ.3, Αντ. Σάκκουλας, Αθήνα.

Γραμματικάκη- Αλεξίου Αν. (2002), *Διεθνής διακίνηση πολιτιστικών αγαθών και ιδιωτικό διεθνές δίκαιο*, Αθήνα – Θεσσαλονίκη: Εκδόσεις Σάκκουλα.

Δωρής, Ευ. (1985), *Το δίκαιον των αρχαιοτήτων - Νομοθεσία, νομολογία, ερμηνεία*, Αθήνα - Κομοτηνή: Αντ. Σάκκουλας.

Ευρωπαϊκή Επιτροπή – Γενική Διεύθυνση Εκπαίδευσης και Πολιτισμού (2003), *Σχεδιάζοντας το μελλοντικό πρόγραμμα για την πολιτιστική συνεργασία στην Ευρωπαϊκή Ένωση μετά το 2006* – Έγγραφο δημόσιας Διαβούλευσης, Βρυξέλλες: Ευρωπαϊκή Επιτροπή.

Κόνσολα Ντ. (1995), *Η διεθνής προστασία της παγκόσμιας πολιτιστικής κληρονομιάς*, Αθήνα: εκδ. Παπαζήση.

Λιγωμένου, Α. (1997), 'Κράτος δικαίου και προστασία του πολιτιστικού περιβάλλοντος', *Διδικ* 9.

Παπαγιάννης, Δον. (1995), 'Ο Πολιτισμός στην Ευρωπαϊκή Ένωση – το κοινοτικό κεκτημένο και οι νέες ρυθμίσεις', Αθήνα: Αντ. Ν. Σάκκουλας.

Παπαγιάννης, Δον. (2000), 'Η ευρωπαϊκή πολιτιστική πολιτική σε σχέση με τη Συνθήκη του Μάα στριχτ και του Άμστερνταμ', in *Συγκριτική ανάλυση των κοινοτικών πολιτικών Ελλάδας και Ισπανίας σχετικά με τη Συνθήκη του Άμστερνταμ, την εισαγωγή του Ευρώ και την πολιτιστική πολιτική*, Αθήνα: Ευρωπαϊκή Επιτροπή (Αντιπροσωπεία στην Ελλάδα) και Πρεσβεία της Ισπανίας στην Ελλάδα.

Παπαγιάννης, Δον. (2004), 'Η έννοια του πολιτιστικού αγαθού στο κοινοτικό δίκαιο', in Ε. Τροβά (επιμ.), *Η πολιτιστική κληρονομιά και το δίκαιο του Ευρωπαϊκού Κέντρου Δημοσίου Δικαίου*, Αθήνα: Εκδόσεις Σάκκουλα.

Στάγκος, Π. (1986), 'Η ελεύθερη κυκλοφορία των καλλιτεχνικών αγαθών στην κοινότητα και η πολιτιστική διάσταση της ευρωπαϊκής ενοποίησης', *Ελληνική Επιθεώρηση Ευρωπαϊκού Δικαίου*.

Index